RECYCLED MEM...

a collection of cycling stories

Compiled by: ISABEL WOODS, MAY FARRAR, RAB COLLINS and BILLY KIRK

Special thanks is due to the writers Tom Morgan and Hugh Robinson for their valuable assistance.

Published by Shanway Press 2010

ISBN: 978-0-9560101-7-9

Category: Cycling
        Historical
        Ireland

Title: Recycled Memories - A Collection of Cycling Stories

Compiled by: Isabel Woods, May Farrar, Rab Collins and Billy Kirk

© shanway

Cover picture: Snowed up Near Saintfield Co. Down 1941

dedication

The Night of Nostalgia' in February last year was aptly named, for many of those involved in cycling since a Reunion in 1998 have sadly passed away. The Guests were hushed and silenced for a few moments that evening, while the names of those who had died were scrolled down the screen and read out by Billy Kirk. Each and every one was filled with a sense of great loss - it was a poignant moment for every person who was in that room. Those men who have passed away would have had so many stories to tell. But sadly their stories will remain untold and are now lost forever.

  We dedicate this book to their memory and also to others who have passed on and whose names we may not be aware of.

BOBBY CONN	TOMMY MOORE
STANLEY CONNOLLY	JIM McBRIDE
JOE CRAIG	JIMMY McCORMICK
BILLY DOWDS	FRANK McKEOWN
TOMMY GIVAN	FRANK O'BRIEN
JOE HADDEN	GORDON REID
CHARLIE HENDERSON	WILLIE REILLY
CYRIL HENRY	TOM SMYTH
SAMMY HOUSTON	TOMMY TAYLOR
BILLY HUDSON	BILLY VOKES
ERNIE LAVERY	GEORGE WILKES
JOHN MOORE	

Contents

foreword

Inspiration for this book *Recycled Memories* came about in a vey simple way......
On 25th February 2009 a special event was held at the Marine Court Hotel in Bangor.
It was a Night of Nostalgia for cyclists and was presented by Ards Cycling Club.

The idea behind the event was conceived by Billy Kirk and overleaf you will read more about it.
It was a huge success and certainly an unforgettable night. When one looked around the room at
so many well seasoned faces - many of whom could not even recognise each other - it was all
quite moving. Sadly the evening passed all too quickly.
But thankfully a further idea was born that night...

Why not approach these veteran cyclists from the Fifties and Sixties and invite them to submit
stories and photographs of their cycling days? The call went out and the response was
overwhelming!

So these are the cycling stories. Some short, some lengthy, some happy and some sad - but all
worth reading. The book is interspersed with tales of great legendary cyclists of the early nineteen
hundreds.

We thought this additional material would add great interest to the book.
We hope the pages are a trip down memory lane for you the reader and trust you will enjoy
reading it as much as we enjoyed putting it together!

ISABEL, MAY, RAB and BILLY

Preface

from President of World Cycling - *Pat McQuaid*

I think most of the readers will be well aware that I come from a cycling family. As a child, initially in a pram, then as a toddler and later as a young teenager I followed my father Jim around Ireland, north and south, as he competed in grass track meetings, in the Phoenix Park on his fixed wheel winning the Hercules Cup or Grand Prix of Ireland or up at Orangefield, Belfast.

This was before television and play stations and cycling was one of the most popular sports in Ireland with crowds of upwards of 50,000 people watching an evening race in the Phoenix Park on a regular basis.

There will be many in this book who were around those days: Alfie Sterne, Jack Johnston, Geordie Wilkes, Geordie Wilson and more whom I remember as a youngster. They moved aside to allow the likes of Davy Kane, Morris Foster - Big Mo as he was affectionately known, Joe Smyth, the Caldwells et al before more recent riders such as Billy Kerr, Aidan McKeown, Archie Cunningham and the rest.

All of these legends plus many others have carved their part in the history of Irish cycling. They have graced the roads of Ireland with distinction and have competed successfully on many Irish cycling teams on many continents of the world as well as of course representing Northern Ireland in such as the Commonwealth Games.

Although born and bred in Dublin as a child of Northern Ireland parents I could actually have qualified to represent Northern Ireland in the Commonwealth Games. It was discussed over dinner on a couple of occasions but considering the political situation in Northern Ireland during the seventies it was felt, and unfortunately I must say, we wouldn't follow that path. As a cyclist all I wanted to do was race my bike.

I won my first senior race in Northern Ireland and remember it to this day. It was on the Dundrod circuit and I ended up in a break with all the greats of the day Big Mo, Wee Joe, Kaner, Taggart plus others. I remember well at some stage having to come off Mo`s wheel and as usual Mo wasn't sitting on the saddle but rather standing on the pedals as he charged through on a massive gear. He looked around and let out a few of his famous grunts and gestured for me to come through which I ultimately did. However it wasn't long before I sought another wheel to come off.

As a young 18 year old from Dublin they didn't reckon my chances in a sprint but uphill sprints were, throughout my career, my favourites and I took off around 150 to go and no one came around me. I must say I was chuffed going down to Dublin that evening, as of course was my father driving the car.

Following that I always enjoyed the weekly trip north for the Saturday race. The religious restriction actually gave us top cyclists a great opportunity because we were forced to travel north on a Saturday where all of the best riders in the country would race against each other and then the following day all the Northies travelled south.

A couple of weeks after winning in Dundrod I ended up in a break in the latter stages of the classic Tour of the Slade in Blessington with Kaner and Wee Joe and the two of them on the last lap worked me over attacking one after the other forcing me to chase. In the last kilometre Kaner was away in what looked like a winning move with Wee Joe content to look for me to chase. I eventually took off in the finishing straight and a dying Kaner looked around and thought he still had enough only to be caught and passed on the line whilst he had his hand up in the air in victory. That was sweet and we talked about it many times after.

I grew up in politics with my father Jim and my Uncle Paddy constantly involved – the N.C.A, the C.R.E, the N.I.C.F. and all the issues surrounding them being discussed in our house over every meal. I suppose one could say it gave me a great grounding for the politics I deal with now on a daily basis.

It certainly gave me a great love of my sport because all I wanted to do was ride my bike – North or South didn't matter as long as the competition was good – and believe me it was. I carry that philosophy into my daily work now as President of the UCI. Any decisions I have to make are based on sport first and what is best for cycling. I can thank all of those competitors in Northern Ireland and also those important officials who assisted in one way or other in carving out my career.

They were and are great people and I cherish all of the memories. Irish cycling and world cycling is indebted to you all.

Pat McQuaid

Union Cycliste Internationale

Oh that my words were written!

Oh that they were inscribed in a book!

Oh that with an iron pen and lead they were graven

in the rock for ever.

JOB 19 v. 23 and 24

introduction

I felt more than pleased when I was asked if I would write the Introduction for this book.
Others insist that I am the one to write it - probably owing to the fact that I have completed 'seventy five' years on racing bikes, plus 'half a million miles' in that time. Well I can tell you there wasn't much leisure about cycling until about seven or eight years ago when I reduced down considerably on the miles.

At over eighty years of age, I was covering eighty to ninety miles frequently on a Sunday!
Anyhow miles don't matter now as it was here, after almost seventy years, I soon discovered what 'Leisure Cycling' really meant in terms of enjoyment. Instead of the old Primus stove which was a 'must' at the start, I use the small stainless steel flask and tea bag. When you stop at a selected spot to enjoy the lunch, you very often open up another aspect of enjoyment - that is the friendship one. I am often very lucky to get going with only three or four 'stoppings', but a few of these would be old cycling friends. I have also had upwards of twenty from walking clubs stop a few times.

From the late Twenties to the late Sixties, these were the last decades when the huge touring clubs, twenty to thirty members, at a pace to suit the slowest, could be seen on many roads on a Sunday. Usually on the Antrim and Coast Roads, the Mournes and Omeath and Carlingford.
Right back before the First World War, Belfast was spattered with Cycling Clubs. I have figures to show that there were four times more cyclists registered with these Clubs than what there are today.

Throughout my life, cycling has brought me much pleasure and fulfilment. I sincerely hope you will find a lot of pleasure in reading this book and that many good memories of your cycling days will be stirred up in your heart while you read.

HARRY McCARTNEY
Cycling Historian

The Night of Nostalgia

In February 2009 Ards Cycling Club presented a Night of Nostalgia. Billy Kirk, with the backing of Club Committee set about organizing the Event and with invaluable help from son Brendan and daughter-in-law Bronagh, the evening came to fruition. An open invitation was sent out to all club cyclists, past and present, to meet in the Marine Hotel in Bangor, County Down.

 The response just snowballed, so Billy had to change the room size TWICE from the original one which he reserved, as the replies of those who wanted to attend came rolling in. The final number who attended 'The Night of Nostalgia' was around 150. It was wonderful to see so many of the 'Old Timers' present. They came from far and wide that night. Billy Kirk had received a DVD from Morris Foster which was originally a super 8 cine move filmed by Marshall McAdam during the 1953 season to celebrate the Cyprus Club, a 21st Anniversary. The film was converted to a DVD by the Kings Moss stalwart, Millar Wright. A selection of photographs from the treasured scrapbook of Jim Crawford were also on display.

There were so many at the Night of Nostalgia that two photographs had to be taken by Jim Lavery.

We had refreshments of tea and biscuits and of course the renewal of old acquaintances past and present was the highlight for many. The evening finally ended when Morris Foster addressed the gathering and thanked them for making it such a success.

He in return received a unanimous applause, the audience acknowledging his past performances in competition and also his valuable contribution to the sport of cycling in general.

Morris deservedly was a recipient of an MBE in 2006.

The Night of Nostalgia passed all too quickly but thankfully the seed for this book was sown that evening and it is wonderful to see it come to fruition.

RAB COLLINS

Cyclists' Reunion 1998

Ards cycling club's second reunion (organiser Billy Kirk) took place on 18th March 1998 in the Strangford Arms Hotel, Newtownards at which 167 old cyclists were gathered.

The first reunion was a film show in the Tudor Cinema, Comber on March 7th 1997 at which 95 people packed the little venue until it was standing room only. See page 377. An examination of these photographs brings it home just how quickly we lost so many great contemporaries and friends, whose stories departed with them.

Mistaken identity

It was in a Time Trial on the Antrim Road in the mid Fifties that I punctured near the Randalstown Road turn. As I had no means of repairing the puncture, I thought - how will I get back to the Crown & Shamrock dressing facilities and my car? So I shouted to one of the riders (as he left the turn) to tell one of my friends at the start/finish to fetch my car and come out to rescue me.

  Now my car was a very rare model. A 1946 Standard 12 Drop Head Coupe, cherry red Tourer.
I think I only saw one other similar car during the years I was driving mine.

After a time the Standard 12 came into view. I thought I would put a little humour into the situation, so I pulled my racing shorts leg up and stepped a few feet on to the road and thrust out my thumb. Low and behold it wasn't my car! I couldn't believe it! The same model and colour. It must have been the only other one in Northern Ireland. Needless to say I got a quizzical dirty look from the driver. I could have been arrested for soliciting! My car of course did arrive a short time later and all was well.

ELLIOT MATTHEWS South Lurgan CC

(After I left Lurgan to live in Belfast in 1955, I joined the East Ulster Road Club/Cyclists Touring Club).

Elliot Matthews rides a massed start Hillsborough 1953-54

Roy Tweedie

Roy - Bicycle Race 1953

Roy Tweedie was a member of the Belfast Cycling Club from 1953 and lived in North Queen Street, Belfast. He took part in club events and was a regular member on Sunday club runs. He was employed in the Electrical department in Harland & Wolff. He married his wife Mary in Belmont Presbyterian church and resided in the Holywood Road area. They decided to emigrate and sailed to America on the RMS Queen Mary in 1963. Roy worked for an electrical company in America until his retirement and continued to cycle and kept an annual record of his yearly mileage which was very impressive. In 1984 Roy was a voluntary assistant to the cycling track team in the summer Olympics held in Los Angels that year.

Roy and Mary celebrated their Golden Wedding anniversary in 2009 and Roy still cycles; he has also taken up flying light aircraft and frequently attends a local flying club.

Roy and Mary are enjoying their retirement and would like to be remembered by friends and anyone who knew them and would welcome any communication with Belfast.

RAB COLLINS

Emigrating to USA 1963

Profile of Pat McQuaid

I suppose once in a life time you are requested to write a unique piece about a friend and colleague who has gone to the top of the tree in his chosen sport.

Naturally, I am not talking about the publicised sports that grace our networks on a daily basis, year in year out! No, we are in the world of cycling that fills our lives with happiness and gossip for the best part of nine months every year. Presumably all and sundry realise that Patrick McQuaid the eldest of nine children is president of the Union Cycliste Internationale and is now in his second term of four years. But. Oh! Where did it all begin for the son of Madge and the late Jim McQuaid? There have been acres and acres of news about the chief of the UCI, but from the humble beginnings of cycling in the late 50's, the young Patrick was influenced by his uncle Paddy. As was the custom and practice of time, both Jim and Paddy were regulars on Irish cycling teams. It was in or around 1959 that Paddy was away in Italy, Milan to be precise. The McQuaids, even in those days were household names when it came to cycling. The bould uncle clapped his eye on a mini bike in a shop window in Milan. Naturally the asking price of the 'cinelli' was out of order, but the bould Paddy with his powers of persuasion managed to strike a deal and the rest is the journey of a life time for a bike and all who cycled it. This machine was unique in those distant days and it was inch perfect for Pat who was the envy of all the kids in the neighbourhood. Of course it was a regular feature of the McQuaid household to barrel into the mini grey van belonging to Madge who would drive the family to various road and track locations. In tow went the bike whilst they sucked up the atmosphere of the meet. That 'Cinelli' was worth its weight in gold as Pat was as happy as Larry to cycle around as he waited for his dad to finish the race. So, basically that was where the love affair with cycling took root. Believe it or not that same bike was a hand me down to all the six brothers who at one time or another got their freedom to cycle around. Interestingly, talking to Pat's mother Madge who has just come back from South Africa on that same topic of the bike; "David my grandson also took his first cycle on that same bike. Maybe in time they'll put it in the museum as a fitting memento to a son of Ireland who climbed to the highest office in the pantheon of cycling". Chatting with various members of the family, the one message that came across loud and clear is that none of the McQuaid siblings were pushed into cycling. I suppose they just drifted in and once you got the bug there was no turning back. Mrs. McQuaid tells me the story of going off in the grey van every Sunday morning with the family in tow. Of course their dad the late and lamented Jim McQuaid was a top race cyclist and represented Ireland on many occasions. I suppose I would need reams and reams of paper to log the details. As children they would see their dad winning races on numerous occasions and like any child the appeal of success invariably gets people into cycling.

As in Pat's case he would have come to prominence in the late 1950's when he won a Tailteann Gold medal and the presentation took place on Jones Road which was home to the Gaelic Athletic Association. Can you imagine the thrill of that Irish victory. Yes indeed it was in the genes. I enquired of him what it was like in a household where invariably the topic of cycling would be talked about. "The family had a shop in Fitzmaurice road and on a regular basis cyclists would call in to see dad. They were the greats of former years and also observed that they had respect for him as a family man, a cyclist and a bread winner. "There was never any pressure on us to get involved in cycling, but it was the discipline that mam and dad showed in our years of growth that stood to the entire family. "Of course we enjoyed our cycling in our early years with no pressure to be successful, but that all changed when I went into the junior ranks. I would have to say that winning the 'Junior Tour of the Slade' which started and finished on the Belgard Road in Tallaght was the springboard that more or less catapulted me into the main stream of competitive cycling. And as they say the rest is history," said Pat. McQuaid the cyclist certainly established himself in 1973 when he not alone won the Raleigh Dunlop Tour of Ireland but added the national championship to his list of wins which were beginning to clock up. Then in '74 he done the double with a second Raleigh/Dunlop win and the following year went for the unique treble. But, it was not to be as he crashed out when in a commanding position on day four of the event in West Cork. Unfortunately for him, he went into a bend with wet leaves on the ground and the foliage overhead had not dried out the road and down he came, by a unique set of circumstances he was the only one to bite the dust and the treble was the talk of the afternoon in Bantry Hospital. But that is for another day and maybe, yes, maybe I'll do the story of a young cyclist who had stars in his eyes and for Ireland Inc. made the breakthrough.

TOMMY CAMPBELL, Cycling Correspondent for Irish Cycling.com and Sunday Independent

More thoughts on Pat McQuaid
by Michael Concannon

My period as President of Cycling Ireland coincided with some of the most interesting events that have happened in the world of cycling. At the top of this list has to be the election of Pat McQuaid as President of UCI. It was my great honour and privilege to nominate Pat for the job not once but twice. The lead up to Pat's first election saw us do a deal of canvassing on his behalf. What sticks out in my memory of that time was the extraordinary degree of affection that both Pat and Ireland were held in by cycling people all around the world. This, and of course more importantly, Pat's history of excellent work in the years leading up to the election saw him elected with an overwhelming majority. In my dealings with him since on behalf of the members of Cycling Ireland I can testify that he has remained a steadfast supporter of the sport in Ireland and indeed he looks to be briefed regularly on what is happening here. His readiness to meet with and sort out difficulties for Cycling Ireland members gives us all a boost of self esteem that is very useful in these gloomy times.

And with those kind works it is appropriate that we know that despite his high office, Pat McQuaid remains a true friend of Irish cycling, but he has a big heart that embraces cycling the world over. Trust me that is a safe pair of hands.

A long way from Glasnevin to Switzerland

Madge McQuaid on her visit to son Pat's Office.

Aigle in Switzerland, set in idyllic surroundings, is the nerve centre of world cycling. Standing in the car park with the slight wind whistling around you and watching the massive trees swaying without a care in the world, you might never know that beyond the revolving doors and on the second floor is the office of the President of the Union Cycliste Internationale, *Pat McQuaid*, the Dubliner who has pressed all the right buttons in the process of his elevation to the post of supreme commander. (Not his words, but mine).

Naturally the woman behind the throne from birth was his mother Madge.
I caught up with her at a wedding of one of her many grandchildren recently.
I asked how she enjoyed her visit to Aigle. This was our conversation:

"Yes. It was simply amazing when I first visited the home of the UCI and that of Pat and his wife Aileen in Vevay. I could have been in the Phoenix Park, such was the greenery. As for Vevay, that could have been in Bray, County Wicklow where Pat spent many a long evening in the home of Nancy and Pat Ryan who always had plenty of 'lemon curd' on tap.

It is a parent's dream that their children have a healthy lifestyle and a job to put bread on the table. I know it has been a long road, but never in my wildest dreams did my late husband Jim and I think that he would be in control of cycling at the highest level. After all in my estimation this was the remit of the Europeans who have had their finger on all the pulses. To think that he is in charge! My biggest regret is that 'dad' was not alive to see it.

The building is so expansive and it has all the facilities. My guide on the tour of the building was Aileen who, on the face of it was very well known to the staff. It just goes to prove that behind every man is a good industrious woman.

*Sitting in a sumptuous leather chair in his office surrounded by memorabilia from all over the world, a head came around the corner. It was his Private Secretary, Audrey and she said: "**Mr President, just to let you know that you will not be disturbed**".*

Indeed Pat McQuaid was having a very important meeting with a very special lady – his Mother.

The Wall of Death

One day in the early 1980's in the course of my work for the N.I. Tourist Board I happened to be in the company of Frank O'Neill (now deceased) owner of the Londonderry Arms Hotel, Carnlough.

Reflectively Frank said to me, "I believe you're a bicycle rider". When I replied "Yes, all my life" he began to tell me about old friends from the Dungannon area whose names were Jim and Paddy McQuaid and were bicycle racers.

My amazement at his knowing these illustrious men in the days before their move to Dublin in 1945 paled into insignificance when he further told me the brothers had ridden the 'Wall of Death' (in a travelling fairground) on their racing bicycles!

For those who may not know, the 'Wall' was a tight, circular, vertical track around which a stunt motorcyclist rode, centrifugal force keeping him in place. I recall childhood memories of the visits to Newtownards of possibly the very same fairground, always containing the Wall of Death.

Phone calls to Dungannon found confirmation of this hair-raising story, from the older generation, of course. One of these sources, also named McQuaid, but strangely not a relation, told of more recent occurrences: Particularly Jim's sons Kieran, Pat and Oliver coming on their bikes from Dublin to visit their aunt in Dungannon and phone calls from Jim to his sister asking had they arrived yet. Checking up, no doubt, not only on their safety, but also on the speed of their training!

Jim McQuaid's widow Madge, now into her 90's remembers the excitement in Dungannon when the brothers McQuaid performed their astonishing feat all those years ago.

BILLY KIRK

The tandem trike

My story goes back 50 years or more. A lifetime ago. Ronnie Millar and 'yours truly' were cycling on a club run. Ronnie was involved in racing on a bicycle which he had converted into a trike.

An idea came to Ronnie. How about getting a loan of a tandem and converting it into a tandem trike? (Never heard of before) As Ronnie's trike was a conversion set, we took the conversion off the bicycle and attached it to the tandem. I must say we thought this was brilliant. So without much ado the day arrived when we 'hit the road' (excuse the pun). This strange piece of machinery caused quite a stir among the passers bye on the road as we rode all the way to Dundalk and back home again.

The Tandem Trike

We cycled about 100 miles that day. Both of us had the same pedal action which made it easier to handle. I was on the front and Ronnie on the back. Must say no trouble on route and we both enjoyed the experience.

JOHN CORRY   Cycling Touring Club

C T C Run
The Lakes, England 1952.
L-R: Ken Blair, John Corry,
Paddy McAteer,
Davy Oldham,
John Riley and
Elliott Matthews.

Camping at Tyrella (mid 1950's)

Instead of the usual Sunday Club Run it was decided to have a camping trip to Tyrella Beach. The arrangement was to have all the gear taken by car and the tents erected on Saturday afternoon. We duly arrived in Downpatrick where some of the party decided to go to the dance in the Town Hall and check out the local female talent! The rest of us rode on to Tyrella, had a brew up and eventually settled down for the night. The 'Dancers' arrived well past midnight having lost their way and cycled more miles than necessary. During the early hours it started to rain which got progressively heavier and two of the tents proved less than waterproof. The remaining tents had to take on the extra guests and a most uncomfortable night was had by all! Around dawn most emerged stiff, sore and tired but after hot tea and food our spirits improved. The 'Dancers' had to take a lot of stick for getting lost but gave back as good as they got. To my knowledge camping was never mentioned again!

BILL McKENZIE   Ards Cycling Club

The timekeeper is always right

One Sunday morning we were riding a 50 mile Time Trial on Antrim Road. There was a Scotsman riding called Ben Balneves.
He asked Tommy Taylor what was his time?
Tommy replied: "You did a 2 hr. 4 mins."
 "There must be some mistake" said Ben.
 "I never did a 2 hr 4 min in my life!"
Tommy replied "Well, you have done one now"

 Typical Tommy Taylor – straight and to the point. You never questioned Tommy Taylor's timekeeping!

GEORGE WILSON   East Tyrone CC

GEORDIE WILSON *(aged 79)*

Veteran Cyclist from Cookstown
Pictured here training in Donegal
last year
An Honorary Life Member
of East Tyrone CC.

A Member of the Club for 59 years
And still turning the pedals.

People ask me how I kept at the
Cycling game for so long.
I tell them it's the Friendship
And the Camaraderie among
Cyclists.

To a cyclist it's the BE ALL,
END ALL of your life, really.

Geordie Wilson's fathers' story

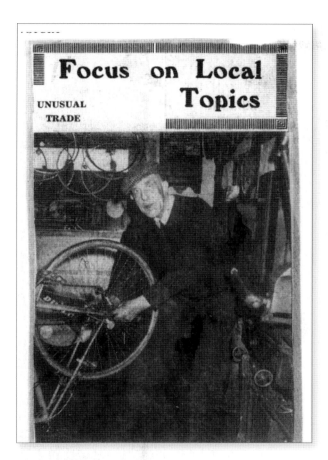

Focus on Local Topics

UNUSUAL TRADE

ONE of the few people in Northern Ireland still making bicycle frames is 71-year-old Billy Wilson, of Oldtown Street, Cookstown.

Under the trade name of "Star of Tyrone," his cycles have taken part in races in many parts of the British Isles and it was on one of them that Tommy Talbot, of East Tyrone C.C., set up a new record in the all-Ireland hill climb championships.

A native of Moneymore, Mr. Wilson has been in the cycle business since the end of the first world war, in which he served with the 10th Inniskillings. He came to Cookstown in 1922 and began making his own cycles in 1935.

Although he has made cycles chiefly for members of the East Tyrone Club, his customers over the years have come from as far away as Belfast and Lisburn. In addition, he made quite a few frames for members of the Forces when they were stationed in the district.

In his earlier days Mr. Wilson was a racing cyclist himself and he recalls the formation of the East Tyrone Club which at that time had its headquarters in the yard at Tullylagan Manor. His club mates included Cyril Henry, Wesley Henry, Sidney Milligan and Matt Millar.

Mr. Wilson's bicycles certainly stand the years well, for when I called with him this week he showed me one made in 1948 and the framework is as sound as the day it left his workshop.

For many years he was well-known in the district as mandoline player and, along with Billy and Eddie Forsythe and Willie Johnston, he was a member of Mowillian Melody Makers, who played at dances throughout South Derry and East Tyrone.

This is the front cover of the very first issue of THE ULSTER CYCLIST Showing a Hercules Bike. Only three issues were published in April, May and June 1935

Isolated

The Ballymena Road Club was training one Sunday in the Sperrins. One of the riders punctured in the village of Sperrin in the mountains. He asked the woman in the shop could he use the airline. "Airline"? the woman replied. "There's not even a bus service up here!"

GEORGE WILSON   East Tyrone CC

East Tyrone CC 60th Anniversary Dinner in 2007

The great Sean Kelly pictured here with (left) Geordie Wilson and (right) Jim Slaine - another stalwart in East Tyrone CC and a hard working member for over 50 years.
Geordie Wilson was Sean's cycle Mechanic in the 1975 and 1976 Tour of Britain Milk Race and have been friends ever since. Sean was Guest of Honour at the Dinner in 2007.
At 10.00 am the following morning he took the Club out for a 40 mile run on the bikes
That cleared a few heads after the dinner!

An Unlikely Pair

It is early spring 1959. Two ambitious N.C.A. men leave Ireland to seek their fortune in the northern Spanish city of Figueres.

They travel with a third man who plans only a short stay, Ronnie Williams of the Tailteann C. C. Dublin.

In those days, although N.C.A. riders could not be selected to ride for their country, many, if not all European countries turned a blind eye to rules against the N.C.A., there was sympathy for the rebels. Spain seemed to give them a special welcome.

Few examples, however, can be cited where N.C.A. men rode as domestiques on the pro teams, but the two hopefuls were aiming at this market.

The contrast between the background of the two men could not have been greater: One was the son of a Belfast Orangeman from the Grosvenor Road, who himself had got as far as celebrating the 12th as a 'Juvenile', while the other's father was a Republican socialist who owned a pub in the town of Killorglin in County Kerry.

Frankie Thompson of Belfast rode for Windsor C. C. He showed great promise until a suspension in 1956 sent him into the ranks of the N.C.A. whereas Kerry's Gene Mangan was already a star of the Ras Tailteann, rode for national C.C. Dublin and sprang out of the same nationalist tradition which produced such great cyclists as O'Hanlon, Flanagan and Kennedy.

After a promising first two weeks Thompson's campaign was abruptly halted when he crashed in a race in southern France. In Frankie's words "*we were riding in a race in Perpignan and were about 25 km into the race. I was in a break of 12 guys and pushing up a hill. I touched the back wheel of one of the others who cut across me. Down I went and broke my arm for the third time*"

The required surgery was only available in the French city of Pau – 200 miles away across the Pyrenees.

Frankie remembers that Gene travelled in the ambulance with him to Pau, came to visit regularly on his bike (taking a taxi part of the way) and generally looked after his interests.

Thompsons words again: "*When I got out of hospital the President of the cycling club in Figueres picked me up and took me to his home. I stayed there for two weeks while Gene sold my bike to raise the money to get me home to Belfast*".

Meanwhile Gene Mangan was getting such good results that an upgrade to his licence was required. Frankie tells how Mangan advised him to rejoin the N.I.C.F. at home as the best way to progress his career. He saw this as the mark of a fair and open-minded man.

Mangan was disillusioned when he heard that questions were raised with the U.C.I. by the C.R.E. regarding his proposed new licence. He returned to Ireland in June – just in time to see his friend Frank Thompson take the yellow jersey on stage 4 of the Ras.

BILLY KIRK

A Tour de France

Six Lurgan lads prepare to leave for a Touring holiday in the French Alps in July 1952.
They are, left to right:
Pearse Tipping, Stevie Nelson, Elliot Matthews, Jimmy McKenna, Jack Higginson (from Moira) and Bobby Martin.

The six Lurgan men at the summit of the Col du Galibier in the French Alps. They are seen at the Memorial to Henri Desgrange, founder of the Tour de France.

Elliott Matthews said:
"We wanted to sample the excitement and atmosphere of the Tour de France and to ride some of the major roads in the Alps. Our plan was to use boat and train to get to Marseille on the Riviera, via Dublin -London - Paris, cycle the Riviera to Monaco, then proceed north to the Alps, taking in the Col-du-Vars, Col-du-Izoard and the Col du Galibier. We then proceeded into Switzerland, Lausanne and back unto France to Pontalier to end a most memorable Tour.

The Tour was won by the great Italian Fausto Coppi - his second victory in the great event".

Whatever happened to track racing in Northern Ireland?

In the early 50's the only type of track racing was on grass and every athletic meeting had both runners and cyclists using the same track.

The R.U.C. sports meet at Ravenhill was very popular with cyclists and the crowds were immense - something like you would see for an Ulster Rugby match these days.

Then the big star on grass was Billy Sands of Windsor CC. I remember him getting a standing ovation from the crowd after winning the 'DEVIL TAKE THE HINDMOST' from the front! No small thing in those days, 1952. It was my first race and I lasted half a lap. However in those days Dublin riders dominated sprinting. Jim McQuaid of Emerald CC Dublin was Irish National Sprint Champion although that title never went south again after 1953. Jim's son Pat is now World President of U.C.I. the governing body of world cycling. Our only other track was the Grove. It was half a mile round and far too long. It was laid with brick dust from the nearby brickworks on the Limestone Road. When you finished your race you were completely covered in red dust which stuck to your sweat and made you look like some kind of alien.

And your poor bike! Every moving part was clogged.

By 1953 Lisburn opened a proper banked tarmac-finished track. Portadown followed and although the first All Ireland Sprint championship to be held in Northern Ireland was staged there, it had not been banked enough. It also had a chain link fence round the perimeter which was dangerous for the riders. Hilty Smith of the Northern CC lost half his ear after crashing into the fence in the 1955 semi final of the sprint championship.

The Orangefield track was opened one year later, but it was not built properly. The banking in the final bend was flattened too much (bad design or lack of money from the Belfast City Council)

As a result, a fast rider coming out of that bend was thrown out towards the fence and had to slow down instead of going all out for the line. Chris Hoy would have ended up in Grand Parade!!

The Lisburn track remained the best venue although it now seems to have fallen into disrepair.

We appear to be the only country in the world without an indoor cycling track and after the successes of Chris Hoy and our own Wendy Houvenagle it seems we have missed out a lot.

I spent 1956 in Denmark. I was invited there for what the Danes called a revenge match after I had beaten their National Champion in Milan at the 1955 World Championships. Going to Denmark to race for a season was a big eye opener for me. I stayed with a family in Aarhus and shared with Australian John Tressider who at that time was No.2 in the world. Cycle track racing in Denmark is a National sport with super stadiums and of course it is all about money. It is run like greyhound racing with betting on every race - very controlled, very professional.

whatever happened to track racing in northern ireland?

I spent all of 1956 in Aarhus and Copenhagen and made many friends there who have changed my life.

Just a little anecdote of how things have changed...I got a letter from the secretary of the N.I.C.F. to tell me I was the only Irish cyclist picked for the 1956 Olympic Games in Melbourne later that year. The problem was that they had no money and could I get myself to Australia under my own steam in time to compete!! No Lottery funds in those days.

LEO FEENEY Abbey CC

Typical photo finish Denmark 1956

1 Rudy Vorster *South Africa*
2 Myself
3 Oriani *Italy*

A picture of myself courtesy of Belfast Telegraph, doing a lap of honour after winning the 1957 sprint title (Note the crowds)

Billy Sands on Wallace Park Track 1952 - 1953

Jim Darragh - Northern CC, Leo Feeney - Abbey CC
and Hilty Smith - Northern CC

Luck of the Irish (Tour of Britain)

The ill luck which had dogged the Irish throughout the race was still with them, even after they booked into their hotel in Southport.

Mechanic George Wilson was tending their bikes outside. He turned his back for a moment and looked around to see five boys pedalling away on five of their six bicycles. A handy policeman gave chase on foot and a police car was soon there. The bikes were recovered and three of the boys were apprehended. The only machine not taken was that of Archie Cunningham from Belfast. He was the only Northern Ireland rider in the team.

"Maybe they thought it had a bomb in it!" he cracked later.

GEORGE WILSON   East Tyrone C.C.

'It's never too late'

Like many kids of my generation - 1950s-60s - I had a bike and most days rode to school. The school playing fields were several miles away so once a week we had to get ourselves there and back for rugby or cricket practice and cycling was the best means. After a few years I took up rowing and as I lived within walking distance of the river the bike was put away and forgotten about.

Jump forward forty years and I find myself overweight and out of condition, but watching the Tour de France on television I decide to get my daughter's mountain bike out and give it a go. To my surprise and delight I manage a few miles without collapsing from exhaustion and, what's more, I find I really enjoy the experience. Each day I travel a little farther and soon find myself looking forward to each outing.

Then for Christmas my daughter bought me some proper cycling kit. Proper clothes deserve a proper bike and I sought the advice of cycling friends. Should I buy an urban bike, a hybrid, a mountain bike? With one voice they all advised a road bike for - as one of them put it - 'the day will soon come when you'll want to go faster'. So, cheque book in hand I set off to the bike shop and come way the richer for an aluminium and carbon framed bike with drop handle bars and 27 gears. Finished all in black it looks ready for action - but will I be up to it? Will it be like switching from a Ford Fiesta to a Ferrari?

Never will I forget the first time I mounted it and felt it spring to life under me. It seemed to be taking control of me, and as my confidence grew I ventured farther and faster. Soon I learnt to take on the challenge of hills and to enjoy the thrill of the descent. My collection of colourful lycra grew and I upgraded my rims and found I could go faster still. I began to learn the particular vocabulary of the bike - top tube, bottom bracket, seat post, and I found a use for the French I studied all those years ago - bidon, sportive, derailleur.

About this time I'm offered the chance to take early retirement and I jump at it. Now cycling is no longer confined to the weekends and summer evenings, but whenever I choose I can take to the roads and discover the rich variety of landscape all within a few miles of where I live. (However I still feel uncomfortable cycling on a Monday morning when all the world is back at work. It's hard to break the habit of a life time.) Now when I am not out on my bike I'm thinking about getting out on my bike.

What have been the biggest hazards I've had to face as a returning cyclist of mature years? Firstly the discovery (which the motorist can largely ignore) that many of our roads are in a truly dreadful condition. Each journey has the potential to end in a fall on roads which are repeatedly dug up and crudely repaired, to say nothing of manhole covers which are lower or higher than the surrounding surface but rarely on the same level. We are promised more cycle paths (which would be fine so long as they are maintained), but most of our riding will continue to be done on the open road and until surfaces are improved cycling will remain a hazardous pursuit. And the second hazard - the frequency with which dog owners do nothing to control their animals when cyclists are nearby. We have all encountered the dog which suddenly dashes in front of us forcing evasive action and putting our fragile bodies at risk.

However these hazards are more than compensated for by the many pleasures of cycling. There's the friendliness of (most) other bike riders who greet you with a wave or a nod, who stop to offer help if you seem to be in trouble, or who just fall in beside you for a chat as you roll along. Then there's the fun of seeking out unfamiliar roads and destinations, and if there is a coffee shop to be sampled along the way - so much better. Cycling can be both a solitary and a shared activity and last summer saw me tackle my first sportive when with 1000 others I lapped the Lough, and although soaked to the skin I have seldom enjoyed a day out more. I may travel at only a fraction of their speed but I can truly feel one with the great cyclists of the past and present.

Any regrets? Yes of course - the forty wasted years when I could have been
cycling but wasn't - but as the old song has it - 'it's never too late'.

WESLEY McCANN

Hudson – 'King' among cyclists

An article taken from IRELAND'S SATURDAY NIGHT 1974
It was written by Stanley Martin, a Columnist in the Magazine.
Stanley was one of the greatest Cycling journalists
of our time.

Not always taken seriously, probably because of his erratic form over the years and often not properly appreciated despite his undoubted ability, Billy Hudson (Cyprus CC) must, by his championship winning record-breaking performances in recent seasons, now be fully accepted as one of Irish cycling's outstanding short-distance unpaced riders of all time.

In May this year he completed a hat-trick of wins in the N.I. 25 miles time-trial championship - having also taken the Irish title in 1969, and nine days ago he capped his '25' prowess by becoming N.I. record-holder in 57 minutes 5 seconds.

A '50' TIME

Also this year he won the Irish '50' championship, at which distance he already stood as the fastest-ever Irishman by his 1 hr 58 mins 39 secs. in 1969.

Last month he broke the Northern Ireland time trial record with 22 mins 58 secs and he further reduced these figures to 22 mins 34 secs on Thursday last.

He is already the N.I. 10 miles and 25 miles unpaced record-holder on the track.

Few, if any, cyclists in Northern Ireland train more relentlessly and vigorously than this ultra-fast enthusiast from Bloomfield. His aim has always been concentrated upon all-out speed and time and again he has suffered frustration when the fast revs eluded him in time-trials, or his impatience with the sometimes sluggish pace of massed-start racing trapped him into early all-out abortive solo win-or-nothing attacks too many miles before the finishing line.

In the recent 84 miles Regal Grand Prix, for example, he rode himself to a standstill - building up a colossal lead of seven minutes before the 40 miles point when a trimming-back of speed at half this advantage may well have secured him victory.

Despite this lack of judgment, so often apparent from the sidelines, he is still a worthy contributor to the massed-start branch of the sport. It is of course his unpaced speed, delivered in a fluent straight-pedalling style with a minimum of body movement, which makes this popular Cyprus personality who is always immaculately attired and with machine invariably spotless, an outstanding figure – as his list of records and titles well proves.

Another press cutting stated:
Super fast East Belfast cyclist, Billy Hudson, now living in Yorkshire had a great win in yesterday's Leeds Wellington CC 25 mile time trial on the Boroughbridge course. Using big gears of 114 inches and 106 inches, Hudson clocked 53 mins. 46 secs. a personal best by two minutes.

Dave Kane and Billy Hudson at Orangefield track.

Christmas is always dry, crisp and sunny

The week before Christmas 1957 three teenage members of Cyprus Cycling Club decided not to spend another boring Christmas at home. We were John Snowden, Norman Cordiner and myself, Austin McNally. We would spend the holiday in Learmount Castle Youth Hostel. Why not? Isn't Christmas always dry, crisp and sunny? The morning of the 24th found us riding towards Antrim, saddlebags packed with Christmas fayre, including a frozen chicken. How we were going to cook it, we had no idea. By Templepatrick a fine mizzle began, by Antrim it was a horizontal sleet. Undeterred, we rode on to Toomebridge where the snow was lying an inch deep on the road. At Maghera we were ready for a cup of tea but, being Christmas, everywhere was closed.

However, Christmas spirit prevailed and a gentleman took pity on us and invited us in for tea. We didn't have to be asked twice. We dried our socks and shoes at his fire and an hour later we thanked him and headed out into the fading light and ankle-deep snow. The Glenshane loomed: a steeper, narrower version than the modern Pass. All traffic had stopped. We could just about ride up the centre of the road with frequent stops to clear the snow from our mudguards. By this time it was looking a bit like Scott of the Antarctic. The sensible option would have been to turn back – but cyclists don't turn back. Between riding and walking like what seemed forever, we reached the top in total darkness and a full-scale blizzard. We decided that the situation was not great. What we needed was a plan. We knew that there was a quarry further down and the suggestion was made that we battle on and spend the night in one of the sheds. Ah, the optimism of youth! At the gates of the quarry I volunteered to go in and have a look. Bad idea. Five steps in, the ice under the snow gave way and I went down into eight inches of icy water. Cycling shoes with holes along the sides and white cotton socks were not quite the thing for this situation. A cosy night in the quarry shed was a non starter. We headed down towards Dungiven, snow knee-deep, bikes now having to be carried on our shoulders.

We had all gone very quiet. We had a lot to think about. Then we noticed a dim light further down. We reckoned it was either a house or we were hallucinating. We weren't sorry when we came to a gateway. There was no way we could bring our bikes up the lane for it was blocked with drifted snow. We left them on the road. That night we truly had the luck of the Irish. The tiny house was completely covered in snow but the heat of the fire inside had melted a corner of snow from the top of one of the windows. It showed enough light to lead us to the house. We dug out the door and knocked. It opened and the snow tumbled into the hall. The farmer's wife stood there, astonished, but, again with Christmas spirit, she hurried us in to meet her husband, her adult son, and an enormous turf fire. They were the Flemings, a family of sheep farmers. (We contacted them in the summer and discovered that they had lost 400 sheep that night – but saved three lambs). They fed us and we bedded down in the warm living-room, after being instructed to keep the fire going all night with peat from the store.

Christmas Day arrived. Guess what? Dry, crisp and sunny.

We shared the Fleming's breakfast, thanked them and went off to find our bikes. They were totally buried by the blizzard that had raged all night. We dug them out, hoisted them on our shoulders and trudged off towards Dungiven. We encountered a group of igloos and as we clambered over the top of them we discovered they were actually abandoned cars. As we entered the village of Dungiven the locals looked at us in disbelief.

Who in their right mind would be coming down from the Glenshane Pass in those conditions? The Hotel was open and, over tea and toast, we reckoned that we'd give Learmount Castle Youth Hostel a miss – for that year anyway. We were told that a train from Limavady Junction to Belfast was possible. We had no way of contacting our families for all the telegraph lines were down so we set off for Limavady and home. Limavady Junction was not in Limavady. It was near the coast of Lough Foyle, four miles away and was like something out of a cowboy picture. A railway track crossed a snow-covered plain from the East and disappeared West, intersected with a tiny building, a platform and a Station-master.

We bought tickets and waited.

Hallelujah! The train arrived!

During the journey we emptied our saddlebags, ate our Christmas fayre,but threw the uncooked chicken out of the window.

It was tea-time when we got to York Street L.M.S. station where we went our separate ways.

Learmount Castle Youth Hostel 1960

I arrived home in some trepidation, thinking that maybe the police and rescue services had been alerted. I needn't have worried for I was met by my Mother saying:

"The weather was so bad we didn't think you'd be back for a day or two".

AUSTIN McNALLY

Original Club Cyprus CC
Present Club North Down CC
The Cyprus CC was formed in Belfast in 1932
and I joined it in 1958.

Cyprus CC on tour

Cyprus CC in
Co. Tyrone 1952
Left to right: Roy
Erskine, Hugh Wilson,
Gordon Reid,
Harry Vance,
Charlie Bateman,
Alex Dickson
(behind Vance) two local
girls identity unknown,
Roy Hamilton, another,
Donald Stewart,
Another and
Davy Crothers

Cyprus C C
At a bridge over the
river Mourne at Sion
Mills   This later
became the Hanging
Bridge.

The girls in Donegal are not so slow

One of the red letter days in our cycling calendar was the Easter Tour.

Because we only had four days from work and because the high speed Ferry had not been invented our Easter tour destination was generally to Donegal. So it was that on Easter Saturday 1941, I was one of a group of seventeen to twenty year olds who met at 7.30 am at the Great Northern Station and boarded the train for Londonderry.

We had planned and booked to stay where we could in Hostels, but on Sunday evening we were staying in B & B in Donegal. When we had eaten and spruced ourselves up, four of us sauntered into town to survey the local talent. Being Sunday everything was very quiet but we encountered four local lasses looking in the window of the local ice cream parlour. They were extremely friendly and after a bit of chatting up we took them into the shop for a 'Melancholy Baby'. They cost ls/9d each and tasted like heaven as we hadn't seen ice cream for ages. We learned that the only entertainment in town was the local film show and how fortunate. The show would be starting in 15 minutes.

Off we went, each with a chatty friendly girl and expecting at least to have a snog in the gloom of the cinema. Inside the door a man at a table relieved us of 2 shillings a head. (3s./9p spent on this already but it would all be worth while) We then passed along a passage to the auditorium which was screened off by a heavy curtain. Through this into the cinema where we hoped to do some heavy petting, only to be confronted by the local priest who directed "Boys to the left, girls to the right" and parted us permanently. I can still hear those girls giggling as they rushed to join their friends in the right hand side of the cinema and regale them on the way they had taken in the sharpies from Belfast!

ROBERT HILL   North Down CC

East Ulster Road Club 1953
This club became the N.I. branch of the C.T.C.

Memorable trip to France

On the Paris tour 1949

Left to right:
Sam Hood, Gordon Reid, Jackie Fee,
Davey Crothers and Joe Stewart

In July 1949 a number of Cyprus Cyclists travelled (with their bikes) on the boat over to England. Jackie Fee, Gordon Reid, John Harvey, Davy Crothers, Joe Stewart and Sam Hood. We cycled down to Dover, making various overnight stops en route and staying mostly in cheap accommodation. We made the crossing from Dover to Calais. In Paris we went searching for certain specialised parts for the bikes. i.e. gears, etc. We also purchased coloured racing jerseys which we decided to immediately wear while cycling. We were surprised when some bystanders started to cheer when we rode past them – they mistakenly though we were part of the Tour de France! We spent two weeks in the vicinity of Paris and Brest. Cycling was very tiring due to the extreme heat in July and we were unable to visit as many places as we had originally planned to see. Nevertheless everyone enjoyed the tour and we returned home with many happy memories of our time in France as you can see from the photographs.

JOHN FEE Cyprus CC

Members of Cyrpus CC 1944

They had been to Portrush for the day and were heading home.
This photograph was taken at the Frosses near Ballymoney.

Left to right: Roy Erskine, Walter Mills, Bob Hill (aged 17) Davy Crothers, Jim Smiley (?)

Willie Weir

The Kircubbin shoemaker, Willie Weir was the great cyclist of the Ards Peninsula in the early years of the last century until the first years of the Great War.

Born on 14th January 1894, he started racing in 1910 on grass tracks at various parish sports meetings all over the area. He was known to bring home prizes such as Wag-at-the-wall clocks, tied to his back with baling twine. In fact he won three of these in his career – one of which still exists in the home of his son, John.

He also rode road time trials and is reputed to be the first person to get under the hour on the Portaferry Road – for 20 miles! These efforts may have been in Belfast C.C. club races. He only joined the club as a non-cyclist in 1940 when his sons, Sandy, John and Will took up the sport and became members, but he was a long serving vice President. John, his second eldest, had a notable achievement in 1943 when he won all Belfast C.C.'s trophies in the one year – one of them outright.

Willie and his daughter Hannah performed as turn stewards for Belfast, Cyprus and (later) Ards Cycling clubs, whose 20 and 25 mile events turned at Kircubbin's Main Street and Saltwater Bridge.

When Ards cycling Club was founded in 1944, Willie soon became a member, eventually becoming President in 1947. I well remember him timing my first efforts on the Portaferry Road.

He followed many sports with enthusiasm, especially boxing. Rinty Monaghan, who became World, European and Empire Flyweight Champion in 1948, was his hero. That year Weir travelled to the Olympic Games in London. He misjudged the money he might need, returned home with enough spare cash to buy the 'Weir Cup' for Ards Cycling club – a trophy still raced for to this day.

Willie Weir

His daughter Hannah tells a nice story of one of her father's trips to Belfast to see Rinty Monaghan fight. It was on 23rd March 1948 when the Belfast man defeated Jackie Paterson to take the above titles at the Kings Hall. She tells that the family were anxious when Willie failed to get off the last bus from Newtownards. When one and two o'clock passed with no sign of him they became increasingly worried and were taking turns to run to the door to see if he would appear. Finally at 2.30 am. they saw a dark figure on an oversized bicycle come labouring up the street. It was him. Exhausted and dishevelled, Hanna also noticed he was not wearing his soft hat. He explained that the trolley bus journey from the Kings Hall had not been in time for the last bus 'for Newtown'. However he caught another trolley bus to Dundonald and from there walked to Newtownards. He called hopefully with a friend who lived in a tiny cottage at the flood-gates. There he was offered the loan of the big bike upon which he just about made it home. After excitedly telling them all about Rinty's great success, Hannah, still a teenager, cried out "But Daddy, what about your hat?" Whereupon he replied "Oh, that. Sure I threw it up in the air and it didn't come down".

BILLY KIRK Ards C.C

John Weir, Willie's son writes ....

"I started racing 1937-38 with Maryland Wheelers along with my brothers Sandy and Will, Charlie Henderson, Tommy Givan, etc. In 1941-42 I joined Belfast Cycling Club whose club races were run on the Portaferry Road.

During the War sports meetings were held at Celtic Park, Windsor Park, Dunmore Park, Dixon Park in Ballyclare and Gibson Park. I rode at all these venues. I was not very successful on the track due to an early accident at Castlereagh Park when a cane rim broke and I had a serious crash. I lost confidence and from then on put my emphasis on Time Trials on the road.

My first 10 mile Time Trial with the Belfast club was 26 minutes approximately. Over the next few years I got down to 24 mins. 56 secs. – done one night in an open event when my minute man was Tom Smyth from Bellaghy.

He caught me and I tried to stay with him, not taking shelter however.

My first 20 mile effort in the Hanna Cup was a disaster! I fell at Greyabbey corner on the way out then at the turn in Kircubbin my father was handing me a drink when I touched him with my front wheel and came down again. On the way back I fell at the school corner in Greyabbey. What a night! But I finished third.

Hannah and John Weir, daughter and son of Willie Weir.
They admire a clock won by their father in 1912. Willie Weir rode 20 miles in 56 mins. to take home the beautiful time piece, tied to his back with baling twine.

In 1942 I won the Neill cup which if you won on two successive years you got to keep. It was a desirable trophy and I made sure it was mine by winning in 1943, by one second from Issac Matier. That was the year I won all the available Belfast C.C. Cups.

I raced a lot on the Antrim Road while riding for Northern C.C. Billy Dowds was the man to beat and Northern was his first club. The 25 mile record in the early Forties was 1 hr. 1 min. 37 secs. by J. Beattie but Dowds eventually took the record in 1950.

My best for 25 miles was 1 hr. 4 mins.

I rode 2 or 3 50's on the Antrim Road. In the first one I started too fast and 'blew up'. I came back to Glengormley on the back of a tandem, pushing very little!

My father had a bike presented to him by the Triumph firm. They had painted "A RACING BIKE FOR A RACING MAN on the down tube".

JOHN WEIR

Willie Weir and Members of Ards Cycling Club

Left to right: Jackie Wilson, Billy Kirk, Willie Weir, John Fennel and Ian Croft in 1956, after Kirk became Irish 25 mile champion and Kirk, Fennell and Wilson were team champions.

The Guinness Wheelers

On horseback: Gordon Reid, Norman McNeilly, Vinty O'Brien and Danny Hall

Lady and her shiek: Davy Crothers and Vinty O'Brien

Swim suits: Joe Stewart, Jackie Fee, Davy Crothers, Norman McNeilly? Vinty O'Brien John Harvey and Roy Erskine

Around 1947/48 myself and some lads from the Cyprus Cycling Club headed for a tour of Southern Ireland. Joe Stewart, Jackie Fee, Davy Crothers, Vinty O'Brien, John Harvey, Roy Erskine, Norman McNeilly and Danny Hall. We decided to name ourselves "The Guinness Wheelers" as quite a lot of the Black Stuff was consumed during the tour!

We stayed in various guest houses between Monaghan and Galway, then headed down the coast to Lahinch and Lisdoonvarna. While there we partook of the water from the famous health giving sulphur wells but we all agreed it was not as good as the Black Stuff!!

While in Ballybunion, Davy Crothers and Vinty O'Brien tried their hand at 'Dressing up', Vinty as a Sheik and Davy in female attire – actually using the sheets from the bed!

We cycled on, taking in the Cliffs of Moher and Killarney and again everyone agreed they had a wonderful time and returned home tired but with happy memories.

JOHN FEE   Cyprus   CC

In the heat of the moment

One Sunday morning in 1953 we decided to cycle round the Glens of Antrim – the wrong way. i.e. Up the Coast and down by Ballymena. Our 'clique' included Jimmy Mullan, Dan McArthurs, Bobby Darragh, Tom and Albert Douglas and myself.

We set out in light rain at about 10.30 am leaving Beresford Street where I lived, up Albany Street, left up Agnes Street, across Crumlin Road, up Cliftonpark Avenue, across Cliftonville Road, down on to the Antrim Road, up to and down Fortwilliam. There Albert and I decided to put on our capes.

We mounted our bikes again and decided to take a short cut down through Mount Vernon housing estate which had only footpaths and was all down hill. We were flying down these hills to catch up with our mates when Albert came off his bike on a sharp corner.

I pulled up and returned to the scene and found Albert doing an Indian hula hula dance under his cape and yelling in a foreign language. When I got him cooled down (figure of speech) and asked was he going round the bend, his reply I cannot repeat.

Apparently when he fell off his bike he landed on his back side and his box of matches for his cigarettes had gone on fire in his hip pocket!

WILLAM LIVINGSTONE Cyprus CC

Back row:
Jackie Fee, Joe Graham,
Jackie Lewis, Jimmy Robb, myself,
Albert Douglas,
Dan McAuthurs,
Billy Hanna,
Billy Moreland

Front row:
Bobby Lewis,
Jimmy Mullan, Jim Douglas,
cant remember??

'Roamer'

'ROAMER' was the pen name of Bill Murray who was a member and Vice President of the Belfast Cycling Club from 1930 to 1997. He was an enthusiastic tourist and travelled the length and breadth of Ireland by bicycle. His sketch book was always in his saddle bag where ever he chose to go, from which he produced numerous paintings in oil and water colour.

In the 1940's he did line drawings for the cover of the Official Circular which was a monthly magazine of the N.C.U. and the R.T.T.C., produced and edited by Joe Bell of the Windsor C.C. with the help of various members from other Clubs.

We thought it would be appropriate to reproduce some of Bill Murray's articles and line drawings for your appreciation.

Lunchtime near Sneem Co Kerry

The story of Woburn House

When I joined the Belfast Cycling Club the main problem was keeping the boys together during the off season

The club-runs then were confined to Saturdays which terminated at the end September, so something had to be done to keep the bunch together during the winter months. We struck oil through the efforts of our treasurer Jimmy McCoo, who was never a man to be put off a good idea. I think it was the way the big man Jimmy Blair called on him to see what he could suggest and our treasurer rose to the challenge. His family friends rented a house on the Woburn Road which was between Millisle and Carrowdore and it was used as a holiday home at weekends and during the public holidays. We began the first of many happy weekends there and as the weeks went by it soon took on the appearance of a Youth Hostel, with bunks etc. to accommodate up to sixteen or so.

At the end of the following March, old Hair-Oil (Sammy) gathered his forces together and suggested we renovate the house for the incoming tenants. We arrived with the various implements of our trades and set too with gusto. I was allotted 'Old Bill' as my helper to do the paper hanging and that worthy helper quickly attacked the old wallpaper with the cook's egg turner – stripping everything including a lot of the plaster as well. There was general chaos. I was using the table as a pasteboard and had the first sheet well pasted and dripping and proceeded to the nearest wall to continue operations. In my haste amid all the general confusion I didn't see my industrious mate working in the very spot which I had selected to start. The result was disastrous as Bill didn't take too kindly to being covered with paste and he burst his way through the paper and grabbed my paste brush and walloped me with it.

I am sure he will have a good chuckle to himself when he recollects the mud-pack I gave him that day.

Then there was the breaking-up parties and what fun we had at those. They were held on the last weekend in March. We had music with the aid of 'Kibby's' gramophone, whose complete repertoire seemed to be two old ditties which I will never forget. 'Texas Rangers' which was Gerry's favourite and 'Never take a bath till you need one'. I can still see Gerry with his old briar sitting in the chair singing himself to sleep and riding down the trail with those rangers.

There was the week-end that Isaac and I laid in grub for sixteen and waited in vain for the rest of the boys, so we just stuck the pan on and proceeded to fry every thing in sight. How we ever made upstairs beats me, but we must have as big Guy came hammering on the door on Sunday morning about 1 o'clock and proceeded to root us out of bed.

What happy memories of those winter nights I have when Tom, Isaac, Bob and I met on Saturdays at North Road on the Upper Newtownards Road in the afternoon as we were the advance party because some of the rest of the main party worked in the afternoons. George, Jimmy and Sammy would arrive about tea-time, nursing bruises from playing cycle polo, while others would arrive later. It wasn't long before the pan was on the stove and full of floating sausages (torpedos as Tom called them). Then the only noise was the rattle of knives and forks on the plates.

After everybody had satisfied their hunger and thirst there only remained the cutting of the cards to see who got the lowest one, then he had to do the washing up of the pan, cups and plates.

Other memories too of the night the ghost walked (hence 'Spook-villa') and the last flitting with 'Old Bill' mounted on the arm chair on top of an assembled bed and wheeled down the road at 11.00 pm on a winter's night. Those were the happiest days of my life.

ROAMER   (Bill Murray)

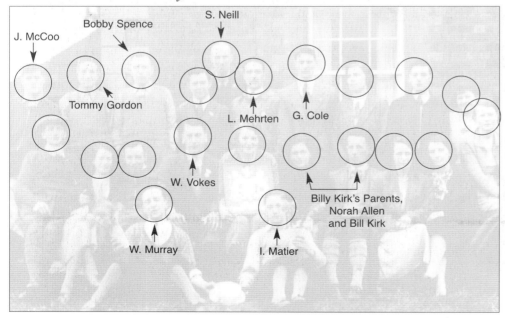

J. McCoo
Bobby Spence
S. Neill
Tommy Gordon
L. Mehrten
G. Cole
W. Vokes
Billy Kirk's Parents, Norah Allen and Bill Kirk
W. Murray
I. Matier

A group of Belfast CC members mark the occasion of the 43rd anniversary of the club at Woburn, near Millisle in 1935.

the story of Woburn House

Bill Murray 1935

Isaac Matier With Bill Murray 1935

Spook villa 1935

Not a sound was heard in the stilly night,
not a soul in the Villa awake
While even the mice would have thought twice
to come out and nibble the cake.

On the sleepers the moon shone its eerie light,
then suddenly one of them stirred
What was that at the window in ghostly attire,
as they watched it the vision was blurred.

Now I'll tell you Bill Murray's a strict TT since
he tasted McKay's Double Bass,
When he saw that sight he was far from tight
and his eyesight was still first class.

He got both Cole and Matier awake and
calmly he quelled their fear
Like warriors bold they stood in the cold and
watched for that ghost to appear.

Our three young gallants had not long to wait
for that ghost very soon re-appeared
It stood by the sash and was gone in a flash its
appearance was certainly weird.

Can you picture those three in their little short
shirts ready to do and to dare,
Cole had the poker and shovel in hand, while
Matier grabbed the back of a chair.

From its head to its toes was a mistily white,
the watchers were fairly enthralled
But in one fleeting glance, they saw just by chance,
that the ghost was nearly bald.

Now the ghost got too chummy, Cole gave it the
dummy and caught it mid-rift to his credit.

Now if ever you sleep at Spook Villa at night
and the moon shines down very clear,
Keep your eye on the cook, he has hair like yon Spook and
methinks you will have nothing to fear.

ROAMER

Spook villa 2007

Now sub-divided into 3 dwellings at 47 Woburn Road, Millisle, this is the house made
available to Belfast C.C. in the early 1930's by Jimmy McCoo.
By co-incidence the dwelling on the right is occupied by an ex-cyclist Don Wright who
was a member of Ards Cycling Club in the 1970's.

The photograph is by Billy Kirk who was overcome with emotion when he found Spook villa, especially when he realised his parents had
sat almost exactly where his bike was placed two years before his birth.

So many memories

A training run near Morrisville, New Zealand

Cormac McCann, Vanda McVicker, Mark Kane, Andrew Moss, Alister Irvine
(Out of picture: Joe Barr and David McCall)

When the letter came in from Isabel (Woods) about Memories of Cycling I said to myself where would I start? I remember cycling down the Portrush Road to Morrison Cottage near the end of August 1954 as the Ballymoney & District C.C. was running a Time Trial on the Portrush Road course. It was on a standard BSA Cycle that had been purchased in Jim Warnock's in Main Street, the main BSA Agent. But why was I there? Well I had been to Dundrod for the Ulster Grand Prix and three riders had been killed and earlier in the year six lost their lives in the Isle of Man T.T. I had this interest then in the Two Stroke motorcycles because at the Farm Engineering Class that I had attended at the local Technical School, a course far ahead of its time set in motion by the foresight of Commander D.C. Quail and taught by Mr. Holmes. At the course we had done a lot of work on the Two Stroke principle of combustion and as DKW were to be at Dundrod, I went there by bus to spectate, near the Hairpin. As a result of this I became Secretary of the B & D until the end of 1959.

I then branched out on my own, first with Route Wheelers and later with Team ROUTE CRT and this gave me a combined Forty Eight years of Memories.

The first rider that I helped was Stephen McDowell just down the street and around the corner into Meetinghouse Street. Just a few weeks ago at the 2009 Tour of the North, Stephen who had taken me out in his car to the Vanishing Lake to see the Stage told me the story of how he burned the ass out of the teapot after his first 100, he was in such bad shape.

Then there was the evening that one of the Route Wheelers put rub on the wrong parts at a Track Meeting in Portadown and again in Portadown when Rommy Rauneyt was stopped by the RUC on the way back in from the Regal Grand Prix and he blew the cigar smoke all around the Officers face to cover up some other fluid intake!

Time moved on and I did as mechanic. Five Tour of Scotland's and one Tour of Britain. One of the T of S was the same year as the T of B, as well as a pre Commonwealth Games R/R in Edinburgh. The Scottish tours brought some great memories. Like the evening Dave Kane came to me to say his frame was cracked. A new frame was brought to me in my bedroom and then it was down to the basement in the YMCA in Sauchiehall Street in Glasgow and they kept me in coffee most of the night so as I could get Dave's bike ready for the morning stage. The late Liam Horner, keeping the doorman at the Hotel in Kirkcaldy talking about haggis while Peter Doyle's bike was pulled up to my bedroom window and into the bedroom so as I could get it ready with 28/28 wheels for the morning T.T. The stage down into Dunbar when the Cech's went through a hedge and came somehow out by a gate and finished in the bunch. The "S" bends down to the T of B finish in Birmingham when Noel Gallagher wrote off another frameset and some teeth. But I had a bike built for the next stage.

The Bath Road 100 with Morris Foster and the ride from Heathrow to Steatly Y H will always be remembered.

The evening two young women from my home town walked into the Mount Smart Stadium with the Northern Ireland Commonwealth Games team in Auckland New Zealand. The nine weeks in New Zealand and the Sunday night dinners out at Annie's is where I will end, as it is the lasting memory.

WALLACE McNAUL

The delph egg

From the early 50's to the mid 60's our Club (then St Gabriel's CC) had an annual cycle camping tour in Southern Ireland during the 'July Fortnight' – always on a tight budget.

On one occasion, 1964 Barney reminds me, there were just four of us. Brian F and I were joined in Killarney by Barney H. and Tony B who had been racing 'down South' earlier. We were camped beside a little stream a few miles from Killarney along the Castleisland Road in a three man tent. We were young and slim then! Having a rest day before riding on, we went into Killarney for a look around and a bit of shopping; particularly looking for a pump washer for a Primus stove (hard to get). About to give up, we entered one of those sell-everything shops which were a feature of the South and, praise be the shopkeeper found one after a search. While he was rummaging around I noticed a basket full of delph eggs and decided to play a prank on Brian (who was a humorous guy unlikely to hit me – also smaller!

We had earlier decided to have a light tea of boiled eggs, bread and cheese and this was a golden opportunity. Making an excuse I went back to the shop and carefully selected the most natural looking egg with no seams. (I should mention that real eggs cost 3d (old pennies) each, while the delph variety cost 2 shillings – eight times as much)! Back at the tent, around teatime, we each helped prepare the meal – one to slice the cheese, one to slice and butter the bread, one to rinse and fill the teapot and egg-pot and the fourth to light the Primus stoves. The eggs were placed in the pot and put on the stove to boil and we sat talking about going to the dance that night and what our chances were of romancing the local belles.

When the eggs had boiled for a couple of minutes I asked Brian to kindly rinse my enamel mug in the river as it was a bit grubby. Once his back was turned I whipped one egg out of the boiling water, concealed it and replaced it was the delph egg. On Brian's return, Barney helped the joke by saying he hoped that the eggs weren't boiled for too long. Tony doled out the bread and cheese. Barney poured out the tea and I dealt out the boiling eggs – giving Brian the dummy and hoping aloud that it wasn't too hard boiled (struggling to keep a straight face).

We had no eggcups and Brian held his egg in a towel and, talking away, started to tap it with a huge soup spoon. (He had no teaspoon). After a little while he noticed he was making no headway and started hitting it harder – eventually saying there was something wrong. He hit it again with an almighty clatter which exploded the thing – sending splatters of broken delph everywhere.

Needless to say, Barney, Tony and I were rolling about splitting ourselves laughing till the tears ran – even more so when Brian said he thought the shopkeeper had included the dummy by mistake – and renewed even more when he heard it cost two shilling and he was annoyed that we had let him wreck the thing so he couldn't get a refund! Believe me it was a lot funnier at the time than writing about it now.

Alas Brian is no longer with us and Tony is in Canada, incapacitated by a car accident. Only Barney and I are still glad to be active – long may it continue.

PS To this day I can't say whether Brian actually knew what was going on and played along with it (to the hilt)! If he did we were the ones who were had, but it would have been an Oscar worthy performance.

BILLY SMYTH   St. Gabriel's / Pheonix CC

To Prove a Point

Joe Graham of Northern CC started cycling with the NCA in 1947. He rode the first Belfast to Dublin massed start in 1949 and was good on both road and track. Also a good time trialist, he broke the hour for 25 miles in 1951 but was stung by the jibe, always used by the 'official' cyclists (NICF) in those days that the NCA timed their events with the town hall clock. He came across to the NICF in 1952 to prove a point.

His first outing was an Ards CC '25' on the Portaferry Road on 5th April 1952 which he won by 42 secs. from Rab Collim of Cyprus CC with Davy Martin of Windsor 3rd.

A colourful extrovert who exuded zest and happiness he had a very modern relationship with his first wife in which they could bring their extra-marital friends to meet each other.

In 1967 he immigrated to Dorset, Ontario, with his second wife Mary, where among other occupations he became a stage Hypnotist and Hypnotherapist, abandoning his original trade of joiner. He also became a coach for one of the Martial arts, dying in 2002 upon returning home from an instruction session with a children's' group. He was eighty.

BILLY KIRK

L-R: Charlie Henderson, Joe Graham, Billy Kirk and George Wilks - 1999

Wheeler dealer

Dennis, Mike and the children in Carrigart.

In April 1985 I took my wife, Pauline and our two young children on a weekend trip to a friend's cottage near Carrigart in Co. Donegal. It was great weather but the heat of course made the journey even longer, especially for the kids, so that by the time we reached Carrigart the promised ice-creams were very welcome. As usual on such a weekend I had taken a bicycle in the hope that I could get a few miles in while Pauline took the children to the beach. It was while we were sitting in the car with our ice-creams that a strange, 'gypsy' looking man tapped the window of the car indicating that he wanted to speak to me. With some trepidation I rolled down the window to be greeted in a barely understandable accent. His name, he said was Dennis and he wanted to buy the bicycle perched on the roof of my car.

wheeler dealer

Initially, I was taken aback but also relieved that this was all he wanted. I told him that the bicycle was not for sale, but Dennis was not taking NO for an answer. By way of 'breaking the ice' so to speak and with perhaps a hint of black-mail, he insisted on buying us all another ice-cream. At least the children would not say NO. And so it continued there on the main street of Carrigart. Dennis was obviously determined to get the bicycle and I was equally determined that it was not for sale. The dealing continued, his 'banter' was infectious and within a short time I realised that we were in 'danger' of becoming friends – not a good idea in the middle of financial dealings. We had still not reached our destination and so with a promise that I would consider selling after the weekend, we drove the last few miles to the cottage. Dennis, not wishing to lose the chance at the bicycle insisted on following us to the cottage, whereupon Pauline made it clear that there was to be no more talk of bicycles that day.

The next morning was beautiful so with a blue cloudless sky and sandy beaches nearby Pauline and the kids headed off, while I went for a spin on my bike. When I returned, he was there sitting in the car waiting for me. Pauline had not returned and so Dennis and I exchanged pleasantries and then of course he launched into another attempt to buy my bicycle. It turned out that he was the local 'bicycle dealer' though he didn't have a shop, preferring to buy and sell from his home. By this time my curiosity was raised – after all I was a bicycle dealer myself and so by the time Pauline returned I had agreed to go with him to his house. It was well off the main road and as we pulled up I could see that he was having an extension built and we were about to find out why.

Once inside the tiny cottage it was for me like an 'Aladdin's Cave'. The place was packed with bicycles of every make and size! They were hanging from the ceiling, pushed into corners, crammed into his already tiny kitchen and even on the staircase.

Dennis helped to get bicycles for the local racing fraternity and also bought and sold all types of bikes at Christmas time. He was a real wheeler dealer!

We squeezed up the stairs past handlebars, frames and all the usual bits and pieces that I was familiar with and there on the landing was a bicycle I recognised instantly – it was Morris Foster's old 'curly stay' Hetchins. Here in the middle of nowhere was one of the greatest Irish cyclist's bicycle.

Dennis had seen it advertised and had travelled to Morris's house at Glengormley to buy it and now it lay rather sadly in a tiny cottage in remote Donegal. The day was, for me at any rate, proving to be interesting. However, the best was yet to come. Dennis in return for us coming had assured us that he would make some tea. He enquired if we both took milk and then lifting a grotty looking pot he bid us all to follow him to the 'byre' where he set about milking a cow. Naturally this was entertainment for the children but as my eyes grew accustomed to the gloom I spied a beautiful antique oak Victorian sideboard. It was covered in straw and splashed with cow manure, but it was a beauty. I knew it could be restored and so hiding my excitement, I casually enquired if it might be for sale. Dennis stood up and with a sharp intake of breath replied that he knew "it was very, very valuable".

"As valuable as the bicycle?" I countered and so began our dealing in earnest.
Back inside the house Pauline for some reason declined the tea while I just managed to close my eyes, think of the sideboard and drink it. It was a done deal – the sideboard for my bicycle.

I left the bicycle there and returned with a trailer two weeks later for the sideboard which we have to this day in our house. Now without the straw and manure it is much admired and quite apart from its value, is a reminder of a very interesting weekend in Donegal almost twenty five years ago.

MIKE McCONAGHY

p.s. The bicycle had been a second-hand Falcon racer traded in for about thirty pounds.

Crilly's Ferraris

Bobby Crilly from Ladybrook Park on the Upper Falls Road won the N.I. junior road race championship in 1956.

A member of Western C.C. he often trained with Tommy Burns of the Windsor C.C. who was his best friend. In later life he developed an obsession for Ferrari sports cars, owning many different models down the years, while living in the working class housing estate where he kept the vehicles.

At his funeral in 2004 there was an ostentatious celebration of his life in the form of a group of at least six Ferraris and a Maserati, all revving up their engines in front of his home, before setting of in convoy to the cemetery followed closely by 20 old cycling mates on their bikes, the cars driving at not much over tick-over speed!

BILLY KIRK

A visit from the banshee

*In the 1950's, St. Gabriel's CC alternated Sunday
club runs with weekends camping (Summer) or
Youth Hostelling (Autumn/Winter/Spring).*

On one such weekend in early Summer 1953 (?) the camping section went to Camlough, near Newry where we had a frightening and unexplained experience. Our campsite was a little overgrown triangle of land between the Jonesborough Road and a small road at an angle. There was just enough space for the two tents to be erected at angles to each other and a few yards apart. So on one side of the Jonesborough Road was our campsite and on the other was a swamp.

There were eight of us – four in each tent and we were young, fit and slim, non drinkers and good-living. I don't remember all the names, but my tent included John McF, Paddy W and possibly Joey D. After our evening meal, cooked over the Primus stoves, we ambled around Camlough which in those days was (still is?) an important farmers market town with, it seemed, every other building a pub. After that we strolled the couple of miles into Bessbrook - a mill town built on model lines and with nary a pub! Arriving back at the camp about 9.30 pm, tea was made and after some chat we went to bed. We always read in bed – with a candle stuck on a plate – until sleep took us, when we settled down. At some time in the dark hours, I woke up with a cold fear! Across the road – from the swamp – there was an unearthly wailing the like of which I'd never heard (no – not cats, nor foxes, both of which can sound 'unearthly' and which I'd heard before). Lying there in a blue funk (as the saying goes), I was petrified. Just then I became aware that my companions were awake and we whispered our fright to each other. Meanwhile the sounds became louder and moved from the swamp, across the road and approached the tents. Even more frightening it seemingly halted somewhere between the two tents! We heard the inhabitants of the other tent shouting at me to stop, thinking I was carrying out a practical joke (as I was known to do on occasion). We replied that it wasn't me and proposed going out to check. The only snag was that we had no lamp, though the other tent had one. However they declined to come any further than the door of their tent, shining the lamp into the undergrowth, where we saw nothing. The sound remained somewhere very close, not lessening and we accepted that there was nothing to be done. After a period, the visitant moved back over the road to the swamp and the noise dwindled away. Sleep was long in coming that night!

After 50 odd years, I still don't know what it was and the fear is remembered. The swamp is still there - the 'triangle' even more overgrown – and I could take you to it tomorrow!!

BILLY SMYTH   St. Gabriel's/Phoenix CC

The Saints C.C. of Twinbrook

Eddie Rafter and the Twinbrook cyclists at the Abbey Lodge Hotel, Downpatrick - 1984

After getting the wanderlust out of my system: driving buses in London, Merchant Navy and finally ten years in Germany, I decided to high-tail it back home and settle down. I was now an old man of forty four. I bought a bike in Munich and decided to start off where I left off. i.e. back to the world of cycling in dear old Belfast! To break me in, so to speak, I toured from Munich to Nice via Garmisch, St. Moritz, Genoa and St. Remo, returning up along the Rhone River to France and east into Switzerland and Germany.

When I got back to Belfast the few remaining of our family were living in Twinbrook which is very handy for cycling, being so near to the country.

The kids seemed to be a lot better in those days of no drugs or cheap alcohol and it wasn't long before they noticed me going out on the racing bike with the full kit of clothing. The "Mister, Mister" questions soon started and they seemed genuinely interested, so I suggested a cycling club. They took to the idea like fish to water! We went and had a word with Father Mullan and he was delighted and got us the use of the Sports Hall in the school for a couple of nights a week. We called ourselves THE SAINTS.

It was Autumn and just the right time to get them all started on the winter training scheme. They were very excited about the prospect of getting away to all the towns and villages and pitting their strength and speed against all corners. These kids had hardly any experience outside Twinbrook or West Belfast due to the troubled times, so as well as a great healthy pastime, building independence and strength of character, it was also a very important exercise in cross community relations. In this context, I overheard a conversation on the way home from a race in which a youth proclaimed to his friend, "I never saw a Protestant before"!

Now before I go any further I have to state that I couldn't have handled it by myself. Luckily I had great assistance from a few old hands from former days. Men like Jovial James (Junior McLaughlin) and Bobby Crilly of "Ferrari" fame *(see page 61).* Bobby won the first race I ever rode - The Northern Ireland Junior Road Championship 1956. Then we had the evergreen Bo Graham and Paddy Mooney, son of Mickey who had held the Yellow Jersey in the RAS 1956. And loads of Dads and Mums all gave great assistance. But the biggest challenge of all was soon to face us. Back in those days frames and accessories were gold dust and how and where were we going to find racing bikes for twenty five to thirty kids? The problem was resolved by the cycling fraternity in general. The word got out that any sort of stuff was welcome, even if it needed repaired. The response was great. Attics were invaded and ancient frames and sprints and all things under the sun began arriving. I could do a bit of brazing and buckle fixing and many hours were spent getting the youngsters equipped. As a matter of fact it led to me getting interested in Frame Building and Wheel Building which inadvertently created a livelihood for me until recently. Bobby Magreechan of Ards C.C. built me a perfectly engineered Frame Building jig and Fork jig and with advice from Eddie Curran (an old time Frame Builder) and also Mervyn Hall, I soon got the rudimentaries of building rough and ready machines. (And thankfully of safe and strong construction) Geordie Wilkes was also tinkering with re-sprays and the building of a few frames and we had a great relationship comparing ideas etc. The actual cycle training on the road was done on Saturdays and Sundays or if they happened to have holidays. Rollers were used at night in the Sport Hall and plenty of five-a-side football. It was agreed that to get to the races it would be mostly – ride there – race – and ride home!

Paul Slane wins the 1991 Tour of Armagh. Twice `Irish road race champion, he showed great versatility by also taking the `Irish 25 mile time trial'. A protege of Eddie Rafter, he was a member of the Saints CC in early teenage years. He appears in the group photograph of 'The Saints' in front row, second right. He now runs a flourishing cycle business in Andersonstown, Belfast.

the Saints CC of Twinbrook

We must have had reasonably good luck with the weather because I cannot remember many soakings.

If the venue was over twenty five miles then we had to find transport. Old trailers and vans were commandeered and we always seemed to manage.

Geordie Wilkes thought it was fabulous that they rode to most of the races because right from the start The Saints were cleaning up in all the races. He criticised the other Dads for driving their kids to all the races, pointing out that The Saints method paid dividends. Geordie called a spade a spade!

So for a few glorious years The Saints ruled the roost in the Ulster Schoolboys events. And to crown it all, Gary Syminton won the All Ireland Under 12 Championship at Mondello Park. Alas he was disqualified for the "two hands in the air" victory salute. But anyway we got a special medal for him and crowned him king, regardless of the rules. The most successful product of the Club has to be Paul Slane. As a senior he won the All Ireland Senior Road Championship not once, but twice! Plus many other big Events including the Tour of Ulster and lots of representations on the National Squad. So there you have it! I can assure you that there's great talent out there among the kids if only enough adults would give of their time to guide them in the right direction. And maybe more so now than ever when one considers the temptations the youngsters are subjected to.

EDDIE RAFTER

Pen drawing by Frank Patterson - from the Patterson Book, Temple Press 1948

'Drum-ups' and coined phrases

"You wouldn't see that in Australia" became a catch phrase in the 'Belfast'.

One of our members had emigrated to Australia or Canada and Bobby Collins and I think that it was Arthur McShane. As the Club Run breasted a hill and the panoramic scene or view unfolded before us, someone was sure to call out: "You wouldn't see that in Australia".

I digress for a moment…

Maybe it was his subtle way of discouraging any more of our friends from leaving us. It wasn't only the boys who went off to seek work and hopes for a better life. The girls did it too. Nora Porter was a lovely and popular club member. She lived in Aberdeen Street, the next one to Isabel's home at Dundee Street. Norah went off to Australia. We were all shocked and saddened when we learned that she had died of cancer shortly after emigrating.

My very first cycling (though neither of us were in a cycling club at the time) pal was Peter White who lived in Newtownbreda. We were in the 42nd Scouts and Rovers together and I recall our farewell cycle ride just before he was setting off for Australia. We went off to Lisburn via the Hillhall Road and then Ballinderry and Portmore, the wee Lough at Lough Neagh. It was a lovely calm summer evening – spoilt by the swarms of Lough Neagh May fly. They got into our hair, down our open-necked shirts and above all, into our mouths (and me a vegetarian!) In Australia he wrote me for a while and enclosed photographs which demonstrated that he was enjoying his cycle touring. Sadly the letters stopped and only months later did I learn that he had died.

Another close, non club cyclist from Newtownbreda went off to New Zealand but sadly he too died of Leukaemia. No wonder I've no notion of emigrating!

MORE ABOUT CATCH PHRASES

Anyway, back to Catch Phrases peculiar to our Club. We had a Dickie McIlvenna who at every Drum Up would get his little frying pan out and so was born the call "Get the pan on Dickie". Sometimes altered to "Dickie, get the pan on".

But what of those Drum Ups? They probably hold the fondest memories of my cycling days. Every Club had their own favourite spots to boil the can and heat the beans or soup. When I joined the 'Belfast', short club runs and long Drum Ups seemed to me to be what cycling was about. Only later when I realised that it was miles I needed, if I was ever to achieve any sort of success in racing, did I join up with Maurice Clarke, Jackie Martin, Leslie Bingham etc. and leave the comfort of the camp fire early and take the long way home. When I tell you that our club run in those late Forties only went as far as Rademon Estate just outside Crossgar and barely twenty miles from our starting point at the Thompson Memorial outside the B.B.C. in Ormeau Avenue.

The Doyen of the Belfast's Oldies, Bill Murray, had a cottage near-by, aptly named Landscape Cottage, for William Otway Murray was not just a house painter and sign writer but a very accomplished artist who had taken lessons with the likes of Maurice Wilkes, and J. Humbert Craig, etc. etc. We would lie on our cycle capes under the big conifer trees with our cigarettes and pipes and set the world to right. Heated debates between Conservatism and Socialism, watching the sparks rising from the fire, disappear with the almost clear smoke, into the darkening evening light made it quite a struggle to leave this idyllic scene for another fifty to sixty miles detour home.

a 'Drum up'

It may have been Bill Murray's respectability and persuasive ways that had gained us permission from the Estate's Owner, Lady Reid to Drum Up in her woodland. It was beside the bridge at the bottom of Church Road, off the Ballynahinch/Crossgar Road. The Estate later became the home of Mr. King of Osborne King and Megran, the well known Estate Agents and Auctioneers.

It was then that we started to Drum Up in the gateway entrance into the Old Graveyard at Kilmore.

Not so private or comfortable but maybe, and I say maybe, for I have no proof one way or the other, it was not acceptable to allow a Drum Up in one's Demesne. It hardly came 'with the Deeds'.

CLUB CAPTAIN FRED COLLINS

That gateway spot brings to mind our beloved Club Captain, Fred Collins. He always had a wee newspaper parcel containing a few sticks and pieces of old cycle tyres with the wire cut off, to help the fire along. Ash saplings from the hedge opposite the graveyard had been cut and left lying in the field and I gathered some of these and was in the process of breaking them up into suitable lengths when my mates said that I was stupid. That the Ash was too green (it was the winter) and wouldn't light. I however, being an ex Boy Scout leader, knew better! Green Ash is one wood that can ignite easily when lighting a fire.

Kilmore was and still is a lovely village and occasionally and especially the Sunday run before Christmas, the Captain would lead us past the usual Drum Up spots, into Kilmore Village and into the yard at the rear of Cis Masons Pub! Soon we were sipping bottles of stout and sitting around the "out of tune" piano, our glasses adding new ring stains to the already well marked piano lid. Dougie Patterson played all the grand old sing along tunes.

Our other favourite Drum Up spot was at the River Bridge at Clonvaraghan.

RABBIT SHOOTING

Bobby Smith and Harry Reford used to bring their 'Two Twos' down for a weekends rabbit shooting to 'the wee house' at Clonvaraghan. Many a Drum Up ended in chaos as we all scattered to take cover behind the trees as the Two Two ammunition exploded in the fire Hardly a wise prank but when one is young one doesn't think before acting. I think that Clonvaraghan and all the happy memories of that place has been adequately covered in another article in this book.

TEN GREEN BOTTLES

I recall getting a puncture after leaving Clonvaraghan and heading into Leitrim village on our way home via Banbridge. I was never allowed to fix a puncture when with the Club, someone invariably told me to "Stand back, you're only a Gardener." Well as I leant against the roadside grassy bank, I saw that most of the riders, apart from my thoughtful Knights of the Road, had ridden the last 30 odd yards into the village and were nonchalantly leaning against the front window of the Pub and Shop.

 I glanced up again and this time saw only four or five figures, where there had previously been six or seven. A further look and low and behold two or three were left. This time I watched and to my annoyance (but on reflection, not with surprise) saw the remaining lads slide along the wall until, backs to the door, the door opened a wee bit and they backed in. It was like 10 green bottles hanging on the wall – and then there were none. The Club knew exactly where one should get a puncture!

 When I started to go out on the bike with John Kennedy, Bill Murray and Leslie Merthen and headed towards Lady Reid's Estate at Rademon, we used to call in to the Post Office at Listooder where the late (indeed almost all my named people in this piece) are now sadly 'late'. Tommy Rea always had a case or two of bottled stout. Romantically one could call it a Sheebeen. Here we could also get the odd bag of sweets without coupons, for the War, though over, had left us with many things still rationed. Eggs we used to get just outside Dromara and over aged bacon at Barney McVey's wee shop at Clonvaraghan.

FAVOURITE

The 'Belfast' always loved County Down. Especially its back roads as they followed the up and down terrain of the Drumlins. Seldom did we venture into Counties Armagh or Antrim, though when we did, the Captain always knew where we were to Drum Up, be it on the way out of Randalstown, beside the Glenwherry River, or on the homeward run down the Antrim Coast Road.

There are so many things that one misses as one gets older, but top of the list are the Drum Ups!

PETER WOODS   *Belfast C C*

Lifesaving at foxford

July 1955 was a real scorcher and St. Gabriel's CC was on its annual July fortnight cycle camping tour in the West of Ireland. Foxford, County Mayo – where we camped for two nights (with a rest day) proved a very hospitable village, where the people went out of their way to make we young travelling strangers feel welcome. It is/was famous world wide for the Foxford Woollen Mills - as well known in its day as Waterford Crystal/ Belleek Pottery etc. The incident which comes to mind occurred during a conducted tour of the famous Woollen Mills to which we were kindly invited.

Our guide was an affable young man called Brian who gave us plenty of information on the history of the mill, while conducting us around the various work and store rooms. We were passing through a large room filled nearly to the edges by deafening machinery which had to be squeezed past. Passing along one side, someone noticed Brian bending over, apparently to inspect the machine. To our horror we realised that in fact the corner of his coat had been caught by a slowly-revolving roller and he was being drawn into it. We shouted and yelled to try to get the machine stopped and tried to drag Brian clear. But no one heard us above the clatter of the machine and we were in despair, for by this time the coat had tightened up to such an extent that Brian could not get it off.

Thank God for our camping custom of the time, for George M was luckily carrying a sheath knife (used for opening tins) which, with great presence of mind he whipped out and sliced the tail off the coat! At the cost of the coat, Brian's life was saved and George was the hero of the day.

To cap a happy ending we had a whip round and presented Brian with £5 for a new jacket – in those days that would pay for a good one!

BILLY SMYTH
St. Gabriel's/Phoenix CC

The Frank Patterson
Book, Temple Press

The Little Book

On the way home from one of our winter runs, we were approaching Ballynahinch when a B Special waved us down and demanded that we put our lights on. Peter (Woods) our Leader took out his little book and indicated that it was two hours before lighting up time. The B man still insisted and demanded to be obeyed. At this point Peter put his leg over his bicycle and started to move off.

The B man produced his pistol, pointed at Peter's back and called for him to stop. Peter rode on and only when the B man put his pistol away did the rest of us continue on our way. We went straight to the Ballynahinch Police Station and Peter reported the whole incident. He followed this by a letter to the appropriate authority. A wall of silence followed. I lost faith in our system of Law and Order from that day.

DOUGIE KNIGHT   Belfast CC

A hot day at Skyview restaurant

(When asked where we dined we always replied: THE SKYVIEW)

Drum-Up – the highlight of the day. For the un-initiated this is the time of the day when club cyclists stop for soup and sandwiches and assorted delicacies. I had just received a consignment of a new compact item called 'the collapsible cup'. I produced some of these at a drum-up and was immediately inundated with orders. However, when a few of us were drinking our tea from them screams would have been heard from some distance as they almost simultaneously collapsed.

After reading the small print it was obvious that they were only suitable for cold drinks! Unsurprisingly the orders were withdrawn! I had just become a vegetarian and with evangelical zeal was preaching during our drum-up about the uselessness of white bread and said "you might as well eat paper." In the Belfast CC you make statements like that at your peril! As we were ready to leave, Maurice Clarke said "Save the News of the World, I might get hungry on the way home". During a discussion, I foolishly quoted Freud and for the next hour it was "Do you like boiled eggs"?

No, I'd rather have them Freud" "I'll see you on Freuday"

And so it went on......I grew up very quickly, thanks to Belfast CC

DOUGIE KNIGHT Belfast CC

The Mercian

One Saturday in July 1958 I cycled from Belfast to Newcastle County Down to stay in my first Youth Hostel.

A life changing experience. Only two years earlier I was in Whiteabbey Hospital, the Whiteabbey Sanitorium as it was known then. I was very young and very ill. For months I could not put a foot to the floor. On my discharge I was told to avoid getting wet, avoid chills and not to 'over do it'. Youth Hostelling on a bike, in all seasons and all weathers was not on this prescription. Avoid getting wet – not easy on the Antrim Coast Road when a severe cross wind from the ocean would drive the rain in under the plastic cape. Avoid chills – in winter the dormitory windows in Learmount Castle Youth Hostel had ice on the inside of the glass!

Sometimes during the summer months I would leave Belfast at 6.00 pm on a Friday, cycle to Mellifont Abbey Youth Hostel near Drogheda, stay the night and be in Dublin by lunch time the next day. Travel all the way home on Sunday, work on Monday, meet the boys on Wednesday night, a short run down the Strangford coast, back by Donaghadee, Newtownards and home. Perhaps this was 'overdoing it', but I was never fitter or happier!

In the early Sixties we led an unrestricted life. No risk assessment forms to fill in, no boxes to tick and no health and safety officer telling us how to climb into a top bunk or jump out of it.

There were dry toilets in some Hostels, fetching water in a bucket, arriving to find empty gas cylinders – so what? – light the fire and put the pan on. After the meal, a story, a joke or a song was enough. With 65 miles behind us that day against a head wind and showers, we didn't need rocked to sleep.

On a bike I was one with nature. My very breathing was in harmony with the pedals. Dropping down from a 9,000 feet Alpine pass I could hear the roar of a mountain river, or the sound of cow bells in the distant valley.

June 1966 I flew to Paris, wheeled the bike out of the airport and headed south to Spain, re-crossed the Pyrenees and headed north for Norway via Toulouse, Marseille, Lyon, Basel, Strasbourg, into Denmark, Gottenberg, Oslo, turned west into Norway, Bergan, Dover, Maidstone, Heathrow and home.

When I was on my back in Whiteabbey hospital, to cough, hiccup or laugh caused me pain. I'm still grateful to Nurse Boyd in Ward Four for all her loving care and attention and grateful for mates, who to this day still make me laugh even though the old jokes are painful!

That bike, my Mercian, with her slender front forks and scrolled lugwork all in a lovely colour of purple and gold was part of me and we both belonged to the countryside, not only of Ireland but of Europe. For very little outlay the bike gave me a profound love of nature, lifelong friendships and health.

RAY ELWOOD *Artist* NEWTOWNARDS

A page of Advertisements taken from THE ULSTER CYCLIST in the mid 1930's.
They make interesting reading.

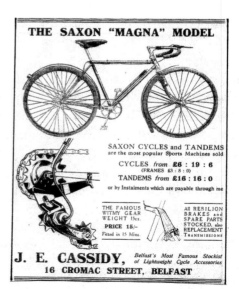

Some cycling memories 1948 – 1960

1948 My first contact with the cycling world was during my early days starting my working life.

I was working as an office boy aged fourteen on board the HMS Eagle aircraft carrier at Harland and Wolff. I was employed there until I was able to start my apprenticeship at sixteen as a Mechanical Engineer. I became friendly with an engineer on board the ship who lived in Lisburn and cycled to work every day. He took his tea break in the drawing store where I was employed and he was always talking about his weekend outings. He seemed to have travelled all over the Province. I talked more about his activities to my parents than what I was doing at work! My eldest sister must have been telling her boyfriend about how I was carried away with these cycling stories for, to my surprise, he arrived one day at our house with a BSA sports cycle – rather old but in good order. I certainly could not have afforded to purchase one – my wages were ten shillings a week. That started me on twelve very enjoyable years devoted to cycling.

BILLY CALDWELL Cyprus CC

1949 MY INTRODUCTION TO CYPRUS CC

L-R: Herbie Holden, Tom Allingham, Bob Collim and Tommy Talbot

One evening on our regular evening runs along with a neighbour, Newell Moore who also was interested in cycling, we met up with a club cyclist, Roy Erskine. He was on his way home on a training run. Roy invited us to his club – Cyprus – which we accepted. We met the members such as Gordon Reid, John Harvey, Hue Wilson and many others all of whom gave us all the encouragement necessary to become good club members.

At weekends - youth hostelling. During the week, training sessions and eventually, road racing.

I was unable to purchase a racing cycle as

I was now starting my apprenticeship and still not earning a pound note. I managed to buy a new frame (five pounds) and each week I bought a part for it until I had a good racing bicycle and really felt like a member of a racing club. I have had some moments never to be forgotten that I would like to share with those who read this book.

1952 A DISAPPOINTING 100 MILE RACE

I entered my first 100 miles race on the Antrim Road. I had an early start – third on the sheet.

The turn was about three miles after the fork on the road where one road takes you to Coleraine and the other to Ballycastle. When I got to the fork where a marshal normally directed you on the right road, no one was to be seen. I followed the route – I was to keep to the left but after arriving in Coleraine, I realized I had taken the wrong road! By this time I had covered fifty two miles and was now out of the race and had to turn around and head home. When I arrived back at the fork in the road there was the marshal doing a good job directing the competitors on the right route. Asking him where he was when I arrived at that point, he said he must have been over the hedge as he had the call of nature. He had seen me but being indisposed was unable to call me. Fifty miles back to the start and out of the race. I never competed in another 100 miles race again!

1954 GOOD FRENCH

Myself and Newell Moore (1954) headed off to France on a two week cycle tour. We crossed on the ferry to Le Havre. On board the ferry we met up with another cyclist, who I believe was a teacher.

As we had planned to stay in Youth Hostels, he suggested that it would be a good idea if we could at least ask the way to the Hostel in French. So with great patience the teacher instructed Newell on how to say, in French, "Could you show us the way to the local Youth Hostel please"? Newell rehearsed this over and over again until he had it word perfect.

On our arrival in France and reaching our first stop, Newell went into a small shop and with his perfectly spoken French, asked the way to the local Hostel. He was clearly understood and the shop keeper immediately replied in very good French that he did not know. But of course Newell had no idea what the shopkeeper was saying. Strangely enough we had not thought of this and felt very stupid. We had a good laugh after the event and did find our way to the Hostel, as we found there was always some one who understood English. If not, we just showed them our Youth Hostel card and this normally did the trick.

PEA SOUP

On the return journey from France we got the train from London to Liverpool. The train was the corridor type and served snacks. Short of cash, we ordered soup which we brought back to our carriage. Newell, fussy with his food, decided that he did not like the pea soup and rather than carry it back, he lowered the window and dumped the contents out. Within minutes a very irate passenger charged into our carriage looking for the culprit who had chucked the soup out the window. His shirt and coat were green as the contents had gone into his compartment as he had the window open.

Newell was very apologetic but did not manage to calm this person, who said he was going to report us at the next stop, but never did. However when we arrived in Liverpool we must have been the first off the train and on our way – just to be sure!

1956 FIRE WORKS

We were at the Youth Hostel – Learmount Castle, close to Londonderry with the Cyprus CC. This was to all Hostlers thought to be haunted! We were all sitting around the large open fire burning, I think, logs or peat and telling stories. The room was very poorly lit. Gordon Read left the room momentarily and returned unknown to us with a mouthful of paraffin oil and from behind everyone, Gordon spat a mouthful of paraffin onto the fire. The fire exploded, sending ashes and smoke all over us! The panic was lively – shouting and laughing and finally Hue Wilson, Eddie Harvey, Jack Mills and others chased Gordon through the building. Gordon is no longer with us but will always be remembered by me for this amusing incident on our club weekend outing.

NO TIME TO BE BORED

I can not understand the youth of today regularly complaining of being bored. I had no time to be bored. My weekend routine was with other cyclists heading off on Saturday for a training run – anything up to fifty miles, or taking part in a road race.

Sunday was the relaxing day out. Setting off for Ballycastle non stop, having a grub-up on the beach or in a field. On round the coast to Carnlough, stopping at Granny Smiths for snacks or lunch.
Then on to Ballygally where we played cricket or leap frog on the beach. Back on our bikes and headed home, a round trip of over one hundred miles and enjoyed every minute of it. No time to be bored! I can not think of any other sport or activity that could offer such friendship, healthy activity, knowledge of the countryside and lasting memories as club cycling does.

BILLY CALDWELL   Cyprus CC

Racing whether the cows come home, or not

About 1955 or 1956, Ards CC held a Handicap Road Race on a little circuit close to Clandeboye Estate.

This is the account of what happened coming to the finish. The scratch riders were Billy Kirk, Jack Wilson and John Fennell. These three had caught and dropped the other groups and had about a half mile to go. What we did not know was, the local farmer, ignoring the pleas of Charlie Henderson and other club officials, turned his dairy herd on the road. The herd filled the little county road and were coming towards three fast moving cyclists, who were going towards the herd of cows!

As the three of us were starting to wind up for the sprint, we all saw one another. I slammed the brakes on, but Jackie started shouting and waving his arms. The front cows stopped but the ones behind just kept pushing forward! Billy started yelling and waving so the cows in front tried to turn around against the cows wanting to come along the road to get to the byre. This was when all hell broke loose! Cows were on their hind legs, trying to climb over other cows! I had climbed up a bank into a hedge.

I wanted no part of this! All of a sudden this big cow, udder full of milk and milk squirting out of the teats, ran up the opposite bank and jumped over a barbed wire fence and back into the field she had just come out of. (Thank goodness she didn't tear her udder). A gap opened and into the middle of this mass of cows went Jack and Billy. They were going for the finish line no matter what! How they got through I don't know. But when they did, they were confronted by a very angry man waving a stick and two farm dogs going crazy trying to get these cows sorted out. When order was restored and tempers calmed, I picked my way through a mess of leaked milk and cow manure to see who had won. Maybe Billy Kirk remembers!!

Other races were run on this nice little circuit and the only thing the race organizers needed to know was WHAT TIME IS MILKING TIME?

JOHN FENNELL   Newmarket Eagles, Ontario, Canada
Also: Abbey CC Maryland Wheelers
Route Wheelers, Shorts Athletic Club

A chance meeting with Mick Murphy

My cycling had always been a provincial affair. Hostelling, touring, club runs with the Belfast C.C. and eventually racing with 'The Ulster Ladies Road Club'.

I progressed to long distance place to place records. In 1953, all under the auspice of the Northern Ireland Cycling Federation (N.I.C.F.) I knew little or nothing of the National Cycling Association (N.C.A.) although familiar with the top N.I.C.F. riders in the 1950's, I had no knowledge of the outstanding cyclists in the N.C.A. This was all to change fifty five years later through unexpected circumstances.

My daughter Vera has a lifelong friend whose sister lives in Killorglin in Co. Kerry. Her husband bought two of my books WHEELS OF CHANGE (published in 2008) one for themselves and the other for a friend and neighbour, Gene Mangan, who in turn sent me a book 'The Ras' by Tom Daly.

During our 2010 holiday at our daughter Sheena's home near Skibbereen West Cork, Peter began to read this book to me, as my sight denied me this pleasure. We got to the sixth chapter which was a mini biography of Mick Murphy, entitled 'The Iron Man'

Mick won The Ras by 4 mins. 44 secs. In 1958 in spite of the terrible injuries he sustained in stage three, as a result of which he had to be helped onto his bike and into his yellow jersey at the start of the fourth stage!

Tom Daly's description of this man, who became a legend because of his prowess as a cyclist and his eccentricities and dedication, fascinated me. Little did I know that within a week I would be given the opportunity to meet this man.

During the holiday we had arranged to spend two nights with good friends who lived in the Inny Valley in South Kerry, not far from Cahirciveen. On our last evening a neighbour Michael Murphy called in for a bit of craic! When The Ras came up in general conversation, Michael informed us that he was related to 'The Iron Man' and would do his best to get me an audience! Not an easy task I was led to understand. Before I could say 'Quick Release Hub' I was being driven over the mountain to Mick's humble abode. Peter's brother Brian who was sharing this holiday with us along with his wife Flo, very thoughtfully accompanied me. He and I waited in the car outside while Michael had a lengthy conversation with Mick and eventually we got the 'thumbs up'. What a thrill it was to meet this unique man who gave us a hearty welcome, having cycling interests in common was our bond. It was a most enjoyable, enlightening and entertaining visit. Conversation was non stop and could have gone on to the wee hours. I was privileged to be shown "the secret of his success" (in his own words) – his gym. At the age of seventy six he can still lift the massive homemade weights, some of which he made at the age of 12! It was a really wonderful experience to have talked with him in his own home and one which I will never forget. Brian has made sure of this, as to my surprise he has this memorable evening captured on film.   *ISABEL WOODS*

(I am looking forward to meeting Gene Mangan to thank him in person for the gift of The Ras book. He is another legend of this race, having been the first and only rider to win four consecutive stage wins in a Tour. Gene was also renowned for his unselfish integrity – a true sportsman. It was he who first described Mick Murphy as 'The Iron Man'- a name that has gone down in cycling history.)

A memorable evening in Wallace Park

The first 25 miles that I rode on the Antrim Road, I didn't have a clue how to ride that distance and did it in 1hr. 5 mins. 25 secs.

Never hurt so much in my life! Riders like George Wilkes and Frank McKeown gave me tips on position and training and gradually more speed and stamina started to produce better results.

Track racing was the next thing to try and this led to getting into trouble at a track meet at the Wallace Park track in Lisburn. Five of the world's best Sprinters were brought over by the N.I.C.F. and when they came onto the track to warm up, everyone else was called off. Temptation is a terrible thing because when they came round to where I was up the banking, I dropped onto the end of the line. How many club riders can say they rode 6 laps with Reg Harris, Bardsley, Ogna, Morettini and Gaignard? It was worth getting threatened with a year's suspension. (Peter Woods will remember this)

Riding Club 10's, open 25's and 50's and the odd road race – at which I was just awful – struggling up the Deer's Leap on Dundrod, I thought I'd try a 12 hours. This was when I found out what pain and suffering was about! Riding a saddle that was an absolute ruin, caused so much pain that I thought I'd done permanent damage to the old water works. All food was gone, so I stole an apple from Spud McKeown – just as he was going to take a bite. This bit of thievery saw me through to the finish at Templepatrick and I finished with 232 miles. The race was won by Tom Allingham with, I think, 257 miles.

The next milestone, if this is the right term, was an attempt at the Irish Hour Record. The standard was set at twenty five and a half miles and attempted at Orangefield. Jim McCormack worked out a schedule and one evening I had a try. Unfortunately I missed it by ten yards. But what a memory! We are missing a lot of the men who led the way and gave us encouragement and were the first to congratulate you when you beat them. These are things you look back on: Club rides into Armagh, The Glens of Antrim, The Ards Peninsula and of course, the men who, when they stopped racing, became organizers and officials and have kept the sport going. We can't thank them enough.

JOHN FENNELL

A tale of Ards Cycling Club

Hunger knock is not a very pleasant experience – with bare knees and empty stomach, one hopes they can make it home. But one of our club mates solved the problem when he found a large orange by the roadside. He lost no time peeling it and went on his way refreshed. A Club member was on his way to a weekend meeting. Something startled a young fowl in the hedge and it darted across the road. It stuck its head in between the spokes and was beheaded. The Member gathered it up, stuffed it in his saddle bag and continued on his way.

And another short story.
Returning from a Sunday Run and a couple of miles from Ballygowan, we were whispering along at our leisure. Suddenly a man in a Sunday suit and a hard hat walked out in front of us! He never looked to see if anyone was coming. We all piled into him! He ended up at the bottom of the pile with a big dent in his hard hat. Sam Pollock said "Are you all right Sir?" and he proceeded to take the dent out of the hard hat with his fist. The man replaced the hat on his head and continued on his way, without a word. We spent some time with a spoke key truing up buckled wheels!

VICTOR HAMILTON

Roy Erskine leads Norman Surplus in a road race around 1949.

A club run that went off road

It was a club run, somewhere in County Armagh The two boys at the front were moving at a good speed, when someone shouted "For God's sake slow up, this isn't a race!"

Now fixed wheels are great for slowing a bicycle provided you don't sit back on it too much, which I did. Shouts, yells and noise of bikes hitting the road ensued! When we at the front stopped we were the only two actually on the road. On each side of the road there was a ditch – a deep one – with almost vertical sides and a lot of water. Riders started to appear from the ditch, dragging bikes and every single one was very angry. A lot of religious words were being used. Every one got sorted out, but was not willing to accept my apologies. We took a head count. One was missing. There was a man and his family out for a walk and he shouted that someone was upside down in the water at the bottom of the ditch. If I remember rightly it was young Dermot Hoy. His feet were strapped in tight and he was not able to free himself. He was frantically trying to twist enough to get his head above the water. Luckily we just dragged bike and him up onto the road and made sure he was okay. John Magill and I were not allowed to set the pace for a long time, relegated to the back of the line – disgraced. You sometimes do things without thinking, but hopefully you learn. Thankfully we finished the club run a bit wiser but all in one piece and looking forward to the next Sunday.

JOHN FENNELL

Enrights discovery

Spotted on a headstone in Glasnevin cemetery (Dublin) by Con Enright in October 2009 while researching his own family:

ERECTED BY THE CYCLISTS AND ATHLETES OF IRELAND IN MEMORY OF A STERLING SPORTSMAN, ATHLETE AND GENTLEMAN - JOHN LEOPOLD DUNBAR, OFFICIAL HANDICAPPER, IRISH CYCLISTS ASSOICIATION, EDITOR 'IRISH SPORSTMAN' BORN 12th September 1857 - Died 1st April 1891.   (Aged 33 years) Editors brackets.

The overcrowded elevator

Two Champions! Maurice Foster and Isabel Woods.

I have travelled with cycling teams to many races down the years and there have been many mishaps and amusing incidents. This particular one happened in the Sealink International Races in the early Eighties. They had decided to run a couple of stages over on the Continent from Ostend down to Calais in France. Our accommodation was in a village west of Calais and we had the Scottish team for company. It was only a small Bar/Café Tea Room with a few bedrooms outside and no evening meal, so they had arranged that a number of teams would have a meal in their large building which they took us to in convoy. The building itself was like one of our Mill buildings in the city, about ten windows along its length and carried up uniformly for about four floors. When we went outside there was a big open area about the size of a tennis court and the only furniture in it was a desk, where a Secretary checked your name off and four large settees which were placed in the shape of a cross in the middle of the room. We were shown into a side room where we had a meal that I don't think anyone will ever forget! The first course was oily fish soup. Well have you ever had a plate of 'cold liver oil'? and that was just the start. The meat dish wasn't much better.

When we had finished we came out and sat down on the sofas to await our escort back to our digs. The door opened and this bloke came in with his arm around a blow up doll which was fully inflated. The 'girl' had bumps in the right places, even if some had been exaggerated a bit. She looked very life-like even without her clothes on! He walked over to this door which we hadn't taken much notice off. It was unusual in that it was the normal height, but less than a couple of feet wide. When he opened it, there was a small lift. I can only think that it had been a food lift to serve the floors above and had been re-designed to take a couple of people. The more I thought about it the more I smiled because two people standing facing each other would have had to hold their heads to the side to keep their noses from banging against each other in the middle! Anyway when the bloke stepped into the lift and pulled the doll in behind himself, the door wouldn't close! When he pulled the arms in, a leg would shoot out and when he got the leg back in, an arm would shoot out again! This went on for a couple of minutes but to us sitting on the sofas as quiet as mice, it seemed an age. The girl at the desk had kept her head down, pretending she was going over her figures, but really she was peeping over the top of her glasses, watching all that was going on. The lad got out of the lift and backed the doll in first and decided this was going to work. So he stepped back and made a rude sign towards the girl, then he stepped on the toes of the doll, held her arms up and pushed the button with his elbow to a huge cheer from all of us on the sofas.

Back to the Café again we sat down at a table for a yarn with the Scottish manager etc. when the Masseur noticed a large glass boot up on the shelf, advertising a local beer. It held two and a half litres and it was supposed to be a feat to drink the full of it in a certain time. It was like drinking a yard of ale only the thick rim at the top of the boot made it so much more difficult. However the bar man filled it up and true enough he downed it in the allocated time. When I heard him say 'fill her up again' I knew it was time for bed. Needless to say that the next morning they strapped him in the back seat of the team bus and he slept through the next stage. What an eventful evening it turned out to be!

MORRIS FOSTER

Smyth's Hotel in Carnlough

I'm sure a lot of us 'old' cyclists will remember Mrs. Smyth at Carnlough and her wonderful dinners.
This memory is about a group of Abbey CC riders on a Club Run around the Glens one Sunday in 1950's. It was a bit overcast when we started out but stayed dry until we hit the big Glen. The skies opened and the wind started to blow. Capes went on and the rain got heavier and soon it was blowing a gale. The rain was bouncing off the road and the wind lifting our capes, resulted in all of us getting soaked from our feet right up to our chests. We made it into Carnlough and slopped our way through the door into Smyths Dining Room.Now Mrs. Smyth was not a very big lady, but could be very outspoken "What are you boys doing out riding in this weather? Have you no sense? Get out of those wet clothes – Right now!" We were all sent upstairs to get stripped off, gave our clothes to her girls and arrived back into the dining room wrapped in a variety of blankets. A table that had roast beef, turnips and potatoes greeted us. Our clothes were on clothes horses in front of a roaring fire, steam wafting up to the ceiling. It was something to see the expressions on the faces of people when they came into the dining room. People who obviously had more sense than us – they arrived dry – by car. Mrs. Smyth explained that we were just silly cyclists and said "Don't be worried about the sight of bare torsos and legs. They are quite harmless!" The storm passed and dry clothes were put back on and hugs were given to Mrs. Smyth and the girls. We left Carnlough a lot more comfortable than when we arrived.

JOHN FENNELL

This photo taken June 2009   Still fit and active and riding with Newmarket Eagles CC in Ontario, Canada

Reunion at The Crown and Shamrock

John Fennell and friends at the Crown and Shamrock Public House (one-time changing rooms for cyclists at Glengormley). with proprietor Rosemary O' Boyle.
L-R: Davy McNutt, Billy Kirk, Morris Foster, Wallace McNaul, John Fennell, Rosemary O'Boyle, Jim Maguire, Bill Campbell, Billy Jebb and Maurice Donaldson.

Earlier this year Billy Kirk arranged for me to meet Morris Foster and what a surprise when we drove into the Crown and Shamrock and there was Morris Foster, Maurice Donaldson, Davy McNutt, Wallace McNaul, Jim McGuire, Jim Lavery, Billy Jebb and Bill Campbell. We had a great chat about the changes that have taken place in the equipment. Carbon fibre and the type of training and nutrition and we all agreed we were doing pretty good in our day with 531 tubing and Williams steel chain sets. We all thought we had gone to heaven when we saw the first alloy chain sets. Do you remember when we got an extra hub and we had ten gears? Now there are eleven and they are all on the back hub.

Left to right:
Jim McGuire and Davy McNutt of Windsor C.C.   Jim Lavery of Banbridge C.C.
John Fennell, Irish 25 Champion 1957, 58 and 59.   Maurice Donaldson, Maryland Wheelers,
Morris Foster, Old Bleach and Cyprus C.C's.:   Wallace McNaul, Team Route, Ballymoney,
Bill Campbell, Maryland Wheelers.

They are studying result sheets and other memorabilia from early days.

A character

Photo of Mike McConaghys shop
It was at 7 Movilla Street in Newtownards

Some years ago I owned a bicycle shop in Newtownards. Bicycles had been a big part of my life but that is another story. Like my father, I never threw anything out: old screws, bits of metal nuts and bolts cluttering up my workshop in tin cans, glass jars and cardboard boxes. It made things difficult to find, however generally customers were patient enough to wait through my searching. This was in the days before the throwaway society. I now regularly see perfectly good bicycles dumped because the tyres are flat. Many of my customers became good friends and in those days when my mind was sharp I remembered most of their names, even after several months of absence.

However one person in particular, even though I never made a penny of profit from our transactions, I will never forget. My shop had an old fashioned bell on the door and one day just as I was having my lunch, it rang. Cursing the timing I went out to met an elderly gentleman. He had been taller than my six feet, though his age left him slightly stooped so that we were now eye-level albeit staring through his terribly thick glasses. He was unshaven, smelt of tobacco and his teeth were dirty and tobacco stained and like my own, leaning like old tombstones. But his manners were impeccable and within a short time I was fascinated by his politeness, his demeanour and above all his obvious intellect.

Jim as I came to know him was dirty, some would say filthy, but as I later came to know, his poor sight prevented him from seeing the stains and general dirt that he both wore and carried.

He asked me for some unusual parts and when I was able to provide them his enthusiasm was obvious. He then inquired where he could obtain several parts that I knew were very unusual. My interest turned to curiosity and I inquired why anyone, particularly and with due respect, someone of his age should be searching for these odd parts? His answer was amazing.

Jim's age coupled with his poor eyesight was about to cost him his driving licence and so he was determined to find another way of travelling in and out of Newtownards. He was building an electric bicycle! By this time I was hooked, lunch was forgotten so when he asked me to come and see his project I did not need a second invitation. I immediately put a CLOSED sign on my door and followed Jim outside to where he had parked an ancient scooter. Declining his invitation to ride pillion I started to follow on my bicycle - a very slow three miles to his house on the outskirts of Newtownwards. If Jim had a dishevelled look, then his house was to say the least, sad.

He had never married so cleaning and dusting was not high on his priorities. The walls, shelves, doors, everything was coated in a layer of nicotine. It was like stepping back in time. I could hardly contain my excitement as the garage door opened and there it was – his electric bicycle. He apologised that this, his prototype was not running but that it did not matter. I could quickly see that the idea, the design and the mechanics, with a little bit of tweaking, would work. It was a big old policeman's bike to which Jim had attached a basket in which he had a car battery. From the battery two cables ran along the frame to a car starter motor fixed over the rear wheel, which in turn, by a system of cogs and chains propelled the bicycle. The ingenuity was wonderfully simple and though heavy, after some minor alternations, Jim was mobile again sans licence. Impressed as I was with Jim's electric bike, it was as nothing when I came to realise he was fluent in several languages, had read all the Classics and taught himself to play the piano.

We became firm friends and sometimes I joined him for a glass of neat whiskey hoping he had sterilised the glasses which we used.

When Jim passed away there were very few people at his funeral and I felt very sad that such a talented man died in such miserable circumstances and for his electric bike to end up in the skip.

MIKE McCONAGHY

Story of the Gordon family of Hillsborough

One wet morning last November, Peter and Isabel Woods and May visited Billy Gordon in his home in Lisburn. We were greeted warmly and the cold, miserable weather outside was soon forgotten as we embarked on a trip down memory lane. Billy has such a wealth of stories inside him - we could have sat and listened to him all afternoon. Which we did!

He has lived alone since his wife died earlier last year. Yes, life can be lonely at times he confessed, but he does not sit in the corner and fret over days gone by. Far from it. In retirement he has not been idle. He proudly showed us the Grandfather Clock he made and a beautiful rocking horse that sits proudly in the hallway of his home – made to perfection. Billy and his brother Tommy had dreamed some day they would make a rocking horse and Billy finally fulfilled that dream. There is a lovely story about the rocking horse and it's worthy of telling and is included in this book.

He is presently working on an Irish Harp. What a task! But not to Billy.

He has a Library of books – all neatly shelved. He has also written Journals of his travels and experiences throughout his life. What a lovely treasure to leave to Grandchildren. His computer and desk share the same room. A very tidy home. No clutter whatsoever. I was duly impressed.

Billy and Tommy Gordon's father was born at Annahilt in 1868. He started a blacksmith business in 1890. He moved to Reilly's Trench, Hillsborough in 1900 and then to Arthur Street, also in Hillsborough in 1916. Billy recalls how their father ran 4 miles the morning he heard the shop in Hillsborough was vacant. He didn't want to miss it, and he didn't!

In one of his many beautifully written journals Billy writes: ...... *during the 1880's when father decided to become a blacksmith, he was indentured to a Mr. Phillips for seven years, five to general jobbing and two years to horse shoeing. He lived in with Phillips and his wages were two pairs of moleskin trousers a year and at the end of the seven years a £5 note. The indenture meant that he had to complete his apprenticeship with Phillips to qualify for his trade. He told me that he was the only one ever to complete his full time with Phillips, as Mr. Phillips was a very demanding and hard taskmaster. Several lads had tried to serve their apprenticeship with him and had not been able to stick the pace. They left and there would be little for them to choose from, it was either go to farm labouring or join the army.*

Tommy left school at 13 and brother Billy left at 13 ½ and both went into the blacksmith's shop to learn the trade. The smithy was in Arthur Street in Hillsborough and their home was next door. There were 22 houses in total in Arthur Street - a short street with 11 houses on either side. At one time their father could have bought the whole street for £100! But remember a £100 was a lot of money in those days! Nowadays these tiny, quaint, stone built houses can fetch very high prices.

Billy Gordon welding a frame in his workshop.

Hillsborough was once known as 'a one horse town'. Now it is the most desirable village in Northern Ireland in which to live.

In 1950 Billy went off to work in England. He was employed by Jack Taylor who was a specialist cycle engineer and owned a small workshop at Stockton-on-Tees. Here we quote from Eric Waugh's article from Belfast Telegraph written some time in the 1950's.

Back in 1947 William Gordon finished sixth in the Belfast to Dublin cycle race. It was the nearest he ever came to star billing in the strenuous world of competitive cycling. But it was only a failure in narrow sense; for since then he has bent his interest to a much more practical and exacting application.......Now Gordon used his acquired skill to produce the feather-weight racing frames of light alloy steel beloved of the clubman. The lightest weigh no more than 20 lbs.. In this way steel more than fills the need opened by the disuse of the old cane frames and wheels. They were never quite strong enough. With a steel frame are combined parts made of aluminium – wheel rims, chain sets and handlebars – which are given a polished finish. The completed machine is one where non essentials are sacrificed to lightness and the fleetest which can be devised without the addition of a power unit. Gordon likes to think that his success has come from giving the enthusiasts just what they want. It has meant patience and a meeting of exacting requirements. The reward he finds is the championship performances of local riders who use his machines. The gold lettered transfer which is the mark of his craftsmanship appears on the cycle used by the champion of the Irish track league who rode into the winning position last month. A few years ago, says Gordon, there was a young fellow who won both the junior and senior massed-start championships on one of my bicycles. His name was Tommy Burns and he was just 17. That was in 1953. However in this case, he is sure it is a record which will never be equalled.

Tommy Gordon at the workshop with beloved dog Penny

During that year long period in England Billy picked up great knowledge in the art of Cycle building. His employer recognised him as a 'natural' and confessed that Billy knew more about welding etc. after six weeks than he himself had learned in a lifetime.

Due to family commitments, Billy returned home to Hillsborough and he and his brother Tommy decided to go into the cycle building business. He recalls the Monday morning in the month of January when he and Tommy opened their shop. There wasn't a single order in the book. However, word soon got around, the orders rolled in and soon they were making 5 frames a week – all individually tailored to suit the rider.

The frames were not built on a jig (too rigid) explained Billy. With the experience they had gained in their father's blacksmiths shop, combined with the skills he had learned in England, the brothers understood the nature of the steel, its capabilities, its temperament and its resilience. All frames and forks were lovingly and expertly made by hand and every customer was important to them.

Frames and forks were stove enamelled and painted in any colour the rider wished.

Billy recalled how he dreaded some riders coming in to collect their cycles.

He remembered one customer in particular, (who shall remain nameless) who would collect maybe 3 bikes at a time and un-ceremoniously shove them into his van! Billy winced – even today as he recalled those incidents of many years ago, and he can still hear the scrape of metal against metal as the bicycles were thrown into the van. How irreverent it was, he added, shaking his head.

He recalled that Harry McCartney was a pleasure to work for. His bicycles were immaculate and so was he. The brothers were actively racing by this time and their sister Margaret was a competitive rider. They founded the Couriers Road Club and they had notable success. Tommy Burns, he mentioned in particular was a great rider.

Many of the famous Gordon Bicycles are still around today. Jerry Beggs owns 22 bikes. Most of them have been lovingly restored.

Gordon Brothers built 4 tandems and Billy has a tandem that has never been ridden.

His son Ken has his last bicycle.

Billy Gordon on his bike.

The Gordon's workshop at Arthur St., Hillsborough as it looks today. Once this building was two storied. Billy Kirk took this photograph and this is Billy's bike in the picture!

Gordon Brothers ceased to trade in 1994. Tommy died in 1986.

Again Billy writes in his Journal of his deep affection and respect for his brother Tommy:

Cycling was one of the greatest things ever to happen to Thomas and I, always enjoying every minute on our bikes. It wasn't just a case of cycling for each others sake, we were in unison, both loving our work and both loving our cycling.
It also meant we worked together, we cycled together, one always helping the other, that also was our life.

Between them they had clocked up 103 years of blacksmithing and cycle making.

They made over 700 bicycles down the years and loved every minute of their work.

Their father always taught them:
If you can't have the best of everything, then make the best of everything you've got.

Billy summed it up by adding: Its not a bad yardstick to measure life with, at least you wont fall behind with the monthly payments!

MAY FARRAR

GORDON CYCLES

Manufacturers of High Grade Racing and Sports Cycles

BALLYNAHINCH ROAD, HILLSBOROUGH,

Co. Down, Northern Ireland.

Directors : W. J. GORDON, T. D. GORDON.

RETAIL PRICE LIST—*November, 1953*

SPORTS MODEL - - -	£7 19 0
CLUBMAN MODEL - - -	£10 15 0
MODERN LADIES' MODEL - -	£13 5 0
CURVED TUBE MODEL (Welded) -	£12 0 0
SUPER VELO (Track) - -	£11 5 0
MADISON (Track) - -	£13 19 0
TIME TRIAL MODEL - -	£12 5 0
INTERNATIONAL MODEL - -	£12 19 0
GRAN PREMIO MODEL - -	£14 19 0

GRAN PREMIO MODEL, ANY COLOUR SCHEME PANELS LINING NO EXTRA.

ALL OTHER MODELS—EXTRAS

HEAD PANEL, 5/-   SEAT PANEL, 5/-   LUG EDGING, 7/6.

ALL MODELS LISTED ABOVE ARE BRAZED LUG MODELS, EXCEPT CURVED TUBE MODEL.

WELDED MODELS CAN BE MADE AS ABOVE, EXCEPT MODELS GRAN PREMIO, SPORTS AND MADISON, AT —— A CHARGE OF £1 LESS LIST PRICE. ——

ALL FRAME SETS ARE FINISHED IN HARD GLOSS ENAMEL OR FLAMBOYANT FINISHES.

CHRONE PLATING TO ANY MODELS.

FRONT AND REAR ENDS, FRONT FORK ENDS, EXTRA £2 5/-.

"THE LEADER" PRESS. DROMORE

The yellow jersey

I left Orangefield Boys School in the early sixties, arranging for any examination results to be sent to my home. Despite nearly five years of French lessons the only words I was familiar with were the ones I had poured over in the French cycling magazines of the day.

Mike on his bike

My hero in those years was Jacques Anquetil, the charismatic super fit French cyclist who had just won his fifth Tour de France and I was going to emulate him. I lived and dreamt cycle racing then, imagining myself adorned in the Yellow jersey at the front of the peleton as we climbed yet another pass through the French Alps.

Opportunity had presented itself a year or so earlier when the local Co-op on the Beersbridge Road needed a bicycle messenger for after school hours. Heaven sent, such joy – what more training could one ask for, pushing a fully laden messenger bicycle up Bloomfield Road every afternoon and then perhaps a run to Portrush and back on a Saturday. It was certainly enough to make me the fastest time trialist of my age in the country at that time.

I do not recall much sign of anxiety from my parents as I prepared to set off alone to France. Perhaps the world was a safer place in the sixties and in particular, Europe, much chastened by the countless rows of simple white headstones now standing in Flanders fields. Eventually the day of my departure arrived and despite protestations I rode off alone on my bicycle down Ravenscroft Avenue and along to Belfast Docks. A ferry crossing, a train journey and then across the English channel – I was in France. Nothing to it. All I had to do was win a few races and that Yellow jersey would be almost within my grasp. Quickly I was racing, too quickly, my lungs bursting, my leg muscles burning and sweat blinding me as I desperately tried to keep the pace. The speed was electrifying - these men were from another planet! Each start was as if my body had been catapulted from a gun, while my mind and my eyes tried to catch up. I was shattered – disbelief turned to disillusionment and then some anger. Not at my fellow competitors but rather at my own naivety.

My meagre, though hard earned 'wad' of French franc notes was dwindling, while the prize money I was counting on, amounted to – exactly NIL. 'Misery' as one Mr Micawber famously put it. My cycle run back through France was somewhat more leisurely. It had been if nothing else a great adventure – and may even have helped to put a wiser head on young shoulders. My father was at work when I reached home. Without a key, I had to knock, but the smile on my mother's face at seeing me again was something else. She was quick to console me and then in an instant retorted "If it was only a yellow jersey you wanted, why didn't you just ask".

MIKE McCONAGHY (Mike the Bike)

the final page of advertisements from The Ulster Cyclist Magazine, dated 1935 - hope you enjoyed these.

Shattered illusions

When we were in our teens, my brother Stewart and I were very keen cyclists. We lived in East Belfast then and so every Tuesday evening we would make our way to the cycle racing track in Orangefield Park. There, hanging on the wire fence we could watch the local stars swerve up and down the banking, their wheels flashing past only inches from our noses. Stewart and I readily made new friends amongst the spectators and it was not long before we all joined the local cycling club, the now long gone Belfast C.C. Speaking for myself, I think it was one of the best things I ever did.

All of us lived within a mile or so of each other, nothing when you had a racing bicycle, so at week-ends a crowd of us would set off to explore the highways and by-ways of County Antrim and County Down. It was not unusual for us to cover a hundred miles in a day, the camaraderie was great and we learned to fix punctures, broken chains and all those wee dodges that the present generation seem to know nothing of. At the end of a long day we would astonish our parents, many of whom did not possess a car, with tales of where we had been. They hardly believed that we had cycled to Portrush and back or round by Newry and Rostrevor - some places they themselves had only read about.

And so it was that one Saturday we set off for Carnlough on the beautiful Antrim coast. It had been the winter of the big snow – 1963 - and though the main roads were clear it was still several feet deep on the fields and hedges around us. Soon we had left Belfast far behind heading for Ballymena, Broughshane and on towards Carnlough.

It was a bright sunny day as we rode shoulder to shoulder up over the glen. The snow was getting higher and higher on either side of us until at one point we could all have been professionals riding through the French Alps. Eventually we arrived in Carnlough and as usual stopped for refreshments at the local 'wee' shop. This one in particular was known for the pretty young girl behind the counter. The ringing bell on the shop door announcing our arrival, she emerged from the back to greet us again, smiling at what must have seemed a right bunch of 'ragamuffins'. In those days most of us could be said to be good-looking, but all of us were still shy, so we would form an orderly queue giving each of us a long look at the local beauty. Chocolate bars never took so long to choose and we even took our gloves off so that in transferring our meagre few coins we might actually touch hands. But it was all useless. That day she had only eyes for one, not me, but my brother. As we all shuffled past her it was clear – she could not take her eyes of him. Outside, Stewart was crowing and crowing like a cock-pheasant.

"Did you see that, did you all see that?" he crowed. "Someone lend me a tanner, I'm going back in to get her name"   It fell to Sammy to burst his balloon.

"Here's the tanner, but first you'd better get rid of that big green thing hanging from your nose!"

MIKE McCONAGHY

The 'glibe' races

SCRABO.

These were a series of cycle races which were held in the 1920's and early 1930's that were organised by a band of enthusiasts on a course between Newtownards and Comber.

The Glibe was an old unused quarry in the town land of Ballyalton. The start and finish was at the gates into the quarry on the Ballyalton Road known locally as McMaster's Hill – so the riders had a downhill start and an uphill finish. The race consisted of three laps of a square course, which was a total distance of about ten miles. It was a handicap event of three groups of riders, starting at different times with the scratch bunch conceding about six minutes to the limit men.

The Handicapper was Isaac McDonald and Bobby Graham had the task of raising the prize money for these events. Another popular person was John McNaull, who encouraged new riders and offered advice on racing tactics etc.

The events were held on Wednesday evenings in the summer months and the riders were generally local lads and of course a number of pot hunters from the surrounding town lands. Before the start of the first of these races, very few people knew about it other than a selected band of would be competitors, as it was a rider to rider invitation affair. Many of the inhabitants living in the district knew very little about what was taking place, but when strangers began appearing about the district, the people were inquiring what was happening. If the police got to hear about it, who knows what the outcome would be? It had been agreed that nobody outside the organisers and riders should be told anything about it. Of course as the inhabitants of farms and houses around the course heard about the race, they got alarmed for their cats and dogs being strewn all over the place by these mad hooligans tearing around the roads! However they were consoled by the organisers and their pets were kept in a safe place until such times when it was safe to let them loose again.

There was also some who thought the country side was theirs and nobody had the right to interfere with their way of living. After that first race which was won by Victor Buckley (who was on the limit of the handicap) riding a Hercules bike with hub brakes and upturned bars, the news must have travelled fast. A number of strange faces were seen in the area inquiring where the course was and when the next race was waking place.

The following week saw a lot of the locals making improvements to their machines – such as fitting dropped bars and toe straps. Some even resorted to drilling a lot of holes in the saddle pillars and doing away with unnecessary nuts and bolts to make their bikes lighter!

Buckley won the second race also, but with a reduced handicap allowance. He was caught on the last lap by W. Coey but managed to stay behind him until the finish and just pip him on the line which made him unpopular with Coey - whose remarks after the race are unprintable. The following Saturday the situation was reversed when they were both competing in a two mile race at Castlereagh Park track.

Most of the bikes had a single fixed sprocket, but as these races continued more lightweight machines with multiple gears began to appear and some of them were Humber, Enfield Bullet, New Hudson, Elswick Hopper and B.S.A.

The third of the 'Glibe' races saw a number of strange competitors checking in with the handicapper, paying their entrance fee of one shilling and six pence and who were put in with the scratch men as their form was unknown. Before the race began some of the local residents mentioned that two riders were practising around the circuit one day before the event and they lapped the course in half the time! This caused much concern until it was revealed that the riders were Jimmy Guthrie and Freddie Frith on Norton motor bikes!

The winner of the two previous races, Victor Buckley was busy making final preparations on his machine.

The 'glibe' races

He bought new bars, a new chain and toe clips and he also changed the sprocket to give him a bigger gear. He also lowered the saddle a little to see if it would help him when climbing the hills. But alas he was a non starter after all that, because a Clydesdale horse trod on the front wheel of his bike prior to the race. This event was won by Charley Henderson from W. Coey and Johnny Brown, who were among the scratch bunch. It is said that Johnny Brown once raced the train between Dundonald Station and Comber and beat it!

There were reports that a lot of riders were making much use of oil - such as Olive oil, Vaseline and even Brilliantine hair oil for lubricating purposes and some were also using liniment and embrocation which was applied to the legs to loosen the muscles. Some said that the local chemist was running low of supplies and had to replenish his stock.

Around harvest time the Wednesday night events were not readily available as the farmers had to work late to get their crops in and the farm yard horses and carts would be using the roads. The roads would also be in a mess as the farmers travelled back and forth from fields to farms.

The International Tourist Trophy car race was an annual attraction and the race consisted of a number of laps of a circuit - starting in Dundonald, through Newtownards and Comber and was held on a Saturday. During the week the roads were closed on a couple of evenings to allow practising and while the cyclists were training around the Glibe, the roar of the racing cars could be heard loud and clear.

In between the Wednesday night events, there were other similar ones organised in other areas on different nights. These were held in places such as Clandeboye, Greyabbey, Ballyhalbert, Moneyrea and Killyleagh. This stimulated a lot of rivalry among the surrounding areas.

The 'Glibe' races continued for some time and eventually the N.C.U. informed the organisers that they disapproved of their racing and this brought the events to a close.

This article is compiled from some extracts of a record of events which was written and kept by Mr. Victor Buckley, of Comber who was the winner of the first two races as well as some later events. These records were passed on to Charlie Henderson who in turn left them to Billy Kirk for safe keeping.

RAB COLLINS

A road too far

*It was 1963 and at the age of sixteen I, like most young
lads looked forward to the week-end dances.*

The popular one was at the Belmont Cricket Club on a Friday night and the great thing about that dance was that most of the girls were local. This meant that if you were lucky you could walk them home with or without your mate or her friend playing gooseberry. It was good fun and pretty harmless stuff. But then Sammy Houston's Jazz Club opened in Great Victoria Street in Belfast and it was suddenly the place to be. However the downside was that the girls came from everywhere and you certainly couldn't walk them home.

One night I was dancing with a particularly pretty girl and when I asked if I could leave her home she replied: "Certainly, if you fancy a bus ride to Londonderry". I was gob-smacked – no chance there! In those days I thought Londonderry was just inside the Arctic circle! It turned out that she was in college in Belfast and was going home to the village of Eglinton the next morning. Not to be put off and in a show of bravado I replied that I would cycle there the next day.

Early Saturday morning found me pouring over the vague map she had scribbled on a scrap of paper and the enormity of my rash promise started to sink in. She lived in Eglinton which at a rough guess was at least seventy miles from my home in east Belfast. However, within an hour, spurred on by bravado and dare-devilry, I was on my way. I had an old George Elrick bicycle with a fixed gear of 66 inches and a big leather saddle bag for my sandwiches. Antrim, Maghera, the old Glenshane Pass and eventually Dungiven was reached. According to my 'map' I had to turn off to the right about half way between Dungiven and Londonderry and make my way over the hills along very minor roads. By now most of my sandwiches had been eaten but I had not much further to go and after all I had this gallant, romantic notion that I was doing something heroic.

Eventually I reached, after some directions from locals, the farm house where I hoped the girl from the night before would be. I can still remember the look of disbelief and amazement on her face when she opened the door! Maybe it was as much to do with the fact that I was wearing an old pair of "holy" tights given me by Hilti Smyth, the track rider.

Her father and mother listened in almost disbelief as to where I had cycled from while I bathed in a warm glow of admiration from the girl. Shyness, I suppose, was the main reason for not accepting more hospitality, though with a handful of biscuits I was soon on my way back home with not even so much as a peck on the cheek for my efforts!

I decided to go home by Limavady and then over the hills and into Ballymoney where my uncles had a farm, but all was not going well. I was running out of 'steam' and more importantly – time. I had no lights and so at Ballymoney I decided to press on towards home still twiddling my low gear fixed wheel. Ballymena was reached, but I was a 'gonner.' I had nothing left to eat, no money to buy any food and I had the 'knock'. Struggling towards Antrim I eventually almost fell off my bicycle about three miles short of the town. I lay there on the footpath until I could summon enough strength to pick and eat some blackberries from the hedgerow. How was I going to get home? I do not know how long I lay there but eventually a black car stopped (they all seemed black in those days) and a man came over to ask if I was alright. I was not of course, and when I told him I had no food nor money he kindly helped me back on the bike and asked me to follow him slowly into the town. We stopped about half way up the hill in the Main Street of Antrim on the left hand side and he brought me into his house. I can still remember the big fry he made me but sadly I am not sure if his name was Frank O'Brien or if I am clutching at straws. In any case he saved my day. Soon I was out on the road again and thanks to him I made it back to East Belfast and home. My parents took some convincing as to where I had cycled that day on a single speed fixed wheel, but when I collapsed onto my bed I was sure my legs were still turning! Was it worthwhile? It certainly was. The girl and I were married some six years later.

MIKE McCONAGHY

Glackin's folly

Paddy Glackin from Gamble Street on the edge of Belfast's Sailortown began cycling with Northern CC. but later entered the ranks of the N.C.A. in the Elk Road club in 1957.

Always one for the latest training tips he was told 'a big one' by a club-mate that the pros massaged their legs with lettuce leaves soaked in vinegar. Shortly after he received this piece of mis-information, a group of his mates arrived unexpectedly at his home one day to urge him to go training with them. Through the kitchen window they spied him in the act of applying the lettuce treatment!

When they entered, after a panic stricken clear-up by Paddy, the room reeked of malt vinegar. With difficulty they contained their mirth.

BILLY KIRK

The Harry Mussen story

There is a long established and popular group cycle ride which departs from Bangor every Monday and Thursday mornings and tours the roads of the Ards Peninsula.

Self styled 'The Wrinklies' due to the advanced age of many of its devotees, it stops for refreshments at Fynn's Factory Shop Café in Ballywalter, with thirty five miles covered and about fifteen to go. On 29th November 2007 a special party was held at Fynn's to mark the 80th Birthday of Bob Hill from Bangor, the oldest member of the group.

At this gathering of about 30 people, just as everyone was about to tuck in, the retired journalist, John Hicks sat down opposite me. He said he had just met a man down in the shop whose father had been a cycling champion in the early 1900's. The man, attracted by all the parked bicycles had told Hicks about his father and mentioned the name Mussen. This rang a bell with me and I thought "This could be Harry Mussen's son." With some excitement I asked was he still in the shop, but John told me he had left. However the following morning I rang the nearest 'Mussen' in the phone book and was amazed to find, in one phone call, the man whose father had been the legendary Harry Mussen from Dunmurry, who has represented Great Britain in the London Olympic Games of 1908, and Ireland at Stockholm in 1912.

Harry Mussen

the Harry Mussen story

Victor Mussen with his wife, holding his fathers photograph

Spitfire Pilot

Before I recount the stories gathered from Victor Mussen at 25 Shore Road, Millisle, and his lovely collection of memorabilia, I should say that Victor's life was of equal renown, but in a completely different arena. He was one of the great band of fighter pilots who defended us from Nazism, flying, in his case, Spitfire fighters. At a recent Ards Air Show to commemorate the 60th Anniversary of the end of the War, he took the controls of a

Spitfire at 81 years of age. His exploits are given a full chapter in "Ireland's Aviator Heroes of World War Two" by John C. Hewitt, self published by the Author in 2003.

The Huguenots

Harry Mussen was born in February 4th 1876 to Publican Henry Mussen and Mary (nee Chestnut). His pub was in the village of Dunmurry and was called the Dunmurry Inn.

The Family Tree show that he is descended from one of two brothers who landed with the Williamite forces under Schomberg at Carrickfergus in 1688. Huguenots by religion, they were fleeing from religious persecution in their village near Thionville in Northern France – close to the border with Luxembourg. They had earlier been expelled from Luxembourg with their father Jacques, mother and two other brothers- victims of the same intolerance.

Records do not show if they actually came under arms, or indeed, whether they took part in the campaigns. What is known is that they survived to settle in the Lisburn/Derriaghy area bringing the skills of weaving with them.

As time passed their contribution to the life of the community became considerable, not only in industry and commerce. A list of Church Wardens in Lisburn Cathedral contains 10 Mussens serving in the century from 1756 to 1856 – in which year Harry's uncle, William Mussen was the incumbent.

Young Harry went to school near Hillhall where the family lived. As he grew into a teenager he helped his father, also called Henry, in the business of running a successful public house. He displayed skill and willingness for all kinds of work, both at the Inn and at home.

Ireland's Saturday night of 2nd July 1898 reported that Harry Mussen first turned pedals on a Penny Farthing, later to be known as the 'old ordinary'. However he did not race on the high machine and it appears the bug did not really bite until the arrival of the chain driven safety bicycle on which he won his first races at Dunmurry in 1894 in the colours of Dunmurry C.C.

The pneumatic tyres

Those first races took place just 5 years after the historic occasion when Willie Hulme became the first man to race on pneumatic tyres – the invention, of course, of Belfast man John Boyd Dunlop.

Hulme was captain of Belfast Cruisers C.C. and the venue for his race was Belfast Queens College Association Sports on 18th May 1889. By 1894 everyone was using a bicycle pump and solid tyres were history.

Mussen's 1894 wins were achieved with minimal training. It was 1898 before he began to take it seriously, winning the prestigious Magowan cup in a 50 miles road race.

Although an excellent short distance racer on road or track, Harry soon showed a preference for long distance riding. This may have been partly a response to the public's amazement, especially in those days, at the very idea of covering 100 miles (or more!) on your own steam.

Tandem racing was common in the early days of cycle sport. It is, therefore, hard to be sure which of his rides were true unpaced efforts. His medal collection in some cases state the full facts, so a reasonable assessment can be made, based also on the fact that Irish and Provincial Championships were known to be un-paced. For example in September 1896 and August 1898 he rode 50 miles in 2 hrs. 53 mins. and 2 hrs. 48 mins. while also in 1898, he covered 50 miles behind a tandem in 2 hrs. 13 mins. Astonishingly he rode 50 miles tandem paced on the track in l hr. 57 mins. 36 secs. in 1899.

Crucial to young Mussen's success throughout his racing career was the encouragement and support of his father who gave him time to train and rest, provided, of course, he 'turned his hand' to a reasonable degree and kept up to date with the needs of the business.

Among Harry's rivals and contemporaries in the North was Shafto Kerr from Belfast who started out as a member of Spencer Street C.C. in 1892. He was a great all round distance rider.

From the Dublin area was R.J. McCready, again a very consistent winner at the long distances. He was, subsequent to his racing career, the founder of 'The Irish Cyclist'. This admired journal continued publication until 1952. The most amazing Mussen contemporary of all, however, was 'The Balbriggan Flyer' Harry Reynolds, a member of Wanderers C.C. Dublin who became Ireland's first and only world track champion. This was on 15th August 1896 at the one mile distance in Copenhagen, Denmark.

At the medals ceremony the organisers began to play the British National Anthem, whereupon Reynolds threw his bicycle at the Officials and created such a furore that proceedings were halted until an Irish ballad was found to placate him! Perhaps it was Danny Boy? Needless to say, on his return to Balbriggan he was feted as a hero. To this day his portrait hangs in the reception area of a Balbriggan hotel.

The Englishman Leon Meredith

Also contemporary with Harry was the Englishman Leon Meredith who was 7 times World Champion in the 100 km motor paced event on the track, as well as gaining 9 British Championship Golds. It is a measure of the standing of Harry Mussen that a challenge match took place in England between the two. The 6 ft. 2 ins. Meredith proved superior, but the Irishman was not disgraced in the David and Goliath encounter – Mussen was a diminutive 5 ft. 4 ½ ins. Victor Mussen vividly remembers his father's description of the race and saying "A good big 'un will always beat a good little 'un'"!

The governing body in Ireland at the time was the Irish Cyclists Association. Each Province had an independent centre and ran its own championships, as well as the main body running National championships. Mussen's medal collection contains 3 National Golds: 100 miles in 1903, 50 miles in 1904 and 10 miles in 1905.

There is also an I.C.A. Ulster Gold for 10 miles in 1904.

Although times are not engraved on these medals, with good fortune his 1903 100 miles time is seen on the YMCA club medal and shows that he set a superb Irish record of 5 hrs. 19 mins. 12 secs.

In the early years of the new century while still a Member of Dunmurry C.C. he became a second claim member of the Irish Road Club, Ulster Branch.

Late in 1902 he joined the YMCA C.C. in Belfast, whose medals, mentioned above, were an artistic delight.

His training methods reveal some modern ideas: He fitted weights to his training bike and rode hard sessions behind a tandem.

A few years into the new century Harry's reputation had grown so much that the English cycle maker Rudge-Whitworth presented him with a made to measure bicycle that became his pride and joy!

He did so well on the machine that the firm later presented him with a special gold medal for his achievements.

His list of cups won outright grew: The Graham, The Magowan, The Barry McIvory, 2 Irish Road Club Cups The McConville, The Londonderry The Steel and Sons and The Dunville. One of his wins was the Rudge Whitworth cup for 100 miles. He won in 5 hrs. 40 mins. with Shafto Kerr in 3rd place.

His most notable feats during the period 1899 – 1908 were great time trials at all distances from 10 to 100 miles as well as the gruelling 12 hour event. His figures for various distances were:

> 50 miles in 2 hrs. 38 mins. in 1900
> 100 miles in 5 hrs. 19 mins. in 1903
> 198 miles in 12 hours in 1908

He also set some marvellous place-to-place records in the closing years of his career.

Among these was a tandem paced ride from Belfast to Dublin and back of 12 hrs. 20 mins. during which he also set the one way time of 5 hrs. 39 mins. This ride improved the 10 year old figures of the Dubliner, J.A. Healy by more than one hour. Prizes were substantial in those days and many useful and valuable household items could be won, as well as the silverware. Later when Harry Mussen bought the house which would much later become the Beechlawn Hotel in Dunmurry, the main bedroom was entirely furnished with prizes he had won on his bicycle.

London Olympic Games

The pinnacle of his career, however, was his selection to represent G.B. at the London Olympic Games of 1908. His event was the 100km track race at Crystal Palace. The usual road race was omitted, unfortunate in that Harry's abilities on a hilly road circuit might have led to better results. Mussen qualified 13th in his heat of 30 riders and went into the final with high hopes of a medal. A German competitor, riding either carelessly or maliciously, edged the Dunmurry man off the track.

He crashed heavily and was unable to finish.

In 1912 he had the honour of travelling with an Irish Team to the Games in Stockholm, Sweden.
It is not known whether he was Team Manager, Coach, or simply honoured guest.
The Team was: R. J. McCredy (already mentioned above), B.J. Doyle, the brothers M. and J. Walker (all from the South of Ireland), Frank Guy of Belfast C.C. (who would later break some of Mussen's records)

In that same year (1912) Harry's father, Henry Senior, died. Although already deeply involved in running the Dunmurry Inn, Harry now took full proprietorship. Married since 1909 to Maud Gilmer, Harry had retired from bicycle racing the previous year – following the London Olympic Games. They began their family with Arthur in 1910, followed by Georgie in 1912, Rita in 1914, Victor coming as an after thought in 1923.

Pigeons

Despite his domestic and business responsibilities his need for sport persisted. First with pigeons and later with greyhounds he excelled. Although this was through the efforts of other creatures it is clear that his application of intelligence and science to all his projects would always bring good results.

His pigeon lofts at Dunmurry soon became renowned throughout Europe and his birds gained legendary successes. By 1914 he had a 2 ½ page advertisement in a typical copy of 'The Racing Pigeon'. In that same year one of his birds set a speed of 2744 yds/mins while flying from Malahide in County Dublin to Dunmurry. The birds' name was Lufthansa but was promptly renamed Malahide after its great flight. This world best was recorded in the Guinness Book of Records from first publication until a Canadian bird eclipsed it in 1983 with 2892 yds/mins. (Work those speeds out in m.p.h. yourself!)

Turning to Greyhound Racing

Family life or the outbreak of World War One did not dampen Harry's sporting enthusiasm.
After the cessation of hostilities, however, he began to take a greater interest in greyhound racing. The pigeons were still cared for but were placed under the care of other handlers. It was not long before his dogs were winning races all over the country, just like their feathered contemporaries. They benefitted from Harry's installation of a fully equipped dog track in the grounds of 4 Dunmurry Lane, complete with 'the hare.' A notable result was his dog 'Magull' taking 3rd place in the Waterloo Cup race in England in the early 1920's. This was the race famously won three times by 'Master McGrath'. In 1923 his greyhound 'Mill Street Masher' won the Belfast Telegraph Cup outright at the Mourne Park Touring Club.

In the mid 1920's Harry opened another Pub in Dunmurry. Naming it the Greyhound Inn he had it decorated to celebrate his passion for greyhound racing. A picture of his most successful animal appeared in frosted glass in the main doorway.

In 1927 Harry's wife died suddenly when young Victor was only 4 years old. For a year or more he mourned her loss but as often happens, Harry met another, while at a Coursing meeting in Kilkeel. She was the daughter of the owner of the Kilmorey Arms Hotel in Kilkeel. Her name was Essie Stevenson and Victor fondly remembers her taking him into Belfast to buy his first school uniform. Indeed Victor insists she was a very caring stepmother.

Harry Mussen never forgot his cycling days. He was often seen standing at the door of the Greyhound Inn waving greetings to two wheeled athletes as they passed through Dunmurry village. The cycling Historian, Harry McCartney from Donacloney reports this memory from the 1930's. He has always regretted not stopping to engage the old master in conversation. I myself recollect conversations with the Kircubbin cobbler Willie Weir who was President of Ards Cycling Club in the 1950's and 60's. He was Timekeeper and also acted as turn-steward for various clubs who used the Portaferry Road for Time Trials. These were mostly the Belfast and the Cyprus Cycling Clubs. His own cycling career co-incided with Mussen's and he always referred to him as "unbeatable". This Willie Weir, incidentally, had been the first person to break the hour on the Portaferry Road – for 20 miles! That was in 1912.

Harry persisted with his twin interests right through the 1930's and the Second World War. He supervised the handling of the pigeons which had now fallen to his son Victor. People remember him walking his dogs on Dunmurry Lane all through those years in which he remained fit and well.

Son, Victor Mussen holding the Harry Mussen Trophy. at Ballinderry Antiques

However, Victor Mussen relates that in late 1951 his father began to experience what was thought to be indigestion, but which turned out to be Angina pain. In the early weeks of 1952 he was forced, under doctors orders, to have some days bed rest. As it turned out there was a Coursing meeting due to take place at Crebilly, near Ballymena. Victor, naturally was charged with taking the two star greyhounds to the meeting where they both had convincing wins. Victor had the great pleasure of bringing back the good news to his ailing father.

On the morning of 8th February 1952 Victor was bottling Guinness in the back of the Greyhound Inn when the phone rang. He was summoned to come home at once as his father had taken a bad turn. On arriving at Beechlawn he went straight to the bedroom where he was met with the question from his father "What's wrong?" His reply was "Not a thing." He took his father's hand and within a few minutes and even fewer words, Harry Mussen was dead.

Some months after the funeral Victor and his sisters Georgie and Rita donated a trophy to the memory of their father. The East Ulster Road Club was to promote a Belfast to Dublin Time Trial. It was initiated on 27th June 1953. This first version was won by Billy Jebb in a time of 4 hrs. 12 mins. 47 secs. Unfortunately this long place-to-place time trial which was complicated to run, began to receive low entry numbers. The emphasis was beginning to switch to mass start road racing. Consequently the Harry Mussen Cup was left without a race after only four events. In 1954 and 1955 it was won by Tom Allingham of East Tyrone C.C. while the last version was won by Maurice Donaldson of Maryland Wheelers. The event record was held by Allingham in the superb time of 3 hrs. 58 mins. 47 secs.

Towards the end of the 1950's the trophy was forgotten. It was known to have been at the premises of the cycle dealer J. E Cassidy in Cromac Street. Very early in 2008 while I was working on this story, Victor Mussen was told that a Mussen trophy was in the collection of Ballinderry Antiques. I phoned them and the voice at the other end said: "Yes, I have my hand on it right now".

On 1st February 2008, Victor Mussen and myself visited the Antique dealers where we found not only the Harry Mussen cup but also the Belfast Telegraph cup won outright in 1923 for Hare Coursing.

BILLY KIRK

Medal presented to Harry Mussen, by the Rudge Whitworth company

Harry Mussens beautiful Belfast YMCA Medals showing inscriptions on back.

Bill Jebb (Kings Moss C.C.) the first winner of the Harry Mussen Trophy for the Belfast to Dublin time trial in 1953.
He is on the start line at Finaghy and he is being held by Billy McCormack of the promoting club – East Ulster R.C.

The Mussen Memorial Perpetual Trophy

Belfast to Dublin records

Belfast to Dublin or VV Record Holders Since 1900

Date	Name	Club	Classification	Time
1904	A J Healy	Irish Road Club, Dublin	Private trial	6.08.39
1907	H Mussen	Irish Road Club, Belfast	Private trial	5.39.30
1908	A J Kettle	Artane CC, Dublin	Private trial	5.33.00
1913	F H Grubb	England	Professional PT	5.21.00
29.8.1925	K Young	Northern CC, Belfast	IRC First Competition	6.00.00
30.8.1926	J McCartney	Irish Road Club	IRC First Competition	5.30.00
30.8.1930	B Kidd	Kilmore CC, Lurgan	IRC First Competition	5.18.17
31.8.1935	V Piggott	Belvoir CC, Belfast	IRC First Competition	5.02.45
17.9.1935	H Opperman	Australia	Professional PT	4.54.36
28.8.1937	V Piggott	Belfast	Irish Road Club Competition	4.58.50
21.9.1938	A Donegan	Portarlington SW	Private trial	4.33.00
26.8.1939	V Piggott	Belfast	IRC Competition	4.53.31
26.8.1944	W Dowds	Lurgan	IRC Competition	4.52.04
26.8.1949	I Matear	Belfast CC	IRC Competition	4.38.47
27.8.1950	G Wilkes	Windsor CC, Belfast	Private trial	4.32.00
11.10.1953	Mrs I (Cle) Woods	Belfast CC	Ladies private trial	4.56.00
4.10.1964	D Kane	Northern CC, Belfast	Private trial	4.29.00
11.10.1964	M Foster	Cyprus CC, Belfast	Private trial	4.24.00
10.10.1971	D Kane	Northern CC, Belfast	Private trial	4.21.00
5.11.1995	T Evans	Banbridge CC	Private trial	4.00.28

Belfast – Dublin – Belfast

Date	Name	Club	Classification	Time
1907	H Mussen	Irish Road Club, Belfast	Private trial	12.20.00
27.7.1936	J Lamont	East Ulster CC	IRC Dublin Competition	12.09.15
26.8.1944	J Gray	Northern, Belfast	Return PR trial	10.51.24
28.8.1948	I Matear	Belfast CC	Return PR trial	10.22.50
4.10.1953	J Hadden	King's Moss CC	Private trial	10.17.00
12.9.1954	Mrs I (Cle) Woods	Belfast CC	Private trial	11.47.00
8.10.1967	M Foster	Cyprus CC	Private trial	9.21.00

The hero

It was the penultimate stage of the 1957 RAS.

The weather was foul – cold, wet and miserable ...

... and my bike was feeling like a torture rack after a week of long hard stages. One of my team mates, Paddy Glackin was having trouble with his machine and when he punctured for the second time, he asked me to stop with him. We were somewhere between Clonakilty and Kilkenny and taking into consideration the distance to the finish and the conditions I gave him my spare tub and suggested he tag along with some of the stragglers and get to the finish. He climbed off as we were going through a small town where the locals stood out in the rain to cheer us on. (I heard the rest of the story from Harry McGurk and his assistant manager, Joe O'Doherty). They stopped to help Paddy with all the people gathered around in anticipation. His bike was made ready and he was regaled with food and drink and shouts of encouragement. A clean jersey was produced and Paddy stripped to the waist and stood against the car flexing his bronzed muscles to the delight of the onlookers, while Harry and Joe dried him off. He pulled the fresh jersey over his head, forgetting their own time in the rain. Someone ran out from a nearby pub with a glass of brandy and the hero downed it and with much back slapping and cries of "He's a great man" and "God Bless You" he took off like a man possessed, with the cheers of the onlookers ringing through the sodden town. Harry and Joe who were thoroughly soaked by then took their leave from the excited crowd and set the Ford Anglia after the rider towards Kilkenny As they rounded the first bend in the road, our hero was standing and flagging them down.

"I think he's packed it in" shouted Joe.

"What'll we do?" asked Harry. "What'll we do?" retorted Joe. "Run over him!"

I'm glad to say they didn't but the language must have been choice in that Ford Anglia heading towards the finish. Later he confessed he only did it for the benefit of the onlookers.

Paddy is gone now but he was a showman to the end.

BILLY CANNING
Windsor CC ELK RC and Phoenix CC

Champions Night in the Windsor C.C. clubrooms in Great Northern Street, Belfast.
Left to right: Sam Neill, Belfast C.C., Aubrey Brown, Easte Ulster R.C., Jackie (John) Fee, Cyprus C.C., Albert Ewart, Maryland Wheelers, Jimmy McCoo, Belfast C.C. (All back row)
Joe Craig, Northern CC., Billy Sands, Windsor C.C., George Wilkes, Windsor C.C., Davy McNutt, Windsor C.C.

Champions Night in Windsor C.C. clubrooms in 1950
Left to right: Jackie Fee, Cyprus C.C. N.I. 100 miles T.T. champion. Frank McKeown, Kings Moss C.C. N.I. 25 T.T. champion. Billy Sands of Windsor C.C.
Stalwart Timekeeper, Tommy Taylor, Kings Moss C.C. and Norman Surplus

Racing and touring photos from the 50's

Dundrod 1953
George Wilkes (cape) Tommy Burns,
R. Vennard, Frank O'Brien, P. J. Glackin (peeping)
Herbie Holden, W. Canning and Martin McKay

*P J Glackin and W. Canning, Bangor Erris,
Co Mayo 1953*

*Windsor Club Run (Early fifties)
Included: A R Bobby, Tommy and John Sands, Mona
McNally, soon to marry Rab Collim,
Ray Carroll, W. Canning and Davy Martin*

*Leo Feeney, Rab Collim, Ray Carrol, AR Bobby,
W. Canning with Maurice Jackson and the two
Maureens at the back*

The ultimate embarrassment for a cyclist

In the early sixties Billy Knowles and I entered for the Northern Ireland 50 mile TT championship, promoted by Ballymena Road Club.

So early on Sunday morning we set out to ride from Woodvale Road Belfast to Ballymena. I started two minutes behind Morris Foster, the defending champion. I caught Morris just before the Glengormley turn. Unfortunately going around the turn steward the bike slipped from under me as the road was wet. While I was on the ground with Paddy Megahey taking photographs Morris passed me again. I remounted and actually started to gain on Morris! However about Templepatrick Morris started to go away from me again. What I didn't know, I was suffering the onset of hunger knock.

Through Antrim and on towards Randastown I really began to suffer and then on a small rise on the road I suffered the ultimate embarrassment of a racing cyclist when a lady on an old 'Sit up and beg' bike, complete with shopping basket passed me on her way to Church! Luckily for me around the next corner I spotted Billy Hudson who was watching the riders go by. He fed me with a couple of sandwiches and I received sufficiently to go on to the finish, recording a 2 hour 8 minutes, or thereabouts. Guess who won? 'Big Mo' as usual.

Then Billy and I were faced with the ride back home. Again, no motor cars in those days.

LESLIE WHITE
Ex Maryland Wheelers

Leslie White - Craigantlet Hill Climb (probably 1956)

Mushrooms

Recently I was showing American friends of mine around 3500 miles of lovely scenery - mostly in Ulster with three trips into Eire.

At Ballyhornan on the banks of Killard, I spied some mushrooms which reminded me of an amusing incident a number of years ago in the club. We were making out the season's run-card in the club-room one evening and we came to the 27th August. Gerry Kirk informed us that that date was his birthday, so he was granted the choice of the run and he chose Downpatrick, adding that he would treat us all to ham and eggs that day, so naturally we all agreed and looked forward to the 27th. I was a late starter but travelling by Killinchy and Killyleagh, I arrived in time for tea, carrying a capful of mushrooms and the pockets of my coat were loaded also. I had picked them from a field on the road to Killinchy. When I presented them, Gerry got the proprietor to fry them and we had them with the ham and eggs and at the finish there was nothing but empty plates – even Leslie enjoyed them. There were a few enquiries as to where I got the mushrooms so the lads decided to visit the field on the way home. So on arrival at the field, we soon had a few bags filled when the farmer arrived on the scene. Gerry Nicholson and I held the fort, while the others made a getaway. So after a brief pow-wow, the old boy took a seat on the dyke to recover while we gracefully climbed the gate back to the road again. Well, we all went on our way rejoicing with our mushrooms for another feed of them when we got home. We discovered later that the bags we put the mushrooms in were supplied by Leslie Merthen who had dropped behind in Downpatrick to get them while the rest of us thought it was a 'quick one.' The members present that day were Billy Vokes, Tommy Gordon, Billy Beattie, Jimmy Blair, G. Nicholson, Spence, McKibben, Neil, Gerry Kirk and Leslie Mehrten.

SAM NEILL 1920's - 1980

Archie's slogan

In 1980 when the colourful Archie Cunningham won the Tour of Ireland he took the lead on stage 5 in an audacious breakaway group, overtaking England's John Parker, who later founded Parker International Cycles. He found his nearest challenger was Alan McCormack, son of the famous John Joe. In the hotels at succeeding stage ends he appeared in the evenings with his dressing gown emblazoned with the slogan: '*Not an inch, McCormack!*'

BILLY KIRK

Strange beds

To the touring cyclist, one of the main items on their agenda is bedding down for the night and this though brings to mind many strange beds which may have been encountered during holidays.

The first to my mind was also the most comfortable and it was called the 'Hole in the Wall' and we slept in it during a tour of the Highlands at Crain-Larach , after receiving a terrible soaking over Rannoch Moor in a 'Scotch Mist.   Then there was the 'Heath Robinson' type which we encountered in Louth. It gave up the ghost under the weight of Fred and necessitated running repairs in the 'wee small hours' and a rather rapid leave taking of the premises next morning. The same thing happened on one of our first Easter Tours in Donegal with the club.

   This being the occasion when a genuine four poster Queen Anne ended up on three legs, old Billy jumping in was too much for it.

   My first experience of the comforts of hay stacks was one night when we had to leave booked-out Killarney at about 10.00 pm to wend our way via the Windy Gap to Peg O'Connor's of Sneem.

   The road beyond the Gap was terrible and my companion and I had to resort to climbing up each signpost with a bobby-dodger, to see where we were. It must have been two or two thirty a.m. when, both tired out, we entered a fertile valley in the mountains with the moon breaking through the heavy cloud beaming on a beautiful field of new mown hay. Without a word, John and I dismounted and turning to me he said "Do you see what I see?" Needless to say I did and so leaving the bikes on the road, we made a bee-line for the stacks. In less than no time all one could see were four cycling shoes protruding from the bottom. But the observant farmer who was coming home after a 'Do' came over to investigate and I was rudely awakened by someone trailing me out, feet first. When he saw the cut of us he laughed loud and long and then began apologising. But notwithstanding his offer of a bed up at the farm, we clung to our hay stacks and only the terrific heat of the sun at ll.00 a.m. made us come into the open again. Next day we reached Peg's in Sneem for breakfast and over ham and eggs we explained what happened and that wise old lady just shook her head and bemoaned the fact that a grand bed went unslept in.

BILL MURRAY   Belfast CC 1930 - 1997

There was another occasion, when owing to unforeseen circumstances we had to bed down on the floor of a small cottage and not knowing the place was rat infested, we left our eats beside us. I had strange impressions during the night and I kept imagining that someone was swiping 'things' off me. This was verified when we surveyed the scene of destruction that greeted us in the morning. Only the bones of the meat we had was left and the bread had also vanished. The rats must have had a jamboree over us as we slept!

AND YET ANOTHER...

Another strange bed we stopped in was at Big Guy's weekend abode at Kilclay in Clogher.
This turned out to be an apple shed and we slept on empty sacks with tons of apples all around us.
As Hughie said "What more could anyone want, but a sore tummy". And we got that too!

ROAMER

OFF THE BEATEN TRACK—

Cyclists of 1907 *(Taken from a copy of The Ulster Cyclist in 1935)*

In an old newspaper dated 29th June 1907, we read of the following clubs:

Y.M.C.A., Eastern, Landscape, Distillery, Victoria, Bloomfield, I.O.R. Belfast, 9th Old Boys, Western, Southside, Ivy, Lisburn, Caithness, R.I.C., Dunville, Barbarians, Vintners, Irish Road Club and Mossley. How many of those clubs exist today? This old newspaper contains a report of a sports fixture held in Wallace Park, Lisburn in aid of the County Antrim Infirmary.

Some of the cyclists who won prizes at this meeting were 'stars of the wheel world' in those days. Then there were splendid tracks like: Glentoran, Ulster and Ballymena cement track to train or race on. Amongst those mentioned were John Robertson (Y.M.C.A), H. Murray (Bloomfield) W. Dugan (Irish Road Club), J.P. Mullan (Mossley) Sam Cochrane, (Ivy) H. Neill (Lisburn), Andy Patterson (Bloomfield) T. Breen (R.I.C.) C. Leighton (Bloomfield) J.A. Fee (Ballyclare) R. McBride (Ulster) W.H. Kerry (Bloomfield) and R. Collins (Y.M.C.A).

In comparing the time with the 1935 times we find that in 1907:
Mullan of Mossley (150 yards) won the mile in 2 mins. 14 3/5 secs.
In 1935 Harry Crawford (Ivy) at Lisnagarvey Sports on the same track won the mile off 140 yards in 2 mins. 12 3/5 secs.
Whilst also at Lisnagarvey Sports in 1935 the two miles was won by H. Crawford off 340 yards in 4 mins. 31 secs.

So apparently the riders of 1935 are at least as speedy as those in 1907.
This old newspaper contains in its advertising columns announcement of sports meetings such as:
The Giants Ring Sports, Belfast Grocers Assistants Sports, Tyrone County Infirmary Sports, Celtic Sports, Tyrone Farming Society Sports and Bangor Sports. Most of these meetings featured £10.10s. first prizes for the principal races, but of course there were big crowds at every sports meetings in those days. In the Club Runs announced for the 29th of June 1907, we read that the Landscape (mixed) Club are going to Crawfordsburn. Perhaps the short distance of the run was to spare the ladies any discomfort, yet the stamina of the fair sex of the present day is undoubted, when we consider that week in and week out, summer and winter, we have them riding to the Glens of Antrim, Kilkeel and even Portrush and returning the same day. We also read in the paper of the Dunville Club having to postpone their previous weeks run because of the weather and this was in the month of June!
So perhaps the present day cyclists are just as hardly as the cyclists of bygone days.

E. NEILL   *Hon.Sec. Maryland Wheelers*

A tour I remember

The 'Day's Plans' Co. Kerry
photo with the Oil Lamp

Jogging down memory lane is no doubt one of the most pleasant tasks of the cyclist and the following is an account of one of my first tours which I'll always remember. It was July 1936 that Isaac and I set out to get our first glimpse of Killarney. Our travelling companion being a tent, blankets, canteen set, primus (nearly all borrowed) and the healthy sum of 50 shillings in the kitty plus the unbounded optimism of youth. We must have cut a queer figure as we headed for the Border, under capes and southwesters, to the accompaniment of frequent clangings from the rear of our protesting steeds, but we never even noticed. An old C.T.C. Diary which I have reveals that we had our one and only cafe feed at Short's Cafe in Dundalk. Then we travelled by Ardee and Kells to Ellenstown where we spent the night on top of the winter feed in a barn. The mileage being 98 soaking wet ones.

The entry for *Sunday* reads: Head for Mullingar, band in square, so miss road and have a ten mile detour before hitting main road at Kilbeggan (still raining merrily). Through Tullamore (I was tee-total in those days, so missed the famous dew – disastrous!! To Birr, then over part of Bog of Allen to the village of Burrosokane. Here we shared the floor of a stable with horses whose faces would have looked much better than the unmentionable half they confronted us with. We slept on the cobble stones with a handful of fodder and the tent as covering and I got a rude awakening in the early hours of the morning by something pressing on my wind-pipe. I must have been dreaming about Sweeny Todd so can be excused for the howl I emitted. Isaac flashed the torch and its beam picked out the huddled shape of the servant-girl who had fainted right away. She had set the bike on top of us, but believe me the chain ring was far to real an imitation of the demon barber at his work for my liking. Mileage: 80

Monday: Head for Nenagh, then right to Bushfield, Birdhill, Annacotley and Limerick (we scrounged tea here). Then through Newcastle, Abbeyfeale to Farranfore (rain again), so we pitched tent in a sensible place under a hay shed. Mileage: 92.

Tuesday: Dropped down (sure feel like it) into Killarney, then via Muckross and Windy Gap to Kenmare then through Tunnelrock to Glengarrif. Beautiful night, so camp on hillside overlooking bay, Isaac says he knew it couldn't last raining, it was bound to turn and you know, he was right. It run and ran down a hillside and hit us for six – blankets and all.   Two wet miserable lads ran up and down that field to try and get heat up in the wee small hours.

Wednesday: To Bantry, Bandon (cold wind and showers, then teeming all the way to Cork). Pity we couldn't stretch it and get digs, but fifty bob even in those days wasn't elastic!
So we made for Middletown and fall in with four of Glasgow Wheelers who are also bankrupt and cheesed off and together we hunt for a barn. Get put up okay

Thursday: Waterford, Wexford to Killane, which village is quarantined with typhoid epidemic, so raise a gallop to outlying farm where we spend the night in a hay-loft and are nearly blown out by heavy storm during the night. Mileage 52

Friday: Through Carlow and Wicklow to Bray.
Saturday: To Dublin and visit the Zoo, then up to Louth and Castlebellingham and camp in a field (first dry night). I'll pull the curtain down here on Sunday's ride home with 4 1/2d between us, or you might get the knock too. My companion of those days went on to become one of our most prolific record breakers and only recently we were recalling that early tour with much amusement.

'ROAMER'

BILL MURRAY   Belfast CC 1930 - 1997

Cyclists services

In the winter of 1956, the Rev. Dr. A L.Agnew held a Service for Cyclists in 'All Souls' Non Subscribing Presbyterian Church in Elmwood Avenue, Belfast. It was suitable for all Denominations.

There was a turn-out of 150 Cyclists all in touring clothes. Soup and sandwiches were provided after the service and we then left for a combined Club Run and Drum Up which everyone enjoyed.

In March 1957, Cyril Henry organised a similar Service in Cookstown at First Presbyterian Church conducted by the Rev. E Morrison B.A. BD. Jim Slaine (East Tyrone) and I were asked to read the Lessons. A similar Service was held in the Roman Catholic Church in Cookstown at the same time.

Everyone met up afterwards and went of for the usual Club Run and Drum Up.

Two more Cyclist Services were held in 'All Souls' in 1957 and 1958 which attracted an even larger attendance.

ISABEL WOODS   Belfast C.C.

Cyclists prepared for their Sunday Run following the Cyclist Service at All-Souls.

Cookstown Sunday Service

...om various parts of the Province who attended morning service in First Presbyteria
Church, Cookstown, on a recent Sunday.

*Peter Woods and Isabel Woods with son David
and Rev. Dr. Agnew and his wife
Dr Isabel Caldwell after a Sunday Service at All
Souls Elmwood Avenue Belfast.*

The reluctant performer

In the winter of 1955, the Rev. Dr. Agnew (affectionately known as 'The Dr.') had another cycling idea!! He asked me if I would perform on Rollers, on stage, during the interval in his Christmas Pantomime 'Robinson Crusoe'. I flatly refused! He was a man who liked to get his own way and wouldn't take NO for an answer. After a lot of persuading, including a 'sob story' that funds had to be raised to save the Church Hall, I relented with misgivings, as I didn't relish being exhibited. To add insult to injury, he insisted on a display of trophies and certificates at the last minute. This ordeal was more stressful to me than any records attempts, including the End to End!!

ISABEL WOODS   *Belfast C.C.*

Isabel Woods on the rollers at the Pantomime interval

If it's pottering you're after ....

To really enjoy your cycling you must have another hobby which you can pursue while on your journeys awheel. This is an oft quoted phrase that I have found out to be substantially true nevertheless. My original hobby, even before entering the joys of wheeling, was sketching and I can say that I have never really lost my early love of trying to depict the colour and beauty of nature.

But there have been others which gave as much pleasure too, which I will tell you of. For instance, there was the time that Walter,* and I used to dabble in what one might loosely describe as Archaeology and we would begin by pouring over an O.S. half inch map of Down and pin-point a certain area where Druid Circles and Cromlech were marked, then set out awheel to investigate.

We had great fun in our "excavations" until one Sunday we failed to locate one near Drumkirk which we knew to exist, so we took to the fields in our enthusiasm to find it. Now the fields hereabouts are mostly arable and are diligently sowed with crop each Spring and we had traversed quite a few before we noticed a hump in the middle of a lovely field of cabbages. We uncovered the topsoil and find our Druid Stone. This must be something good, we thought and straight away started digging underneath, ruining several head of cabbage. We must have been quite near the 'fairy gold' when there was a loud shout from the edge of the field and a corpulent figure came tearing down on us! We didn't stop to explain as he had probably never heard of Druids and by the look of him he didn't want to, but we took to our heels and ran. I believe we would have left Steve McCooks standing that day and on reaching the bikes we didn't stop on this side of the Quoile Bridge.

Another hobby was following a river from source to estuary and this is most interesting as very often the course leaves the road and one has to consult the map to pick it up again at the nearest point and generally these roads are well off the beaten track. We had a grand club-run one day tracing the Quoile which, incidentally, rises on the Lisburn side of Ballynahinch at Annahilt and comes quietly along as a stream to the edge of Montalto Estate and crossing the road at the cricket ground, straggles along the Crossgar Road where it goes well inland via Listooder, Kilmore and Annacloy to Downpatrick and the Lough. It would be hard to find a more peaceful spot than quaint old Steam-boat Quay where the river finally merges into the grey waters of Strangford.

Then there were other phases of bird-watching (not the type you mean dad, sit down) and the search for a rare species of black-bird called the ringed-Ousel. Manys the day Alec and I toiled along the roads watching for one to appear and funny enough, after Alec had found his particular bird and hatched several fledglings, I was lucky enough to see two of this type of bird in the space of a few weeks. Which goes to show lads, keep looking at the winged variety.

Then there was the craze for finding old right-o-ways which often took us through old farm-yards and other out of the way places. Sometimes we prowled around looking for old coaching highways, which a century ago rang to the echo of bugle and bell.

You can take your pick of this lot and I'll be more than surprised if you don't get twice the fun from your journeys awheel.

'ROAMER'

BILL MURRAY Belfast CC   1930 - 1997
Walter was Bill's brother. He was a famous cross country runner and champion from Ballyclare.

Bill Murray's line drawing

Jack Johnston

An article written by Stanley Martin in the Irish Cycling Review and published in 1987

As though to jog old memories of his many fine performance of past years, Belfast man, Jack Johnston (Cyprus CC – Heatco – Nubrick) made a brief return to racing in 1983 at the age of 43. He took the Irish '100' title in 4 hrs. 16 mins. 31 secs. beating runner up Martin Quinn of the same club by 2 mins. 27 secs. Three weeks later he won the NICF road championship round nine laps, 67.5 miles, of the Dundrod circuit. 'Big Jack' who served on last years Irish Tripartite Committee, has carved out many racing distinctions. Most of his career will not be familiar to the majority of those at present in the sport. Here are a few highlights along the way, which may give some measure of this outstanding all-rounder.

It was the 1960 NICF-CRE national road championship and the race had gone into the last of its five 25 miles laps. Ahead loomed the long arduous Deadman's Hill climb near Newtownhamilton, Co. Armagh. Through the distance and uncompromising terrain most survivors were tired. Then Johnston, just 20, and in his own words: "green as grass in the finer points of road racing tactics, I took off". Up the leg-breaking Deadman's, I could hear someone shouting and roaring behind me. I looked back and it was Peter Crinnion (Bray Wheelers). He was calling for me to slow a little so that we might set up a dual effort. From Peter I immediately began learning a lot about breakaway riding. It was a sweltering hot day. I felt I was the strongest and decided on what should be my winning move. I had it all measured in my mind. At the appropriate moment the gear-change, then the almighty burst of effort and I surged out in front. Alas, it all went wrong! What I thought was the finishing line, wasn't! We were in a kind of Square and I had slanted off at the incorrect angle! Ron Killey (Isle of Man) shouted to me. I swung round a monument, rejoined the proper path on a slightly uphill contour as the others began edging past. It was impossible to raise a second such effort and I was fifth to finish. Less than two seconds behind winner Wes Mason (England). What a feeling of despair!"

Now we run on past many other episodes in 'Jonty's' eventful racing days. Winner while on holiday in France 1963 of the GP de Plevenk. 37th from 140 starters in the World championship at Renaix, Belgium that year. Also in 1963 he lasted 11 days in the 14 day Tour de l'Avenir when another Belfast man, Ian Moore was the Irish team's only rider to reach the overall finish in Paris. Wins in abundance at home, of course. In one sequence he chalked up six successive victories.

In 1964 Jack became only the second Irishman, after John Lackey (Dublin Regional) in 1961, to win Northern C.C.'s high-class Easter Tour of the North which had been running annually from 1955. Then with high hopes, off to France, he joined the independent (semi-professional) ranks with the Union Cycliste Briochine club at St. Brieuc, Brittany. There were good days – a couple of wins including le Prix de la Madeleine – but bad ones too. Some illness, loss of form and purse misfortune. It was really the wrong set-up. We didn't get into the right events and there was a kind of 'Mafia' at work. Perhaps we didn't take it all seriously enough. A somewhat wasted period, he reflects.

In 1966 Jack was back on the home scene, reinstated as an amateur but barred from representative teams and championship events. In that season's Easter Tour of the North he finished second by 12 secs. to Liam Horner (Lorraine Club) who, an individual entrant, retained the leader's jersey against all the odds during the final stage.

A year later and Big Jack treated us to the greatest Tour of the North epic of all. It was Easter Tuesday in Omagh and a light covering of snow lay on the ground when the field sped off on the fourth and final Stage of 82 miles, eastwards to Carrickfergus. Alan Mellor (Manchester Regional) had the yellow jersey with Andy McGhee (Glasgow Regional) reigning Scottish champion and 1966 Tour of Scotland winner, second at 54 secs. Peter Buckley (Manchester), 1966 Commonwealth champion was 3rd at 1.30, followed by Ian Thomson (Glasgow) at 1.32, Alfie Sterne (Belfast Regional) at 2.07, Steve Chivers (Cyprus CC) at 2.25, Jimmy Leitch (Glasgow) at 2.32. Nigel Dean (Manx RC) at 2.56: George McBean (Cumbernauld) at 3.03. Then came Johnston, 10th, at 3.14 and next were Noel O'Neill (Bray) at 3.20 and Peter Doyle (Dublin Regional) at 3.23. Across the hills to Cookstown on the thawing snow the race winged along, 27 miles in 56 minutes. Buckley soon afterwards remarked to Johnston "you're quiet today, big fellow" At Ahoghill roundabout Jack skidded and fell, leaving him with one hand lacerated and a thigh showing red through his torn shorts. Remounting, and with a circular-saw noise emanating from slightly damaged chain-rings, he charged after the peleton and went straight past. Noel Taggart (Belfast), 17th on G.C at 7.15, was ahead and Jack joined him. Together they went 10......20......30..... secs. - up round the Ballymena detour. There were 27 hills left with two King of the Hills offering 10 secs. bonus on each, plus l min., 30 and 15 secs. for the Stage placings.

Johnston, 3.14 behind on GC still appeared to be without a mission. Even if he could collect maximum bonuses of 1.20 he still needed a 1.55 advantage over Mellor to snatch victory. With eight other riders in between. Along the rising Larne road they pounded in cold sharp rain, turning right for the Collin Mountain, its summit lost in driving sleet. Johnston and Taggart were tough hard roadmen of speed, strength and determination. Real 'big league' riders. At the top they were 1.20 in front, 15 miles to go. Now Johnston was in with a chance. Their descent on the treacherous surface was hair-raising in the extreme as they sought to gain every possible second of time in dreadful conditions. Taggart was left with nine miles remaining, as Johnston powered on to the final climb at the head of Snowey Glen. Then he was on the last 800 feet drop to the sea-front finish at Carrick's ancient Castle. Frozen, soaking wet, bruised and cut, he awaited the men who mattered. Next to arrive were Mick Brown (Nottingham RC) Owen Davies (East Coast Olympic) and Dave Watson (Gosforth RC) all at 2.14. Johnston was the overall winner. Mellor finished in a group of eight which included Irishmen Doyle, Chivers, Wallace Caldwell (Ballymena RC), John McCarthy (Obelisk Wh.) and Harry Dawson (Bray) at 2.50. A memorable never-say-die performance indeed by big Jack, victory by 54 secs.

Jack Johnston

over runner-up Mellor, all in that dramatic last hour.

That 1967 Tour of the North took place on March 25-28. Two months later, on May 28, Johnston won the Irish (NICF-CRE) "25" championship on the Derry-Limavady course in 57.30, then the fastest-ever '25' by an Irish rider on Irish roads, if I am not mistaken. In the North, nearly 12 years earlier, Billy Kirk (Ards CC) had clocked 58.28 in September 1955 on 82.8-inches fixed using wired-on tyres and that was the recognised NICF record until Johnston's flyer shattered it. Also in 1954 Billy Dowds (South Lurgan RC) won the Irish '25' title in 57.56, outside NICF territory on the Navan Road.

Johnston was cleared to ride national championships only on the evening before the 1967 '25'. First of the top-seeds to finish on that sunny morning on Foyleside was: Morris Foster (Cyprus CC), 16 secs. outside Kirk's long standing NI best with 58.41. Peter Doyle, on multi-gears, knocked this aside with 57.55, faster than those 1954/1955 rides of Dowds and Kirk. Then came Johnston, on 90 inches fixed, 57.30. The foundations of this result had been laid on the harder 12.7 miles outward leg where the turn times were Johnston 30.50, Doyle 31.30, Foster 31.40, On the final list Reggie Kearns (Irish RC) was fourth, 59.13, followed by Joe Smyth (Cyprus) 59.34, and Ernie Mark (Ballymena) 59.59.

Afterwards Jack set about establishing his own Heatco business and rarely raced again. And when he decided to prepare for another spell of competition in the 1983 season his training was disrupted by two severe accidents in the winter when he twice was knocked down by motor vehicles. Once he was hit from the back and on the other occasion the vehicle suddenly veered across his path. But he wouldn't give up and came back to win the Irish '100' in what was his first-ever attempt at time-trialing over that distance, and take the NICF road crown which he had last held 16 years earlier.

Jack's long list of successes included events which have disappeared from the calendar. Tour of the Gaps and Tour of the Seaside in the South. Tour of Mid-Down and Tour of the Glens in the North. Once, back in 1961, he was best in King's Moss CC's 72 inch medium-gear '25' in 1.2.29 which represents a high-degree of fast-pedalling. He was a strong fearless trackman too and possesses a bagful of championship medals won in a variety of events.

All this, and he only joined Cyprus CC in the first place, to be a social member!

Jack Johnston bicycles, Dallas, Texas

Jack opened the door and peered into the derelict building. He weighed up his options. It was Spring 1988 in Dallas, Texas. Temperatures were high, but below the 105 degree summer temperatures that were to come. JACK JOHNSTON BICYCLES, Dallas, Texas was about to become a reality. After months of planning and construction work, Jack signed a five year lease. In the summer of 1988, Team Jonti, our bicycle club was formed, the shop was damaged by a tornado and we were broken into twice. Armed for protection Jack and his son slept in the store at night until they could get a proper security system installed. A year later when closing the store for the day, Jack was persuaded to hand over the contents of the cash register. He thought this would be a good idea because the recipient of the money had a gun and was screaming like a maniac. Truly, this was a great adventure! Belfast, Northern Ireland with its unpredictable weather and political unrest was a distant memory. During 1992, Richardson Bike Mart, the largest bike shop in Texas opened a location across the street from Jack Johnston Bicycles. They sponsored Lance Armstong. His fame was on the rise and it was hurting Jack's sales, so something had to be done. He dusted off his road bike and set his sights on the 1992 Master's World Championship in San Diego, California. After six months of intense training he was ready. He went to San Diego and won his event. He returned with a gold medal. With articles in the local newspaper and photo ops around Dallas, business improved. The strain of working 60 to 70 hours a week running a bike shop for 15 years prompted him to sell the business in 2002.

"Lets get into the car and drive all over the USA and find somewhere really nice to live" he said to his wife Patricia. "Do you really mean that?" she asked. Two days later at 11.00 am. they were eating breakfast at the McDonalds - 200 miles north of Dallas at the beginning of their 6000 mile search for a new home.

Myrtle Beach South Carolina (aka golf capital of the world) was home to Martin McKay and Michael Horgan. They were both top track cyclists in Northern Ireland in the 1950's and 1960's. Jack and Pat visited them and were hooked by the climate and relaxed pace of life. So they purchased a house beside the beach and settled down. Riding bicycle on the beach and through the neighbourhood every day is enjoyable and good exercise. But Jack needed something else to fill out the rest of the day. So in 2004 he started a new business venture called MCM Services. The company provided plumbing services and mosquito control services. His son Aaron joined the business a year later. When the recession hit in 2008 demand for plumbing and mosquito control services dropped. So they searched for a new service to provide. New bicycle paths had just been constructed in Pawleys Island and more people were riding bikes. So in November 2009 they decided to put their cycling knowledge and experience to use by opening a local bike store to serve the community. Whether its fixing, renting or choosing a bike, they can help. Aaron came up with the name Cyclopedia, which means bike smart. The doors opened for business in December 2009. Check us out at www.cyclopediaonline.com

An article from a Dallas newspaper.

Ballycarry weekend

Often I wish I had kept a diary of my cycling episodes during the past thirty years as the different events could be brought to mind more easily.

Time dims ones memory, but as I read your articles by 'ROAMER' vivid recollections come to mind. Once we spent a weekend in Ballycarry and our sleeping quarters were above an outhouse of the farm and were approached by stone steps which led to a large room or kitchen. The room next to it was all fitted out with wooden bunks around the wall. Before retiring to bed that night after the others had bedded down, I stoked the fire and put some sticks on the lower part of the oven for Sunday morning. I then did a few odd jobs and eventually crawled into the bottom bunk about an hour later. I had hardly got my head down when I heard a noise like a bolt being drawn and, as our bikes were in a store out in the yard, I got suspicious. I slithered out of bed again and crept down stairs then out into the yard which was lit up by a brilliant moon. I checked on the bikes and they were safe enough. But I strolled around to make sure there were no prowlers about.

  I then made my way upstairs again and as I was going through the open door, the light house at Blackhead flashed its beam and it was then I observed the reason for the suspicious noise. The latch on the oven door had not been properly secured so when the heat of the oven increased it had slipped out. I was just getting back into my bunk
when a voice from the bunk above whispered

  "Did you see anything Sammy?"
"Nothing" I replied.
"Your dammed soft"
he said
  "I wouldn't have gone down there for a fortune!"

STAR OF DOWN
Alias SAM NEILL
Belfast C.C.

WOT! NO CLUB RUNS
B.M.

The wee black can

THE "DRUM UP" —

B.M.

Whenever and wherever a cyclist tours, one piece of valuable equipment always accompanies him….. a wee black can. It has millions of counterparts in many circles, the ceremonial teapots of china, shining silver on drawing room tables, modern electro plated companions of the fireside, but none to compare with the 'old black friend.' Road men use it nevertheless, travellers, tramps, working men not catered for in canteens treasure it and to many it is invariably associated with: "I remember well the day…." or "I mind the time…." A worthy place the "black can" has in most memories. This piece of equipment is called many things, but its proper name is 'Drum' and 'drumming up' is the term given to brewing tea, but to cyclists it still remains the wee black can. Nearly everyone who has tasted the rich strong beverage, brewed over a wood fire will agree with addicts that it is the only way to make good tea. Its shock tactics on the nervous system of the fatigued, are so exhilarating that the wee can could well be called a life-saver.

A tin of beans or soup which is easily heated and quickly opened with little trouble is a constant companion to the can by the fireside. The can was once a shiny tin also, but after a few days boiling by the outdoor fire, it became a smoke burned chalice. As it becomes more and more blackened in the smoke of a thousand fires on the edges of hills, roadsides, forests and fields and while we sit marking the years with pints of the dark golden tea in wet and dry, warm and cold weather, the wee black can becomes our talisman. It travels with us on all our expeditions, north, south, east and west. Its handle bent to suit a strap or grip, its shape often queerly altered in the whims of a days touring. When emptied it is usually thrown aside while we sit eating our sandwiches, exchanging yarns and arguing who is going to be the fastest rider in the club next season. Lying on the grass or on the roadside it doesn't look strange, noticeable nor out of place for these are its natural surroundings. It blends with the ageless earth like a symbolic vessel of ancient ritual, temporarily discarded, its memories linked up with quiet companionship and cheery milestones on life's undulating road.
With affection then and something of reverence we salute…THE WEE BLACK CAN.

RAB COLLINS Belfast C.C.

Maybe its a mug's game

Start of I.R.C. 100 race Fortwilliam August 1941, left; Bill Murray. Others unknown

As my first and last love has always been touring, nevertheless riding against the watch has also provided amusing and painful memories too.   Never having enough speed to warrant being off scratch, my time-trial days began and ended at best being dubbed a middle-marker.   But what fun we had in pre-war days! Once while riding in a Maryland Open '50', Roy and I were at the tail of a very large field. I, being unfortunate enough to have those two great road-men, Vic Piggot and Bill Kernaghan of Belvoir Club, immediately behind me in starting order. Well, anyway, they let me get to the Temple before passing me. I though I had stopped! I carried on to the check at Randalstown and then back to Antrim, where I beheld Roy sitting on the verge.

"Pack it" he shouts. "It's a mug's game". "I never packed yet and I'm not going to this time" I replied. He then flashed two half crowns from his black Alpaca jacket and shouted "Would that coax you?"

Yes friends, that, and the fact that he was outside the local, did all the coaxing that was necessary and we discarded tubulars and disappeared inside in our tights. In no time at all I was in complete agreement that it was a mug's game and when we came out after being treated several times, anyone could have bought two racing machines quite cheap. We arrived back at the dressing rooms in Glengormley in time to see the last man off the premises.

There was another day when I took possession of a new Osgear and rode it in one of the old Ivy Club's 'Open 25's.' I had it in top most of the way to the turn and dropped it down coming home at Antrim Hill where I broke the chain and a kindly motorist gave me a lift to the finish. Isaac and a rider called McClinton of Northern volunteered to push me down to the dressing rooms but as we reached our destination, a Peeler stepped out and nabbed us for riding three abreast. McClinton was the first to give his name and address. Isaac nudged me and gave a knowing wink and I straight away re-christened myself Duff-Gibson and he followed with Felix O'Neill. The addresses were just as fictitious too. We didn't see our friend until the next "Open" when he came across to where we were stripping and he sure made our ears red with the dressing down he handed out. He had been to Court and been fined seven shillings and sixpence and they were still looking for Duff- Gibson and Felix O'Neill! We had found these 'handles' very appropriate when we were accepted by the limb of the law previously.

On one occasion in another Open '25' we had persuaded old 'Hair Oil' to make a come back.
He got a bad dose of the 'bonk' at the 'Half Way House' and was up to his neck in the well that lies opposite. I still think he'd have finished if he had gone across the road for a few minutes.

Then there was the Dunlop Cup '100' which was run-off over the old course, I had stages of the 'knock' but with the lads whipping me on vocally I managed to finish. So with Isaac placed second and Roy well up we landed our first Team prize in Open Competition for the old 'Club' and you can bet we were proud that night. Yes, there was sure grand fun up the road those days and there is yet, but don't you agree that the Riders take it far too seriously nowadays… Or maybe it's still a mug's game.

ROAMER

Expedition Gobbins

One Saturday afternoon early in May 1954, the sun was shining so I thought I would go for a ride ...

.... along the Antrim Coast. I went down into the village of Whitehead and after wandering around decided to walk along the pathway by the shore to the Blackhead lighthouse. When I got there I didn't feel like walking all the way back again, nor did I feel like daring the idea of cycling along the somewhat narrow strip of concrete separating the cliffs from the sea. The only alternative was to climb the steps up to the lighthouse and hope that there was a way out up there. I picked up my bike, which was by no means a light one and started up the wooden steps. The sun was very hot and the old bike seemed to get heavier every minute, so I stopped for a rest on a sort of ledge. When I looked down the sea appeared an awful long way off and I began to feel a bit queasy. Heights always make me feel dizzy. I began to wish that I had never embarked on this climb, especially when I realised that I was nowhere near the top. But I never would have the nerve to retrace my steps, so I had to go on.

Feeling a bit panicky, I began to rush and suddenly I slipped. For a brief moment I was precariously balanced on one foot and how I regained my equilibrium I don't really know. However, I reached the top – 160 steps approximately and was soon able to get back on the road. The next place I came to was the 'Gobbins'. Leaving my bike I went down onto the shore. There wasn't a soul about - everything was quiet except for the crying of the gulls and the lapping of the waves against the rocks. Suddenly I was surprised to see two goats roaming around and went over to stroke one. A very tame animal, I thought, until it began to butt me. The other one then came over and the pair of them followed me to an iron gate-way which led to some caves, but the gate was locked. The goats were apparently annoyed at the presence of a human being encroaching on their ground, but before they could attack, I had beaten a hasty retreat. By this time the sun was going down and it was beginning to get dusk so I wended by way homeward.

BERYL HILL Belfast CC

Irish Junior Road Race Championship Banbridge 1972

Left to right:
Oliver McQuaid (2nd)
Sean Kelly, Carrick Wheelers R.C. (1st)
Alan McCormick (3rd)
Course: Banbridge,
Gilford, Scarva

Sean Kelly, Carrick Wheelers Road Club
Irish Junior Road Race Champion 1972
Banbridge, Gilford, Scarva Course
In the background is Paddy Sullivan
(Note Sean's hand knitted jersey – a labour of
love by someone close to him!)

Editor's note: These negatives only
came to light after Kelly's great
professional career was over.

Up at the front

Fixing the Puncture

Don't let the title mislead you. This is not an article on the geographical position of men in some theatre of war, but I can't help thinking there is a terrible similarity at times when I am up at the front on a club run. "Well, how do you come to be at the front?" you may ask, but what I want to know is how do the rest of the club get to the back. After a little observation I am amazed at the ability of the rest of the members. They have Reg Harris licked when it comes to track tactics, such as standing still, or out of the saddle manouvering for a position at the back. So being a novice at these track tactics I have no choice but to become sucker No.1. Don't say it! I know there are always two at the front of a club run and you want to know how he comes to be there with me. This member, my friends, is the most callous in the club. Up he comes beside me with a gleam in his eye which tells me I am to be his victim for as long as I can suffer it. After leaving town he gradually begins half-wheeling which provokes a creature within me and before long the whole club is gliding along about 'evens', but still intact and orderly. After a couple of miles of this my morale and energy levels content are very low. Aching legs, back and bleary eyes, that's me. But what about your man beside me, how is he faring? My view point being from the handlebars he looks alright, so do the other club members and I decide one of two things: either somebody is hanging on to my cape-straps when I'm not looking, or the rest of the members are real sadists in disguise, and I go for the sadist theory. On and on I struggle and then it happens. A faint bang inside my head, a burst blood vessel, surely not? Then through the faint babble of voices and easing of pace it slowly dawns on me – a puncture at the back of the club, thank goodness.

P.S. The only people who enjoy hearing your troubles are doctors and lawyers – they get paid for it.

FRED COLLINS   Captain Belfast CC 1950's

The other me

5-4-3-2-1 Go!

That being the Time-Keepers's farewell I am away on a time-trial to battle against the watch, plus.

Out of the saddle, getting the revs up and then sitting down to settle-in, I become aware of a most discouraging passenger. It's me. The other one. This passenger, a very talkative fellow, jeers and gabbles at me through the whole race, knowing I am compelled to listen.

"Come on now" he says. "Put up a good show until you reach the first bend, then you will be out of the time-keeper's sight" On rounding the bend he continues "Alright, ease of, they can't see you now, what are you riding for anyway? You're not fit enough for this game. When did you train? Get wise to yourself man, pack it now before you reach Greyabbey. What about that hill this side of Kircubbin? Terrible drag that, it will pull the legs out of you. It might even rain when you're out near the turn and you know how miserable it is riding in the rain. Stiff wind against you too, but it will help you coming back from the turn, this is, if you can reach it. Give in now. Its about two miles back to the start What is that noise just behind you? Sounds like the whirr of wheels. You are caught already and only two miles out. Why not pack it in now. You have no chance of even a fourth handicap. Got your second wind now? You might catch your man, but not on that bike. It must feel like pushing a tank. Lift your head and have a look in front. There it is. That hill. But there's a drop down into Kircubbin, so hammer on. Here is Kircubbin now, so impress the locals. Pep it up a bit and keep the agony grin from your face when going through. Bluff them, make it look easy, but for the benefit of the other riders look as if you are trying hard. Careful now. Don't knock the turn-steward down. Give him your number with a smile and homeward bound. But there is something wrong! That wind is still blowing in your face. It changes round like that every time you race. Near the finish now. Just round the corner. Well, maybe it's the next one. Bad course for bluffing you like that. That's the finish now, so look good. Work up a bit of a sprint. Finally work up a voice that the time-keeper will hear when you shout your number."

Thanks to my companion I still hold my honoured position on being the slowest man.

FRED COLLINS Captain Belfast CC 1950's

World championships 1959

World Championship Zaandvort
Holland 1959
Left to Right:
John Joe McCormick,
Sam Kerr,
Sean Fox, (Mechanic/Masseur)
Ian Moore and Jim McGuire

This was taking place in Holland. After winning the 200 km National Road Race Championship in the Phoenix Park Dublin, I was selected to be a member of the Road Race Team representing Ireland.

The other Members were Sam Kerr, Ian Moore and John Joe McCormick. We all flew out from the old Nutt's Corner Airport to Schipol in Holland. Then on to our hotel in Amsterdam. John Joe and I were sharing an en suite bedroom. Our first experience of such luxury! John Joe needed to use the en suite bathroom and after about fifteen minutes I needed to go myself. However, John Joe was refusing to open the door and let me in, despite my pleading that I was getting desperate. At long last he opened the door looking very sheepish. He said that the toilets in Holland were strange and pointed to me the problem and when I looked into the en suite I saw what was embarrassing him. He had left a rather large deposit in the Bidet!

JIM MAGUIRE   Windsor CC

Only Ten Guilders

World Championship 1959 - The great Shay Elliott
Irelands First Professional Rider *(Photograph submitted by Jim Maguire)*

After a few days familiarising ourselves with the beautiful city of Amsterdam, one night after Tea, we decided to go for a walk in the city centre. Everybody, including Billy Kirk, ventured into the 'Red Light' district. We all strutted down past the girls in the windows and doorways, looking very confident and mature, but really gob-smacked at all the sights (Not very Northern Ireland!) John Joe McCormick decided to enquire as to the prices and one girl shouted back "TEN GUILDER".

  John Joe shouted back "I'll give you FIVE" and we all panicked in case she said "Okay!"

As we were all as green as cabbages and wouldn't have had a clue what to do – even though we were well out of our teens!

JIM MAGUIRE   Windsor CC

My first tour *by* MARSHALL McADAM

My first tour of Ireland was in the 1940's. ?????? and I on the tandem with Alex Dickson and Billy Murray. We set off for Dundalk and arrived about 5.00 p.m. on a Saturday evening. Walking along the street we stopped and met two girls and asked them if they knew somewhere we could site our tent. One of them told us her father had a butchers shop in the town. So we made our way to the shop. On seeing us he said, "Bring them up to the Farm". We all made our way to the lane at the back of the town were the butcher had his yard and fields. The girls had to hurry home, but Billy made a date to see one of them later on that evening. We erected the tent and found the nearest café. After the meal we set off around the town. Bill went to meet his girl. Later we went back to the tent and Billy arrived home. We looked forward to a good nights rest, but the chapel bell rang every hour and disturbed our sleep. On rising we packed the gear and walked to the yard to find the butcher and thank him and say goodbye. Two men standing in the yard. They had a rope round the neck of a cow and through a ring to the ground and a burly man with a large hammer was ready to strike it on the head! As fast as we could we collected our gear and bikes and were away down the street.

Next day was Dublin and looking for a cheap B and B we saw one at five shillings for a double room. We put our bikes and gear in the yard at the back of the house. We found our room, washed and changed into our longs and set off to see Dublin. We had a meal and back to the B and B, noticing that the stairs were slanted and not too safe because the building next door had been demolished! Later we noticed the door had no key so we pulled a set of drawers across the door. It was another not too comfortable night. Up early for breakfast and on the road again. Next stop was Boyle and arriving in the area we looked out for a camp site. We went up to a small cottage and got permission to put our tent up. Again looking for a good night's sleep. On rising we found there was a heavy mist and we needed to dry the tent. We went to the cottage and a little old lady came to the door. We told her what we wanted. She brought us in and poked up the peat fire and said "You should bring your bikes in too!" The tents were dried and we thanked her and were on our way this time to Bundoran. Having had a slight accident on the way down while we were riding on a rocky road, I hit my foot on a rock. My shoes were split very badly so I had to buy a new pair of shoes in Bundoran.

The following day, coming through the Border at Belleek the keen eye of the Customs Official noticed the new shoes and told me I would have to pay five shillings. I produced a five pound note and of course he had no change. He made me go to the village and get the note changed. The money paid over for the shoes, we were soon on our way again. We passed through Enniskillen and then discovered we had trouble with the rear tyre of the tandem. It was a slow puncture, but we pressed on. We were somewhere around Portadown and darkness was coming down so we looked for some where to put up for the night. Spotting a farm by the roadside with some barns we slipped in and stayed there until daylight. We packed up and moved on and by keeping pumping up the rear tyre we managed to arrive home by lunch hour. We were very relieved, but we thoroughly enjoyed our Tour.

Co-operation North

MAGHERACLOGHER Co DONEGAL

B.M

An early departure – with Betty, my youngest son, Ian Alister, his Canadian cousin, Russell and my bike in the old Maxi. The frame had been built to my spec. by John Crawford of "Wester Ross" – he took my old trike frame in part exchange! Actually the frame was conceived at Aultbea, but born in Yorkshire where, disenchanted with Scotland, they moved back to. Saturday morning, roads quiet. Took the roundabout outside Ballymena sharpish – the young policeman informing me that "Your driving leaves much to be desired, sir". Cut the speed (for a couple of miles) but wasn't I running late to join the happy gang gathering at Belfast's City Hall – for the 8.a.m. start of Co operation North's first exchange between cyclists from the 'North' and 'South.' My participation partly in celebration of my 50th, and soon I found myself riding alongside Tom

Smyth, ten years my senior. He kept threatening to turn up the rate on his pacemaker and had a young Kings Moss female with him. We soon gathered up another young woman, a novice who had been riding on her own and this group stayed together. Ashamed to admit that I don't remember the girl's name – but there's a lot I don't remember, these days. Climbing Newry hill and I heard Cyril Henry remarking that you can tell who's getting it tough by the way they clash their gears!

On my best Belfast-Dublin time trial I rode 76 fixed. That was when the start was at the GPO in Royal Avenue and you finished in O'Connell Street – on a Saturday lunchtime! Tommy Allingham had me well beaten, despite falling (pushed?) as he negotiated a parade in Newry town. Tommy looked like a schoolboy and was one of the East Tyrone "trio" including the other Tommy (Talbot) and Jim Slaine. Tommy Talbot was the one who continued competing (successfully) well into middle age. It was Jim who was Billy Dowd's minute man in a twenty five when Dowds didn't catch him.

WE told Billy that this was Jim's first time wearing real cycling shoes – and next week he was going to try toe clips. Cyril Henry, of trans America fame ended his days looking after his wife and nipping over from Cookstown to John Smyth's very superior bike shop in Moneymore with the wheels he regularly built for him. John is a son of Tom Smyth.

One evening there seemed to be something special going on at his shop so I drove over with John Jones. It turned out that John Smyth was introducing a range of Italian frames. Discovered afterwards that the rather slight young man who shook my hand was Stephen Roche!

I rode the Inishowen 100 with John Jones in miserably wet conditions.

It was the day after the dreadful accident at the nuclear power plant in Chernobyl. John, who was a senior lecturer in Chemistry at the University of Ulster, told me that they found rain water in Coleraine contaminated by 'fall out' such that it would be unsafe for sheep to drink. Our bike ride was in aid of the Ulster Cancer Foundation. A strange irony. We seemed to be favoured by a light Northerly wind and the fast boys had bunched up, dead set on doing 'evens' all the way. At Dundalk, at the feeding station, we encountered the lot who had a harder ride from Dublin. At least they had the consolation of anticipating an easier run back the next day. Our wee group made it quite comfortably to Dublin and to the Halls of Trinity College. Tom and I were sharing and the girls similarly occupied an adjoining flat. Quick showers were taken and before dandering out along O'Connell Street looking for a restaurant, Tom, with his years of bitter experience in such matters, guided the girls in the art of leg massage. A grand meal, then fairly early to bed in readiness for the gathering in the morning at St. Stephen's Green for the ride home.

RONNIE MILLAR

Attempt at trike record

This is a photograph of me after finishing an attempt on the 12 hour trike record. No one else had been daft enough to try this in Ireland so they gave me a 'Standard' to meet. I beat this by about thirty miles – but I'm not going to tell you my distance! Also on the picture on the right: Jimmy Keenan, a good rider in his day and very active as an Official. Looking over my shoulder is Jack Lamont. I think he held the Belfast to Dublin at one time. Not sure about the other chap.

RONNIE MILLAR

A great CTC man, Steve Dobson, helped me with my Attempts. He and his wife, Nell lived at Glengormley - near to my finish on the Ballyhenry Road (unrecognisable now) I suddenly felt pretty groggy so they took me to their home for a lie down. A couple of years ago I visited Neill after a long absence. Steve had died long before and she was about ninety. We had a great chat (with a twinkle in her eye she reminded me of the day I finished up in her bed) and getting quite late in the evening, I felt she might be wanting to go to bed and was about to excuse myself when she apologised saying, she had a meeting to go to! Nell died the next year. A wonderful woman.

RONNIE MILLAR

We've been taped

In 2009 these words could mean many things, from being recorded by a CCTV camera to being tied up by home intruders, but in 1958 it had a different meaning for two members of East Tyrone Cycling Club. They had travelled to Cardiff to see the 1958 Commonwealth Games at which fellow East Tyrone Cycling Club member Tommy Talbot and Leo Feeney had been selected to represent Northern Ireland. Tommy was competing in the 4000 metre Pursuit and the ten mile Scratch Race in Cardiff's Maindy Stadium. The two East Tyrone spectators had lodgings in Whitchurch, Cardiff, but got an invitation from members of the Northern Ireland team to visit them at the Games Village at Saint Athan's RAF Base near Cardiff Airport. The pair enjoyed seeing the leading sporting personalities and also the food. It was fairly recent after rationing and the food was spectacular, especially things like peaches and cream, but all the grub was wonderful. In the evening they were told they could stay overnight in a spare room in the Northern Ireland cyclists' hut, which they accepted. Later that evening the two interlopers were near the entrance to the Games Village waiting to see our cyclists returning from a training run. A group of Welsh Games Officials wearing their blazers were in the vicinity when one of the two overheard a Welshman saying "That's them!" Panic, fuelled by Gatecrasher's Guilt, set in and he made himself scarce. When a second gatecrasher returned to the room they hoped to use that night, a hand pulled the overhanging bedclothes on one of the beds and a face appeared saying "We've been taped"! Sleeping on the floor under RAF beds is not to be recommended but anyway no search party arrived.

Next morning, wearing borrowed tops emblazoned NORTHERN IRELAND, they joined the Northern Ireland Cycling Team in one of the dining rooms. Suddenly a shower of Games Officials, Pressmen and Photographers swept in accompanied by none other than the Duke of Edinburgh. What a relief!

The prey was not the gatecrashers, but Sharon Davies, the Golden Girl of Australian swimming, much fancied for a Gold Medal. The Duke spotted the NORTHERN IRELAND tops and headed for our table, followed by the Officials and the Press Gang. The first one he spoke to was the Gatecrasher who had heard the remark which led to a night spent under a RAF bed.

"Which event are you competing in?" asked the Duke. The answer he got was "The Road Race"

After a few words to other diners the Duke left, but the Press and the Photographers did not. They wanted to know what 'He' had said, but it was denied he said anything.

At home next morning the other Gatecrasher's father was looking at the Belfast morning paper 'THE NORTHERN WHIG' when he exclaimed "That's Tom's head!" In the photo he was looking at was the Duke, the 'Road Race Rider' and others at the table, but the back of Tom's head was toward the lens. It might have fooled others, but not his Dad! In turned out that the blazered Welshmen had been waiting for a party of Welsh Oarsmen returning from training on Lake Bala in Central Wales. Being taped could have been worse!

TOM ALLINGHAM

The Gatecrashers were
George Wilson and Tom Allingham

(Right) **Duke of Edinburgh
And his dad was right!
Tommy Talboty turned up this
photograph of the Duke and the
back of Tom Allingham's head is
instantly recognisable.**

Tom Allingham

Newspaper photo of Tom Allingham Jim Slaine and Tommy Talbot.

Tom Allingham was a great long distance Rider. He won the 1954 N.I.C.F. 'Best All Rounder' competition which was based on a years performance of 50 and 100 miles and 12 hour Events. He set a new record with an average speed of 22.764 miles per hour.

In this same year the East Tyrone Cycle Club Team of Tom Allingham, Jim Slaine and Tommy Talbot also set up a new Record with a combined speed of 22.166 miles per hour.

Northern Ireland cycling officials in the mid 1940's

A group of N.I. Cycling Officials
Seated (Left to Right) - R. Irvine, J. Keenan, J. Lynn, E. Neill and J.E. Cassidy.
Second row - W. Thompson, E. Gracey, W. Black, A. Moore, W. Cairns, G. Fee, F. Kernohan, J. Higginson and H. Smith.
Third row - J. Hughey, A. Gregg, W. Braithwaite, R. Bratten, T. Stewart, J. McCoo and A. Magee.
Fourth row - F. McKeown, B. Hughes, H. Crawford, J. Watson, W. Guilfoyle, T. Guilfoyle, C. Andrews and T. Taylor, W. Adams and J. Galbraith.

Back row - T. Robinson, A. Simpson, H. Boyle, S. Neill, S. McCartney and W. Smith.

Irish road club 1910

I. R. C. Dublin and Belfast Teams 1910

Charlie Henderson

Charlie Henderson, founder in 1944 of Ards Cycling Club was born in Ballycullen on the Belfast side of Scrabo hill.

He rode his first bicycle races in the nearby townlands of Ballyrainey and Ballyalton in a series of short road races on a course known as "The Glibe". They were unofficial events, not under NCU rules. One day the race coincided with the famous Ulster T.T. car race and the riders could hear the cars roar along the Comber/Dundonald road.

Charlie became good on road and track and he had been on the team of workers who laid Newtownard's Castlereagh Park cinder track. Everyone said "Henderson knows every little fault and bump and that's why he's so good on it.

Among many silver and bronze championship medals his best result was winning the N.I. 3 mile championship at the NIAAA and NCU shorts on 15th August 1942, riding for Belfast C.C.

BILLY KIRK

Quite a lady

Mrs Ena McKeown (nee McClure) qualifies for being the most continuous racing lady cyclist in Northern Ireland.

Mrs Ena McKeown, Londonderry to Belfast
3hrs 45 mins.
She broke standard time of 4 hrs by 15 mins.
Timed by Mr E Lavery.

Her racing career covered twenty years. She started Track Riding in the mid Thirties and was Time Trialing up to the mid Fifties – winning numerous prizes in both. She holds the Derry to Belfast Record which she set in 1953.

I first met Ena at Trinity Harriers Club in the winter of 1948. She noticed that my sister Nan and I arrived on our Ladies Sports Bicycles. Ena was a member of 'The Ulster Ladies Road Club' and was on the lookout for lady cyclists to ride in the club's novice five mile Time Trial which was to be held in the Spring of 1949. She wouldn't take "No" for an answer, so we promised to take part. Our bicycles enabled us to escape from the city and enjoy the pleasures of the countryside. Hostelling added a further advantage to the joys of cycling.

Boarding the aircraft for France In 1953, a Bristol 170 freighter of Silver City Airways. This airline also flew in and out of Aldergrove Sydenham and Newtownards.

True to our word, Nan and I turned up at the 6th Milestone beyond Glengormley for the Novice Five mile Time Trial. Having got a 2nd placing in this event, encouraged me to try again. In due course a racing bicycle was purchased and Time Trialing became a ritual.

In 1950 Ena persuaded me to join the Belfast CC of which she was also a Member, the ULRC being a second claim club. This has given me many years of great pleasure, lasting friendships and wonderful memories.

In 1953 Ena and her husband Billy – better known as 'Spud' McKeown invited me to accompany them on a cycling tour to the south of France. It was a wonderful experience. Billy was a hard taskmaster and on one occasion we had to face a long arduous climb in the gruelling heat. There were very welcoming Hostelries at various intervals en route. So needless to say, Ena and I insisted on taking advantage of these. After the third stop for orange juice, Billy's patience was wearing thin and he was disgruntled at the lack of progress. So at the 4th stop, instead of orange juice, he set two large glasses of shandy or beer in front of us. This did the trick. Our thirsts were quenched and no further stops were required!! On another occasion when we stopped for lunch in the scorching sun (mad dogs and all that) Billy took a notion for chips. He wasn't given the name 'Spud' as a nickname for nothing. He got the Primus going and proceeded to fry. Panic broke out as the grass verge caught fire and was spreading fast. We pranced about frantically to stamp out the flames. Fortunately a National emergency was averted.

Ena and I have still some things in common. We are both visually impaired, but this doesn't prevent us keeping active. We both dance weekly, albeit different styles. Ena likes Old Time and Modern Sequence. I enjoy Set Dancing and Old Traditional Irish Solo Dancing (Not the ringlet and spangles kind)

ISABEL WOODS   *Belfast CC*

The ferry waits for no man

Sketch of Strangford by Ray Elwood

Ards CC Sunday Tour to Tyrella mid summer 1950. The late Davy O'Neill and I owned a pre war Raleigh touring Tandem which we used on some of the runs. We arrived and spent the day at Tyrella – heading home after 6.00 pm but stopped at Ballyhornan as the Georgetown Victory was ashore. It was a World War Two Victory ship. We spent too much time there and suddenly remembered the last ferry left Strangford at 9.00 pm. It was only a motor boat then and as anyone who knows Strangford slipway, as soon as we hit the slippery slope, we put the brakes on and next minute we were in the tide which was on the turn and up to our waists in water! So we had a wet cycle home from Portaferry to Ards. Among some of the ones who had a good laugh were Ken Hedley, Ivan Dempster, W Heron, the Gourley brothers, Dickie Weir, The Anderson brothers, The Morrison brothers and Sammy Houston. Some who are now deceased.

W M McBRATNEY Ards CC

A great cyclist

Leslie Bingham was one of the fastest Time Trialists in the Belfast CC in the 1950's.

When he joined the Club it had 69 members and 29 Vice Presidents. This is not so surprising as it was formed in 1892. Leslie had previously been a member of the Short and Harland CC. In 1951 he took out his first Racing Licence. He had purchased a Raleigh Lenton Bicycle frame for £15. 5. 2 and a jersey from Gordon Cycles for £1.1.6 and a second one for £1.0.0.

In a Belfast CC Open 25 miles TT in 1951, he was 24th in an entry of 68. He improved steadily and in 1954, in the first race of the season - a 25 mile medium gear TT run by Kings Moss CC - Leslie's claim to fame was beating the great Billy Dowds who dominated the 1950's. Leslie's time was l hr 3 mins 8 secs. Second was Tommy Talbot l hr 3 mins 11 secs and third was W. Dowds l hr. 3 mins. 37 secs.

The following year, 1955, in this same medium gear event, he won again in spite of riding with a broken arm in plaster. He returned a time of l hr. 5 mins. 4 secs.Second was R Collim l hr. 5 mins. 27 secs. Third was J. Slaine l hr. 5 mins 34 secs.

In 1954 an unrestricted open 25 mile TT was run by Belfast CC with an entry of 97 riders. W. Dowds winning time was l hr. l min. 7 secs. Second was J. Slaine l hr. 1min. 44 secs. Third was T. Talbot in l hr. 3 mins. 1 sec. Fourth L. Bingham l hr. 3 mins. 24 secs.

Even for a 50 mile TT entries ranged between 70 to 100 riders.

Then in an N.I.C.F. 50 miles TT in 1954 Leslie was placed 5th behind W. Dowds.

During this era, Leslie brought much acclaim to the Belfast CC.

This information has been collected from a diary Leslie kept in 1954 and old race result sheets he was able to produce regarding this period.

ISABEL WOODS   Belfast CC

Leslie Bingham Medium Gear 25 mile TT 1955 wih arm in plaster.

The other Leslie

We cyclists, both ex. and active will know of Leslie Bingham – who in two consecutive years won the King's Moss Medium Gear '25'.

The second time with his broken arm in plaster! He won his own Clubs Tour of Mid Down and married his childhood sweetheart, Avril. Although Leslie had little or no 'Irish' connection, apart from his notion that his family was a very distant and far removed member of the much hated and oppressive Bingham Landlord family from the Belmullet region of West Mayo, he was to become very much an 'Irish Man'. He and Avril attended Irish language classes. He was determined to master the traditional music. The Flute and Tin Whistle were his forte. Like many a father he had high hopes that he could pass on his love of traditional music to his children. His daughter Tara achieved many championships on the Flute and Whistle and is now a much sought after Tutor on these instruments. Also with son Terry on the Concertina and Ciaran on the Fiddle, Leslie's ambitions have been fulfilled. Leslie was a Marine Electrical Engineer and for a spell he worked on Belfast City Council vehicles. He was based at the Gasworks. Often he told me of the odd looks that he encountered from his workmates when they found him listening to Ceili music from Radio Eireann on his radio! In those days few, if any, ex Ship Yard or City Council workers would have been 'inclined' that way.

The young Leslie that I knew had another great passion and that was fishing. To this day he loves nothing better than to get away to Lough Glencar in County Sligo at his Great Aunt Alice's farm house. This lady was also Tom Allingham's Great Aunt!!

 The melting pot for many traditional musicians in the late 1960's and early 70's was Pat's Bar in the Docks area of Belfast. Leslie and quite a few other cyclists would have met there on Friday and Saturday nights to enjoy playing music together. Brian Lamont, son of old time rider, Jack Lamont and Billy Bothwell were but two that came to mind. Billy Bothwell continued cycling up to his death a few years ago. A young seventeen year old lad, Dermy Diamond was a regular player in the Pat's Bar sessions and although starting off as a guitarist and mandolin player, he eventually moved to become a talented fiddler.

In 1977 he married Leslie's daughter Tara and the hopes that Leslie had for traditional music to be a firm fixture in the Bingham family, were firmly set when Dermy and Tara's two children, Danny and Helen also became talented musicians. But don't think that life is all music and pub sessions.

Professor Dermot Diamond D.SC; PHD; M.SC; BSC; FR.SC; MICI; CHEM. President of Research, Dublin City University, he is at the top of his game. A published and acknowledged leading light – Internationally in Biosensor Technology.

PETER WOODS   Belfast C C

the other Leslie

Pensive one of Leslie, the fisherman

Leslie (left) fishing with a friend, Glencar June 1956

Leslie and daughter Tara on their flutes

Short tales

Our gathering 'spot' was in front of the Newtownards Town Hall doorway. One evening some of the boys went to the cinema. While they were at the show one or two boys got hold of a bike and hung it up on the iron railings above the doors of the Town Hall. When he came back the hue and cry went up! We were having a good laugh at him until he looked up and found it. Tears were nearly flowing. Another time they played a trick on another one (again he was off chasing girls). While he was away they changed his wheels round, also the handlebars and seat. He didn't accept it too well as he was going to leave a girl home!

The old Ghost Train

The line was closed and they were removing the sleepers. At night the waiting room was often used as a 'love nest.' One night it was full of courting couples. I was with my mate Jim Savage (he was called Frangio after the racing driver) Jim said out loud "THE OLD GHOST TRAINS COMES DOWN THIS LINE EVERY NIGHT AT THIS TIME!" Well all of a sudden there was this rumbling and sure enough the train came through the station. Well, they all scampered out of that station and run like rats off a sinking ship – yelling and scared stiff. Needless to say the most of them were Ards CC Members.

I have happy memories of the good times we had at Ards CC Good luck to the club.

ALICE HOEY (Nee Beckett) Past Member Ards CC

Going over to France July 1955 For the Tour de France

Alice Hoey in July 1955

Hunger and the large pan loaf

Ehrenbreitstein Castle (Youth Hostel), Koblenz, Germany

One day in July 1957 two cyclists, Austin Reid and myself (21 years) who would later join the Belfast Cycling Club set off from Belfast for Ostend – the Port on the Belgium coast. There we began a touring holiday on our sports bicycles, visiting Southern Belgiam coast, Southern Rhineland and Northern France. We eventually cycled 1210 miles in 13 days and visited many cities and towns on route. It was a wonderful experience for the two of us and we stayed in Youth Hostels at night where we bought our breakfasts in the mornings.

At lunch times we usually stopped at a restaurant or café to buy our main meal of the day. This occurred at about 1.00 – 2.00 pm depending on where we were. One day an event happened which I never forgot. We cycled from the German city of Trier, (near the Border with Luxembourg to Koblenz situated at the junction of the Moselle River with the Rhine (Trier is reputed to be the oldest city in Germany and is the birth place of Karl Marx *editors note*). It was a lovely sunny day and the pair of us cycled on after lunch. The distance was approximately 110 miles mostly alongside the meandering River Moselle where the sides of the low hills on either bank of the river were covered by vineyards which produces the German white wines.

Eventually after a long tiring day we arrived in Koblenz at about 8.00 pm in the evening. We headed for the Youth Hostel which was in a castle called "Ehrenbreitstein" on a high hill overlooking the River Rhine. We were very tired and had to dismount from our bicycles and push them up the steep road from the River Rhine to the top of the hill about 300 to 400 feet above river level. When we arrived at the castle we were in a state of extreme exhaustion. After enrolling in the Youth Hostel for the night we had our supper. One large pan loaf consisting of 30 slices of bread. We put butter and jam on each slice of bread before we ate it. Austin Reid ate exactly half the loaf - fifteen slices! But I could only eat fourteen and a half slices despite being urged on by Austin to "Finish it up!" I was really amazed that two people could eat a large pan loaf at one go especially as it was only their SUPPER! That night there was a Fireworks Display on the castle walls but I was so tired that I couldn't make the effort to get up from the table and go outside to watch the Display. Such were the joys of cycling!!

Next day we headed off down the River Rhine towards the City of Worms.

It is always interesting to learn what cyclists from the Fifties are doing with themselves these days. That is, if they are not still riding around the countryside.

CYRIL MORRISON

CYRIL passed on this information of how he now spends his spare time: He has a great love for water colour painting, sending us some very good photographs of his paintings. However, black and white doesnt do them justice. An even greater passion of Cyril's is calligraphy. For the past eight years he has practised under Gayner Goffe from England and has spent 10,000 hours of practice over that period!

Editors Note

'Shoah' The Holocaust
by CYRIL MORRISON
The murder of the Jews
Calligraphy-Sharpened "Italics"

St Columbs Park Londonderry
by CYRIL MORRISON

The unfinished time trial

Stanley McMullan, John Boyd and Cyril Morrison
After Belfast CC 10 miles TT Saintfield Road 7th March 1959

One summer day in 1960 three members of the Belfast Cycling Club cycled out together from Belfast to the 10th Milestone from Belfast on the Lisburn to Moira Road. The three were: Stanley McMullan, Louis Fairley and Cyril Morrison. All were relatively new to bicycle racing and Stanley was looked on as a good prospect having just completed a 25 mile Time Trial in just over 1 hour and 4 minutes on the old Glengormley to Antrim course in his first ever Time Trial. At that time Willie Kirk etc. were doing under the hour for the distance depending on the weather conditions.

This was the usual winning time at this distance. Stanley had recently ridden a 10 mile Time Trial in about 22 minutes 30 seconds. The idea was for Stanley to be timed by his two friends doing a 10 mile Time Trial (out and back) on the flat Moira Road to see if he could get his time under 22 minutes. Eventually Stanley pedalled off from the 10th Milestone. Our expectations on that day were very high for him. We waited in expectation as 20 minute passed, then 21 minutes – but no sight of Stanley. Then 22 minutes became 23 minutes which in turn became 24 minutes. We suspected that something must be wrong. As 25 minutes passed we decided to cycle out the Moira Road ourselves. Traffic passed us going in the opposite direction towards Lisburn, including an Ambulance. We thought nothing about it.

Then at roughly 14 miles from Belfast, we noticed a crowd of people standing around a motor car parked on the other side of the road and facing Lisburn. The rear and rear window of the car was all stoved in and a wrecked racing bicycle was lying on the ground behind it. We immediately recognised Stanley's racing bicycle and asked the people there what had happened. They informed up that a cyclist had crashed into the back of the stationary car. So Stanley, with his head down watching his pedals turn, but not looking forwards up the road, had crashed on his way back to the 10th milestone after turning at the 15th milestone. We were told that the ambulance (which we had seen) had taken Stanley to the Lagan Valley Hospital in Lisburn. We then cycled off to visit Stanley who had received severe bruising to his face, upper body and arms. So he never did finish the un-official Time Trial on the Moira Road much to our great disappointment.

CYRIL MORRISON   *Belfast CC*

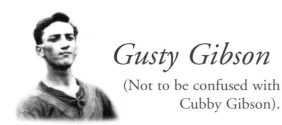

Gusty Gibson

(Not to be confused with Cubby Gibson).

Gusty and his trophies

Gusty Gibson, who ended his days at Ballybeen, Dundonald, but whose birthplace I do not know, was a prolific winner of bicycle races at Parish Sports all over the Ards Peninsula in the late 1920's and early 1930's. Venues such as Kircubbin, Portaferry, Portavogie, Ballyhalbert and Ballywalter were his happy hunting grounds, but he also had many successes at Downpatrick, Shrigley and Temple.

Most of this racing was on grass tracks but there were also events on short road circuits which took them through the small villages and countryside and brought the people out to cheer. Bookies were almost always in attendance in those days. Gusty's career was prior to the Charlie Henderson, Tommy Givan era by ten years or so.

One evening in the mid 1970's I chanced to be in his company in the Devonshire Arms Hotel, Newtownards, when he related to me this quaint little tale: A friend and himself were cycling down to Portaferry to compete in a grass track meeting. They stopped at Saltwaterbridge to make tea and eat their sandwiches, so as to 'have it well down them' before the races. It was a beautiful sunny day and as they sat munching, it happened that two pretty girls passed by. Never one to pass up nice company, Gusty hailed them and drew them into conversation in which the boys told about their race meeting and their hopes for the day. Hearing this, one of the girls asked would they be racing against Paddy --------- and if so would they be sure to beat him! She explained the reason for her spite was the man had jilted her. She also said if they beat him she could guarantee the nicest meal they could wish for. Gusty told me he personally beat the man and sure enough they enjoyed a slap up feed – compliments of the girl's mother. With a twinkle in his eye he led me to believe the meal was not his only reward that day!

BILLY KIRK

The Hanna Cup

Mr James Hanna was elected as Vice President of the Belfast Cycle Club in 1900 – the year in which he presented The Hannah Cup for competition. It was decided by the Club to award the Cup to the winner of an Unpaced 20 mile handicap race held on a track. There was also a 20 mile Motor Paced race for the Duffield Cup. Both events were held on the track at Glentoran Football Grounds.

The 'Hanna Cup' race was changed in 1903 to a 20 mile Un-paced 20 mile T.T. to be held on the road – starting just outside Newtownards, through Greyabbey to Kirkubbin at which point it returned to the start. This was the first ever, out and home, unpaced road time trial in Ireland and it was always held on the Ards Peninsula. It was not competed for in the years between 1915 and 1918 - World War One. B.C.C. Members who won the Hanna Cup more than once:

W. Vokes	5 Times
F. Guy	3 Times
T. Teuton	2 Times
M. Stevenson	2 Times
T. Young	2 Times
J. Mckee	2 Times
S. Neill	2 Times
W. Rea	2 Times

Billy Vokes with the Hanna Handicap Cup. The only man to win it 5 times. On left is Billy Rea who won the Hanna Handicap Cup on 2 occasions

Father's and son's who won
The Hanna Cup were: T. Watson and M. Watson. S. Neill and D.Neill.

The Belfast C.C. celebrated its Centenary in 1992, as the Club had ceased to be active by then.
A discussion took place regarding the disposal of trophies. It was decided to offer the trophies to a young active Club to be competed for, as this had been the intention of those who had donated them in the first instance. These Trophies, plus the bank balance of the Belfast C.C. were duly presented to the Belvoir C.C. who shortly afterwards, handed the Hanna Cup back as they didn't want the responsibility of such an historical Cup. At present the Hanna Cup is in the custody of the Ulster Folk and Transport Museum at Cultra. It is their intention to put it on display in their cycling section, along with a short history of the Belfast. C.C. To date this had not been done, but we have been assured that they will fulfil their promise soon. It is a fitting resting place for this fine trophy as Sir Robert Kennedy whose home was Cultra Manor had been President of the Belfast C.C. from 1912 to 1937 – a total of 25 years!

The man who stole the show

In 1999 the Northern Ireland Cycling Federation celebrated its 50th Anniversary.

To mark the occasion a Golden Jubilee Gala Dinner was held in the Stormont Hotel in Belfast. A large number of members both past and present turned up for that event. A prominent cyclist from each decade was asked to relate the highlights and outstanding personalities that they had encountered during their ten year period.

The Northern Ireland Cycling Federation was formed in 1949, so the first Speaker started with the Fifties. Then followed the Sixties, Seventies, Eighties and finally the Nineties, which brought us right up to date. Each Speaker brought their own style of presentation and it was very interesting for all those present. When the Master of Ceremonies asked if anyone else would like to contribute, we were greatly surprised, as was his wife and daughter, when a gentleman from our Belfast Cycling Club table, who had required a little assistance on arrival at the venue, sprang up unexpectedly. He mounted the platform and made his way to the podium – completely unaided. It was Billy Vokes from Lisburn - an old member of the 'Belfast' who was in his late eighties. Billy had been one of our fastest men (cycle wise) breaking many records and winning numerous trophies. He was a popular club man known for his humorous story telling.

He rode a tandem with his wife Nancy on the back seat. On one occasion, when stopping momentarily at a railway crossing, the Station Master, seeing that the expected train was not in sight, opened the small pedestrian gate to let them through. He didn't want to detain them and not having dismounted, Billy cycled onwards. When he had covered a few miles and not getting a reply to a question, he looked around to see an empty seat. Nancy had hopped off like a butterfly at the crossing. You can guess the rest! Nancy was not amused at hearing this story being told to the audience, but many hearing it were. Billy then proceeded with his speech: "having listened to the progress of cycling over five decades from 1950, I'm now going to represent the 1930's".

Billy's speech was by far the most entertaining that evening. I only wish it had been recorded. It was full of humour as would have been expected of the man. The manner in which he related his experiences held the audience spellbound. The younger of those present were amazed at the difference between their present day cycling lives and that of yester-years which were more basic.

The 'old' cyclists thought nothing of riding to Dublin to compete in a race the following day and then riding home by moonlight. They were made of stern stuff! Billy Vokes speech stole the show and for which he received a standing ovation.

Extracted from Isabel Woods book 'Wheels of Change'

The human spear

Cyril Morrison

Austin Reid

One day in July 1955 two cyclists Austin Reid and myself set off from Belfast for Ostend in Belgium.

Our reason was to go on a cycling touring holiday of Northern Belgium, Holland and Northern Rhineland in Germany. Together we cycled 900 miles in 13 days and this was the first cycling holiday that either of us had undertaken.

In fact the previous distance that I had cycled was from Belfast to Bangor, County Down and back – a distance of approximately 25 miles. On this solo ride I had collapsed by the side of the road at Holywood on the way home – not knowing why and certainly not knowing that I had got the 'Knock' as it was called by racing cyclists in those days. (The 'Knock' occurs when the body has used up all its energy resources and can be overcome by eating bananas, chocolates or sandwiches as one cycles along the road). However I loved travel even then at the age of 19 years – my idol being Marco Polo of Venice who travelled overland all the way to the Palace of the Emperor of China in the Middle Ages and then years later returned home again to Venice. However to resume the story….

Austin and I were cycling on the ubiquitous cycle paths in Holland one day. On one side was a very busy arterial road built of red brick paviors bedded in sand as all the main roads were at that time. On the other side of the cycle path was a narrow grass area beside a canal of about 10 to 15 feet wide. I do not know how deep the canal was. I was in front with Austin riding behind. Suddenly there was a loud bang. Austin's front tyre had burst! He was flung forwards off his bicycle and I saw his body flying through the air nearly horizontally with his head slightly downwards towards the ground. His head appeared to me just like the point of a spear and his body shape closely resembled that of a spear shaft. Needless to say he hit the ground with a bang but as the ground between the cycle path and the canal was just grass he wasn't badly hurt. However he was very lucky that he hadn't been catapulted into the canal itself. A great stroke of luck as neither of us could swim! Getting to his feet we took out of our saddle bags a spare inner tube for our tyres which we had with us and after repairs we cycled on once more. However I can never forget the near miss when Austin could have ended up in the canal with possibly disastrous consequences for both of us. So we continued toward Amsterdam…

CYRIL MORRISON *Belfast CC*

The Hairpin at Dundrod circuit during The Irish Road race Championship 1954. the winner was Shay Elliott. L-R: Harry Lane, Alex Geddis, Roy Erskine, Jackie Wilson, John Smiley and W J Dowds is in there.

Memories of cycling

After taking up cycle racing with the East Tyrone Cycling Club and competing in Club Time Trials, no dressing rooms meant changing at home or behind the hedge. There was also very little motorised traffic on the roads in those days. A few of those competing were equal in ability with one or another.

When lining up on the roadside waiting for the Timekeeper to say "GO" two were waiting. One of them said in a sarcastic manner to the one behind him, "Take a good look at that back wheel for that is the last of it you will see this evening!"

STALWARTS IN THE CLUB

Cyril Henry was an enthusiastic Chairman of the Club for many years and a worker raising money etc. He was held in high esteem by all members. He turned up on many occasions and being present at Open Events encouraged us to bigger efforts. The principal family within the Club were the Talbots, with the four brothers: Tommy, Bobbie, John and Ronnie competing. Their mother Mrs. Talbot was most supportive of her boys and other members of the Club. When we club members were competing in Open events Tommy provided his van for transport and Mrs. Talbot always sent one or two flasks of hot tea for all to enjoy after the events. All concerned brought their own eatables.

TIME TRIALS

'Sunday Runs' were the 'in' thing during those days and, for us, even the 100 miles Time Trials on the Saturday. Distance usually 80 to 100 miles. Some of the destinations for the club was Belfast via Lisburn. Returning through Antrim. Newcastle via Banbridge. Londonderry via the Glenshane Pass. Through Omagh to Cookstown. Enniskillen or Beleek, through Fivemiletown via Omagh to home. Newry via Portadown, home by Armagh. Dundalk via Newtowhamilton homeward by Newry. During my first 100 mile Time Trial in late 1953, I got the bus from Cookstown to Randalstown – my idea. I needed a warm up prior to the start. The dressing rooms being in Antrim. I finished with a time of 4 hours 36 minutes and some odd seconds, being sixth in the event. During the last leg of the course on the Belfast Antrim Road, Joe Hadden passed me at Muckamore with words of encouragement "Keep it going!" Being far through strength wise, I appreciated those words. After the event I cycled the 35 miles home!

During the Fifties traffic on the roads was increasing, hence Time Trialing events were changed from Saturday afternoons to Sunday mornings – early. During this time Tommy Talbot was preparing for marriage, requesting an early start, so that he would be home in time for him and Sylvia to go to Church. As I have stated after the race all of us were in the vehicle preparing for the welcome cup of tea. George Wilson was along with us and looking around somewhat surprised enquired "Where is Tommy?" One of the party explained that he was away home to go to church and George replied "That bloody man is away to hell altogether!"

DUNDROD CIRCUIT

Having memories of the Northern Ireland Road Race Championship on the Dundrod circuit, I was lucky to be in a four man break over the Deer's Leap on the last lap. I do not remember the names of those along with me. I was in third position over the climb. A helper handing a drink to the cyclist behind me informed him "There is a medal in it for you" Not being a sprinter I realised I must open the distance between him and I, so while he was having his drink I seized my opportunity. And it was a long hard grind to the finishing line on the Dundrod circuit!

OPEN EVENTS

Travelling to participate in Open Events prior to Tommy Talbot acquiring a van for travelling had its problems. Especially the 100 mile Time Trials. Living 5 miles north of Cookstown, I'd cycle 7 miles to meet with Tom Allingham and Tommy Talbot. Then a further 8 miles to board the train at Dungannon. Arrive at Victoria Street Station in Belfast and cycle to the Crown and Shamrock Dressing Rooms. Competing in the 100 mile events meant missing the early train back to Dungannon. Therefore I had to wait for the 10.00 or 10.30 pm. returning to Dungannon at around midnight. Then sort out lights etc. and cycle another 15 miles home arriving about 12.30 am. Sunday morning . A total of over 140 miles.

JIM SLAINE   *East Tyrone CC*

Monaghan's memory

Brian Monaghan of Newry Wheelers who won the NCA Tour of Ulster in 1956 was a dedicated NCA man all his cycling days.

He remembers two races taking place on the same circuit in County Meath in the early 1960's. One was run by a C.R.E. club and the other by the N.C.A., the interesting fact being that the races ran in opposite directions on the same roads. The tough climb of the 'Naul' was on the course and he says it was amazing for one group of racers to be labouring up the ascent while the others descended at more than 50 m.p.h.

Brian thinks the winner of the NCA race that day was Seamus Kennedy but is not certain.
He also says that, considering the political tensions between the two bodies, the day went off quite peacefully.

BILLY KIRK

Reminiscences

Thinking of the late Tommy Smyth of the Kings Moss CC and having a friendly chat I recall that in time trialling Tommy gave it his all.

He said to me "It's a great sport and no one is pushing you".
Then went on to say "There is no point in finishing with the shade in your hair!"
Being friendly with Jim McBride also of the Kings Moss CC I enquired what he did for a livelihood.
His quick reply was "A Fitters Get". Being a country man I didn't understand. So Jim explained. "It was a job. Get me this……. or Get me that………"
On another occasion in the dressing room at the Crown and Shamrock, Jim and I were getting on our shorts and racing vests. Then I noticed Jim putting a ten shilling note into his pocket, so I enquired "what was the idea"? Jim replied "If anything should happen to me or the mechanics of the bicycle, the money is adequate to pay my fare home from the furthest point on the course"

During the winter of 1953 and spring of 1954 I had been training with weights and playing table tennis and was reasonably fit.
  In an early season 25 mile time trial I came second to the great Billy Dowds of Lurgan.
I treasure this photograph (opposite) of us both cycling together from the Finish on the Ballyhenry Road.
Another photograph I also treasure is being third in the 1954 BAR team of Allingham, Talbot and Slaine.
The distance involved 50 – 100 miles plus 12 hour time trials.

JIM SLAINE   East Tyrone CC

Club comradeship and loyalty to your fellow member

The only road race I won was a selection event for the 1958 British Empire and Commonwealth Games in Wales. During the early stage of the event I was finding the going tough but I improved as the event progressed. Eventually I forged away on my own with approximately two laps to go. Staying away to the finish. My club mate, Tommy Talbot was listed as a possible team member for the Games. Therefore he was in a quandary as to chase or not. But the agreement between Tommy, Tom Allingham and myself was that if anyone of us was away from the bunch that we would not assist in bringing the bunch up to the one away. Our motto being: ***Ride for one another***
And Tommy being a superior cyclist was selected, to my relief.

JIM SLAINE   *East Tyrone CC*

Only road race I won crossing finishing line
Event promoted by Maryland Wheelers

Finish of 25mile 1954
WJ Dowds 1hr. l min. 7 secs. J. Slaine   1hr.1 min.44 secs.

Silly old trout cartoon submitted by Ronnie Millar

Little gems

Inseparable

When I joined the Maryland Wheelers we used to meet on the Sunday morning in Donegal Square East. This was in the days when most club folk wore plus fours and a Continental sweater.

There was a chap in the club called George Gilroy who saw a friend on the other side of the road. This friend was going to the Methodist Church and George decided to go over to speak to him.

He got his bicycle and wheeled it over and when he returned, Tommy Givan asked him "Why did you take your bike across the road"? George replied "Without the bike I would feel like a cowboy without a horse!"

Pedal Pushing

In the days when we used to race on a Saturday afternoon and go out on a Sunday to get the 'miles in', I used to do a lot of cycling with a chap called Guy Crawford who unfortunately died at a very young age. We had an Open 100 TT on the Saturday and been up to Portrush on the Sunday and coming down the Coast Road, Guy complained that his legs were sore and said he was going out the following night to get his own back on his legs! I never knew whether Guy or his legs were the victors!

Eddie McArdle

When Eddie McArdle rode the 24 hour he stopped around midnight for a short break at the Crown & Shamrock. He asked for a leg of chicken and was told in no uncertain language by W.L. Smith that it was a chicken he had, not a centipede! (He had asked for a leg of chicken too often!). When he was leaving to continue his ride a lot of the boys were taking his photograph. Eddie being the gentleman that he always was, slowed down and asked if they got him alright.

Smyth's Café

In those days Smyths Café in Carnlough was very popular with cyclists. We were having lunch there one day – a four course lunch for half a crown (twelve and a half pence in present money) There was a very nice young girl who was old Mrs. Smith's Grand Daughter. She later married Harry Shannon of the Maryland. Anyway when she was serving she spilled some soup over Billy Bracegirdle and apologised. But Billy told her not to worry as he had another two suits at home. When she was out of ear shot he said: They were boiler suits!

BILL CAMPBELL   Maryland Wheelers

Bill joined Maryland Wheelers in 1946 as a long-distance specialist. He rode many 100 mile and 12 hour events. His first 100 time was 4 hrs 54 mins 7 secs, and he rode 221 1/2 miles in 12 hours, both in 1946. He won his first 12 in 1947 covering 223 miles, exceeding 20 mph, for the first time, in 1950 with 241 miles and improved to 244 miles in 1951. In 1956 he was NI and Irish 100 and 12 hour champion, repeating the feat in 1958. In 1963 he set up a p.b. '12' of 251 miles 266 yds to win the NI Championship - also clocking a pb '100' of 4 hrs 27mins 20 secs to take silver in the Irish Championship.

Tour of the North '61

I have a couple of stories I would like to share with you relating to my racing days, so long ago!

The first one is about the Tour of the North 1961.
Stage One finished in Bangor and John Lackey of Dublin won the sprint against the whole army cycling union team
Stage Two crossed the Glenshane Pass and John was delayed.
Immediately his "Teammate" Sonny Cullen attacked and John lost the overall lead.
Stage Three went up the Springfield Road and at the top K.O.M Peter Gordon beat Jim Hinds.
Immediately I attacked with Kevin Fairhead and Jimmy Kennedy, Dublin. Jimmy had to stop – mechanical problem and Kevin and I rode on to Lurgan where I took the prime. I relaxed but Kevin pushed on. Next thing a break caught me with Frank Thompson, Ray Auld plus two English riders. We worked well and caught and dropped Kevin. I rode very hard and we eventually dropped down from Scrabo into Newtownards. I was in front and John on my wheel. I heard him say "Go Don, go!". I went and John didn't chase and by the time the others decided to chase, it was too late. I won this stage. John was 1st overall.

Afterwards I realised John had rewarded me for working so hard. In a real sprint John could have beat any rider in the break with one leg. Oh, yes, Peter Gordon was one of the English riders in the break.
He went on to become British Champion.

DONALD STEWART
Cyprus CC (at this time)
Northern CC (later)

Tour of the North 1961 3rd stage. John Lackey leads Donald Stewart on his left

Taking the final climb

My second story relates to a three day race around the Dublin area.

After two stages I was leading John Joe McCormick of Dublin by 30 seconds. The next rider was about 3 minutes back.

Stage three started and finished in Dalkey and took in quite a few climbs in the Wicklow mountains.

Jimmy Kennedy and I attacked right away and after Bray there was a small group of us. Included in that group was a very light English rider - I'm afraid I cant remember his name. He later became English Hill Climb Champion. He pushed on the climbs and eventually got 3 firsts. 9 points. Meanwhile I was picking up placings on the climbs and we caught the hill climber and then dropped him. Approaching the final climb of the day I had 6 points and if I could win on the final because of my placing overall, I would have 9 points to equal the English rider and would win the K.O.M.

I talked it over with the other riders in the break and since none had any chance of getting 9 points they all agreed that I should take the final climb. Except ONE. An English rider.

He said that the hill man was his mate and he was not going to let me win if he could help it.

On the climb I was leading and approaching the top. I went for it - the English rider on my wheel.

He must have been really close and when I accelerated he touched my back wheel and crashed.

He got back on to the bike but I got my 3 points and said how sorry I was. But I got the overall K.O.M. even though I had to knock somebody off to do it. I did not mean to do it. I swear.

DONALD STEWART
Cyprus CC (at the time)
Northern CC (later)

Donald Stewart T.O.N. 1961
Donald Stewart won the stage
and finished sixth
John Lackey won overall

The Hub was the monthly Magazine of the Belfast Cycling Club.

It was first printed in 1954 and below is printed the front cover of the first issue which came out in January of that year. The cover depicts the Coat of Arms of Belfast City.

The Club had to ask permission to use this Coat of Arms on their badge and permission was granted.

Rab Collins was the Editor and the Magazine was produced on a Gestetner. Forty copies were produced each month, members picking up their copy on club nights. Postage at that time was probably 2 ½ pence. Members contributed stories and news items each month and probably the greatest contributor of all was Bill Murray, writing under the pen name: THE ROAMER

The Magazine ceased to be published in the Seventies.

Nostalgia

I was terribly sorry that I missed Billy Kirk's evening of filmed nostalgia. No one is into nostalgia, memorabilia, sentimentality and history more than me, so you can imagine how I felt when the Bangor evening clashed with a very important alternative engagement. The idea that Isabel and May contact everyone requesting us to contribute to a proposed publication of a collection of essays, jokes, anecdotes and short stories related to cycling seems a grand idea. Despite having some past experience in the field of cycle sport journalism, I now am shy to put my memories on paper, not the shyness of modesty, but because I realise that every time that I try to write down some little snippet of a story, my memory fails to provide the necessary accurate detail that is essential to allow the piece to stand up to the scrutiny of my contemporaries. Knowing that once started, I could take up more than my fair share of space, I think that I'll jot down memories of moments - just as they come into my head. One story prompting another and hope that my contribution stimulates others.

LATE STARTER

My cycling came later than most others. I learned on a second hand cycle, with straight, BSA handlebars. Wobbling along the back roads around Cairnshill and where the Four Winds now is, through hedges at corners, overbalancing off the towpath into the Lagan canal near 'the Pound' on the Hillhall Road, coming to the surface and finding my head and shoulders up through the frame when I surfaced was quite a fright, but worse still was the knowledge of the ticking off that I knew my mother would give me. I'm almost certain that she was psychic, for that morning she warned me not to go riding on the Tow Path. When a kind gentleman delivered me to our home at 'The Inns' bike sticking out of the boot of his car, he urged her to not be cross with me, but be thankful that I hadn't been drowned. Eventually I bought my first real bike. A Parkes, I think it was, out of Eddy Cassidy,s Cromac Square shop.

In due course I fell in with a couple of lads from the Breda Park area. --------Blaney and ------- Henning. (Now you can see what I meant when I said that the memory would let me down)
Next I started to go evening runs around the maze of back roads of Carryduff, Purdysburn, Moneyrea, Ballygown etc. with John Kennedy and Bill Murray – two members of the Belfast CC.

Through their company and example, I learned of the wonderful joy of companionship that cycling brought. I joined the club and that autumn, rode my first race, 'A Rough Stuff', the forerunner of cycle cross and mountain biking, but in those days done on ones ordinary bike, with a low geared fixed wheel.

Rough Stuff!

Peter Woods

It wasn't long before I bought my first road frame, a Mercian, followed by a track/time trial machine. £15 to £17 would buy a decent '531' frame and selecting ones own choice of wheels and all the other components, one could be kitted out for around a total of £37 to £50. I even bought a wee black 'Geordie Stone' track frame and have fond memories of riding down the Saintfield and Ravenhill Roads with my stripped down 'Stone Special', track wheels over my back, no brakes and feeling really the business.

I loved the grass track and have even memories of riding a 'black meeting' at Drumalig Sports - where Cyril Johnstons is at Carryduff. I got a fourth and brought home a glass jug! I was chuffed. I though that a 1st, 2nd and 3rd would leave me out with 4th, but no, I proudly presented my mother with the jug.

I recall riding a 'Black' 10 mile TT, Saintfield to Crossgar and back.

There were many lads who turned up at 'Black' meetings, trying to look like country bumpkins on old dirty bikes and thus got a decent allowance from the handicapper. There was an odd feeling of excitement in partaking in something that could loose your 'official' standing in authorised NCU Races There was a rider called Davy Allen who, or so I heard, always had one member of his family licensed, the rest stayed outside the regulations and rode all the local 'Black' or 'Flapper' meetings.

Nevertheless the grass track meetings continued at the RUC Sports at Balmoral, Ravenhill and I even took the bus to Loughery Sports where there was lots of rises and dips in the terrain, not to mention the cow pats. One event I can recall, or think that I can, was the Albert Foundry Sports where the going was so wet and muddy that one rider, I think it was someone called Kelly lapped his cane rims with bands of binder twine thus giving a degree of traction. I cannot recall whether he won or not.

PETER WOODS

The 'Belstaff' waterproof long coat

Not the most modern of gear, but it is what Peter Woods wore when acting as a motor cycle pillion race marshal at massed starts.

A 'Belstaff' waterproof long coat, bought in Eddy Cassidy's shop in Cromac Square and a black beret worn 'Basque' fashion was his attire for riding 'shot gun' on Archie Boyd's motor bike.

Archie, like many more, gave freely of his time and were truly the unsung heroes of road racing.

ISABEL WOODS

Peter Woods in the coat

LEARNING FROM THE EXPERTS

I had come to the sport at an age older than others and so was very open to being influenced by the top riders and here again, I hope my memory doesn't let me down.

Davy McNutt, Davy Martin, Billy Sands, Raymond Carroll, Billy Dowds or Jimmy or W J as others called him. Frank McKeown, who you would know for certain it was he who was coming up behind you for you could recognise the swish, swish, swish of his wheels as he had a riding style that rode his bike in a slight weaving path rather than the straight smooth style of most others. I often thought that had there been coaches around as today, Frank would have been much faster than he was. 'Sausage feet', 'Funty' Joe Craig - all heroes of my early years.

David Woods as a toddler

Charlie Montgomery leading Tommy Givan in the massed start championship at Ards Airport the night that the thundery black clouds come down so frighteningly close, but it was the knowledge of all us spectators that Tommy Givan would come off Montgomery's wheel and add yet another title to the already long and illustrious career that I learned of from those of his admirers. Peter Gaynor, a rider who no matter how much effort he was making, never opened his mouth. Always breathing through his nose! I think I recall someone asking him and having it all explained as he was very scientific!

KNICKNAMING

I have always had a rather silly habit of knick-naming people and so gave my eldest son David, the nickname 'Dede le Duc' after an old pro rider who had a make of toe straps named after him. I had great ambitions that my children might achieve in the sport what I had never had the talent to do and I even got David a little Italian child's bike before he could even walk.

It came out of Dougie Knight's Cycle shop on Great Victoria Street as did the sidecar that we attached to my Mercian, thus allowing our touring and Sunday runs to continue until the family numbers increased to the point that we no longer were able to.

CLUB RUNS

Important and exciting as competitive cycling was, it was the Club runs on a Sunday that really cemented the bonds amongst us. What devilment we got up to! After a walk through the woods, or up the mountain, one could often return to the drum up fire to realise your bike was no longer leaning against the tree where you had left it. Nowhere was it to be seen. Everyone ready for the return journey home and still no sign of the trusty steed. Lift your eyes to the heavens and yes there it was, hooked up to the top of a 30 or 40 feet tree! Bean tins with their lids off would be set upside down over lit squibs, placed upright into the soft ground. Then it was a case of whose tin was shot highest into the air when the firework exploded. Harmless enough a bit of fun and certainly less frightening when someone would place the red burning tip of his Woodbine to the blue touch paper of the squib and surrepticiously slip it in under the flap of some unsuspecting rider's saddle bag. I recall even an empty syrup tin, with some water and a handful of dry carbide placed in it, the lid tightly pressed down and the lot tossed into the stream. Boom! And the shockwaves would bring a few stunned trout to the surface. Totally illegal, needless to say.

CHILDHOOD

Being born in 1929 doesn't leave a lot of room for much physical activity at this end of the eighty years, but it does leave one with a wealth of memories of early childhood. Only one of cycling I may say. I can recall my father bringing me home from Magheragall Parish Church after Sunday 11.30 am morning service. Oddly enough I have no recollection of how I got there, but I remember that I sat on a cushion, tied on the cross section of the handlebars, or was the cushion tied to the top bar? The two things that I do remember clearly were that as father mounted the bike, a rook or jackdaw dropped a 'you know what' on his Sunday hat and shoulder of his jacket. The other, that I got the top of his boiled goose egg when we got home. I was fortunate to have spent my childhood near Ballinderry, outside Lisburn among the Agricultural community and to be able to recall many traditional farming activities – cutting a grass seed crop by reaper and tying and stooking the sheaves. The reaper being pulled by horse. Horse ploughing. Corn cut and sheaved by a horse drawn binder. Hand milking of cows, haymaking by reaper, buck rake, tumbling paddy. Hay stacks, brought from the field by ruck-shifter, barn dances after harvest. What a blessing to be that old!

However I had better finish with my last cycling anecdote. I hope that I'm accurate in this.

At the start of a 25 mile TT this tall newcomer of the Old Bleach Club from Randalstown, wearing ordinary black everyday shoes and I have a notion, no toe clips, set off. Tommy Taylor remarked:
"There is the beginning of a new era. What will he do when he gets kitted out?"

PETER WOODS   *Belfast CC*

MORRIS FOSTER *by Isabel Woods*

How right he was......
The cyclist's name was Morris Foster, Cyprus C.C. The top man of the Sixties. In Harry McCartney's opinion, Morris was "The greatest ever Time Trialist". He won 26 Time Trial titles and was winner of "The Bath Road 100 Miles in under 4 hours. He held the record for: *Dublin to Belfast   Belfast, Dublin, Belfast Irish End to End*

In 2006 he was a worthy recipient of an M.B.E. Morris is currently writing his own story which will be a great read for everyone interested in the sport of cycling.

Morris Foster with his trophies

The Workers

This picture shows a typical Monday morning throughout 2009 - 2010 when Isabel, Rab, May and Billy met around the Woods' big kitchen table at Lisnoe, Lisburn to work on this book. At the end of each session their reward was tea, fresh bread, cheese, tomatoes and onions, followed by Nan's (wife of Rab) chocolate cake.

Ulster Ladies road club

Many years ago I was given a wooden box containing documents relating to 'The Ulster Ladies Road Club'. (U.L.R.C.) I have tried to write a brief account of its history from the fragmented information in the wooden box. In the early 1930's, ladies interested in cycling would have joined their various local clubs, which would have organised Gents' races. As Ladies were in the minority and being spread among the numerous Clubs, they didn't merit special events. The only opportunity for Ladies to compete was in Track Races, organised by the R.U.C. Sports and others.

Annual 12 mile cycle race - late 1939

In 1937 'The Ulster Ladies Road Club' was formed to promote Time Trial Races for Ladies.
It was decided to make it a 'Second Claim' Club to enable Ladies from any Club to compete while still belonging to the Club of their choice.

Lillie Cumming (Ulster Ladies Road Club) (on left), Winner of the Ladies' Half-Mile Cycle Race, being congratulated by Lillian Neill (Maryland Wheelers), who was second.

Winner Lillie Cumming.

The first President appointed was Mrs Ann Goorwich, of Goorwich's – one of Belfast's top quality stores. The first Race Result Sheet in the Box was for an Open 10 mile Time Trial run by 'The Prescot Clarion Ladies Club' in England. Two Ulster girls went across to compete in an entry of 30 riders. Irene Neill (later Matier) and Ena McClure (later McKeown) They finished 5th and 7th fastest! The next race run by the U.L.R.C. was a 10 mile Time Trial held in September 1937 with an entry of 15 riders. Ella Hutchinson (later Smith) was fastest with a time of 28 mins. 46 secs.

Their first Social event was a dance held in the Orpheous Ballroom that same year with an attendance of 242 people.

In 1938 'Claud Butler Cycles' donated a good quality cup which was presented yearly to the winner of the 'Best All Rounder' competition. Several other trophies followed through the years including the 'Smyth Cup'.

The U.L.R.C. continued to flourish until the end of the 1940 season when like most other Clubs it was interrupted by the Second World War. An Annual General Meeting of the U.L.R.C. was held on the 8th March 1945 and saw the revival of the Club. In 1946 the Club acquired an enamel badge (cost three shillings and six pence each) The design was a winged wheel contained in a semi circle. *(Below)*.

In the early days the Ladies who deserve credit for the survival of the Club were Lilian Neill (Boal) who was a great Secretary. Her sister Irene Neill, Ena McClure and Ella Hutchinson were also stalwarts of the Club.

Bangor Massed Start 12th May 1945.
Irene Neil and Lilian Boal alert the public that
the race is about to start. These sisters were two of the
fastest riders in the late 30's and 40's.

Fixing a puncture at a track race.

Front Row: L to R: Maureen Black, Maureen Osbourne Ena McKeown and Rose Rainey.
Back Row: L to R: Irene Neill. Others unknown.

There was an average entry of 15 riders at this time. In 1951 and 1952 I was unable to compete because of family commitments.

The race result sheets for 1952 are the last ones that I found in the wooden box.

Right: Ella Hutchinson being pushed off in the first race. Ella won U.L.R.C. first Time Trial in 1937 a 10 mile Time Trial with a time of 28 mins. 46 secs. There were fifteen riders in the race

Hopefully missing information will eventually turn up, but maybe not in time for this article. So I can only write about my memories of the next period.

In 1953 I competed in a few of the U.L.R.C. Time Trials while at the same time training for the Enniskillen and Dublin to Belfast records.

Ena persuaded my sister Nan and I to ride in the Club's 5 mile Novice race in 1949.

I got placed 2nd in this Event which encouraged me to try again. In 1950 I won the Claud Butler B.A.R. Cup (beginners luck).

MISS ELLA HUTCHINSON, WINNER OF THE FIRST ULSTER LADIES' ROAD CLUB RACE

In 1954, 55 and 56 as I was continuing with 'Place to Place' Records, I only competed in The National Championships and 'Wearwell Cup' Time Trials. As a result I lost touch with the official running of the club. In January 1958 our first child was born and three others followed in quick succession!

As you will appreciate this left little time for cycling! As far as I can gather the U.L.R.C. ceased to function before the end of the 1950's. I do know however that Mr Tommy Taylor and Mr Sammy Neill were two of our Presidents during this period.

My fellow members of the U.L.R.C. were a wonderful crowd of girls: Good sports, no animosity and great fun to be with. As in the early days of the Club, the emphasis was put on running a really enjoyable social event for the Prize distribution.

The following photographs have captured the evidence of this.

Photo taken at Smithfield, Belfast. Isabel Woods heading for the finish at the G.P.O. in Royal Avenue. (Enniskillen to Belfast race).

Ulster Ladies Road Club Annual Dinner and Distribution of Prizes 1956.
L to R: Maureen Osbourne, Beryl Hill, Nora Porter, Isabel Clements, Hettie Breen, ... Rosaleen
Rainey, Ena McKeown and Ella Smith.

U.L.R.C. Ladies with Timekeepers Ernie Lavery and Tommy Taylor

Timekeepers stories - *Tommy Taylor*

*I think that a great many of we cyclists took
Time Keepers for granted.*

Theirs was a very unenviable task – turning up in all weather conditions with no shelter, except an umbrella, held my someone, to keep the 'Start Sheet' dry. In the 1950's the Entries for a 25 mile time trial were restricted to 120 Riders. 50 mile Events had an average of 70 Entries plus. 100 mile time trial had around 50 Entrants. Having started all the Riders, the time keeper had to wait patiently until the last man or woman arrived back and was clocked in. Tommy Taylor was one of these stoic men who had to be fit in body and mind to endure the elements. He was highly respected for his integrity. He could be called an English Gentleman with a County Antrim accent!

He was selected as Manager for the Commonwealth Games Team in 1958 and would have been one of the longest serving Time Keepers.

Tommy worked in the Accounts Department in Richardson Larmour (Linen). This firm was situated at the rear of the Crown Bar in Belfast.

He swam every day, both winter and summer. He and a brother of Raymond Moore swam in Strangford Lough. No wonder, when we were first told tales of his hardiness, we learned that as a child he had paddled in very cold water.

A book could have easily been filled with his stories alone, if only they had been recorded.

Tommy passed away in December 2001. These few remarks are very inadequate to pay tribute to our past Time Keepers who have not had the recognition they deserved. The success of the riders that they have timed in races has been well recorded, but Time Keepers years of service vanish into oblivion. Maybe someone with more knowledge than I and with more years of experience than I could list and give credence to these dedicated men who had given of their time to further the sport of cycling.

ISABEL WOODS   Belfast C.C.

A Tribute to Ernie Lavery

Northern Ireland Commonwealth Games Cycling Team in Cardiff 1958.   From Left: Tommy Taylor (Manager,) Tommy Talbot, Seamus Herron, Sammy Kerr, Eamon Burns, Martin McKay and Jim Maguire. Note: Their smart blazers were made from 'Mogashel' weave, the world renowned fabric. Incidently Tommy Talbot worked in Moygashel.

Ernie was one of the three local timekeepers, along with Tommy Taylor and Eddie Cassidy who were in great demand for club and open events during the years after the War. From 1945 they applied their services most efficiently without favour or reward. I was asked to write an appreciation of Ernie and I am sure there are others more qualified and capable of doing this than I am, but I can only write about him as I knew him. I first made his acquaintance when he was introduced to our Rover Scouts troop of which I was a member, just shortly after he wad demobbed from the army about 1946. He was a close pal of Bobbie Irvine who was a representative of the Northern Cycling Club to the N.C.U. and was a contributor to the 'Official Circular' which was edited by Joe Bell, a member of the Windsor Cycling Club. Bobbie Irvine's father was associated with the Scout troop and it was he who brought Ernie along to teach the members some unarmed combat for a number of weeks. After he had thrown us about for an hour, we had the pleasure of listening to his many yarns and experiences and if he had been around today he could have filled this book by himself. Ernie came from a family who lived on the Newtownards Road, Belfast and in the 1937-38 years the war clouds were beginning to gather, so a lot of men joined the Territorial Army, including Ernie and an Uncle of mine who knew each other.

Training camps were held in Portstewart and at the end of each course they were paid a bounty. There was much unemployment then which I am sure contributed to the numbers that joined.

In August 1939, those who were finishing their two weeks training which included Ernie and my Uncle, were told to go home and pack a few belongings together and report back in 48 hours - you are in the army now and they were in the Royal Artillery for the duration of the war, that is, the ones who survived. While Ernie was in France and Belgium during the war he met and befriended some people there involved in local cycling and he sent home reports to Joe Bell for publishing in the 'Official Circular' at that time.

When he arrived back home after the war he was once more involved in cycling and became a proficient timekeeper and was usually available when required. Ernie's day job for a while was as a steel erector, working along with his brother Bert and others in the construction of a power station in Belfast. He had the misfortune to fall in which he severed a thigh muscle and I remembered him saying they had a job trying to stitch it together again as it kept springing back like a coiled spring. They must have been successful because he eventually became an invaluable asset to the cycling sport in general. He was a true gentleman.

RAB COLLINS

More about Ernie

Ernie Lavery was another good time keeper. I hadn't known him quite as well as I did Tommy Taylor, who had timed most, if not all the Time Trials run by U.L.R.C. in my era. What comes to mind when I think of Ernie was his great sense of humour! Maybe this is a necessary attribute in the make up of a Time Keeper as Tommy was gilded with this also. Ernie was a Member of my Team acting as Observer when I made my first Attempt on the 24 hour Record. He turned up at the 6th Milestone, Glengormley to push me off with his pockets bulging with licorice.

The licorice came in every shape and form and he supplied everyone with a liberal ration and assured me that I was good for an extra five miles an hour if I included the licorice in my menu!! The weather conditions were atrocious as I set off. Solid rain for the first 12 hours after which it was decided to abandon the 24 hour and settle for the 12 hour, in which I had covered 200 miles. I had arranged for a hot bath at Aunt Mary's house in Rosemount Gardens, off the Antrim Road. The Team were brought inside and treated royally with Ernie in the rocking chair and W.L. as his deputy. The hilarious entertainment lasted for three hours!

As a matter of interest, the 12 hour Record was disallowed as I had covered some sections of the course more than twice. The 24 hours Schedule I was following permitted covering sections of roads 4 times!

ISABEL WOODS Belfast C.C.

W. L. Smith

Ernie Lavery pushing off Isabel Woods at the start of her 24 hour record attempt in 1956.

Ernie and 'W. L.' were two of cycling's most popular characters. Between them they could have filled a book with their humorous stories, examples of which follow in Stanley Martins article 'The Lighter Side' This is taken from the 1954 N.I.C.F. Year Book. When their names were read out by Billy Kirk among the missing at the start of 'The Night of Nostalgia' in February 2009, I felt a deep pang of sadness and loss. The world is a dimmer place without them and many of the others listed that night.

Isabel Clements being pushed off in an U.L.R.C. Time Trial by W.L. Smith in 1950.

His only packing for a cycling weekend was, and I quote, his toothbrush and a spanner.

The lighter side

This extract from the 1954 NICF Handbook is a fine example of the work of Stanley Martin, often referred to as Northern Ireland's greatest ever cycling journalist.

No doubt you will appreciate that in any attempt to set out on paper a few of the more amusing incidents in the sport of cycling, it is difficult to recapture with any degree of success the exact atmosphere and circumstances of the moment and in fact much must be left to the imagination of the reader. It is impossible for the writer to satisfy himself that those who didn't happen to be in on his anecdotes will see the situation as he did.

Actually I didn't fancy tackling the job – and I admit to doing my best to wriggle out of it – but your Editor, Joe Bell is nothing if not persistent and again he won. If he does include this lot in his Year Book, then remember that he decides what is printworthy!

The stories aren't all mine. Billy Smith of Northern, Freddy Redmond of East Ulster and that well known R.R.A. man, Ernie Lavery were present inside a confectioner's van when, for the best part of twenty four houses, the stock of laughs from their combined total of over sixty years club cycling, and my meagre ten, stayed the course without ever running low.

If you haven't guessed the reason for the twenty-four hours sojourn in the van, I'm sure you will when you know that more than the supply of memoirs were gallantly sticking the course. Right! It was Eddie McArdles (Cyrus C.C) successful attack on the R.R.A. '24' and we were the crew.

During the war years there were many mid-week sports meetings throughout the Province under the auspicies of War Weapons, Savings and Welcome Home Committees and a gay spirit pervaded amongst the merry band of riders who frequently took days off work to travel around and compete.

On one occasion, at Ballycastle, the boys looked in at a Fair Ground which was close to the track and stayed longer than they should have. Imagine the consternation and the signalling to one another that went on forty feet up in mid-air when the announcement from loud speakers came clearly to our ears "Riders in the first Heat of the Eigh Eighty Handicap get to your marks". The riders for Heat 1 were then flying at full speed in the Chair-o-planes!

At Portstewart we all had a fair bag of First, Seconds and Thirds and the prize values were higher than usual. At the prize presentation each was called and an official promptly wrote out a cheque for the value of prizes won. This was the job alright, until the inevitable Jimmy Keenan twigged on, and we reluctantly handed back the 'please pay' orders. Thus our amateur status was saved, though J.K. wasn't the most popular chap in the railway carriage that evening going home.

Many of our amusing memories involve Jimmy Keenan, who, through all the years since has remained Official

Handicapper, for he is terribly capable at that unenviable job and it was worth a lot to put one across him – from shifting ones mark-peg a few yards forward to 'jumping the gun' when his back was turned. Needless to say J.K. invariably won the battle of wits, but what fun there was when he came across the track and caught the boys on at their work.

The expense involved by a rider in taking a day off plus rail travel to such venues as Cookstown, Irvinestown and Clough was heavy and on one occasion someone hit on a bright idea and turned up at the station with a supply of potato sacks. Wheels were speedily dropped out and the bikes slipped into the sacks and the party triumphantly tripped through the barriers with their bags over their shoulders to save the price of a bicycle ticket.

One the subject of rail travel: Once in this city there was a 'Quad' – a bike built for FOUR and how the bystanders stared as this monster with four speedy riders up and a long row of twelve or so 'solos' on its wheel would come lashing in from the Moira Road on training nights.

Well, this machine was once ridden to Dublin and the base tube broke in O'Connell Street. To the station went 'W.L.' and the staff were ultimately convinced that such a mount was a reality. Regulations were turned up and it was agreed it could be taken home by train the following night. "Afterall, there's only two wheels, so it must be a bike" said the man. "Fair enough – five bob". But when the four stalwarts wheeled the Quad in next evening, heads were scratched. A dozen hands pushed, pulled, lifted and manoeuvred. It got jammed, stuck and for a while couldn't be moved in or out of the already loaded van. A crowd gathered to see the big operation and steam was being let off in more ways than one. Everyone was advising, considering and directing. Eventually it was got on to the platform again and another van was hitched to the train to bring it all the way back to Belfast. The tears were rolling down the face of Billy Smith as he recalled the episode.

Ernie Lavery has a masterpiece from a 12 Hour of many years ago. A certain rider supplied his pal with a chicken and instructions to hand this up at a declared spot. The rider wasn't very speedy, but lacked nothing in keenness and on this occasion was moving slower than usual. After he became long overdue the helper gave him up as lost and by then, being very hungry himself, polished off the racing man's bird. Just as he'd finished the tasty morsel, he gulped tagain as the rider came in view and exclaimed that he'd have packed long before but for the thought of that chicken ahead – and thanked his pal for waiting. "You may pack right now" said his pal "for I've just polished it off myself".

I wonder if any of you remember the bunch hitting that treacherous bend on the last lap in the Waterworks Massed-start during the Holidays at Home programme during the war and the awful crunch as they piled up when making that final effort for the chequered flag? What a roar there was when one rider sprinted off on another's bike (his own un-rideable) while the dispossessed man turned the air blue with his language!

Strangely enough, while all these incidents were being turned over again, there were other happenings on this particular occasion which, though they seemed serious at the time, since a man's aspirations to the Twice-around-the-Clock record were at stake, can now be regarded as amusing, and not the least in appreciating the humorous side will be Eddie McArdle himself, who topped the existing standard handsomely with a courageous ride of 416 miles.

Eddie has a big army field-flask of special soup guaranteed to radiate new life within fading long-distance racing men. Somehow between the hurricane lamp and the primus stove, which were a small part of the equipment in that bouncing shambles which was the inside of our van, the soup took on a distinctly paraffin flavour. One item of sustenance, by the way, was contained in a white bag, which was thrown into the middle of the confusion as the doors of the wagon slammed when departing from headquarters in the darkness – it was a pillow-case with five loaves of bread inside! Anyway the soup was declared unfit for even a racing-man, and was duly pitched over the hedge at Carneatly. Soon the call came for the soup and it was left to 'W.L.' to brazenly yell "You've already had that". "Sorry, Billy" replied the ever-trusting Eddie and pepped up his pace as though he had. It took us three weeks before we could get round to telling him the truth!

Then there was the chicken – not the one we mentioned before. 'Leg of chicken' would come the call at well spread intervals and after the second, this was answered with a slice from the breast or whatever other part of that chicken came handiest. After five such calls and about fourteen hours riding, Eddie shouted once again, and the exasperated 'W.L.' let loose with "Holy Jerusalem, you've had five off it already – and it wasn't a centipede"/

And finally the tense situation at Carnlough after some seventeen hours on the road. It was a few hours after a wet dawn and the night had been chilling frosty. Eddie was obviously at his lowest ebb and needed a muscle warming rub plus hot tea of the fresh and not flask type. Dry clothes were also required and a call was put through to a restaurant in Carnlough to stand by to receive one roadman in distress.

After all items had been attended to, Eddie's attempt hung in the balance when he seemed reluctant to emerge from the locked toilet. 'W.L.' coaxed him, and then with no response from within, the soft stuff turned to loud threats and suggestions of battering the door in and pulling the rider out. The Proprietress came on the scene and told us we should all be ashamed of ourselves for thus cajoling the poor, tired boy and while we were putting up lame excuses, I believed she even vowed to have 'Cruelty' upon us.

Eddie himself saved the situation by slipping out almost unnoticed in the uproar. He then apologised to all hands for having caused any trouble! He obligingly hopped on the bike and rode the next two hours at 'evens', and the Proprietress was on the street as he returned through Carnlough to give him a shout of encouragement.

There you have but a few from the scrapbook of pleasant memories of those who have, perhaps, been accustomed to times when competition wasn't so fierce, nor the necessity for a serious approach to the game so evident. Still, no matter which way you play this cycling game, every now and again, when you look back, you'll have a laugh.

STANLEY MARTIN

Scars

These are the hallmarks of most cyclists and to my knowledge they are obtained involuntarily.

The usual places they are found are: the head, shoulders, elbows, hips and knees. Whenever I see some scars on a cyclist I wonder what yarns are associated with them. The person to whom these scars belong are usually, in their opinion, not responsible for them. To me they resemble a painting by Picasso – something that the onlooker appreciates only as a disturbance of the flesh, obtained with some pain and discomfort. Whereas the one who carries the scars needs only to look at them and vivid scenes

"A step in time saves nine".

flash back to memory. If you get some on a cycling tour during your holiday break you will appreciate them more than the ones collected on an ordinary club run. Simple because they are better than picture postcards, as they immediately remind you of places where you have been – maybe France, Spain, or somewhere like that, where there was plenty of sun, mountains and glorious beaches and unlike the picture postcard they are handy to carry about with you wherever you wish to go...

The popular way to obtain scars is to overlap your front wheel behind the back wheel of the rider in front of you on a club run or a race, so if he or she switches you will bite the dust. But the guy in front will stay upright and in the process you will bring a half a dozen down behind you!

Another method is to hook your handlebars on to the saddlebag of a member on a club run, or a general sprint to the 30 Signs as the group approaches each town or built-up area, especially if there is a Pot hole or two in the road. If you are successful in obtaining any of these skin decorations, without them being too serious, they will be an instant reminder of the time, the place of their origin and the cause. Anyhow, happy scar hunting to all, but leave me out of the action as I have sufficient picture shows to do me, thank you.

FRED COLLINS Belfast CC

Memories from further afield

Joy McVeigh lives in Ontario Canada. Through Dave Kane and Billy Kirk she heard that a book on cycling memories was being compiled. And not to be left out, Joy has written to us and shared some memories.
My last full year of racing was in 1955, because in April 1956 I met a Canadian named Richard (Rick) Maze and we were married in Belfast in December 1956.

In February 1957, I moved to Canada where we have lived ever since, except for the following two periods. In November 1958 we returned to Belfast for almost a year and where our daughter Lesley was born in August 1959. Her Godfather is Aubrey Brown, an ex-racing cyclist. We returned to Canada in 1959 and a son (Ian) was born to us in 1961. Living there until April 1965 we again left, this time for a seven and a half year attachment to the Royal Canadian Air Force. We returned again to Canada and have been here ever since. I still have my 1955 Diary – the only one that I have ever kept and after perusing it, I am groaning at the daft nineteen year old that I was. The main themes are boys, cycling, racing cycling, dances and more boys. In those days I just thought I was going to live forever and "take no prisoners" seemed to be my attitude to life. However I can be excused because I am a Sagittarian and we are known to have a side that indicates recklessness and tacklessness!

My Diary shows that my racing licence number was 393 and that I belonged to the Ulster Ladies Road Club and my affiliation number with the Northern Cycling Club was 1591.

Early Days
My first bike was a girl's Phillips. I was very proud of it and with it I started to tour. I joined the Youth Hostel Association. I needed another bike and I acquired a pre World War Two Holdsworth for the princely sum of twelve pounds. At the time I probably earned two pounds per week.

The first trip out, luckily with young men of chivalrous character, produced thirteen punctures in about three miles. They fixed them all using spare pieces of leather but finally resorting to stuffing the tires with grass. New tyres were an immediate necessity. At that point I realized that I had acquired a dependant - the bike that would cost me every spare shilling I made for the next number of years. I entered a novice five mile race either in 1949 or 1950 riding the Holdsworth. I won with a time of 14 mins. 5 secs. After the race, I promptly up-chucked! Before the race on the Antrim line, my mother had fed me well – fried eggs and bacon. I enjoyed it better the first time!

However it was at this race I believe that I met Ella and W.L.(Billy) Smyth who were to have a great influence in my cycling days. I also met people from the C.T.C. and have friends from that Association to this day. I hear that Ella recently passed away. I have no information on Billy. *(Billy is now deceased too).*
I think back to their many kindnesses to all the younger cyclists whom they encouraged and the many times that they provided tea, scones and fruit cake for all the wet waifs and strays who dropped in at their home

unannounced. While they gave so much time to the sport of cycling, they also were raising a lovely family. Roy, Patsy and was there a young Billy too?

If there had been such a thing as a life-time cycling achievement award I'm sure that they would have qualified.

Saturday August 13th 1955

Two cycling friends from Dublin were staying at my home in Belfast. They were Doris O'Connor and Marie Kearns. They were dedicated to being good guests and insisted on doing the dishes and tidying up before we left to cycle to Portadown for the All-Ireland Ladies 25 mile Championship.

They weren't racing and because they were touring types rather than racing people, I found myself pushing them, in turns, because they were becoming slower and slower while time was moving on.

By the time we arrived, I was perspiring heavily and hurried to change into my shorts and jersey.

Almost immediately it seemed, it was my turn to start and off I went. Never having raced this course before, I couldn't believe what I was seeing – hills that appeared to be 1 in 7 or worse! I had seen hills like this in Scotland whilst on holiday so why were they now here in Northern Ireland?

I rode on hoping that the landscape would change and feeling distinctly ill from the stress of the prior 28 miles ridden to get to the race. I threw in the towel at the 5 mile mark and rested for a while until I could make my way back to the starting point. The Northern team consisted of Marie Ward and Maeve Lee and myself. Maeve and Marie were disappointed at my failure to complete the race.

Sometimes excuses just don't mean a thing when you have disappointed others! This race was won by Isabel Woods in the time of 1 hour 11 mins and 38 seconds. Congratulations to all the others who did finish despite that nasty course selected by some sadist!

Isle of Man Fiasco

In 1956 I determined that I would go 'offshore' and race in the Isle of Man. To my disappointment, I found that the time set for the 25 mile race would be the day before I arrived, but the track race (not my forte) would be during my time there. In my diary I have noted the financial details:

Plane fare three pounds sterling. Lodgings five pounds one and six for the week. Four pounds eighteen shillings and six pence for spending money. This huge amount of money accrued from a 72 hour week and was saved during a three month period. The time arrived when I would make my debut in an international race. My heart beat faster as the gun was fired and we were off!

The race was soon over and I was in the pack, but not quite last. After the race when I was asked why I was wearing a world championship racing jersey. I was utterly bewildered and replied

"Do you mean this jersey? My mother bought it for me in a sale"!

record of 1955 time trial races

Date	Race Miles	Promotor	Course	Winner	Time	2nd	3rd
05/10	10	U.I.R.C.	New'ards	J.McVeigh	27.53	H.B.	M.Ward
05/19	10	U.L.R.C.	Moira	H. Breen	27.59	M.L.	J. McV
05/25	10	Northern	Antrim	I.Clements	27.41	M.O.	J.McV
06/2	15	U.L.R.C.	Antrim	U. O'Neill	41.59	J.McV	???
06/8	25*****	Windsor	Antrim	H. Breen	1.11.32	J.McV	M.Ward
06/16	20	Windsor	Antrim	J.McVeigh	57.15	H.B.	M.Ward
06/23	25	U.L.R.C.	New'ards	J.McVeigh	1.11.55	------	-------
06/30	30	U.L.R.C.	Saintfield	J.McVeigh	1.26.53	H.B.	M.Ward
08/13	25	All Ireland	Portadown	I.Clements	1.11.38	------	-------
08/20	50	U.L.R.C.	Antrim	OPEN	J.McVeigh	2.24.30	H.B. R.Rainey

In this 25 mile race Isabel Clements crashed and was quite badly hurt.
***** On this line I appear to have a conflict.
My record details are as shown but my actual page of the diary indicates that the race was cancelled owing to an accident to our time keeper T. Taylor. It is possible that it was re-scheduled for another time and that I didn't change the date

The ratings in the 1955 T.T. gave me the B.A.R. title for that year of which I am still proud.

track racing 1955

Date	Distance	Course	Winner
05/18	880 yards	Wallace Park	Marie Ward
06/15	880 yards	Portadown	Maureen Osborne
06/18	880 yards	Portadown	P Corr
07/27	1 mile	Portadown	Una O'Neill
08/3	½ mile	Portadown	Una O'Neill
08/13	5 min pursuit	Portadown	Una O'Neill

On many occasions I think of all the girls and this is what I know about many of them: Isabel Clements married Peter Woods and lives in Lisburn. I, Joy McVeigh, now Maze, live in Brampton, Ontario, Canada. Una O'Neill I believe went to British Columbia, Canada.

Flora Cameron married Sam Young and settled in Montreal, Quebec, Canada. I heard that Rosie Rainey had passed away.   That still leaves a lot: Maureen Osborne, Hettie Breen, Marie Ward, Maeve Lee, Mona and Mary – particular friends of Una. Unfortunately I can't remember their last names, but very nice girls.

I do remember Mary and Ann Morris. I don't think that they raced but they did have beautiful white, matching Claud Butler bikes and they were always beautifully turned out with perfect hair.

  Oh what I would have given for perfect hair? There are other names that have slipped from my memory but just now I have suddenly remembered the Houston sisters from Comber. I'm still in touch with Aubrey Brown and also T.R. (Ronnie) Millar. I met Jimmy Darragh and his wife Vivian here in Brampton many years ago, but Jimmy died at about age 60, maybe some 15 years ago from, I think, a sudden heart attack. He stayed involved with cycling up until his death.

Thank you for allowing me the space to share just a few wonderful memories of cycling in the fifties in Northern Ireland.

JOY McVEIGH

Joy McVeigh and friends, who knows where?

PS: Joy failed to mention that she was chosen as "Miss Cycling" at the Dun Laoghaire Cycling Week.
PPS Once after racing on the Saintfield Road in Belfast, Joy and her colleagues were invited into Peter Wood's father's home for tea and buns. Peter's father asked Joy how she trained?
Joy, without hesitation replied: CORNFLAKES and PARK DRIVE!

Fancy dress on tandem!

R.U.C. Sports, Balmoral Showbrounds. Competitors unknown. 1937 or 1938

St Stephen's Day

Snowed up near Saintfield Co. Down 1941

Christmas is a time when we think of the family circle – parties, celebration and all the good things that go with this special occasion. But for me it is a time for reflection as well and my happiest memory was the St. Stephen's Day when I had my first meeting with the 'Rhymers' who carry out an ancient Irish custom in most peculiar circumstances.

I set off that particular Christmas for Wicklow, which I remember was an extremely cold day with a frost glistening on the hedgerows and the roads as hard as metal. My first stop was at Dromore where I called on an old friend of our Club, Miss Lucy who used to cater for our Club when we cycled there and that good lady soon had a Christmas dinner set up for me in front of a blazing warm fire. When I went to pay her she insisted that it was her little Christmas present to me, but I paid by leaving ample money on the table and rushing out.

St Stephens Day

How we could do with more of those grand old ladies who were true friends of the cyclists. I proceeded on my journey and took the road through Collon and on to Mellifont Abbey, where I spent the night in the hostel, with not even the warden to keep me company. I then resumed my way through Louth to Navan and it was just outside there I met 'The Rhymers'. They were congregated outside the 'local' and were dressed in old huntsmen's scarlet tunics with black cap and breeches and each one carried a long stick on which was impaled a tiny carcass of a wren and on uttering a chant which began something like this:

"The wren, the wren, the king of all birds, St. Stephens Day he was caught in the firs".

To my amazement the landlord came out and invited the entire company in and although I was not wearing the hunting gear, never mind a wren on the end of a stick, I was fairly itching to know what it was all about, so I pushed my way in behind them. Before long I was called into the company and I felt like Reynard the fox with so many huntsmen around me.... After toasting King Wren I was initiated with due ceremony into "The Worshipful Company of Wrens" whatever that entitles me to. There was another toast all round and then the fun started with the red-coats performing all sort of jigs and reels and singing old ballads in return for the landlords hospitality. I even sung a song myself the craic was so good.

The only thing I felt sad about was the wanton slaughter of the industrious little wren, but I was in real jolly company and it relieved the loneliness. I got as far as Greystones on that trip and although I have made a number of enquiries since that occasion I have never met up with or even heard of another company of Rhymers from that day. So if you go touring around Christmas time in the counties of Louth or Meath watch out for the 'wren boys' as the local people call them and you will have a very pleasant interlude in the most jovial company you could wish for.

ROAMER

"THE HARDRIDER"

The reunion

Though turbulent times have replaced the old
And the changing years have taken their toll
There's a special event which we always hold
The annual *Club Reunion*

We gather by train, by bus, by bike
And some laggards would even hike
While to have to work late, why, we would go on strike
To be there at the *Club Reunion*

The youthful brigade and all the heads
The bachelors gay and the newly weds
And a goodly proportion of middle aged spreads
Will be there at the *Club Reunion*

How the hours will fly as past years we recall
And the laughter re-echoes around the hall
For tonight we are young again, one and all
At the annual *Club Reunion*

Then in sorrow we think of dear old friends
Who have travelled the roads to the rainbows end
May they journey in peace is the wish we send
From the annual *Club Reunion*

Yes this is where friendship withstands the test
Where we are only too willing to give of our best
I offer this toast, may we always be blest,
With the annual *Club Reunion*

ROAMER

B.M.

"THE HARDRIDER"

This is a letter from Stephen Roche to Lenny Kirk in August 1980
It conveys so much about the lifestyle of an aspiring professional cyclists.

110 Rue de Bellevue   *27th August 1980*
92100 Boulogne Billancourt,
France

Hello Lenny
Thank you for your letter. I only got it this morning because I am now on a kind of a working holiday in the South of France, just 4 km from Spain. One of the lads went back to Paris last week and returned this morning with your letter.

Anyway, I came here straight from Moscow on 1st August and I stay here until tomorrow when I leave for a three day 4 stage Tour, a little further south. I had my first 6 days here just swimming, lying in the sun and doing a little fishing. Just having a complete break from the bike. I tell you I needed it. I had been racing hard and training since February without a break and with all the travelling I've done it takes a lot out of you, mentally and physically.

Moscow didn't go as I hoped it would. After Belgium, the Tour de Liege, I was really going well. Then the first day in Moscow I could hardly turn the pedals. All I wanted to do was sleep. I couldn't walk any distance, I could do nothing. Billy and Tony were having a great time, sight seeing and all that and I just had no interest. So I think that I must have picked up a bug or something. The Course was hard, a stupid course really, just like a 'Roller Coaster'. However, if I had had the form I had in Belgium I know I could have finished in the first 10. The French riders that I finished 30 minutes ahead of in Belgium, finished 8th, 9th. So after this I was really disappointed. But now that it's over I must look to the next big one.

I have been down here in the South with four other lads of the team. We paid £40 each for to hire a villa here. We also must cook and feed ourselves for the month. After the second week here we started riding critiriums. So far I've ridden about 8 and won two of them. I was placed in them all. Between the team we can win about £15 to £30 a time. So the holiday here will cost me really very little and I'm also having a break from the big ones.

In the last week I've been training hard for a Tour which I start on Friday 29th to the 31st. Just 3 days. But it will be my first big race with all the top 'Freds' together since Belgium. So it will be hard. There are four stages, 3 Road and a 15 km. T.T. So I am hoping to do something in the time trial if nothing else. Our Director thinks that on my own I am one of the fastest riders in France. If I get away from the bunch on my own I can do a bit of damage. In the Crits. down here I can take a lot of Primes just by riding flat out for 10 laps or so. In the two races I won, one was a 2 km circuit. I lapped the break 2 times and in the second it was a 6 km. circuit with a hard climb. I put 6.35 secs between me and the 2nd place rider. If the form is good in this tour I might do something.

After this tour I go back to Paris and ride another tour on the 5th, 6th and 7th of Sept and then to the South to train for the G.P. des Nations T.T. The G.P.de France and then I hope to ride the Etoil de espoir Pro-Am at the end of Oct. So my season is far from over. I hope to be home then by the end of October or early November.

So that's the life story of a 'Fred' in France! O! I nearly forgot. In case you haven't heard, I've signed for Peugeot for the next two years. I get a really good contact. So things haven't gone too bad for me. Also I have had 11 wins this year including two classics, two tours and a few stage wins. To think I only had 4 or 5 wins altogether at home last year. So there hope for you yet. There is a place for McIlroy here next year. Somebody said "McIlroy's flying, Kirk's creeping".
I hope that you can get your problem sorted out okay and get back on the bike soon. I'm sure that you also can do what I've done. (Whatever that is) You have the ability, speed and lots of class. Believe it or not, since we first met x years ago I've always admired your speed and style. So I give you hope, I think you can do something.

Well Lenny, I'll close for now. But when I'm home you must come down for a few days and do some training and talking and all that. Maybe for my 21st birthday on November 28. Were having a party. However, keep in touch.

All the best, your good friend STEPHEN

Lenny Kirk leads Stephen Roche at Cork in 1977 during the Irish Junior Road Championship. Roche won by 1 minute over Kirk

The old faithful

I was passing a second hand shop one day when I noticed a carbide bicycle lamp in the window.

It reminded me of the days when the average clubman looked naked without his 'two piece' and I am not talking about a suit of clothes from a tailor's shop This 'two piece' consisted of a generator, which was fastened on to the top tube of the bike with head and tail lamps mounted front and rear and each connected to the generator by rubber tubes which conveyed the gas to the front and rear lamps. I purchased a set of these in 1935 for the sum of fourteen shillings. The manufacturers name was Powell & Hamner in Birmingham and what a gem those lighting sets were! I had many good years of service from mine until during the war years when the threads on the generator became stripped and it was in desperation I had to look around for a replacement. I wandered around to Gresham Street and in the window of Andrews Cycle shop I saw a hideously shaped carbide lamp which was retailing at five shillings and that being the sum total of my purse, I made a purchase.

The club run was the following day and we met at the Thompson Fountain in Ormeau Avenue where we set off for a weekend in Woburn, near Carrowdore. My latest acquisition was the centre of attraction and the gleaming lamp displayed the name of Bauer, who was a German.

We were due to set off about five o'clock and everyone was eager to see the new German lamp operating, so I confidently applied the match and nothing happened. I then closed the door and gave it a couple more nicks of water and then re-applied a second match. There was a terrific bang and the comments were not complimentary afterwards to Gerry and myself. After a much more subdued approach we finally got it lit and we proceeded on our way. I lost count of the number of times it went out with a lot of hissing and grumbling from its interior, which did not instil any confidence.

At our week-end rendezvous everyone had a go at operating the lamp. Then came the time to start our homeward journey and after a few miles it began acting up again. So when we had a couple more stops to re-light it, Old Bill's patience ran out as he had a date with his girl friend Nancy in Lisburn and before I could protest, my new lamp was describing a beautiful arc into the night sky ending up in the middle of a cornfield. The rest of my ride home was a case of dodging the police which I managed to do with a bit of luck. There was also the good days when the old 'two piece' was very useful when we were camping. The lamp was strapped to the tent pole and the tube ran down to the generator on the ground.

On another occasion while cleaning the container, I was blowing some dirt out of it and I got a particle of carbide in my eye which was painful and necessitated a club mate holding me while another poured caster oil into my eye.

Through all those misfortunes I have never faltered from my love of the 'two piece'. In spite of those isolated incidents which I have recalled about them, to me it was always the friendly beam shining across the lanes which was their greatest attraction.

ROAMER

Newspaper article on the Carbine Lamp

This "tendem" has lately made it appearance in a Massachusetts tow: and is said to career through the street at 60 m.p.h.

IT'S back to the bicycle again. A couple of weeks ago I published a picture of a tandem built for four and the letters came piling in from men who are keen on the good old bike.

First came a welcome epistle in praise of the bike from a gentleman called Ernest McDowell of the Harmony Heights district outside Lisburn. Writes Ernest: "We all enjoyed the article and photo of four on the bike, but you have not made much mention of lighting equipment for these antique models ..."

He went on to add that a friend of his, one John Malcolmson of Rathfriland on the Hill, has a genuine Carbide Lamp (dictionary definition of which is — Carbide, compound of carbon with an element). This lamp, it would seem, is still in working order. Ernest McDowell says he remembers the days of the Carbide Lamp, just like myself.

On a recent visit to his friend in Rathfriland they discussed this mode of lighting and set to wondering if there are many in Ulster who still possess a Carbide Lamp. Says Ernest: "On a frosty night, when you would be cycling without gloves, one of these lamps was

Listen here a while
by Gerald Rafferty

very useful for warming the hands as you pedalled on."

Now I'm wondering if John Malcolmson with the Carbide Lamp can still find carbide to keep his lamp aglow? Is it still available? If so then I'd like to know. As a lad on the bike I had a Carbide Lamp and recall that it went on fire a couple of times along the winter night road. But it gave off a very good 'panoramic' light and not only could you see the road clearly, but also the ditches and hedges along both sides. Anyhow, I hope that Ernie McDowell keeps throwing some light on the Carbide Lamp.

Can you cast any light on the Carbide Lamp?

This week, take a look at the photograph here and I bet you'll have to admit that this is the first time you have seen a Bicycle Built For Ten.

Harry McCartney has been writing to me from Donacloney, now in the Craigavon area. He kindly sent me this old picture of the ten on a tandem taken from a magazine dated July 11, 1924. The title of the magazine was 'Cycling.' The caption with this great photo says that "This tendem has lately made its appearance in a Massachusetts town, and is said to career through the streets at 60 mph." Note the spelling of tandem as 'tendem' (10 on a bike).

Harry McCartney tells me that he has been a club cyclist for almost 50 years, both racing and touring and still engages in both, what do you know. He read my piece on the Tandem for Four and is a friend of Eddie Allen of Dunmurry whom I recorded not long ago as still riding the same bike for 25 years and it ticking away like a Rolls.

Harry says he looks forward to 'Listen Here Awhile' each week (good man Harry, you're not the only one, bless your heart) and mentions my former friend and colleague, the

late W. D. Morrow, who for many years was one of Ireland's best known newspaper scribes. Harry says that WD used to time the Portadown C.C. event when he rode with them in pre-war days.

Harry has been a member of Banbridge C.C. since 1947 and now Club President and Touring Captain and our own cycling correspondent, Stanley Martin, one of Nature's gentlemen, let me add,

highlighted Harry's career in the Pink about a year or so ago when Harry estimated he had cycled 350,000 miles since starting on the bikes. I'm sure there was many a night when Harry used a Carbide Lamp.

☐ ■

Of course, to the fraternity, Harry McCartney is looked upon as a cycling historian, not only in this part of the world but also in the field of international and world events. He says he has been a reader of the magazine 'Cycling' since 1932. A copy of a 1908 magazine contains pictures of the 1908 Olympic Games Marathon in which each competitor was accompanied by a cyclist.

This was the first Marathon ever to be run in England. The 1920 edition had a picture of a gent diving off a 60 ft. springboard on a bicycle and there was another photo of a man riding a bike across a wire rope between two of the then highest buildings in the town of Paris.

Harry McCartney certainly knows his stuff about bicycles and famous cycling events down the years. To quote him again: "Nearer home motor-paced racing took part on the steeply banked track around the Oval before the First World War and evidence of this can be seen in issues of "Ireland's Saturday Night" in 1912."

Well, that was a right while before 'Listen Here Awhile' appeared in the Pink. Sure I'm only a lad when you look at it.

I am very grateful to Harry McCartney and hope to hear from him again. I'm still giving serious thought to going back to the bike, but I am looking out for one of those old-fashioned machines on which you sit upright and which has a good gearcase, broad Brooks saddle, strong frame and strong, straight handlebars. Ah for the days of the Kerry dancing

In praise of Ireland

SLUT VILLAGE CO. DOWN

I recall as a youthful reader of the Bicycle and Cycling magazines, two of my favourite contributors: Ragged Staff (Rex Coley) of the former and Wayfarer (W.M.Robinson) of the latter. The reason that I mention those two authors, although they were English, their favourite touring ground was the Emerald Isle, which was my own favourite haunt. Their reasons were typical of these two widely travelled tourists. First, the completely unspoilt beauty and antiquity of Erin always appeals to the primitive instincts of the true Nature lover. Secondly, the unconscious humour that is found in every corner and can only be described as completely Irish. Thirdly, the world renowned hospitality that is given so freely to every wanderer in our island. These two gentlemen summed it up perfectly.

I still treasure a club runs card of 1935 which bears Wayfarer's signature which he signed for me at a local C.T.C.D.A. sponsored lecture by him in the old schoolhouse on Beersbridge Road, Belfast. It was entitled THE CHARM OF IRELAND.

To get back to the three reasons listed by the cycling authors, I can only recall personal experience which is surely best. On a tour in Connemara, when we left Roundstone via the lovely coastal stretch of Ballyconnelly. The sun was at its zenith and ahead stretched a full mile of rich golden sand with the white gulls sweeping gracefully overhead. The giant breakers were pounding in, but at that distance we only heard a throaty murmur - like a muted section of a huge orchestra. Beyond the breakers lay a huge carpet of Prussian blue. In the midst of this, the surf was like rich trimmings of ermine. As if in relief of that golden strand, we made out the distant figures of women in black shawls and red flannel skirts and bare feet, heaping kelp into wicker creels. A rough little road ran its twisting course like a dirty white ribbon in the breeze to disappear into the blue void of the sky. There was no one but the two of us two and those minute figures on the beach, to drink in the scene of unspoilt beauty.

The humour of the Irish recalls many chuckles, but the loudest and longest concerns a comical situation in which we found ourselves in Narin, County Donegal. A free for all started in the hotel bar when a certain Jim Boyle set about all and sundry to prove that he was the best man in the length and breadth of the strand. He started off by smashing a hole in the sheeted front of the bar and we beat a hasty retreat. The tallest man in the company looked very small indeed being trailed out, feet first. Towards midnight we had a ringside seat while number two victim was carted away. We retired and had just got into bed when an uproar heralded number three being led to the slaughter and after a furious battle, he went the way of his predecessors. We agreed to bolt and barricade our single room, when we were awakened about 3.00 am to an insistent hammering on the door. We looked around the room only to discover the window was too high and the drainpipe too far away, as I thought I was for the next contest on the village green and when I finally got my tongue unstuck from the roof of my mouth, I asked who it was and a voice that could have belonged to Christopher Robin, said that it was the 'Champ' himself - demanding to see me! Ah well, this is it, I though, as I opened the door a couple in inches and to my surprise and intense relief a huge bruised hand grabbed mine and its owner apologised for his unseemly behaviour. Next the three of us proceeded down the landing in pyjamas and knocked up the owner, who was practically dragged from his bed. The yawning landlord, also in his sleeping suit, began pulling pints of Guinness and we had to stay and consume it while all good people were in bed sleeping. So after a couple of drinks we eventually retired.

Lastly, Irish hospitality recalls the day in the Reeks of Kerry when I was cycling on my own in an impoverished and rocky part of the country as one could find. There were small dwellings which were literally perched on the side of the mountains. The thatched roofs were secured by ropes with heavy rocks back and front for protection against the prevailing winds. I sat on the roadside to watch what I had never seen before. A poor family, children and all - trailing the soil from the valley up to where their home was and building it up over the rocks to grow crops. The old man on seeing me called me up and I have never seen such poverty. They made me welcome with a cup of tea and home baked scones and in spite of my protestations would not accept money. I got the children and give it to them, for here was Irish hospitality at its best. I do hope that you derive as much from your Irish travels as I have. So, happy and safe wheeling during your travels.

ROAMER

Herne Hill and BBC letter to Harry McCartney

This was a competition run by the BBC, for the 12 best stories on the most unusual incident in Sport. Harry McCartney's story was selected.

In the final of the 880 yards handicap the riders, with just over a lap to go, came into the home straight grouped together. Suddenly there was a crash, two riders fell, and a bicycle went flying into the air.

Precisely what happened will perhaps, never be known, but the next thing the spectators saw was A. J. Murray riding along the home straight with his head through the frame of the bicycle, unhurt, and wearing the machine across his shoulders like a world champion with his wreath of honour. Neither of the two fallen riders, J. Allen and P. Sopp, was seriously hurt, although badly cut.

In another handicap eliminator, H. Dodds fell thirteen yards before the finish, and slid on his back this distance over the line, but escaped with abrasions.

—J. B. Wadley

Herne Hill and the BBC's letter to H. McCartney

THE BRITISH BROADCASTING CORPORATION

Broadcasting House, London, W. 1

TELEPHONE : WELBECK 4468   CABLES : BROADCASTS, LONDON

INLAND TELEGRAMS : BROADCASTS, TELEX, LONDON

Ref. No: 03/0B/GOP   21st October, 1946

Dear Mr. McCartney,

If you heard our "Sports Magazine" programme on Friday, 18th October, broadcast in the Light Programme from 6.15 - 6.45 p.m., you will know that your story of an 'unusual incident' qualified for the prize of a guinea.

We are therefore pleased to offer you this amount for the use of the story, and I am asking our Accounts Department to forward you a cheque in due course.

Many thanks for sending the cuttings illustrating your 'Freak incident', and I now return them herewith.

Yours sincerely,

Geoffrey Peck
Outside Broadcasting

H. McCartney Esq.,
Clare,
Waringstown,
Co. Down,
N. Ireland.

A day out in Dublin

Photo of Bill Murray and others walking past the Post Office in Dublin with their bicycles

From left: Isaac Matier, Bill Murray, Harry Boyle??

The eternal cyclist

As we are writing about the past we have selected a few outstanding cyclists worthy of note. - Hence the following profiles

Photo of Harry McCartney in a 25 mile time trial on the Moira Road.

Harry McCartney (Banbridge CC) bought his first bicycle, a 'Humber' at the age of 14 in 1934.

In 1935 he changed it for a BSA Clubman. Early in 1936 he was passing through Portadown and stopped to look into Jimmy Fletcher's shop window. On display were 3 of the most modern 'Coventry Eagle' clubman type, lightweight cycles. The frames were finished in the new flamboyant lustre with chromium plated 'Ross pattern' forks. The red one just had to be his. Harry was renowned for keeping both his bicycles and himself immaculately turned out. A few weeks later he joined the Kilmore CC and started racing and joining in the club runs. In 1936 at the age of 16 he rode his first race. In 1984 he rode his last race at the age of 64. During the 1930's bare knees were not allowed when racing and black tights and black jackets had to be worn, so as not to look conspicuous on the road.

What a contrast to today!!

In 1937 the Kilmore CC ceased to be active, so Harry joined the Portadown C.C. It was at this time that Harry introduced a 17 year old youth to cycling – Jim, W.J. Dowds. Billy eventually demoted Harry into 2nd place in the club races.

The outbreak of the Second World War at the end of the 1939 season had a disastrous effect on cycling in general. In Northern Ireland, many of the clubs disbanded. It ended the 1930 decade, which Harry says was one of the most enjoyable. Harry recalls some fellow cyclists who would have agreed with him. Cyril Henry (Cookstown) Tommy Stewart (Ballyclare) Tommy Taylor and Billy Reilly (Belfast) and many others. There was a very friendly and social atmosphere amongst cyclists.

In 1947 Harry joined the Banbride CC and is 62 years a member. In 1970 at the age of 50, his total cycling miles which he has kept a record of, was 350,000 – averaging out at 10,000 miles per year.

After 75 years, Harry is still a cyclist at heart, but not in a chair but on a saddle. He was cycling over 100 miles per week right up to almost his 9th decade! By this time he had covered half a million miles on his bicycle.

ISABEL WOODS

MY FRIEND, SEAN KELLY

*Harry McCartney shares a few words
with Sean Kelly
in this photograph.
In 1972 the young Kelly turned up
for the All Ireland Junior MS
Championship, in Bangridge and
discovered, through an oversight that
he had not been registered to race.
He was bitterly disappointed.
However, Harry spoke to the officials
and Sean was
permitted to race that day.
He went on to win the race!
(See page 137).*

Harry McCartney celebrates his 90th birthday

This photograph was taken on the Portadown-Newry Tow Path, with Moneypenny's house in the background. It was to mark the occasion of Harry's 90th Birthday.

From right to left:
Harry McCartney, his son, Jim, his grandson, Alistair and his great Grandson, Jacob.
To have four generations in a photograph such as this is quite unique.
Harry has been riding racing bikes for 76 years.

Harry's advice to young newcomers

*Don't do as I did! I got my own racing bike on the 24th
June 1934 and in August I rode to the British Legion
Sports at Balmoral Showgrounds and home again.
A distance of just over fifty miles.*

The same year, on Christmas Day, after dinner, I extended this to visit my Uncle who lived just off the Ravenhill Road in Belfast. Almost sixty miles. So right away I was in the 'hard riders' class. If you have just taken delivery of a new cycle and about to venture out, assuming you can already ride one, if you can get to a cycle path this would be preferable to the public road. Start into the headwind, if there is one. It will assist you on the return run. Only go about five miles in total. Rest a couple of days, then go again – increasing the miles a few each time. You will soon build up to thirty miles.

Get properly equipped with a cape and hat. Look at the type of overall cape worn by the cyclists before the B.B.C. News at 6.00 pm.

With the good surface on these cycle paths, mountain bikes with the wide tyres are clumsy and heavy to push. I use tyres less than one inch wide and 100 lbs pressure per square inch. You just float along. Always carry at least one spare tube of the correct size and a pump, making sure the connection is the proper one for the tube. If you don't have quick release on your wheel spindles, have the right spanner to fit the wheel nuts. Also carry two tyre levers, strong enough to remove the tyre. After a short time you may decide to join a cycling club or you may be asked by someone you will meet up with. I would suggest that the Cyclists Touring Club is probably the most suitable for anyone living in the Belfast area. Many of the present day clubs have developed either a racing or hard-riders group, but little, if any, short distance, slower paced leisure cycling. So one has to check carefully to find a suitable club and when you do you will be richly rewarded with the camaraderie of the members. But most of all, enjoy your cycling.

HARRY McCARTNEY

Photo taken late 1940's Note the capes aforementioned by Harry McCartney
4th left back row Jack Watson (Sen)
1st left front row George Houston
3rd left front row Billy Reilly
4th left front row Jimmy Gray

Lurgan Grand Prix 1953

Billy Jebb, (Kings Moss C.C.) leads Billy Sands of Windsor and W.J. Dowds (South Lurgan) to the finish of the Lurgan Grand Prix in 1953. Dowds won from Jebb whose handle bars swung loose in the final sprint. Tommy Talbot (East Tyrone) can be seen with his foot to the ground in the background

Cycling's Almanack

Photo of Harry being held by Harry Kennedy
This photograph was taken at John Beggs race at
Dromore. The date was 25th April 1998 and it was
Harry McCartney's 78th Birthday

Considering the amazing number of miles that Harry McCartney must have covered during his 75 years of cycling (having totalled 500,000 miles up the age of 90) it is unbelievable how he found time and energy for his other interest – the History of Cycling in Ireland. His recall is phenomenal.

He produced a 520 page, comprehensive, chronological history covering 100 years of cycling. Also 36 ring binder files with 200 clear inserts in each, filled with Press cuttings and photographs from newspapers and cycling magazines. In addition there are Entry Forms and Result Sheets of many Races. A wonderful source of reference for researchers. I have referred to Harry's knowledge of cycling as being phenomenal. I can personally vouch for this, as can many others. When asked an unexpected question regarding a Rider or Race, Harry can immediately respond with the Placings and Times of the top Riders and also the weather conditions on the day! Likewise as to the sequence and dates regarding the formation of the Governing Bodies. A really remarkable man.

This invaluable collection took 10 years of diligent research to produce. Truly a labour of love which has never had the full credit or recognisation it deserves!! These irreplaceable archival treasures not only contain Records of great riders performances, but also the history of Irish Cycling's Governing Bodies, which is so convoluted and linked to our political history. This makes it an amazing story in itself! This incredible collection of Harry's is now the property of 'Cycling Ireland' in Dublin. At present it is in the safe keeping of Jack Watson in Bangor, who is the

Secretary of this Governing Body in Ireland. Its final destination is to be the Roche Kelly' House which is the Headquarters of Cycling Ireland in Dublin. When we approached Harry regarding an article for this publication, he kindly sent us his personal file which covered his 75 years of active cycling. From 1934 to 2009! By the way, Harry is a modest man and did not mention his own achievements in his Historical collection!!

ISABEL WOODS

Harry Reynolds

In 1895 Harry Reynolds, from Balbriggen, won the coveted 'Surrey 100 Guinea Cup' at Kennington Oval. The next year, he won 'The World Mile Amateur Sprint title' in Copenhagen. Reynolds might have gone on to become Ireland's first Olympic Champion, had not the ICA and the GAA declined to take part in the first modern Olympic Games held in Athens that same year – 1896.
Racing at that time was mainly on grass tracks while Road Racing took the form of Paced Races.

ISABEL WOODS (extracted from Harry McCartney's Journal)

ALO DONEGAN

Alo Donegan (Swift CC) was born in Laois in 1903. In 1928, at the age of twenty five he took up cycling. He started on grass track and then on road. In 1933 he was riding twenty five mile Time Trials. In 1934 he had the distinction of being the first man to beat the hour in a 25 mile T.T. run by 'The Harp CC' in October that year, with a time of 59 mins. 5 secs. – beating F. Southall's record of 1 hr. 59 secs. set in September 1931. He rode a gear of 88 inches.

In 1938 he beat the 'Dublin to Belfast' Record which had been set up by Victor Piggot in 1937 with a time of 4 hrs. 58 mins. and 50 secs. Alo's time was 4 hrs. 33 mins.
It was 12 years and four top road men later before this record was to be beaten.
    VICTOR PIGGOT tried to re-claim it the next year 1939. His time was 4 hrs. 53 mins. 31 secs.
    In 1944 BILLY DOWDS did a time of 4hrs. 38 mins. 47 secs.
    In 1949 ISAAC MATIER's time was 4 hrs. 38 mins. 47 secs,
    In 1950 it was beaten by G WILKES in a time of 4 hrs. 32 mins.
Only 1 minute faster!
Alo Donegan retired in 1938. The same year that he had set up this record. Harry McCartney met him 25 years later at a race in Phoenix Park and on several occasions after that. They corresponded quite regularly.

He gave a small brown book to Harry in which he had recorded every race on both Road and Track in which he had finished in the top three with details of times. When Alo Donegan died in a Nursing Home in Maryborough, Harry had the little book photocopied and he sent the original to Alo's son – suggesting that he should keep it safe for future generations of the family to see. Billy Kirk borrowed the copy of 'The little brown book' and he gives additional information on Alo Donegan overleaf.

ISABEL WOODS
(extracted from Harry McCartney's journal)

The following two poems were penned by Alo Donegan
and signed 17th July 1983

UNTITLED

It eats no oats, it eats no hay
It's ready harnessed night and day
It needs no smith, it needs no groom
It takes up very little room:
Its temper's good, it wont get riled,
It's safe to trust with any child
It needs no rein, it needs no goad
But little care on it's bestowed:
It cannot kick, it will not shy
It gives one what no wealth can buy;
It needs no physic – will not bite
It's silent, graceful, strong and light:
Delights the young, makes glad the old
It's surely worth its weight in gold

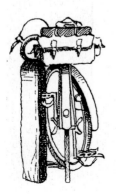

TO MY TANDEM PARTNER

Maid of Dublin, ere we start,
Tell me if thou'll do thy part,
For I think it well to own
I'm not up to it alone.
Hear me ask before we go,
Wilt thy do thy share, or no?

By those tresses unconfirmed
Wilt thou help to shore behind
By that dainty sailor hat,
Wilt thou pedal on the flat?
Though the pace be swift or slow,
Wilt thou do thy share, or no?

Maid of Dublin, it is o'er
You and I must trike no more:
For no matter how we tried,
Our strokes would never coincide.
I must cease to shove thee so
Thou must find another beau.

Photos 1920s and 1930s - *Donegan, Donnelly and Stewart*

Alo Donegan

B. J. Donnelly.
Harp C.C.

Geo Stewart, N.I.
Champion

More about Alo

Donegan was born in Prosperous, Co. Kildare on 6th June 1903. The family moved to Portarlington, Co.Laois some time after World War One.

Following some years of cycle touring he began racing in 1928 aged 25 and became a member of the Swift CC. Possessing great natural ability and strength he was soon winning races on both road and track and showing a special flair for road time trials.

On 30th September 1934 he won the Palmer Cup 25 on the Navan Road returning the sensational time of 59 mins. 5 secs. – setting not only an Irish record, but surpassing the British record by 1 min. 54 secs. One week later he rode a private 50 mile T.T. with full official timekeepers in attendance in which he clocked 2 hrs. 3 mins. 47 secs. again beating the British best by 1 min. 33 secs.

Less well known is that he again broke the hour on 28th April 1935 in the Celtic CC 25, clocking 59 mins. 34 secs. on a gear of 84.8" – lower than his usual 88". Even more surprising is that he did a P.B. 58mins. 50 secs. in July 1935, this time in a private T.T. in a club event.

He was very much in demand in G.B. where he rode successfully on road and track, his riding style and position on the bike being greatly admired by spectators and experts alike.

His record of championships in Ireland include: 3 Leinster grass titles at 2, 3 and 5 miles as well as national T.T. championships at 25, 50 and 100 miles.

In October 1935 he rode the Birchfield 25 at Manchester where he beat the best in G.B. in a field of 100.

Mostly in his last year of 1938 he set some great place to place records:

Limerick – Dublin 1935   5 hours 24 minutes
Dublin - Belfast   1938   4 hours 33 minutes
Cork – Dublin   1938   7 hours 55 minutes
Dublin - Belfast Tandem 1938   4 hours 7 minutes
Galway – Dublin   1938   6 hours 18 minutes
Waterford – Dublin1938   4 hours 14 minutes

In a ten year career his total of 1st places was: 157, 2nd places - 80 and 3rd places: 25

Some of this information derives from a CD sent to me by Alo Donegan's son Gerard in April 2010. This item contained a wealth of detail about Alo Donegan's career.

BILLY KIRK

Geordie Stone's shop in Cromac Square

The pen drawing below of George Stones Bicycle Shop in Cromac Square will evoke memories for many cyclists in Belfast like myself who may be old enough to remember the times during the 1940's and 1950's when Cromac Square and Cromac Street was a 'Mecca' for club cyclists on Saturdays when they would meet at Geordies shop and also at Eddie Cassidy's shop which was only 100 yards away.

Geordie had a workshop where he built the 'Stone Special' and these bicycles were stove enamelled in blue or black. There were always a number of clubmen gathered there to have some repairs done or to try and speed up the new frame they had ordered sometime previously. He was never short of local orders. It has to be remembered that during the war years and even after the war, everything was in short supply which included tubing and chains, as well as spare parts that were vital to the war effort in the engineering industry, so the private sector supplies were very limited.

Geordies shop continued after those years but eventually the whole area succumbed to redevelopment. A number of other cycle traders around the city centre met the same fate through redevelopment or retiring. There was Jimmy McCoo's shop just past the Gas Works on the Ormeau Road. Herbie Knights in Great Victoria Street. Joseph Gass in Kings Street. Andrews in Smithfield. Piddingtons in York Street and Cochranes in Ann Street. Time marches on.

RAB COLLINS

Geordie Stone's business empire is amply demonstrated in this sketch, by the number of shops depicting his name.

Cromac Square by Michael McKernon

David amazes

There was a special gathering in Cormac McCann's home to celebrate his son David's astounding achievements in late September 2009.   Not only did he break Chris Boardman's British '25' record with 45 mins. 54 secs. but also, a few days later, just missed by 3 seconds a top 10 place in the World T.T. Championship. At this celebration we were astonished to realise that David's feats all but co-incided with the 75th Anniversary of Donegan's historic ride on 30th September 1934.

BILLY KIRK

Photos of David in action

B. J. Donnelly, Harp C.C.

In 1896 the year that Harry Reynolds was excelling on the Tracks, another Irish man was born who would follow in his footsteps and be dominant at Track racing from 1915 to 1940.

B J. (Bertie) Donnelly started racing in 1912 at the age of 16. He was told that he was too young for such a strenuous sport and that he should restrain himself until he reached muscular maturity. The following year he had several handicap successes which encouraged him to continue. After competing in four meetings in 1914, he was compelled to rest. The following year 1915, he won his first Irish National Championship. By 1930 at the age of 34 he had won 36 National Championships and hoped to make it 50 before retiring. In 1935 at the age of 38 he won the English 5 mile grass championship which was open to the world. Not since 'Charley Peace' and Harry Reynolds had an Irish Rider competed so frequently and successfully on English tracks. His

B. J. Donnelly. Harp C.C.

first appearance in England was in 1923 when he entered for 'The Rhodes' Gold Cup Race at Fallowfields and finished 2nd to 'Jack Sibbit' in Manchester. He always selected meetings where the competition was hot. Another favourite venue of his was Coventry where he won the 'Jack King' Cup twice and the 'John…..

The Jubilee Vase at Manchester and the 'Lewis' Cup in New Brighton and many others to name but a few of his successes. It was recorded that by 1930 he had won 490 prizes!! He retired in 1940.

In 1942 he came to Lurgan to visit Mr Patsy O'Connor who invited Harry to have tea with them.

Bertie invited Harry to call at his Pub in Sheriff Street the next time he was in Dublin, which he did 4 weeks later when competing in a race. He was warmly welcomed. Harry said he had never seen such a display of silverware! He kept the friendship up until Bertie's death. His son Sean was also a good rider. He was one year older than Harry.

ISABEL WOODS (extracted from Harry McCartney's Journal)

A cyclist who must not be left out

Billy Stewart, when asked to put on paper a few of his memories and to us a bit about his famous father **GEORGE STEWART,** apologised for not being able to write due to ill health. Not wishing to miss out on Billy's anecdotes and pieces of vital memory that so easily could be lost if not recorded, Isabel and I arranged to call with him. It was far from an easy interview, for Billy had so much to tell that by the time we reluctantly left, we realised we would need to have another session and possibly more, if we were to record even part of his very full cycling career. Not to mention his long service to the Commonwealth Games Council.

   During this first interview, Billy kept introducing side tracks and as they were all relevant, I have included them here and underlined the headings.

George Stewart (1893 to 1966) was Billy's father. He had been a very fine track rider and although Billy didn't give us a lot and then only little cameos that we could enlarge on by further investigation through the like of Harry McCartney's records. To put down on paper the snippets that we did glean at that first visit seems the best way to ensure their initial safety.

Cochrane trophy This prestigious cup was won outright by George Stewart and was given by Billy to Stanley Finlay for competition in the Ballymena Road Club in 1994. It was a very valuable cup.
At 42 years of age, George won the 1932 Northern Ireland 5 miles grass track championship. Danny Corr being runner up. George rode a Granby cycle.

The Granby had a double down tube. When the great Australian rider, Hubert Opperman came over to attempt some of the Irish place to place records he saw and coveted George's Granby and wanted to buy it!

While on the subject of famous and valuable trophies, Billy mentioned the huge Ulster Cup donated to the sport by Northern Ireland's governor, Lord Wakehurst, through the good offices of Portadown's Tommy Rainey. It was awarded for the 10 miles Championship on the short lived Portadown track and first won by Jim McQuaid, with Billy Stewart second. Billy won it the following year and Jim Maguire the third year.
Jack Johnston became the custodian of trophies for the Federation but no one seems to know where the cup is now. This in no way casts any reflection or questions on Jack's integrity. Another cup that I remember was the Sunday Dispatch Trophy for the Irish massed start championship. Incidentally it was involved in my introduction to Draught Guinness! Previously I had shunned the 'black stuff' having worries of what might be lurking dead or alive in this liquid that I could not see into! So different to the transparency of lagers and other such 'clear' beverages.

SHAFTO KERR (Receipt for Bicycle dated 14th April 1924)

Memorandum.

FROM

SHAFTO KERR,

Cycle Agent and Repairer.

REPAIRS TO ALL MAKES OF CYCLES EXECUTED PROMPTLY.

18 ULSTERDALE STREET,
CONNSWATER,

BELFAST, 14th April 1924

To George Stewart

66 My Ladys Road

	£	s	d
To 1. Granby Cycle Frame Double D. B.S.A. Fittings No 1327	6	5	0
" 1 Pair. B.S.A. Wheels double sprocket	2	14	0
" 1 Pair Constrictor No 3 Road Racing Tyres	2	14	6
" 1 Pair B.S.A. Pedals 3 3/4 inch		15	6
" 1 Renolds Roller Chain		11	6
Total	£13	0	6

Paid with thanks
14/4/24

S. Kerr

A cyclist who must not be left out

Another cup that I remember was the Sunday Dispatch Trophy for the Irish massed start championship. Incidentally it was involved in my introduction to Draught Guinness! Previously I had shunned the 'black stuff' having worries of what might be lurking dead or alive in this liquid that I could not see into! So different to the transparency of lagers and other such 'clear' beverages.

The Irish Massed start championships were held on a course just outside Dundalk and I had ridden down to act as one of the selectors of an Irish International team. The event was won by Shay Elliott. Officials, riders and supporters finished up in the Lorne Hotel, Clanbrassil Stret, Dundalk for our meal. Shay's father filled the Sunday Dispatch Trophy with Guinness. I nervously sipped it and low and behold, the road to Dundalk became my road to Damascus!

The Lorne Hotel, if its walls could talk would have many stories to tell.

Mrs. McIlduff, the owner was a kindly soul and many joint North/South Official meetings took place in the back room beyond the upstairs restaurant. These meetings were normally after a meal which usually commenced by us hungry riders clearing the piles of lovely brown bread which we buttered and sprinkled with sugar!

There was an annual inter club time trial held on the Newry to Dundalk via Omeath course between the Northern C.C. and perhaps it was the City of Dublin Wheelers (but I am open to correction)

Riders stayed overnight in the 'Lorne'. I recall hearing of stories where Mrs. McIlduff's sister or sister-in-law, would have been known to have 'skelped' with a tea towel, the bare legs of cyclists who should have been in bed rather than cavorting in a state of half undress through the Hotel's corridors. Billy mentioned the Holdsworth Cup, first won by Peter Brotherton. A 'Hill Special' frame comes to his mind, but I failed to note in what context. It now seems that the frame is in Billy's roof space. He recalled that it was all chromed and apart from the forks, overpainted. The fact is that if the paint got chipped, the chrome was revealed below, thus proving that it had been 'chromed' throughout.

Billy mentioned that Peter Brotherton built a Holdsworth frame and that he was the first rider 'to get' a Holdsworth.

The Highland Games were mentioned and Billy recalled that he loaned the great Australian rider, Russell Mockridge, a 'grass tub'. Russell had turned up with 'silks'. It took some persuasion to convince Mockridge that the 'grass tub' should go on the front and not the back!

Hector McKenzie competed against Billy and Mockridge, but I've still to get further data on this. Billy tells of Albert Ewart competing in Dublin's College Park meeting where the U.S.A. Olympic athletes were appearing. As De Valera was shaking hands with one of our riders 'Ewarty' said "Watch out, He's an Orangeman!"

Billy gave long and faithful years of service to the Commonwealth Games starting in 1958 as the Cycling representative on the Northern Ireland Commonwealth Games Council. His administrative talents and voluntary services were quickly recognised and he moved on to become a member of the Commonwealth Games Council, being replaced on its Northern Ireland Committee by Tommy Givan, followed by Billy Reilly, John Snodden, Dave Kane, Morris Foster and Steve Chivers.

In 2007 Billy was awarded with what he feels was his highest honour when the Commonwealth Games Council presented him with the 'Commonweath Sports Award' in association with Clydesdale Bank.

HUMILITY – EQUALITY – DESTINY
William 'Billy' Stewart
Lifetime achievement of the Year 2007

n.b. Other winners were the tennis player, Arthur Ash (posthumously) Nelson Mandella in 1999, Ben Johnston (I wonder did they take the trophy back from Ben Johnston?)
Billy was awarded the M.B.E. that year in the New Year's Honours list.

Billy Stewart and his sister

As I was about to leave Billy at the end of that second visit, he reminded me (and I admit to needing much and frequent reminding these days) about the Saturday he and I agreed to bring a couple of 'super sers' down to N.I.C.F. headquarters in Great Northern Street to heat the hall at what was probably an Annual General Meeting. After the meeting the heaters were carried out, gas bottles separated from the super sers, which we loaded into the car. One cylinder was forgotten about. Later that day half of the street was evacuated due to a Calor gas cylinder 'bomb' being left in the middle of the road! Thankfully it all ended peacefully. As I drove home from Billy's house after my visit, his tale of the gas bottle and the excitement it caused, for some reason or other it brought Billy Braithwaite into my mind. Many a meeting erupted, exploded or was brought to a chaotic halt, when this Maryland Wheeler's delegate came to his feet, to strongly make 'a point of order!'

A cyclist who must not be left out

Billy reminded us that Maryland Wheelers promoted two great track meetings at Wallace Park in the 1953 season which were a financial success. They were funded by none other than the late gentleman of Ulster Cycling, Tommy Givan.

I was only a novice to track racing and will never forget the exit of hundreds and hundreds of cyclists 'racing' back from Lisburn to Belfast in near dark after the events. Sprinting for every lamp post, end of tramlines, traffic lights – it was awe-inspiring, frightening, exhilarating – all at the same time! We filled our side of the road at 12.30 am. and maybe a bit more! No one could have stopped us on those nights!

My contribution with its frequent 'new' items being introduced by Billy has turned out to cover lots, but details little and I don't apologise for that. The Billy that I interviewed was so enthusiastic and anxious to leave nothing out, that I resisted the temptation to edit and 'ghost' write a smooth and polished article.
But, have I done enough to cover Billy and his father's careers?

It was Harry McCartney who provided the fuller picture of Billy Stewart's father, George. Harry described George Stewart as the *North's* equivalent to Bertie Donnelly. They both commenced their careers before World War I but George's suffered more interruptions.
However, he continued winning track championships well into the 1930's.
His principle rivals were: Jack McCartney, Northern C.C., 'Cubby' Gibson, Dundonald and J. Walker of the Belfast C.C.

In 1922, Stewart beat McCartney in the 2 mile Ulster championship. He was second to Walker in the 1923 Ulster championship 1 mile at Bangor and repeated his 1922 title win of the 2 mile at the R.U.C. sports.
At Gibson Park in 1928 he took the 25 mile Ulster title and the following year, 1929 he won the 10 mile championship at the Northern Ireland Athletic Association sports meeting, as well as coming 2nd in the 1 mile title event. But what of Billy's title wins?
In 1953 he took the 440 yards title as well as the Blue Riband 1000 yards.
In 1954, Leo Feeney came out on top in the 440, 880 and 1000 yards with Billy 2nd in the two shorter events. The silver going to him in that years Irish 880 yards and 1000 metres.
By 1955 Jimmy Darragh and Leo Feeney had pushed Billy back to 3rd place and Billy's career seemed to have eased off, perhaps due to his willingness to be involved in the administrative side of the sport.
He joined the track Committee in 1955 and was Executive Committee Member in 1956.
By the way – he was no mean Water Polo player!

A most treasured item in Billy Stewarts collection of memorabilia is a note book containing a beautifully written account of a trip to Killarney by rail and bicycle in 1895 - the work of his grandfather William John Stewart. The collection also contains a membership card of Belfast eastern C.C. and three old club badges from his grandfather's time (see page 365). This is my abridgement of granda Stewart's delightful travellogue.

George Stewart - 25 Mile Ulster Track Champion 1923.

"They left Belfast on the 7.00 am. train and arrived in Dublin, heading off for Kingstown (Dun Laoghaire). They *'were obliged to walk most of the way owing to the repair of the tram line'* On arrival at Kingstown, they had a walk along the Eastern pier of the harbour. Three of the Holyhead mail boats and H.S. Melampus were tied up and they enjoyed the fine view of Dublin Bay from the end of the Pier.

On the walk back to the town, they admired the conspicuous Royal Marine Hotel – so splendid a building overlooking the harbour. After dinner they set off for Bray and hence on to Enniskerry where they visited the Demesne of Lord Powerscourt. They were charged 6 pence at the entrance. They found the grounds beautiful and extensive. A visit to the famous waterfall made him note that the almost perpendicular fall *'had not a great body of water falling at the time of their visit, but during wet weather the volume of water is very much increased'* Next they *'directed their course'* for the Seven Churches of Glendalough. Dut to the road being rough and steep they had to walk, which gave them the opportunity of viewing the charming country with beautiful hills and valleys as far as the eye could see. Later the road ran alongside a moor from where they could see Little Sugar Loaf, a conical mountain devoid of vegetation

They rode on through the villages of Roundwood, Annamoe and Laragh, arriving at Glendalough about 7.00 pm. where they put up at Mrs. Kavanagh's. After a wash and tea they walked through the Cemetary, the Round Tower and noted its good preservation. The valley that they walked along was so narrow that the hills shut out the rays of the sun, giving the place a gloomy appearance. A number of ruined churches gave the valley its name. They returned down the other side of the valley and off to bed. (Even at to-days fast pace, they got in quite a lot in their first day!)

A cyclist who must not be left out

13th July 1895   *Up early and before breakfast took a walk on a road which looks down on another valley running parallel with that of the Seven Churches. This other valley had a scattering of white washed cottages and looked very pretty.*   George's companion said that one very wet night two years previously he and another friend had been given shelter and hospitality in one of these picturesque cottages. After Mrs. Kavanagh's breakfast they headed for Rathdrum, going through Laragh en route. They admired the mixture of mountain, woods and water that made up the scenery. After Rathdrum they rode to the Meeting of the Waters where the 'Avonmore' meets the 'Avonbeg' to flow along the Vale of Avoca. A tree was pointed out to them where Thomas Moore is said to have written his poem, *The Meeting of the Waters*, a celebration of the Vale of Avoca.

On to Wooden Bridge where they thought this the nicest part of the Vale. *'The road overlooks the river, the bright waters of which, flowing through the Vale bounded by hills, clothed with beautiful verdure presents a scene not to be forgotten soon'*

Through Aughrim for dinner at Tinahealy. Then on through Shillelagh, Clongall, Myshall (cup of tea) Fenagh (which they much admired) and on to Bagnalstown.

They had to contend with a head wind all day and opted to overnight at Bagnalstown.

14th July 1885 After breakfast they headed for Kilkenny (which but for the previous days headwind they had hoped to reach by their second night). It was 12 Irish miles distance and with the wind against them,. Their comments as they passed through Kilkenny was *'has a clean appearance with some good buildings'.* At Callan they stopped for some refreshments and then headed for Clonmel. They noted that *water is very scarce on this route and what there is is being bad'.* Dinner at Clonmel, they set off at 4.00 pm. for Clonheen but *'mistaking the way'* found themselves on the road to Cahir'. Too far to turn back so they continued on through Cahir admiring its fine Castle, before making for Clogheen where they thought of staying the night, but opted to push on the 16 Irish miles to Fermoy. They had the Knockmealdown Mountains on their left and in the distance, the Galty Mountains while between our intrepid travellers and the Galtees lay a beautiful, well cultivated plain. Grateful of the downhill run through Kilworth, they arrived in Fermoy about 9.00 pm. and put up for the night in the Blackwater View Hotel. A few Northern C.C. members had arrived just a little while before George on their ride up from Waterford. Tired, they washed, had tea and didn't bother to do the usual evening walk around the town.

15th July 1885 Off for Cork, 22 miles away. They relished the down hill run through Rathcormack, Watergrasshill, and Glanmire. They admired the scenery. The last couple of miles had the view so familiar to those of us who today, 104 years later enter Cork by the same route: The water on our left and those big houses high up on the right.

A place to stay was found, machines '*put past*' had dinner and off for a walk around the city. They admired Shandon church, famous for its chime of bells. They took a trip to Queenstown (Cobh as a friend of mine calls it) and time and space prevents me from giving in full, the pages that cover that visit. After tea they went out again and heard the sweet bells of Shandon and noted that '*they were sweeter toned and better played than the bells of St. Peters in Belfast*'.

It being the eve of the parliamentary election in Cork, there was a lot of stir in the streets, a very bitter feeling existing between the Parnellites and McCarthyites. As we did not belong to either faction we retired to our quarters for the night.

16th July 1885 Out of Cork by 9.00 am and off along the road for Blarney Castle. Road rough and dirty. At Blarney they passed the Mahony Brothers Tweed factory and at the entrance to the castle grounds they passed Sir George Colthurst, the owner, arriving at his ('pile') which dates from 1446. Names down in the visitors book, up the circular staircase, a quick kiss of the Blarney stone and saw the new castle, a modern building having a very fine appearance. Off to Macroom where they take in its castle, the property of Lord Bantry. After dinner in Macroom they headed through Inchigeelagh and Ballingeary to Gougane Barra, a fine mountain lake. (Our Diarist writes so beautifully of all the scenery and in such a simple yet colourful style and such detail that I hope someone someday will let PRONI or Linenhall Library, or even Cycling Ireland, or the C.T.C. have them for publication in full) By the time they reached Bantry Bay darkness had set in. It had started to rain and it was 10.00 pm. when they put up for the night in Glengariff.

17th July 1885 Off at 9.00 am. for Adrigole Waterfrall which was 12 miles away. The rain of last night continued and with capes, from the knees down we were soaked. The road was swimming with water, but a hard clean surface meant we had no slipping. We found the Fall to be veiled in thick haze and noted that when in full flood, this Fall is said to be unsurpassed in grandeur by any other Fall in the British Islands.

After dinner and drying shoes and stockings they we off for Kenmare. Rain off so the run was much enjoyed. Refreshements in Kenmare around 6.00 pm. and off again at 6.20 pm. for Killarney – 21 miles away. By 9.00 pm. we had arrived having covered 80 miles. A welcome bath and tea in Mrs. Johnston's Hotel and bed.

18th July 1885 10.00 am and off in a car (I assume a jaunting car) *shared with two Scottish visitors and up to the Gap of Dunloe. Saw Mangerton Mountain, the Magillicuddy Reeks and Carn Tual. Passed two houses from which the tenants had been evicted. Refreshments in the cottage of Kate Kearney, the present 1895 owner being a grand-daughter of the original Kate! Next a boat trip.* George's description so detailed and lovely that I would doubt if it has ever been surpassed by professional guide books, before or since. *Back to the Hotel, dinner at*

A cyclist who must not be left out

Gap of Dunloe. Saw Mangerton Mountain, the Magillicuddy Reeks and Carn Tual. Passed two houses from which the tenants had been evicted. Refreshments in the cottage of Kate Kearney, the present 1895 owner being a granddaughter of the original Kate! Next a boat trip. George's description so detailed and lovely that I would doubt if it has ever been surpassed by professional guide books, before or since. *Back to the Hotel, dinner at 7.00 pm. a quick stroll through the town and into bed!*

19th July 1885 *Early breakfast, but found the train had gone. Caught the next at 9.30 am. due in Dublin 5.09 pm. where we hoped to catch the Great Northern train for Belfast at 5.30 pm. At Thurles we had time for a drink and some sandwiches, repeated again at Portarlington. Arrival at Dublin 20 minutes later and then cycling to Amiens Street Station we found that the train for Belfast had gone, so, leaving our machines in the luggage office we got some tea and then walked along Sackville Street, returning to get the 7.30 pm. which got us into Belfast at 11.45 pm.*

A short summer holiday, 7 days but what a lot they covered and how much they enjoyed it is so evident in this lovely diary.

We enjoyed our holiday very much, we were very much indebted to the people we met on our way who were very courteous in directing us and giving us information about the various places we visited.

I wonder could we do that trip in 7 days today? I doubt it!

PETER WOODS

A well preserved I.C.A. membership card from 1896.

An interview with Mr. Robert McCann who was an authority on the early years of cycling

In 1953 Stanley Martin of Northern Cycling Club, who was later to become Cycling Correspondent of the Belfast Telegraph, spent an evening with Mr. Robert McCann J.P who had just passed his ninetieth year and he re-lived some of his memoirs of cycling before the start of the Century.

He was an active Timekeeper, Secretary of Woodvale Cycling Club, President of the Irish Cyclists Association and Delegate to the Union Cycliste Internationale.

Prior to 1900 – back to the dawn of the safety bicycle, to the days when there were no motorcars or motorcycles, no street lighting or on lamps required on bicycles after dark and before there was any electric trams. It was a privilege to listen to a description of the pioneer days of our sport.

BELFAST CYCLING CLUBS

In 1896 in Ulster, the number of cyclists affiliated to the ICA (Ulster Branch) was more than 3000. Here are the names of some of the thirty Belfast Clubs at that time:

PREMIER, CRUISERS (President, John Boyd Dunlop, Inventor of the pneumatic tyre) WOODVALE, YMCA, COMMERCIAL, BALLYMACARRETT (later to become Belfast Cycling Club), ORMEAU, EAGLE, OSBORNE, BLOOMFIELD, WEST END, TRINITY, SPENCER STREET (WITH WHOM THE FAMOUS Shafto Kerr commenced cycling), RICHMOND, IRISH ROAD CLUB, SOUTHSIDE, IVY, CLONARD, WILLOWFIELD, NORTHERN (no connection with the present Northern) CPA, ENFIELD, ULSTER, EASTERN, SHORE, YMCA, HIBERNIANS and RIC.

While outside the city, strong clubs operated in Ballyclare, Mossley, Ballymena, Balmoral, Newtownards, Lisburn, Carrickfergus and many other parts.

CYCLISTS FANCY DRESS PARADE

At a rally in 1898, Woodvale Cycling Club had 272 members present and Ivy also had over 200 in attendance. The occasion was in fact, a Cyclists Fancy Dress Parade through Belfast, commencing in Alexander Park. A number of Clubs constructed floats which were supported and propelled by four cycles (the bikes taking the place of lorry wheels, as it were) on which were mounted various tableaux. Woodvale's floats included one depicting the Empire, on which sat Britannia surrounded by the principal Colonial representatives and another supported by four tandems, which carried nothing less than a piano and a pierrot group of eight.

The parade which was watched by thousands, was sponsored by 'Ireland's Saturday Night' and took 421 minutes to pass and with members of the Harriers Clubs collecting along the route. £200 (some money in those days) was taken and presented to the Lifeboat Institution.

an interview with Mr. Robert McCann

RUPTURE IN THE ICA

A rupture within the ICA in the early 1890's almost divided Irish into two separate (North and South) bodies, although of course the Border hadn't been dreamt of then. And close on the settlement of this dispute came a period when all cyclists were banned from competition in England and Scotland. The trouble arose over two flying Irishmen, Charlie Reese and Bob Reynolds, who were sweeping the boards at the principal cross-channel sports meetings. The pair were accused of asking for appearance money at a South of England meeting and were immediately suspended by the English Governing Body (NCU)

A number of years elapsed before everything was finally settled and the two rider's suspensions were conveniently shelved and they later represented Ireland at the Empire Championships (which were held twice in Ulster – once at Ballynafeigh and once at the Oval, Glentoran's Ground)

HARRY REYNOLDS

The only proper hard track in Ireland in those days was at Ballymena. There is evidence of the opening meeting being held on 22nd June 1897. It was within the confines of the present Showground's area. Great meetings were held annually, the most lucrative being on 12th of July when riders came from all over Ireland.

Mr McCann personally timed a number of hour record attempts made by Harry Reynolds who won the World 1 Mile Championship and later became a professional.

One of those bids by Reynolds was made behind a motorcycle which machines were very much an unknown quantity and in appearance were strange contraptions indeed, festooned by wires and levers and suggestive of a mobile telephone exchange. The opinion of the spectators was that while there was no doubt of Reynold's ability to go flat out for an hour, it was improbable that 'the baste' wouldn't last that long! Every few laps, one wire or another snapped and Reynolds made fresh starts with long delays amounting to almost three hours before he finally got a full sixty minutes run behind the snorting and hissing machine to accomplish a new record.

The Summerfield Football Club commenced a match inside the track during Reynolds ride and many times he narrowly escaped being brought down by the ball.

The rider of the motorcycle that day was an English cycling champion called J. Benyon and shortly afterwards in 1906, he raced Reynolds in a 20 mile motorcycle paced match at the Oval in Belfast. Benyon won in 39 mins. 21 3/5 secs. which was, in fact, three minutes slower than Reynolds time for the same distance during his hour record ride in Ballymena. This was the first and the last purely professional race in Belfast. A £50 a side race between Reynolds and Fred Chinn, five times professional champion of England, was proposed later but it never materialised.

MEMORIES

Here are a couple of gems of stories McCann wrote for a magazine some years later. They are taken from it word for word.

THE PUNCTURE PROOF PATENT

As it will be readily understood, the 'puncture fiend' was the main trouble experienced by early riders of pneumatic tyres and, in the case of the old solution-on cover before the detachable one was introduced, repairing a puncture was a fearsome job. Often instead of tackling it, riders would take the train or walk home. Naturally there were many 'puncture-proof' devices but none of them proved effective.

The first I can remember was invented by a local man whose business was in Alfred Street. It consisted of a number of pieces of very thin spring steel which were made to overlap each other like the scales of a fish. It was not a success as the movement of these scales soon cut the inner tube and the remedy proved worse than the disease.

It happened that the Inventor got the idea protected in the Patents Office a few days before the heats of the Magowan Cup were to be run off, which I think was about the year 1895. The races were from Fortwilliam Park to Antrim and the YMCA, Cruisers, Eastern and Woodvale were the competing teams. Between officials, club mates, competitors and others interested in the races, there must have been 300 plus cyclists in Antrim after the finish.

The Inventor had driven down in an open carriage and, after the race, he entertained all and sundry in a right royal fashion and they in turn wished all success to the 'puncture proof' patent.

I had left home without waiting to take my tea and I had to be at the finishing point to help check in the teams placings and, as I felt somewhat 'peckish' I left Antrim with a club mate between ten and eleven o'clock as the jollification was in full swing and at a stage when food was entirely 'taboo'. We had only got as far as Templepatrick when I punctured and, as neither of us had a repair outfit, we had perforce to walk.

After having trudged along for almost an hour, we heard the most appalling clamour behind. In a short time, the cavalcade was abreast of us. At least 100 riders were in the party and, in the midst of the crowd, was the carriage into which about a dozen of the 'boys' had clambered before leaving Antrim. So intent were they all engaged in singing – or trying to sing - the remainder creating as much din to outdo the singers, that they swept past my companion and I 'like Arabs in the desert' and we had to paddle our own canoe.

Time marches on

Rab Collins of Belfast C C doing a lap of honour after winning the All Ireland 660 yars Roller Racing Championship. his time was 22.3 secs (60.53 mph).

While travelling about the roads today it is a welcome sight to see the numbers of club cyclists out training or on club runs. Cycling is now the most popular sport and past time and it receives lots of publicity at present due mainly to the Olympics, when Britain won the most Gold Medals and also the performances of British and Irish riders domiciled in European countries.

The sport has changed greatly with the improvements in frame designs and equipment. Also the accessories and the multi-coloured apparel etc. All of which must make competitive cycling very expensive to be involved in at any branch of the sport. For those who can remember the sport in the 1940's and 1950's they could not have imagined the revolution that has taken place in technology and the general management of the sport of which I concur. It got me thinking of all the changes and I could not help making comparisons between then and now. For instance the multi-coloured jerseys and helmets. The exception being track racing, when competitors wore their club colours and the helmet which were made of padded leather. I still possess one after all these years. The time trial competitors were compelled to wear dark colours and in earlier years the riders wore black tights and a black alpaca jacket which was an R.T.T.C. regulation, as competitors were supposed to be inconspicuous to the general traffic and public on the open highway.

Massed start races were held at the Belfast Water Works on the Antrim Road and Bangor Castle grounds or on other enclosed estates as the Law did not allow massed races on the public roads.

Prize values in club events were meagre which is understandable as the clubs did not have much money in the bank and riders that finished in the first three in a race were given vouchers. Prize values in Open TT's were one pound ten shillings for First, a pound for Second and ten shillings for Third. The vouchers were supposed to be redeemed in nominated cycle shops and stores to purchase cycle parts or goods to value of the vouchers. So if you were a fast rider you could lump all your vouchers together and trade them in for a decent article of your choice. Accepting cash was definitely not permitted and to do so one would be declared a professional. There was always ways and means of getting round the rule, but nobody made a fortune.

Regarding bicycle frames, many riders ordered them from English or Scottish manufacturers, who built them from your own personal measurements which you provided when ordering and the average price then was fifteen to eighteen pounds. The alternative was to order one from Geordie Stone in Cromac Square Belfast, who stove enamelled them and the colour was mainly black. Other frame builders were Thompson from Dromara who built the Star of Down, and the Gordon brothers of Hillsborough.

Today it is quite common to see cars with a couple of racing bikes mounted on the roof racks and some with portable brackets that are attached at the rear of the car to carry a bike to ferry competitors to events. A luxury that many riders in the past would have appreciated.

In 1954 the C.R.E. in Dublin had a presentation of awards for their members in the Archbishop Byrne Memorial Hall in Rathmines. It was on a Sunday night and their special guest was Reg Harris - for appearance only. They invited the N.I.C.F. to nominate a team of two men and two ladies to compete against a Southern team in a novelty challenge match on rollers during the proceedings on the night. The Federation selected Rab Smith and myself from the Belfast C.C. and the lady riders were Roselyn Rainey and Hetty Breen from the Windsor C.C. The late W.L. (Billy) Smyth who was a Northern CC delegate in the Federation was asked to hire a suitable vehicle for the team and he also volunteered to drive us to the venue in Dublin where we duly arrived at the location. The changing room was a minor room at the rear of the main hall where the presentation took place. Reg Harris was introduced to the audience and was acclaimed. The roller contest began afterwards and the N.I.C.F. team won all the events. We then retired to the minor room where a bar was set up with a table loaded with bottles and glasses. There was Reg enjoying a whiskey with other notable people enjoying themselves also. No one thought of asking us to have a drink with them! Rab Smith decided to go to the table and ask if we could have some refreshments. He returned with bottles of beer and glasses which was much appreciated, while Reg was still being regaled by his company.

We left Dublin about 10.30 pm. and arrived back in Belfast at 1.00 am. W.L. drove each of us to our homes. So it was 2.00 a.m. before I got to my bed and I was up again to go to work at 6.30 a.m. on Monday morning. The four of us received no reward whatsoever, except the two bottles of beer that Rab and I got.

I recall this episode to illustrate that no one received expenses or otherwise, that I know of, and so I will conclude this article by wishing the present cyclists the very best of luck and that they may achieve their ambitions.

RAB COLLINS   *Belfast C C*

Ladies Roller Competition with Hetty Breen in foreground.

Stage 1 of the 1986 Tour of Ulster leaves the Abbey Lodge Hotel, Downpatrick. Rider no.9 in the foreground is the late Jim Megarry who won the Northern Ireland Junior Road Championship in 1954. He was riding for Western C.C. which later moved to the N.C.A. To his right is Raphael Kimmage, younger brother of the ex pro and Tour de France rider Paul Kimmage, now a noted journalist and author. Beside Kimmage is Billy Kirk of Ards C.C., while 3 riders to Megarry's left is the great Dubliner, Shay O'Hanlon, four times winner of the Ras Tailteann. *Photograph by Mary Kirk.*

The Christmas Ten

*Ards Cycling Club's Christmas ten miles time trial was
initiated in 1979 at the suggestion
of Rab Dunn, Senior.*

It was intended only as a club event to work up an appetite for the Christmas dinner, but it developed an infectious spirit of its own which attracted visitors from surprisingly far-flung quarters. For example: Mickey Carroll from Maghera in South Derry, Ryan Connor from Ballymena and Tommy Burns and Patrick Morning from Donegal. The formula for the event was simple: No entry fee, but every rider brought a small prize nicely packaged in Christmas paper. These items were placed in a car boot. The riders then drew their prize out at random when their name, time and race placing was called out. After a few years a perpetual trophy was presented for the fastest man and a special prize for the best fancy dress, as people had spontaneously began to dress up. Costumes such as Santa Claus (a bit obvious!) Superman, Mickey Mouse, a brilliant Mr. Blobby by James McFarlane and many more added colour and humour to the occasion. One year a young rider came in full drag with suspenders and all. A lot of the guys fancied him! Hot whiskies became a feature, especially under the Chairmanship of Mike (the Bike) McConaghy.

On a couple of occasions, had I been breathalysed on the way home, I might have been found drunk in charge of my bike.

On Christmas Day 2005 the best costume prize went to Brendan McCartan of Pheonix C.C. for a superb witch outfit: pale green knitted dress, high wellington boots, a truly surreal witch hat and broom, all mounted on a great big ladies sit-up-and-beg bicycle – complete with skirt guard. As it turned out he started about 3 minutes in front of me. He could not go very fast as you might expect. I however, was giving it a bit of welly and was only showing a bit of tinsel wound through my crash hat. At the turn I could see I had gained a lot of time on the 'witch' so I continued to dig in with the hope of catching her before the finish. I could see her skirt billowing in the wind as I sped along the straight at the big stone. Finally I pulled up to her, gasping, almost on the finish line. As I overtook her I suddenly shouted "The spirit of Christmas passed".

BILLY KIRK

No, this is not a sign of Transvestism in Ards Cycling Club, but one of the Fancy Dress winners in the Christmas '10' showing his appreciation of fastest man Michael Carroll, Bann Valley Road Club, South Derry, who timed at 23 mins. 56 secs. in terrible weather.

Left to right: Mr Blobby, James McFarlane Lindsay Gamble No.1 Drag Queen, Bobby Magreechan, Michael Carroll, Russell Moreland No.2 Drag Queen and Daniel Trimble. 4th left wishes to remain anonymous! Happy New Year from Ards Cycling Club!

A Dublin expedition

The Chemico Cup 25 miles time trial was regarded as Ireland's Blue Riband T.T. event in the 1950's and 1960's.

The opening event of the Dun Laoghaire Cycling week drew entries from all of Ireland and Great Britain to compete on the Navan Road, famed as the course where Alo Donegan of the Swift Cycle Club, Portarlington, Co. Laois, became the first person to break the hour for 25 miles.

He clocked 59 mins. 05 secs. on 30th September 1934 to the barely concealed scepticism of the British Cycling press – who were made to eat their words a year later when Donegan went to Manchester and beat all the best English 25 milers of the day. However, Donegan's feat on the Navan Road ensured its reputation as the place to go for personal bests. Apparently its secret was high dense hedges and lack of big hills.

Chemico, the Dublin makers of (believe it or not) puncture outfits, presented the trophy to the County Dublin R.C., promoters of the Cycling week. Cycling Magazine of July 1954 reported that Stan Higginson of Halesowen A and C.C. won the cup that year with a time of 56 mins. 21 secs. – 8 seconds faster than the British record of the time. His twin brother Bernard was 2nd and their club won the team prize, also in Irish record time. I was present, but not competing in 1955 when our local champion Billy Dowds from Lurgan and Cookstown's Tommy Talbot relegated an off form Higginson to 3rd place. Their times were 60 mins 19 secs., 60 mins. 20 secs, and 60 mins. 23 secs.

1956 was my second season of Open racing. I had become Irish Champion at 25 and 100 miles that year, the latter having been two weeks prior to the Chemico Cup. I therefore thought the time was right to make my own challenge for the trophy. So, having pre-entered by post, my girlfriend Mary and I boarded the Dublin express train on the fresh and beautiful morning of 14th July 1956. We had cycled to the railway station from Newtownards that morning and were intent on riding home from Dublin on Sunday after the race.

This was my first railway journey as an adult. It has always retained a special magic in my memory. I found myself comparing it with train rides with my Grandmother Kirk during my mother's long illness and realising how dark that period of my life had been. Often, but more so on overcast winter days, lakes at the edge of the tracks intimidated and depressed me. They seemed to echo the pictures of highland cattle submerged almost to their underbelly, seemingly always present in railway carriages of that time.

On the Dublin train, however, although leaving or entering cities or towns still gave me a feeling of the futility of everything with their endless decrepit backyards steeped in lonliness, the train soon found pastoral scenes with sheep, cattle and horses, sylvan glades, glistening waving crops of wheat, barley and corn, farmers walking behind ploughs or more often driving in front, stooping potato pickers and the odd cart horse marking time as we sped past.

Our bikes, saddle bags packed were still safe in their carriage when we arrived at Amiens Street Station. We unloaded, wheeled them out of the station and set off up Talbot and O'Connell Streets to Parnell Square and Frederick Street where we booked into the great white stone faced Anchor Hotel.

Here we found supreme comfort and a great breakfast into the bargain; hopefully to the benefit of my effort on Sunday. At tea time we found a nice restaurant on O'Connell Street. On our way back to the Hotel I had the uncommon and pleasant feeling that I could relax and breathe more easily in this city. Wondering if this was simply imagination I asked Mary about it. "Yes", she agreed, "there is a nice atmosphere here".

This impression remained with me on every visit to Dublin, possibly becoming more noticeable after 1969 with the coming of the Troubles. Strangely I cannot say I felt it in other places such as Balbriggan or Drogheda. Its cause I cannot begin to fathom, but I could conjecture that if the people are contented and easy going, like they say Dubliners are (or were?) then perhaps it is 'in the air'.

Our route to the start at the village of Ashtown had already been traced by myself in May on the weekend of the Irish 25 Championship. This had been on the directions of the owner of Rutland Cycles whose shop stood on the corner of Denmark Street and Rutland Place. The shop sold all the best racing equipment and was only a short distance from the Anchor Hotel. "Blessington and Berkeley Streets, North Circular and Cabra Roads will lead you to the Navan Road", is clear in my memory. They brought Mary and I to a hive of excitement and nervous expectation which was Ashtown on the morning of the Chemico Cup, 15th July 1956. The place was buzzing with cyclists removing and unpacking saddle bags (in a few cases – car boots) removing mudguards, exchanging heavy wheels for sprints and tubs and changing into silk or woollen racing jerseys and shorts. They were rubbing their legs with everything from Elliman's Athletic rub to Olive Oil and Wintergreen, the acrid smell of which gave dressing rooms everywhere their unique aroma. 'Dressing Room' is perhaps a grandiose term for facilities offered in that time – the Ashtown dressing room was a disused double decker bus.

163 Entries had been received, but only 85 started. They were listed on the large start/result board which was surrounded by excited riders anxious to know their start time and whether they could get time checks against rivals. The main contenders were: myself, who as Irish Champion, was favourite, Tommy Talbot of East Tyrone C.C., Con Enright of County Dublin R.C., Jimmy McGinty of Glasgow Regent C.C. and John Lackey of Tailteann R.C. Dublin.

The start line at Ashtown was adjacent to the western end of Phoenix Park on the left. The road ran parallel to the Royal Canal for two miles on its right, crossing the waterway over a hump backed bridge at Blanchardstown village. Then followed Mulhuddart and Clonee - again almost exactly two miles apart, with Black Bull the odd man out at three miles. After which it was four miles to the turn near Dunshaughlin. These villages could have given an experienced local rider with a handlebar watch a guide to whether he was going well, but competitors such as myself, Talbot and McGinty would only have the 12 ½ mile turn as an indication.

a Dublin expedition

As the lone Ards traveller I had no one to give me time checks on the road. I could not expect Mary to do this complicated task.

My warm up was as much a mental as a physical process. I pedalled along in a low gear, breathing to a tempo of 4 revs in, 4 revs out. This suppressed 'butterflies in the stomach' a symptom of anxiety and fear of the effort. Within a few minutes of my start time I stopped and changed my wheel round to the 15 tooth sprocket which gave me a gear of 82.8 inches. In this matter most of us were behind the times. The great Billy Dowds had understood that a ratio such as 46 x 14 – 88 inches – was better for high speed cycling. Only recently when studying the diary of Alo Donegan did I discover that he also used 88 inches to become the first person to go 'under the hour' in 1934.

I started fast in those days, believing if I didn't I would not reach high speed later. This goes against the current wisdom of accelerating gradually over the first two miles. I reached Blanchardstown gasping for air, yet by Mulhuddart I had my 'second wind' (a term used in those days for getting your breath back) and settled into a fast pedalling rythym. I met Con Enright at one point but cannot remember whether he was in front of or behind me on the course, but he seemed to be 'flying'. All I could do was maintain concentration and hope for the best. I used various aids such as trying to catch my 'minute man' quickly or simply thinking about passing kerbstones or hedge rows rapidly. It was said of Billy Dowds that he could meet an opponent on the road (whose start number he knew) quickly glance at his watch and when reaching the turn be able to judge if he was faster than the other man. People said he was like a computer!

I reached Dunshaughlin without faltering. I clenched my teeth and pushed hard away from the dead turn and was soon speeding half way back to Black Bull, when the thought came to me that Enright, Talbot and McGinty would have to be going very well to beat me. I had fallen into a lovely rhythm in which I was breathing easily and just floating along. Almost like a trance. Through Clonee I kept the sweet spot going but approaching Mulhuddart with 5 miles left I knew I had to raise the tempo. I was soon gasping again but going very fast through Blanchardstown and over the bridge towards the finish with sweat stinging my eyes. I remembered Dowds saying he liked to keep something for the last mile and wondered had I anything left. However I sped into the final mile as best I could crossing the gently uphill finish to enter that strange no mans land which is unique to bicycle time trials; where a contender may have to wait for a long time before success or failure is confirmed. As it turned out on this occasion I knew within 15 minutes I had beaten Con Enright by 11 seconds to take the trophy. My time was 59 mins. 31 secs. to Entrights 59 mins. 42 secs, with Tommy Talbot 3rd in 60 mins 4 secs and McGinty 4th with 60 mins 27 secs. A notable tie occurred for 8th place. Peter Crinnion of Bray Wheelers and Jim Maguire of Windsor C.C. Belfast. Crinnion would later surpass us all. He won the Route de France (Amateur version of the Tour) in the early Sixties. He much later became manager of Continental Pro teams in the late 1980's. Jim Maguire became Irish Road Race Champion in 1959.

I was treated graciously by the Dubliners, especially the Organisers, despite having beaten the local hero. In fact I felt a little pang of guilt, so generous and sporting had been Enright's response to my win.

The crowd at the finish contained many non-racers; visitors from the North rarely saw such gatherings. Many took an interest in my cream Holdsworth bicycle. I noticed a tall dark man of almost gypsy appearance in the crowd. He had dark oily hair, a brown suit so greasy it shone and wore bicycle clips on his trousers. Firmly grasping the handlebars of his high ordinary bicycle and fixing me with wild dark eyes, he said: "Oi don't know hayo you sit so hoigh and ride so haaard". This astonishing and unforgettable man, straight out of the pages of Flann O'Brien, had observed that I did not crouch low and was therefore not aerodynamic. He was anticipating the modern concern with technology which would enter sport in later years. Fifteen years would pass before Len Hiller, physio/trainer of Linfield Football Club, found the reason for my lower back inflexibility. By means of two simple exercises he cured what he called sacra-iliac strain. The result was I could ride in a streamlined position for the first time in my life, but I was then aged 34 and my best years were past.

The prize presentation was very exciting for Mary and me! We had noticed a beautiful chiming clock among the prizes on display and reckoned it might be for first place. This proved to be true, but it gave us the problem of finding space to carry it. The Chemico Cup was not travelling as it had to be engraved. Many items were transferred to Mary's bag until finally we were just able to squeeze the clock into my larger bag.

When all the excitement was over and I had turned my wheel round to the 18 sprocket and fitted my mudguards, Mary and I set off for Drumcondra via Phibsborough where we found a nice restaurant near the Tolka River bridge. It was on the corner of Botanic Avenue. There was an almost continental atmosphere and we savoured more of that nice easy feeling. We ate well to ensure energy for the long ride home, leaving Dublin with a light southerly breeze behind us.

A steady 15 m.p.h. took us through Santry and Swords and on to Balbriggan. Then it was up the 'Washboard' hill, so called because it was deeply ridged concrete which made the clock tinkle away to itself in my saddle bag. After that it was all pleasure until we swooped down into Drogheda for coffee and scones. Next stop was Dundalk for a meal at 5.00 p.m. during which I watched my bike like a hawk, thinking about the clock.

By this time we were both getting tired, but luckily the tailwind persisted. It saved the day for us. The draggy, heavy road out of Dundalk to the Killeen Custom Post was overcome.   We pulled in to declare the clock. Possessing documentation from Co. Dublin Road Club, I was confident there would be no problems. But to my shock, the Customs Officers, dressed almost like sea captains, refused to accept the paperwork and my prize was impounded. No discussion or appeal permitted! Mary and I left Killeen with a sinking feeling in our stomach. It made the rest of the journey seem more difficult, although it did not prevent us enjoying the downhill to Newry.

Some of the long stretches to Loughbrickland, Banbridge and Hillsborough can be boring at the best of times, but with fatigue and the loss of the clock it was even worse that day. We were reminded of the absence of the clock by the lack of the sound of the strikers hitting as I rode over bumps and potholes, as these little sounds had followed us all the way from Ashtown to Killeen. However, we had a sense of achievement when we reached Carryduff a little before 9.00 p.m. although it was turning surprisingly cold for July.

After many brief stops to rub bare legs and hands we arrived in Comber at 10.00 p.m. - extremely cold and hungry, the chiming clock now forgotten! Funds were low but we searched our pockets and found a total of one shilling, enough for one fish with the usual small handful of chips thrown in. To avoid the embarrassment of our poverty, (we could not afford cups of tea) we took the newspaper wrapped fish up the square a bit and divided it between us. A feast fit for a king! Only trouble was Mary later accused me of taking the bigger half of the divided meal. The four miles home was a doddle. We went straight to our separate homes, had tea, bread and jam and fell straight into bed. However I had first to report fully to my Grandmother, with whom I lived at the time, the results of my expedition.

Charlie Henderson, the Ards Club Secretary spoke to the Northern Ireland Cycling Federation about my loss. They in turn took the matter up with G.B.H. Currie, local Unionist M.P. at Westminster who raised it in the House at his first opportunity. About six weeks later I had the satisfaction of calling at the Custom House in Belfast to collect the now famous clock, the whole episode had been reported in the Belfast Telegraph, The Newsletter and the Northern Whig. A sad little postscript is that Mary and I used the clock in our home when we were later married. After some time it became faulty and I pondered on the bumping it received on the rocky road from Dublin. It was placed with a local jeweller for repair but because we inherited another clock from my Grandmother, it was forgotten. When we belatedly went back to inquire we were told the storeroom of un-collected items had been cleared out.

BILLY KIRK

Post Script

In late 2009, worried that my description of the dark eyed spectator at the finish of the 1956 Chemico cup might offend relatives, I rang Con Enright to ask his opinion. A few weeks later he rang me back to say it was alright to go ahead as written. However, I was astonished when he told me the man's name: Johnny Kindillon from Ballymun. Contrary to my opinion he had been a member of City of Dublin Wheelers and raced in the 1930's – the large ordinary bike had put me off the scent!
Con then told me of the long serving committee of the Dun Laoghaire cycling week whose chairman was Bill Slieth. Treasurer was John O'Brien with Nan Lyons Secretary and Robbie O'Connor, Assistant Secretary.

CUSTOMS RELEASE CLOCK

Ards cyclist's prize won at Eire race

When William Kirk, a member of Ards Cycling Club, won a cycle race in Eire last month his prize, a clock, was seized by Customs officers at the Border as he was returning home. His club made representations to the Northern Ireland Cycling Federation and also to Mr. G. B. H. Currie, M.P. for North Down at Westminster.

Mr. Currie took the matter up with the Commissioners of Customs and Excise and has now received a letter from Treasury House, London, stating that directions had now been given for the clock to be released.

In the letter it was stated that under a section of the 1952 Customs and Excise Act no duty was chargeable on articles which were shown to the satisfaction of the Commissioners to have been awarded to a person for distinction in sport or as a record of meritorious achievement. Whether a prize for a sporting event fell within this category depended on the status of the event.

The information that Kirk gave when he arrived at the Border with the clock was not sufficient to enable the Customs officer to admit it under this provision and that was why the clock had been detained.

Billy Kirk
Craigantlet Hill Climb 1956

Treasured bicycles

In 1953 myself and some friends, namely Bobby Watterson, Robert Chambers and a few others went to Gordon Brothers in Hillsborough to order our bicycles.

These were hand made to suit the individual rider and we were very excited at the prospects of taking delivery of these bicycles.

Tommy and Billy Gordon were making around five bicycles each week so we did not have to wait too long. I purchased a road bike and a track bike. They cost me £14.19s. each. That was for frames and forks.

We belonged to the Courier C.C. This club had been formed by the Gordon Brothers, was around for many years and had notable successes. They met in the Church Hall beside Elmwood's the Undertakers in Dunmurry. Our favourite runs at the weekends and on clear summer evenings was around Spelga and Newcastle.
Also in that year the new Cycle Track in Wallace Park was under construction.

The original one was a cinder track and the new track was tarmac - athough many cyclists preferred the cinder one. Reg Harris was invited over for the opening of the Track and I had the pleasure of competing with a World Champion! Arie Van Vliet the Dutchman also rode at Wallace Park. It was a first class venue for cycling and many events were held at the Wallace Park. Spectators loved it and the park would have been buzzing on a summer evening, all gathering to watch the cycling.

We rode a 25 mile T.T. on the Antrim Road, meeting at the Crown and Shamrock.
I wasn't outstanding, but I enjoyed the racing.

Tommy Taylor was the Time Keeper and later in life our paths were again to cross. I was working in Fuel Services and Tommy was employed by the parent Company who was John Hogg and Co. Later I sold my road bike to Raymond Boyd of Lisburn. I kept my Track bike and in July 2009 I gave it over to the original maker Billy Gordon for restoration.

There was a great camaraderie among cyclists in the 50's and 60's and quite often I sit and reflect on all the riders I met over those years.

WILLIAM DOWLING Courier R.C.

Wallace Park cycle track

Many Cyclists who have written stories in this book recall the excellent cycle track in Wallace Park, Lisburn. This is indeed a lovely Park. It was donated to the people of Lisburn by Sir Richard Wallace and I thought you would be interested to hear how the cycle track looks today. Time inevitably brings changes and once the young men of the Sixties could afford to buy cars instead of bicycles, the track became under-used and within a short time it soon fell into disrepair.

Some fifteen years ago the adjoining Cricket Club were seeking additional ground, so a chunk of the cycle track was given over to them.

A children's play area flanks the other side of the cycle track. This 'state of the art' play was completely re-vamped at a cost of a mere £750,000 and was opened on 10th July 2010. It will be interesting to see if another chunk of the cycle track is taken away at some future date.

Perhaps the only encouraging news is that a Soccer Pitch is in the centre of the track. The grass looks very healthy, the turf in the goal mouths in perfect condition – all indicating a pitch that is very under played. Nevertheless it's there - a green space in the hollow of that famous cycling track which holds so many great memories for past cyclists.

MAY FARRAR

Reg Harris at Wallace Park, 1953

How the running track looks today

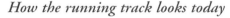

Photo courtesy of Barry Sewell

The first Belfast to Dublin race

This race was held in 1949. It started at Finaghy traffic lights and finished at Whitehouse Traffic lights in Dublin. The race was won by Karl McCarthy from Cork. Sponsors of the race were the Irish Press. Joe Graham of Western C.C. rode an 82 inch fixed gear.

There were other riders from Dundalk and Dublin and the two Gordon brothers from Hillsborough. McCarthy broke away about Swords to win. I cannot recall the other placings.

Belfast, Dublin, Belfast was run in 1950. McCarthy won again. I was second and Cecil Reilly was third. We three broke away before Drogheda, but despite attacking Karl on every hill we could not shake him off. At that time, apart from Jim McQuaid and Shay Elliot, he was the only International Class rider in Ireland. He later broke the 100 mile T.T. record on several occasions. He nearly died after crashing in Belgium.

TEDDY HAWKINS

The names of the three Officials back right of the photograph: Lurgan, Time Keeper Pat McAllister (Western C.C. Belfast) the Organiser Johnny Donaldson, Time Keeper. Riders from the right as you look at this photo: Mick Cahill (Harp C.C.) Karl McCarthy (Cork C.C.) Matt Sands (Western C.C.) Teddy Hawkins (Western C.C.) Herbie Holden, Tommy Moore, Joe Graham. Charlie Copeland, Brian O'Neill, don't know next rider, all Western C.C.

An Ulster Scots tale

It was Jackie Wilson who came up with the suggestion, in late summer 1955, for a trip to Scotland to ride a 25 mile time trial.

Excited by the fact that I had clocked exactly 60 mins. for 25 miles on the Portaferry Road, and that a few others were not far behind, he thought we might win the team, if not the individual prize.

Inquiries revealed an annual event on the Sunday morning of the Engineers long weekend in early September. It was a "25" on a Clydeside course promoted by Glasgow Regent C.C. on 11th September. Our contact in Glasgow was the cycle dealer Tom McGuinness who had a shop in Whitehill Street on the edge of the Gorbals. He had been a good cyclist but was now retired from racing. A great friend of the very popular Billy Sands of Windsor C.C. (Uncle of Bobby Sands, incidentally) Both Sands and he had ridden private time trials in Ards club races, when McGuinness was on holiday in Northern Ireland.

We sailed on the Belfast-Govan ferry on Friday night docking on Saturday morning after breakfast on the boat. We had to face a laborious journey across the city with more than the usual gear stuffed into our bags. Our group of four were: Wilson, Don Barbour and myself from Newtownards, all aircraft workers in Short Brothers and Harlands, and Ian Croft from Bangor, a joiner by trade.

Tom McGuinness found us a nice guest house in Paisley near the Inchinnan course which followed the north side fo the Clyde out towards Dumbarton, over which he drove us, by way of a recounoitre, in his luxury Wolseley 680 on Saturday evening.

Heavy rain fell early on the morning of the race, but it dried out later, providing the back ground to one of the memorable episodes of the weekend. A father and son, both named J. Harvey and member of Glasgow's Ivy C.C. were entered for the event. Just as we arrived in the start area angry shouts and curse words spoken in a broad Govan accent drew our attention to the two men, one old and white haired, the other in his thirties, who were having a quite serious disagreement. It turned out the son had risen early, saw the torrential rain and went back to bed. Later the father got up, saw his son was back in bed and, as the weather had improved, took his son's special racing wheels to the race. Finally young Harvey rose and saw the rain had ceased. He realised he could just make it to the start on time, but was shocked to find his good wheels were missing. Although it was a serious row, somehow it seemed good natured and we all had a quiet and appreciative laugh. It heightened my own appreciation of the sport.

In the time trial I was beaten by Jim Hay of Nightingale C.C. who clocked 60 mins. 48 secs. to my 61 mins. 29 secs. Jackie Wilson's hopes for the team prize were realised. We beat the Nightingale trio by just 19 seconds. Jackie Wilson was 6th in 63 mins. 26 secs. – a tie with another Northern Ireland visitor we had not expected to see there – Gerry McCann of Maryland Wheelers. Ian Croft was 9th in 63 mins. 41 secs. and Don Barbour was 11th with 65 mins. 09 secs. After the prize presentation we returned to the guest house for a wash and meal and then set off for a tour of the scenic Trossachs area. Just as dusk was descending we booked into a Youth Hostel.

The following morning, well rested, we retraced our wheel tracks to Glasgow, just in time for the ferry, on which we experienced a rough crossing to Belfast.

On Tuesday evening we called to see our club Secretary, Charlie Henderson who was over the moon about our achievements After a long chat, many congratulations and tea and buns made by his wife Dorothy, he set about writing his report for the Newtownards Chronicle.

In 1957 Charlie urged us to make a second trip to Glasgow for the same Trade Union weekend.

His hopes were based not only on my National championship wins at 25 and 100 miles in 1956 and my Northern Ireland 25 Record of 58 mins. 28 secs. – set within a fortnight of the first Glasgow trip, but also on the fact that new member John Fennell was reigning Irish and Northern Ireland 25 mile champion.

The stories about the 1955 excursion had been told and re-told, so there was great interest in the proposed 1957 trip. Seven people signed up: John Fennell from Holywood, the brothers Jackie (now John) and George Wilson, George Fitzsimmons, Tom Williams, Don Curry and myself. Although we wrote to Tom McGuinness to get entered for the T.T. we were helped on this occasion by the Scottish International rider Ernie Scally who rode with us all over the Govan area in search of accommodation, also showing us the sights. One of these was the infamous Locarno dancehall which was often the scene of fights among Teddy Boys using bicycle chains, dunchers lined with razor blades and other vicious implements.

Scally finally found us a bed and breakfast in the Broomilaw area of Clydeside. It was in a tenement building in Brown Street whose landlady usually catered for long distance lorry drivers during the week but often had vacancies at weekends. She welcomed the business with the Ards bike racers. We were all crammed into a single small room – one of us sleeping in a hole-in-the-wall while others were on collapsibles brought out of storage. This bedroom was the scene for a great, hilarious happening.

Jackie Wilson was one of these people who fall asleep as soon as their head hits the pillow. Don Curry noticed that Wilson was indeed fast asleep. He suggested we all pretend to be getting up and called on Jackie to "Get up, its breakfast time". After a couple of minutes of moaning, Wilson said "Oh, I will never race today. I feel like I've been sleeping ten minutes". He rose and pulled back the curtains (there was only one tiny window) and it must have looked like early morning. The other thing about Wilson was he was very short-sighted. Without wearing his glasses he did not notice that we were all back in bed. He had reached the stage of pulling on the big hand knitted roll-neck jersey when he shouted "What are you'se guys doing in bed?" When he realised what was happening his language was not appropriate for someone who would eventually become a Presbyterian Minister in Seattle, U.S.A. After that everything was anti-climax, even though we performed well in the time trial and there were other little merriments. In the event, again promoted by Glasgow Regent C.C. I, with the Scottish name Kirk, was beaten by a Scot with an Irish name: Jimmy McGinty returned 60 mins. 27 secs. to my 60 mins. 52 secs. with John Fennell 4th in 61 mins. 12 secs. Wilson, despite the trauma of the previous evening was 8th in 62 mins. 28 secs. We won the team prize by a much larger margin than last time.

The course was known as West Ferry and took the south side of the Clyde out through Gourock towards Dunoon. At one point on the route we had to negotiate a roundabout in Gourock and then proceed to the 12 ½ mile turn. One of our riders, a barber called George Fitzsimmons actually turned at the roundabout and came in with a very fast time, whereupon, after his error was discovered we called him 'The silly roundabout kid'.

An afterthought to this is that one of the characters in the book 'The Children of the Dead End' by Donegal writer, Patrick MacGill was 'Gourock Ellen'. MacGill's theme, writing in the early 1900's was the troubled and arduous life of the Donegal folk who had to travel to Scotland to find work. We also must remind ourselves of the Ulster Plantation to see how the Kirk – McGinty thing came about.

It is ironic that in his day, Patrick MacGill was ex-communicated from the Catholic church for his anti-clerical and socialist ideas – yet now he is a hero of Glenties and Donegal and much farther afield.

BILLY KIRK

Message From Rev. John

From the plains of the USA I want to send my greetings and congratulations on the publishing of so many and such various cycling stories in the North of Ireland.

In particular, I want to congratulate my former team mate and friend of so many years, Bill Kirk. It was through him I learned the ideas of sportsmanship and discipline that must be practiced in order to gain success. I am proud to call him and his wonderful wife Mary, my friends.

Remember always: FAITH sees the invisible
                       believes the incredible
                       and receives the impossible!

Rev. John K. Wilson, Pastor First Presbyterian Church, Kamrar Iowa USA

The Camino

Ronnie Millar on
The Memorable Trip

It was dark when we disembarked from the plane at Bilbao so after straightening Liza's rear gear changer, we cycled only a short distance before camping at the roadside. The lights from the industrial town were a pretty sight in the valley below. I had more miles in my legs than Liza – but she had greater spiritual preparation for our journey. The Camino is the route followed by pilgrims since the supposed bones of St. James were unearthed over a millennium ago, at what is now Santiago de Compostela. We had a fairly tough ride up from the coast to join in at Burgos. Actually it is not one route but several. Almost all originated in, or passed through, France. Although we were joining the most followed route, the one known as the Camino Frances, it is perhaps neither the shortest nor the easiest. A very mixed bag of roads and tracks. Liza had the more informed interest in matters theological/architectural. Mine was more influenced by the old desire to 'get the miles in' but what memories remain are mainly of the fellow travellers we encountered. There was a guy from Madrid who had just completed a one hundred kilometre event – running! Of course he was walking (approved) – covering as far each day as we were on the bikes (permitted) And the charming young German (?) Architect whom I suspected of taking the odd lift. Mostly we camped or used the 'refugios' but, at Leon we treated ourselves to a stay at the five star Parodor. Very impressed at the respectful manner in which our bikes were wheeled in. Mine with underwear hanging from the saddlebag to dry!

The Camino Certificate

At 8.00 pm on 25th July 1988 (St. James' Day) we met our friend Janine and her young son Bjorn on the steps of the cathedral in Santiago, as arranged. Terry Day travelled by the coastal route (risking death by lorry on that busy road). It's remarkable how, considering all the people and places in the world, things so often work out.

P.S. The scallop shell hanging from my saddlebag is traditionally carried by the Santiago pilgrim.
Perhaps I was a bit of a poser – perhaps not.
PPS for those interested, one of the many Web sites: www.santiago-compostela.net/france

RONNIE MILLAR

CAPITULUM hujus Almae Apostolicae et Metropolitanae Ecclesiae Compostellanae sigilli Altaris Beati Jacobi Apostoli custos, ut omnibus Fidelibus et Peregrinis ex toto terrarum Orbe, devotionis affectu vel voti causa, ad limina Apostoli Nostri Hispaniarum Patroni ac Tutelaris **SANCTI JACOBI** convenientibus, authenticas visitationis litteras expediat, omnibus et singulis praesentes inspecturis, notum facio: *Dnum Liza Burrowes*
hoc sacratissimum Templum pietatis causa devote visitasse. In quorum fidem praesentes litteras, sigilo ejusdem Sanctae Ecclesiae munitas, ei confero.
Datum Compostellae die **25** mensis *Julii* anno Dni *1988*.

Secretarius Capitularis

Buddy can you spare a dime?

An extract taken from THE HUB

(Magazine of Belfast Cycling Club) Dated: June 1954

Those of us who have inspected the new club-rooms are surprised at the spacious accommodation.

The rent is reasonable and I learn that a number of members have volunteered to meet this expense by a weekly subscription. That is the spirit of sport, the rest of us will have to help in the matter of fixing it up as a comfortable club-room. Partitions will have to be made at each end so that we may have a committee room and cloak room. We should also like to have a kitchen and tea bar.

The club members in general could help by providing a cup, saucer and plate and perhaps a milk jug, sugar bowl, knife, fork and spoon. Between the partitions there will be a space of 50 feet by 22 feet and a business friend of mine is prepared to supply linoleum at whatever price the manufacturers charge him. We have had a very generous offer which was accepted and that was a hundred weight drum of paint, and also quite a number of rolls of wallpaper.

These at the moment are being used in the decoration of the hall. Another big item is stocking the club-room with furniture, such as forms and tables, which are necessary for social functions. So any ideas for raising money to this end will be duly considered. The easiest method as I can see for making money is to enlist fifty volunteers who are willing to subscribe one shilling per week for one year, which would realise a sum of app. 125 pounds and this would go a long way to cover the cost of all our needs and thus provide us with a first class club room. So let us work together for the next twelve months and see if we could achieve our aim.

Yours in sport
STAR OF DOWN
SAMMY NEILL, BELFAST CC

Pure Poetry

*The Belfast Cycling Club had acquired new club rooms at Beersbridge Road in Belfast.
Previously they had met in a large room above Jimmy McCoo's cycle shop at the railway bridge,
Ormeau Road. The new premises needed a lot of major work done to it to make it habitable and
strenuous efforts were made by many of our members to achieve this. Bill Murray penned this poem
on work in progress on the new hall*

OUR HALL

We may think of the halls of Valhalla
Those mythical lofty domains
Or perchance a magnificent gala
Where only the rich entertains
But permit me to tell you a story
Of loyalty, courage and grit
That went hand in hand with the building
Of the Hall where the Club now sits.

The picture at first was depressing
An air of neglect we beheld
There was little by which to encourage
Our lavish schemes were almost quelled
But our Sec. was not lacking in courage
And the Skipper was not far behind
They set an example of stern resolve
That naught but achievement can bind.

We wielded the pick and the shovel
We frolicked in dust and in grime
And slowly but surely we saw it
Our progress beginning to climb
But old Sam the Gaffer was ruthless
He wanted the job hurried on
So he bawled out the cause of the trouble
The lazy squad Maurice and John.

He loaded up Harry with sand and cement
And hounded old Jimmy below
To brace up the grounds was what he required
And to Sam we couldn't say NO.
He goaded old 'Smudge' till rebellion
And set him aloft mid the tanks
Then he brought him below to dig for the sewer
And the old blighter never said Thanks.

Then March came along all too quickly
With ever so much to be done
The painter was lost for a fortnight
It nearly made Rab Collins run.
But Jimmy he came to the rescue
And wielding the brush with a will
While Sammy he drove them to frenzy
The pace was enough for to kill.

There was Woods making ceilings of fabric
The Clarke fitting scullery sinks
There was Rab filling lights in the toilets
And Fred and John working like Chinks
Then along came the lassies to brighten
The windows with curtain cretonne
And Dinah and Nan they accomplished this
With the able assistance of John.

pure Poetry

We sat down to fish and chips
As twelve o'clock midnight did strike
Provided by Jimmy Blair senior
For lassies and ladies alike
Then Dinah got busy with teapot
And Nan buttered bread by the yard
By gum! How we lapped up that fodder
The going was certainly hard.

So hats off to the lads of the Belfast
And lift to the ladies too
It's lovely of the Club that prevails in us all
And will conquer us fields anew
But this is just one of our objects
A mission that's duly fulfilled
So don't tarry now at the gateway
The rich soil has got to be tilled.

So let us move forward together
And keep the Old Club at the top
With a legend of wheeling behind us
Move forward – it's fatal to stop
There are fresh fields along the horizon
Keep plugging its all in the game
Any maybe some day your successors
WILL SAY -
You built them a Hall of Fame

ROAMER

The opening of 'our hall' (the club rooms) in 1954

BELFAST C.C.

ULSTER'S oldest cycling club celebrated its 63 years with the opening by Mrs. W. Caughey, wife of the president, of its magnificent and fully-equipped clubrooms in conjunction with the dinner and presentation of prizes. Among the 120 present were T. M. Conkey, the club's first hon. sec.; and a host of others who have from two to four decades of others who have from two to four decades membership. In the toast to the club J. Keenan spoke about the unselfish sacrifice of the members who had done so much for the club. He also thought the Belfast club with so many members in the 40-50 age group should start an old-timers' group open to the local clubs. D. Willix in his reply recalled the old history of the club and its associations with the city. Isabel Clements was the star of the prize table, having set up five women's road records last year. The gesture of Mr. Willix in presenting her with his 50-year-old club badge was loudly acclaimed.

The Opening was performed by the wife of Club President, Mrs. W. Caughey She was presented with a bouquet of flowers of mark the occasion

Love at first sight

I first noticed her as I was walking home from work.

There she was behind the counter of a shop I was passing. Its funny I didn't notice her before. Maybe she's new here, but she sure was a beauty and just my size too. If only she were mine I would care for her and attend to all her needs. Even take her with me on holidays, but it's just like me to miss such a chance! Coming home next day, there she was again. So an excuse into the shop gave me a chance to get a closer look. Imagine! She was just an arms length away! A few discreet enquiries and I were informed that I had a chance, because she is still free from the clutches of other men, but not from their attentions.

Now is my chance to get acquainted before the shop closed, I thought. And it was no time until I was bidding good-night to the shopkeeper and walking up the road with her. When the opportunity arose I introduced her to the folk at home and they admired my choice. Now all I need to do is to put the ring on her and show her off to the boys in the Club. Better still, I'll get a double-ring. After all, you're nobody now unless you've got a double chain-ring on your bike!

A CYCLIST   (story taken from THE HUB June 1954)

Amsterdam afterthought

A postscript to Jim Maguire's fine little memoir (page 141) of an Irish teams visit to Amsterdam for the World championships in 1959:

As we proceeded on our walkabout of Amsterdam's street of sin, viewing the wares displayed almost in window dressing style, suddenly the roar of a car engine interrupted our reveries and a red Porche open-top sports car sped round a corner into the street where we stood. It was driven by a prominent French sprinter and before his feet touched the pavement it was as if the adjacent brothel simply emptied its contents of young women on to the roadside where they fluttered like a flock of birds around the cyclist and his vehicle, laughing in a happy and unaffected matter.

We were astonished that a Parisian cyclist should have such a following among the working girls of Amsterdam.

BILLY KIRK   Ards C.C.

Tour of southern France

On a club run in 1954, while stopped for a drum-up, one of the members of the Belfast Cycling Club suggested a tour of the Riviera and another said:

"Aye Devon and Cornwall are very nice", but the other guy chirped up: "I was talking about the French Riviera!" Another member said you would be sure of getting a bit of good weather there anyway and that started a whole debate. The result was that ten members of the club, seven men and three ladies, decided to take up the challenge and that was the beginning of a lot of planning. We decided to fly to Paris, take a night train to Grenoble where our assault on the Alps would start. That would take three days, then we planned to drop down to Monte Carlo and Cannes and cycle round the Cote d'Azur to Marseille. Our first problem was, we had to fly to London, but the aeroplanes in service then were Elizabethans which were unable to carry ten cycles altogether. So we had to remove the wheels and strap them on each side of the frame and turn the handlebars as well. We then took the bicycles to the BEA in Glengall Street in Belfast the night prior to our flight to have them transported to London for our flight to Paris the next day.

On arrival at Heathrow we checked in for our flight to Paris and all our bikes were on the plane as it was a Viscount which was a larger one. When we landed at Le Orly in France we had to re-assemble our bikes before cycling to Paris to catch our night train to Grenoble, at the Gare du Nord. We arrived at Grenoble about 6.30 a.m. and had a quick wash and brush up in the Ladies toilets as directed by the station master, because the Gents didn't have any such facilities! Next we headed for the first eating house we could find to get some sustenance as this is where the Alps begin and is known as Napoleon's route. The Alps are enormous compared to what we ever experienced and the tour took us through the towns of Gap, Deigne, Castillanne and Grasse then drop down to Cannes and Monte Carlo on the Mediterranean coast, where we had our first swim.

There were a number of incidents during that part of the tour. The first was on the 13th July where we stopped in Digne. The town square was decked out with bunting, flags, streamers and a band stand. Later that night there were melodious players and musicians with dancing and singing which created a real carnival atmosphere. It was the eve of Bastille Day. The following night we stayed in Castellanne and the Bastille Day celebrations were even better and went on into the wee small hours.

We had a hard days riding in that section of the Alps and were fortunate to get accommodation for the ten of us together. Everyone was looking forward to a good dinner that night in the restaurant so when the waiter came to take our order he babbled off the menu in French. Arty McShane told him to bring us their speciality. We waited and waited and waited some more, then the waiter eventually arrived with three large platters, tongs small two prong forks and about three dozen snails! There were groans of disappointment from the bunch, then a combined chorus of: "Bring us an Ulster Fry".

About four of us decided to tackle the snails, rather than send them back, while the rest of them got their fried eggs and bacon, but not an Ulster Fry.

The town of Grasse is noted for its Perfumeries and while cycling in that region the air was filled with the smell of lavender and the fields were a purple colour growing the lavender.

Our next stop was Cannes where we checked into a hostel that provided the bare essentials for cooking, sleeping and washing, which is all a cyclist requires. We stayed a couple of nights there to see how the other half lives and enjoyed the sun, sea and scenery. There was a couple of amusing incidents in the hostel. One was the toilet which was out in the courtyard and it was also a shower. The toilet was at ground level with two large foot prints either side where one placed their feet and just squatted. This practice was introduced in the early 1900's by the Authorities to combat the spread of venereal diseases. It was also the mode at other places we stayed in. But there was one thing that one had to be aware of in this toilet and that was the fact that it had two chains which hung beside each other. One for flushing the toilet and the other for the shower. Our Captain, Fred Collins made that mistake, much to the hilarity from the rest of the club, none more so than Arty McShane, who to his own embarrassment did exactly the same on a later occasion! Another thing one had to remember was when the toilet was flushed one had to get out fast if you didn't want a foot bath as well! While we were staying in that hostel there were other non cyclists who were 'bumming' around from place to place by hitching lifts and generally living by their wits. One guy from Dublin latched on to us and was selling *Phillip Morris* and *Camel* cigarettes. Some of us bought them as the French brand called *Gauloises* were worse than *Woodbine* and really earned the nick name of coffin nails! An American warship was anchored in the bay and that was the source of the cigarettes which the Dublin guy was selling. He was obviously making a profit which he said he was going to forward on to a contact in Spain where he was heading to work in the grape fields. The reason was that his six month permit had expired in France, so when he would arrive at the Border he would be fined a sum of money, but as he had none, they would lock him up for a few days and have to feed him. When he would be released his money would be there for him to collect in Spain, after he had crossed the Border.

Another illustration of how some of those hitch hikers survived was when we made a dinner for the ten of us, we purchased meat and vegetables from the butcher and grocer. Then the ladies did the cooking and we were the envy of the other hostellers. When we had our fill and there was some left overs on the plates, a few of the hikers would not let us bin the leavings. They scooped the lot into a large pot along with what they had themselves and heated it into a mush. This would sustain them for the next day on the road to their next stop. We continued our journey around the coast and by this time our group were getting too much sun and beginning to suffer, so anytime we stopped for a break it was always under the cover of trees.

We had a mishap when approaching a town called Frejus. We were going downhill and on entering a sharp left hand bend there was a lot of loose gravel on the road. John Kennedy came down and sustained a lot of abrasions to his leg and elbow which necessitated a visit to the local hospital where he was bandaged up and given an injection which cost the equivalent of two pounds in Francs.

We had an unscheduled stop over here to give John a chance to recuperate so we checked into a local hostel. There was also a large campsite and this suited us fine. While in Frejus there were posters up around the town advertising a 'Bull Fight' that day and someone had told us they don't kill the bulls in France. Anyhow a few of us decided to go and see it, as the only time any of us saw a bull fight was on a cinema screen. It was starting at 4.00 p.m. and the admission charge was 300 Francs (6 shillings). We were in the cheapest part of the arena, but we managed to get a good spot from which the whole show was visible. We were in the shade of a high wall as the sun was at its hottest. A brass band played continuously and struck up a fanfare to introduce the matador and his assistants who received great applause. They presented a very colourful picture in their regalia. Another fanfare heralded the entry of the bull which charged around the ring. Each of the assistants took turns at sticking two foot long darts into the bull's back. The animal was obviously in pain - charging about trying to dislodge half a dozen darts. At this stage the matador took over and proceeded to demonstrate his skill at body swerves etc. and proved to be as nimble as a ballerina. After about five minutes he then levelled his sword at the bull with the intention of thrusting it through a gap between its shoulder blades for an instant kill. In this case he missed several times and he became very unpopular with the crowd who began to shout: "assassin" and "butchere". The bull dropped to its knees a couple of times and each time he tried to finish it off by stabbing it behind its right ear with his dagger, it reared up again. That infuriated the crowd all the more and they began to throw stones and bottles at the matador. The bull eventually died through loss of blood and fatigue, I believe. The gates opened and two gaily decorated Clydesdale horses galloped in with drag ropes which were hooked around the bull's horns and it was dragged away unceremoniously to a fanfare from the band. Its final destination was probably the nearest butcher shop. I did enjoy the more humorous entertainment at the interval when the announcer invited local lads to enter the ring and about two dozen accepted. A bull with its horns well padded was then released among them and it was comical to watch it scatter them and even toss a few blokes over its back. The bull in this case lived to fight another day, but its days are numbered as it will eventually meet a real matador.

In conclusion, I personally thought it was a brutal form of entertainment as the animal was doomed from the moment it entered the ring. When John had felt able to continue after his fall we proceeded on around the coast through Toulon to Marseille. This is a very cosmopolitan city where there was great excitement as France was fighting a war in French Indo-China at that time. They had suffered a humiliating defeat at Dien Bien Phu where they capitulated. Marseille was the main port where their troop ships left for the Far East so the result was many soldiers who were waiting for embarkation to the war zone were spared the journey. When we boarded the night train for Paris the corridors were crammed with soldiers that were being returned to the barracks where they came from. One soldier who was standing within earshot of us asked in very good English where we came from and we told him we were from Ireland. They then asked which part? We said "Belfast". He then informed us he spent a long time in Whiteabbey Hospital where he was treated for and cured of T.B. and that he was very familiar with the area. It got me thinking about all the rich people sending family members to Switzerland to be treated for the very same disease and here we had a French man who had been sent to Ulster to be cured. It must be remembered that here in Ulster and Scotland at that time there was a mass campaign to help combat the disease.

After a day of sight seeing in Paris we returned home to Belfast the next day and I would add that in 1954 we were also in a recession. The Government only allowed us to take fifty pounds worth of Francs out of the country, plus five pounds in sterling which was to be used in an emergency only.

The members of the Belfast Cycling Club who were on that tour were: Fred Collins, David Johnston, Arthur McShane, Rab Smith, John Kennedy, Nora Porter, John and Dinah Campbell. Also Rab and Nan Collins.

RAB COLLINS, Belfast C C

Billy Smyth 'brewing up', 1959.

My first 100 mile time trial

It was 1957 and I had been riding with
Ballymena Road Club (BRC) for the last two years.

By the month of June the season was half way through and I felt now was the time to try my first 100 miles time trial. The only problem was, I lived 25 miles from where the race started. To overcome this, a means of transport had to be found as it was too far to ride before the start of such a long race. Sammy Connor, his brother Ernie and I got a taxi to take us to the start which was at the 6 milestone near Belfast. The race proceeded from there to Antrim, Randalstown, back to Antrim, Ballymena, Ballymoney, Old Portrush Road to Whiterocks. This was the turn around point and was a little over the half-way mark of the race. By this stage I had caught a few of my minute men, but I was beginning to slow down and I didn't feel great. All the drink I had in my half pint bottle and food which was in my jersey pocket was drank and eaten and still I had 40 miles until the finish. It was then I started to recall a conversation I had with a cycling friend about how long it would take me to ride a 100 mile. In which my reply was: if I couldn't ride it in less that 5 hours I wouldn't race anymore! Now I had grave doubts as to whether I would achieve this 100 mile in under 5 hours. I knew I had to struggle on, as riders whom I had caught early on were now catching up and going on.

By this time I was getting close to my home town, which made me feel a little better. Just out of the town, a senior member of BRC was handing out drinks. I don't know what was in the bean tin he handed me, but it went down well. I was starting to pick myself up again and riding well, catching a few riders along the way. At this stage I was getting close to Antrim, still catching the odd rider. After passing through the town I started to feel bad again, I wondered if I could stay on the bike to the finish. I died a lot of deaths from that point to the finish. I don't remember my actual time but I did manage to finish in just under five hours. After a short break in the changing room, it was back on the bike for another 25 mile to Ballymena. I did however continue to race until I was a VET. Competing in a few more 100 miles along the way, in which the personal best time I recorded was 4 hours and 29 minutes.

In all the races which I competed in, the 100 mile which I have described above is the one that stands out most in my memory.

ALAN MARK   Ballymena Road Club

The Isle of Man Express

While leafing through a 1946 June edition of the Official Circular - the monthly publication by the N.C.U. and R.T.T.C. my attention was immediately captured by a pen and ink drawing by 'Herriott', who did many drawings for the covers of the magazine at that time. We have reproduced the drawing at the end of this article. I have no idea where this mode of travel originated but a group of enthusiastic cyclists and four competitors including bikes, hired a fishing boat in Donaghadee to take them to the Isle of Man for the famous international race of two circuits round the island. A total of 75 miles.

The four competitors who were to go were:

John Kelly (Kings Moss), Tommy Givan and Jack Murphy (Maryland Wheelers) and Jimmy Gray (Northern C.C.) Two of them missed the boat as Tommy Givan had a fractured shoulder and Jimmy Gray overslept that morning. It was a happy party as the boat headed out of Donaghadee harbour - some of whom were sailing for the first time. It wasn't long before a few were beginning to feel a bit sick. However, they had no option but to continue the journey which took five and a half hours to reach Peel. When they landed they had another forty five minutes travelling before reaching Douglas.

At Douglas the party were booked into Cunningham's Holiday Camp which was a popular place in those days. Much the same as Butlin's and had all the same recreational facilities and amenities, also dancing till late, including liquid refreshments. The cost for one night stop over plus meals on Wednesday and Thursday was the grand total of seventeen shillings each.

The following morning before the start of the race the French team bikes were spotted outside the hotel where they were staying. The bikes were all brand new Claud Butlers with the latest five sprocket Derailleur gears.

The French riders were Baldassari, Coste and Ferrand who won the team prize and Baldarassi was first over the line by twenty eight seconds from a group of eight riders which was led by Coste.

Our two competitors from the fishing boat, John Kelly and Jack Murphy had very creditable performances which were marred by John getting a puncture at the start of the mountain climb on the second lap. Jack too was unfortunate – he unshipped his chain a couple of time.

After the race our group returned to the camp for dinner and then they were able to have an hour of ballroom dancing before leaving to go to the Palace, where His Excellency the Lieutenant-Governor of the Island presented the prizes to the winners.

The boat party left afterwards and made their way back to Peel to catch the fishing boat for the return trip to Donaghadee at 2.00 a.m. on Friday morning. They had a very rough journey home as some of the waves were coming over the sides of the boat and the cyclists were squeezed below deck and the hatch closed over. They were not at all well. It was a great relief when the boat docked in Donaghadee harbour at 7.00 am where the cycling party thanked the Skipper and crew before disembarking and left for their homes.

This is an extract from a report published by J.H. in July 1946

Submitted by RAB COLLINS

The great W. J. Dowds

W. J. Dowds

In or around 1936, Harry McCartney had the distinction of introducing a young seventeen year old Lurgan boy in the Portadown Cycling Club to cycle racing. His name was W. J. Dowds – better known as Billy or Jimmy Dowds. Much has been written about Billy Dowds and I offer my apologies to previous writers for any inaccuracies or lack of detail that I am guilty of, in this synopsis of such an illustrious career. In the 1955 N.I.C.F. official year book, the editor, Joe Bell captions a photograph of Billy Dowds as 'Surely Ireland's greatest ever Time Trialist.' The same year he was 2nd to Leo Feeny in the pursuit Championship. 2nd to Tommy Talbot in the 50 mile T.C. Championship. Won the N.I. and Irish 25 miles titles followed by up and coming Rab Collim of the Cyprus in both events.

These title races represented a gracious 'bowing out' while showing that at almost forty years of age he could still be 'in and around' the top. Rather than racing on longer than he should and so avoid the anomy of being an 'also ran' to the new generations of Tom Allingham, Billy Kirk, Maurice Donaldson, Rab Collim, Harry Lane, Tommy Talbot, Morris Foster, Sammy's Kerr and Connor, John Fennell and others. 1954 had seen Dowds come 3rd in the N.I. massed start championship.2nd to Tom Smyth in the Irish 100 Time Trial. Win the Irish 25 title in 57 mins. 56 secs.! As well as the N.I. 50 title.

But it was in 1953 that it all came together for him when he lifted the N.I. 25, 50 and 100 mile titles as well as the Irish championships over those same three distances. I have looked through year book championship results and can find no other rider equalling this, at that period. The rise to that 1953 peak seems to have been building up from 1951 when he had 25 wins. In 1952 he was 2nd in the N.I. 50. 2nd in the All Ireland 25. 3rd in the All Ireland 50.

Prior to 1950 there appears to be a gap. Many of the provincial clubs ceased to function until the outbreak of World War Two and Dowd joined the Northern C. C. in Belfast in 1941. By 1943 Dowds was their leading rider. In 1944 he had lst, 2nd and 4th fastest 10 miles Time Trials 1st and 2nd fastest at 20 miles. 1st, 2nd, 3rd, 4th and 5th fastest at 25 miles. 1st at 30 miles. 1st, 2nd, 3rd and 6th at 50 miles 1st and 3rd at 100 miles.

Harry McCartney tells of W.J's 'return' in 1950.

So there must have been a break somewhere along the way between those halcyon days of 1943/1944 and the comeback of early 1950's.

I use the word 'comeback' nervously, but bad memory or not, I do have a misty recollection of hearing about this great south Lurgan road club rider, who gripped the bars well up into their bends – gripped them so tightly and pulled on them so hard that one knew that every ounce of strength and effort was being channelled to his legs to produce a fast but optimum geared tempo. Somehow or other, I as a newcomer to open racing at the 6th milestone just knew that I was in the presence of greatness and can remember being able to sense the atmosphere that surrounded this man.

Perhaps it's best that I leave someone else the task of explaining where the gap years came from and why. I fully admit to delving through the pages of Harry McCartney, Stanley Martin and dear knows who else's notes in an endeavour to try and paint a picture of this great cyclist, without allowing the dry data of times, names and dates to take away the overall stature of the man.

After all, he was a gardener. Elsewhere in this publication I hope the Editors will include some other contributions on W.J. and so we can gain a fuller picture of the man. I will finish on one small anecdote. Elsewhere in this book someone has made reference to Smiths of Carnlough, the well known watering hole, or eating house. This reminded me of another lady called Mrs. Smith who had Tea Rooms in Drogheda.

One day Billy Dowds and I met up to cycle down to Drogheda to ride in an Olympic trial on the Drogheda – Colin – Slane course. We free wheeled down the hill at the bottom of which one could see Smyth's Tea Rooms. No new Boyne Bridge in those days to take the traffic away from the busy main street! We entered, eager for tea and toast. The lady of the house ushered us to a table, all the whilst sniffing hard in an endeavour to keep her runny nose from running further than what would be tolerable! Her head cold was obvious to even the most hardy of us two hungry bike riders, but we hastily made some lame excuse as we retreated and mounted our bikes to head out the course towards the start.

What finally decided us to forego breakfast was that, as Mrs. Smyth proceeded to set the table, she repeatedly wiped her nose with her apron and then proceeded to wipe the cups and plates with that same apron! Billy Kirk tells that the Belfast Telegraph reported how Billy Dowds had raced from his home and had beaten the train on a number of occasions between Lurgan and Derriaghy where he worked at Sam McCready's Rose Garden, depending on the wind direction and the number of stops the train made.

PETER WOODS

A family affair

*Tommy Talbot, ever a stylist, was noted for his incredible versatility.
He excelled at: Time Trialing on the roads, Individual Pursuits on
the Track, Massed Starts, Hill Climbing and Roller Riding*

Time Trials

Tommy joined East Tyrone C.C. in 1948 and started Time Trialing. Over the years he won countless prizes and major awards, including: 5 Gold medals, 3 All Ireland and 2 Northern Ireland.

In 1957 he was first man to beat 23 mins. in a 10 mile T.T. with a time of 22 mins. 57 secs.

He won the East Tyrone's Club's 'Best All Rounder' Competition 15 times!

Track

He had numerous successes on the Track including winning 5 Gold medals, 2 All Ireland and 3 Northern Ireland for the individual Pursuit competitions.

Hill Climbing

Tommy won the Craigantlet Hill Climb 5 times in succession.

Tommy in action

The four Talbot Brothers: Tommy, Ronnie, John and Bobby secured a uique 'all brothers' win in the 1960 Maryland Wheelers Team Time Trial

Massed Starts

He excelled at Massed Starts also and was selected to represent Northern Ireland at the Empire and Commonwealth Games and for Ireland twice in the World Championships. One of these was the 1955 World Amateur Cycling championship in Rome for which he, Bart Sharkey (Dublin) and Shay Elliot had been selected. While waiting at the start in Rome they were attacked by four N.C.A. (National Cycling Association) Members who insisted that they were the rightful Team to be representing Ireland. Tommy was injured in this fight and his bicycle damaged. The four trouble makers and an Official were arrested. Shay Elliot was quickly rescued from this skirmish and competed in the Amateur race. He became a professional later.

Peter and I had planned our wedding and honeymoon to coincide with these Championships. We had ridden out to the Frascati Course very early – hoping to get a good viewing position, but thousands had got there before us. When we got a glimpse of Shay we gave him the usual cheer "Keep er going!" Immediately all Italian eyes were upon us and up went the cheer "Irelande!"

A passage was created for us to get a better viewing position right at the front!

Team Work

The renowned East Tyrone's Team of Tommy Talbot, Tom Allingham and Jim Slaine were a formidable trio. They had many successes as a Team and also individually.

Mrs Leeper handing out certificates

In 1951 they won the Northern Ireland competition record certificate for the best 25, 50, 100 miles and 12 hours. Some achievement! A unique Team in which he was included was that of the four Talbot brothers: Tommy, Ronnie, Bobby and John They enjoyed many successes. Not only as a Team, but also as individuals.

Another very unique Team was Father and son Paul (30 years younger) who competed in 'Two man' events with good results. Paul beat his Dad – albeit by a small margin on other occasions.

Father and son

Rollers

Tommy and Tom Henry set up a new record for a two man 3 hours Attempt. A Charity Roller Marathon. They covered a total of 128 miles and 40 yards. This added n 20 miles to the previous record which was held by Dave Kane and Tom Fletcher in 1970. Tommy was part of another Roller Team which set up a four man 4 hour record. They covered 161 and three eight miles. It was a Sponsored Event to raise funds for the Mary Peters Track in Belfast. The cheque for £100 (worth much more then) was presented to Mary. The other three riders were: Dennis Durbridge, Tommy Blaney and Billy Kerr.

Veteran

Tommy continued to compete as a Veteran with numerous successes and ended his racing career in 'style' by winning the Northern Ireland 'Open' Veterans championship in 1999 at the age of seventy! This was the year he retired from competition in which he had taken part over a period spanning 51 years!

Although retired he still takes an active interest in cycling. He is on his bike most days howbeit in the enjoyable form of touring. When being interviewed in 1999 he remarked that he had always enjoyed competing. Especially against the clock in Time Trials where there was no hiding place. It gave him great pleasure to finish the season with better times than when it started. His best time back then for a 25 mile T.T. was 59 mins. 13 secs. As a Veteran it was 1 hour 4 mins.

He eventually invested in a low profile bicycle with carbon fibre frame and tri-bars and he was able to lower his time by 3 mins. to 1 hour 0 mins. 9 secs. He informed me that when Chris Boardman rode a conventional bicycle when attempting the hour record he covered 49 kilometers.

When riding a low profile bicycle under the same conditions he covered 55 kilometers. I have gleaned the information for this Article from reading through Tommy's scrap books which he kindly retrieved from his attic for me.

A final bit of information which should be included: When Tommy won the first race of his career in 1949 he was earning seven and sixpence a week. The prize money for the race was eight shillings.

This event was an experiment by Cyril Henry to see how many would be interested in cycle racing in his area.

I have only written briefly and would have had to write twice as much to attempt to do credit to his wonderful cycling career.

ISABEL WOODS   (Belfast C.C.)

Mary Peters presented with a cheque: L-R: Dennis Durbridge, Tommy Blaney, Billy Kerr and Tommy Talbot

Tommy Talbot's wheel

This wheel hangs in Tommy Talbot's garage at Randalstown.

Isabel and May visited Tommy's home last summer and while in his garage we spotted this 'wheel' on the wall. And as a matter of interest, one would seldom, if ever see a garage as tidy and organized as Tommy's.

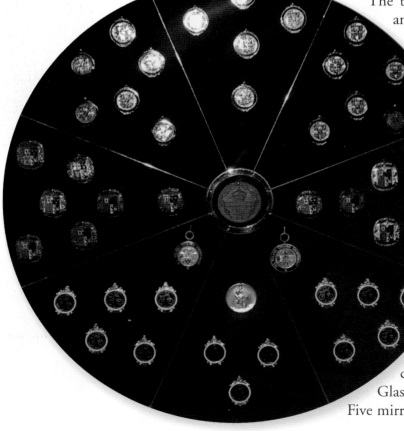

The medals in the wheel came from Time Trials, Road Racing and Track Championships.

The top five sections are a collection of N.I.C.F. and C.R.E. medals from the 1950's.

There is Gold, Silver and Bronze – some are place medals, others are team and N.I.C.F. BAR medals.

The bottom three sections are Veteran Standard medals from 1970 to 1999.

The large medal in the centre is the 1958 Commonwealth Games Commemoration medal.

Every one that was selected for that event received one of these medals.

The wheel is simple to make up:
A tubular rim
Six spokes
The centre is a large flang hub with centre cut out
Three eighth plywood for the back, covered in Royal Blue satin
Glass for the front
Five mirror clips

A short tribute to Cyril Henry

The N.I. Veteran Cycling Team

L to R: Tommy Gibben, Tommy Talbot, Geordie Houston, Bobby Conn, John Snodden, Willie Riley, Cyril Henry, Bobbie Adair Gerry McCann and Davy.........

I personally would like to pay a special tribute to the late Cyril Henry who reformed the East Tyrone Cycling Club in 1948, just after the war years. He introduced me and many others to the sport of cycling in the Cookstown area.

In the early 50's he took me many times to the Antrim Road to ride in open time trials. He also took me and others to the Navan Road. The first pair of racing tyres I had he bought them for me.

He also organized Tourist trials and week-end tours at Easter and to Donegal or Sligo.

I owe a lot to Cyril for anything I achieved in the sport of Cycling.

TOMMY TALBOT   East Tyrone C C

Veteran's comeback

I've entered the Wheelers' 'twenty five',
I'm having another 'go'.
The old pair of sprints look almost new
I borrowed them last week from Joe.
The 'old iron's' gleaming from stem to stern,
And running as smooth as silk,
And just to prove that I can still move
I've been training on bread and milk.

The day of days has at last arrived,
By gum! wont I show these boys
When they see me flash home with a short 'one-one'
They won't half raise a noise.
They've been 'ribbing' me sorely for weeks on end,
With "Make sure you put on your lamp"
And "In case it rains and there's no late trains,
Carry your mum's old gamp.

But I'm happy again 'cos I'm back in tights,
And I'm breathing 'embro' air,
And I'm hearing the banter and chat again
In an atmosphere free from care.
And I'm soon to be off 'cos I've just been told
"Hurry up, you'll be late you know",
So with thumping heart I rush to the start,
Yes, I've only a minute to go.

The timekeeper signals to me "Get Set",
I'll make a comeback you know.
Then the man with the watch raises hand aloft,
"Five, four three, two, one – Go"
A mighty heave at the rear I feel,
Then I'm pedalling along like mad,
If I keep this up I may win the cup,
'Cos the going is not too bad.

At ten miles out my throat goes dry,
"Boy, oh boy, could I go a pint?"
But I grip the bars and resist the urge
Tho' I'm feeling quite hot 'behint'
My mind's made up, it's my day of days,
I simply wont 'pack in',
Tho' its vexing sore when the folk next door
Pass by in a car and grin.

Somebody's shifted 'the turn' I'll swear,
I should have been there by now.
And I'm feeling quite queer amidships
And the sweat's running down my brow.
Och! I'll be as right as rain again
There's the turning steward waving me on
Lost time I'll catch on the homeward stretch,
When my dose of the 'bonk' has gone

But another few miles brings a series of hills
Which I somehow manage to climb
And I glace at my watch in a hopeful way
"Ye Gods, that can't be the time!"
The young 'uns have passed me in ones and twos
But now they are passing in crowds
Oh,, boy, I'de feel fine, if I had for a time
The legs of Givan and Dowds!

The rest of my story is sad to relate
And painful to memorise too;
The spirit was willing, the flesh was weak
And you can't beat the years 'tis true.
But somehow I'm glad I've recaptured the thrill
Of riding against the clock
No more I'm a flyer, so now I'll retire
And watch your 'uns suffer 'the knock'.

And so as I potter among the lanes
And walk every hill in view,
I often remember my time-trial days
And that painful come-back too.
But whether its 'sprints' or 'balloons' you ride,
Wheel lightly or carry a load,
To cyclists all there is but one call
The call of the open road.

ROAMER   April 1946

Isaac Matier, Belfast CC, leaving Mizzen Head in 1949 for his record attempt. Note the rough road surface. He set many other Place to Place records.

World championship - Cologne, Germany

Jack Ryan, Jimt McQuaid, Joe Bell and Frank O'Brien Co. Cork rider
Officials Raymond Moore, Leo Feeney and Marshall McAdam - rider

Having assembled at Belfast we drove to Aldergrove,
flew to London, then on to Cologne.

We were met by German officials and were transported to our B & B and told to report to nearby Cologne Cathedral the next morning at 9.30 am. After a good nights sleep and hearty breakfast we walked to the Cathedral and to Brouett to see the basement which was the German Army Headquarters during the 1939/1944 Second World War.

The Hostess welcomed us as she did every morning and explained what the programme was for each day. That day we were to be brought to a large manufacturing company, shown around and then taken to a lecture from the 'top brass'. One of the party with us, a Dutchman, took over and explained that some of the party were having trouble understanding what they were being told. Everything turned out fine. We were brought to a large hall for dinner and the 'top brass' welcomed us. We enjoyed the lengthy programme set out for us. Then back to the Cathedral and the B & B.

Each day we met at 9.30 am at the Cathedral. Each day was different. We went to Wuppertal to the Sprint and Motorbike Assurance Races and saw Reg Harris beat Van Vliet in the Sprints.

Another day we went to the road race on Germany's Motor Car Race Course. Then a tour down the Rhine and following a train journey we boarded at a large boat at 12.30 pm and sailed back to Cologne with all the meals and drinks supplied free.

Arriving back at Cologne we went to a large indoor Stadium where the cyclists on bikes were playing football. It was very exciting! (Fifty years ago they used to play in Gibson Park).

Another day at the Stadium there were cyclists doing balancing acts on their bikes. It was wonderful to watch. After these events and being brought back to the Cathedral we slipped into a pub for a drink and talk about the day. It was hectic. Up about 7.30 am and in bed at 11.00 pm.

Alex 'gave out' on Wednesday. I 'gave out' on Thursday.

A Burmese girl who was staying in the B & B visited Alex on Wednesday and Thursday. She came to visit us. Her father was a millionaire and she was travelling the world to run a hospital in Burma for her father. Later on that day the gang were asked out and we all went to a restaurant for a meal. We had a brother and sister staying at the B & B while we were there. They were college students and they joined us for the meal. It was a wonderful meal and a great programme of singers and artists to entertain us. We were presented with little mementos of our stay. I received a leather case of nail file and scissors. It just put the top hat on our stay in Cologne. We were sorry to say goodbye to all who had looked after us. We came home from Cologne via London to Belfast.

MARSHALL McADAM

Far from finished

Teddy pictured on top of Ben Nevis after climbing the 'North East Buttress' with son-in-law Kevin Quinn.

Teddy Hawkins was one of those cyclists who sent in material for this publication. It arrived in the form of three and a half pages from the Mourne Observer. He hoped that we could select enough material from the Articles to compile 'The Teddy Hawkins Story'. These were excellent articles by Amy Biggerstaff and Sports Editor, Raymond Stewart.

Oddly enough, Teddy and I were born the same year, 1929. We were both keen cyclists and then mountain walkers, yet I never knew the man. There the similarity ended as I never achieved what he did. Yes I knew of him and his racing career. In those days it was a case of *them* and *us* - the N.C.A. and the Federation. Although cyclists at heart: a win, a crash, or a head wind were the same to us all, the politics of the time overflowed into sport and so kept us from getting to know each other. Teddy had a good career in the N.C.A. and the one outstanding thing that I knew about was his being captain of the N.C.A. Irish Team competing in the 1951 BLRC Tour of Britain. Right from his early days, sport played a big part in Teddy Hawkins life. Despite his love for both Soccer and Gaelic, it was the ban on 'foreign' games that had him barred from Gaelic – on two occasions. He recalls that when the local Soccer team had difficulty in finding a Goalkeeper it seems that "no one ever wanted to take the position because they would always get the blame if anything went wrong" One of the teams offered to produce one on the day. The Goalie turned up alright but he was a Gaelic player and didn't know the Rules of Soccer. During the game he grabbed the ball and ran, hand to toe, up the field. The two teams, even the Referee, just stood and stared in amazement!

Around 1946 Teddy took up cycling. However, his racing career ended abruptly in 1953 after the Tour of Ireland. Teddy had been involved in six or seven bad crashes during his career and it was in that Tour of Ireland that an English rider fatally collided with a run away horse and cart. I recall that the press reports of this tragedy affected a lot of us at the time. Teddy tells in that 1990 Mourne Observer feature of his encounter with Jimmy Saville, the TV Star of 'Jim'll Fix It'. Popular as a D.J., the 'Duke' as he was known then, was a member of one of the teams competing in that Tour of Britain. Teddy adds that Jimmy Saville was a scream and caused a real commotion when arriving for the race each morning. He always turned up in a big chauffeur driven limousine, dressed in a morning suit, complete with bow tie and smoking a long cigar. The driver would go around and open the door. Jimmy would alight, nick out the cigar, strip down to his cycling gear and drape the suit over the driver's arm. During the second stage, after about 50 miles, Teddy crashed, changed bikes and was advised to take it easy as another 'dropped' group was coming up and to stay with them. Jimmy Saville was in this bunch and chatted and jabbered on continually, telling stories and jokes. Their group was last to finish that day and 'The Duke' made a big thing of having a mock fight with Hawkins as they sprinted for the line. He was a real Showman and could manage to achieve more publicity than riders of real ability. Jimmy even made an epic out of coming last!

Teddy had married Sally, sister of Kilcoo bike builder, Pat Rodgers. They had four girls and four boys. He continued in sport, playing Gaelic for Kilcoo and Soccer for Dundrum and Castlewellan.

Obviously not one to lie down or give up his love for active participation sports Newcastle man, Bert Slader persuaded Teddy to become involved in Mountaineering and enlisted Teddy's help in forming the first Mourne Mountain Rescue Team. Later Teddy became its Team leader and held that position for six years.

In 1971 he became the first permanent Warden to run the Northern Ireland Mountain Centre outside Bryansford. As Chief Instructor Teddy has led expeditions to the local Sperrins, Donegal, Kerry and Wicklow to Scotland, The Lake District, Wales, Austria and the Pyrennees. Along with thirty two others he took part in a major expedition to Afghanistan, being awarded a Churchill Fellowship as he was the Team's sole Mountain Rescue Expert.

In the early Eighties he finally resumed cycling, dusting down his 1951 racing frame which had lain untouched for thirty years. With new wheels and the bike updated he joined the local Shimna Wheelers. Not satisfied with 80 mile Sunday Club Runs and on his retirement from the Mountain Centre Wardenship in 1993, he started planning cycle trips that he had always promised himself. But like a lot of us never got around to. With the support of wife Sally and daughter Joanne he did the Mizen to Malin version of the Irish End to

far from finished

End. This five day trip gave him such a kick that he yearned for more.

He realised that while racing and training one has little time for the niceties of touring. As he says himself "with racing all you see is the backside of the rider in front but this gave me the chance to see the country and go at my own pace". Next he had a go at the Lands End to John O'Groats. Camping, Hostelling, Bed and Breakfasting - he completed this classic Route of almost 1000 miles in nine days. Having family both living or working in 'The States', he started planning an across U.S.A. trip from the West. Starting from the appropriately named town of Seaside, Oregon to Washington D.C. in the East. It took six weeks to compete the 3000 miles solo run. At that years Club Christmas dinner, his old pal, Jim Patterson toasted him with "He is a role model for a lot of people. Teddy Hawkins is committed to everything he does. He's been there and got the tee shirt!"

I am well aware that had it not been for those two Mourne Observor Articles by Amy Biggerstaff and Raymond Stewart, I would not have been able to paint any sort of picture of this man of so many athletic talents.

Between the published date of the second Article, 15th August 1990 to Monday 15th August 2009, Teddy like myself has passed from his 60's to his 80th and I know that I have fallen far short of giving all his funny and extraordinary tales that are in those newspaper articles. So I recommend that you use the magic of modern day technology to seek them out yourself.

To get the full story:

Mourne Observer page 46 Wednesday 21st December 2005.

Mourne Observer, page 43, Wedneday 8th August 1990

Mourne Observer page 41, Wednesday 15th August 1990

I was curious…

I rang Teddy today, Wednesday 12th August 2009 to have a chat with him and I am delighted to report that he is as fit as ever. Still on Club Runs and here is an idea to keep enthusiasm up around County down and other similar runs with a specific purpose or interest. He tells me that he is off again to visit family in the U.S.A. with another cycle tour, with family in Nova Scotia. All at 80 years of age!

The 15th August 1990 article will, I hope, sum up in his own words he admits to having a 'fair' level of fitness and adds that the "greater the distance, the more ones strength and fitness comes into it"

He added: "I marvel at the young ones today and the speed and distance they can do in both cycling and mountaineering." He describes exercise as 'a drug' and says that he feels as if he has done something wrong if he fails to exercise. He feels extremely fortunate to have found such a rewarding outdoors career at the

Mountain Centre. His last quote sums up the man for me and his unselfish attitude: "It is with pleasure and delight that I look at the numbers I have got started and see them climbing for higher and far better routes that I could ever climb. I like to see other people doing well".

PETER WOODS   *Belfast C.C.*

One Man and his Bike, Teddy packs his carrier bags for another day in the saddle.

Teddy Hawkins and the Tour of Britain

A few years ago Jim Crawford, originally a member of Couriers R.C. Hillsborough but later Ards and North Down C.C.'s gave me two interesting souvenir booklets. They were the result books of the first two BLRC Tours of Britain, sponsored by The Daily Express. I remember reading them avidly all those years ago as a mad keen 14 – 15 year old. But imagine my surprise and pleasure on discovering that my good friend Teddy Hawkins from Castlewellan had actually competed in those races of 1951 and 1952. He had been selected on a N.C.A. Team, led respectively by Karl McCarthy and John Lackey. I loaned the documents to Teddy and the letter opposite is his reply on returning them to me:

He later verbally recounted an episode which occurred overnight on Thursday August 28th 1952 at Carlisle, Cumbria after stage six. After breakfast on 29th the Irish Team went to inspect their bikes. To their shock they found all their tyres had been slashed. They reported this to the organisers but had no suspicion as to who might have been responsible.

14 Kennedy Estate
Burrenreagh.
Castlewellan
Co Down
BT31 9AN.

Billy,
Thanks for the memories, and for the opportunity to relive those days, so long ago. Despite the fact that the writers didn't get all the facts, I am sure everyone on these races would have different versions of what took place, the crashes, the punctures the misplaced road signs, even internal squabbles between teams and individual riders. I remember two riders fighting with pumps and bottles and then finishing it off with fists at the roadside whilst the race still went on, and they weren't Irishmen. We on the Irish team were, with the exception of Karl McCarthy, not the best Irish riders at that time, but the big stars, mostly Dublin riders, wouldn't travel, "Your just being thrown to the Lions", that was the statement that some of those top men said. They weren't far wrong, to most of us the speed on the first stages took us completely by surprise and added to poor gear choices and punctures almost wiped us out, working as a team just didn't occur, if you punctured, crashed or were dropped, tough luck, you were on your own, our team manager was in a taxi with another team manager and two mechanics. I only saw them at the start and finish any help given to any of the amateur riders was from the Cyclo spares team, anything else you did it yourself. However it was a wonderful experience.
Billy thanks again,
Yours in Sport
Eddie Hawkins

BILLY KIRK

Ireland Team:
The first Tour of Britain 14 day cycle race
August 19th – September 1st 1951

At that time there was no love lost between the NCU and the BLRC. In fact there was probably greater enmity between these two bodies than between the three Irish bodies. However, a nice resolution developed when the manager of the B.S.A. team, the renowned past track champion Syd Cozens offered the Irish team a set of Dunlop No.2's for each rider.

Karl McCarthy age 23 ,Medical student
100—miles Massed-Start Champion 1950
1st—2day Belfast—Dulin and back 1950
1st-- Tour of Tyrone 1951
100 –miles record holder, 50 miles massed start champion 1951

Joseph Lennon—age 23 factory worker
1st Cookstown 50 km
3rd-50 mile Massed –start championship 1951
Mt, Pleasant senior team captain

Joseph Lennon

Edward Hawkins—age 21 Fitter,
All-round Road Champion 1950
50 –mile Massed –start Champion 1950
2nd 100 miles Massed –start 1950

Edward Hawkins

Mathew Sands age – 35, plumber
2nd All –Round Road Champion 1950
2nd 50- miles Massed –start Championship 1951
Captain St ,James,s Gate racing Club, senior team
15 years racing

Matthew Sands

Conliffe Carr—age 23, Farmer
Midlands Cycling Club (attached to N.C.A.I.)
Winner of the Harp C.C. Palmer Cup 1950
Champion of Co,Kildare

His riders were changing tyres every two days, punctured or not.
The tyres were accepted in almost mint condition and the Team arrived at the London finish, eight stages and 839.5 miles later – puncture free!

Irish results:

1951	K. McCarthy	9th
	J. Lennon	30th
	C.Carr	32nd
	E. Hawkins	33rd
1952	E. Hawkins	37th
	C. O'Reilly	39th
	N. Moorish	43rd

In 1951 Jimmy Saville rode the event, listed as Oscar Saville.

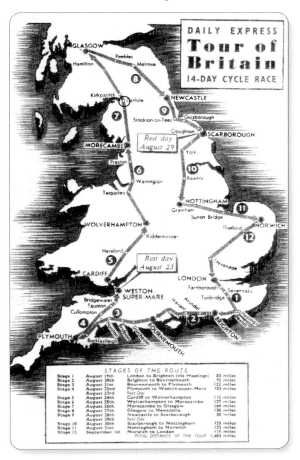

Daily Express Map of England The 14 day cycle race.

Discovering America 1980

In the summer of 1980 five schoolboys from Newtownards were part of the Discovering America Cycling Expedition that rode 3960 miles coast to coast across the USA, setting two unofficial world records for a school group on the way. Here is their story....

The Discovery American group of young cyclists a6t Hazard, Kentucky – the home of the Dukes of Hazard!

A year earlier a group from an American High School had cycled coast to coast in 45 days. Alan Evans (Senior Education Officer with the National Union of Teachers) thought that a London school could beat this. Pupils from Islington Green School (already famous for their part in the Pink Floyd video for Another Brick in the Wall) started preparing. Early in 1980 they decided to invite riders from across the UK to join the expedition and as a result an invite was sent to the Northern Ireland Cycling Federation. The NICF were not interested in the Expedition and passed the invitation to Mike 'the Bike' McConaghy (then Chairman of Ards C.C.) A group of us were leaving Comber cinema one night, having just seen the American cycling film *Breaking Away*, when we met Mike. Fired up by the film, we were inspired by the idea of spending the summer cycling in the U.S.A. Five of us started training immediately under the watchful eye of underage coaching legend, Jimmy Thompson. He soon had us up the Antrim Glens and down over Spelga. By the time Alan Evans came to Newtownards to pick three riders, we were flying! Alan was so impressed he picked all five. The five were Ralph Fowler (16), Ivan Edmonds (16), Alastair Martin (15), Robbie Dunn (14), and Robin Haughan (13). We joined two riders from Wales, one from Scotland and thirteen from Islington Green school.

The route was quite northerly. We started in Washington State on the West coast and rode through 13 states covering 3960 miles in 39 days to finish in Virginia. This is longer than a southerly crossing, but avoids the worst of the summer heat.

Looking back now, the thing that stands out for me most is the generosity of our American hosts. Through Alan's links with American education authorities we were able to stay with American families on over half the nights. They were always very welcoming and kind – especially to the five riders from Ireland. I'm sure we were often subdued, tired and slept a lot, but they always fed us well, washed our clothes and got us to the start in time for the next day's ride. We even stayed with a family in Bloomington, Indiana where 'Breaking Away' was filmed and they had an old flooded quarry on their land where we went swimming, just like in the film.

Our next plan was to cycle 165 miles from Hot Springs in South Dakota to Scott's Bluff in Nebraska. We awoke to find a block headwind and it took five hours to ride the first 60 miles. As we collapsed at the lunch stop there were still over 100 miles to ride. Luckily the wind eased and the route changed direction slightly. As the sun set in a glorious red ball, we descended down through fantastic rock formations into Scott's Bluff, where we were met by a welcoming committee including an enthusiastic brass band, despite being several hours behind schedule. A few days later we rode 215 miles across Nebraska to set an unofficial distance record for a school party and it seemed a relatively easy day.

The only bad moments I can remember were getting abuse from some of the locals as we cycled through the poor, depressed areas of the Appalachians in Kentucky. A bottle thrown from a passing truck smashed on Ivan's handlebars, cutting his hand quite badly. Having said that we entered the town of Hazard a few miles later to another big welcome. Dukes of Hazard was a top TV programme at the time so this was a big moment for us all.

The trip re-enforced my love of cycling – not just racing but touring, exploration and adventure. The bicycle I had used to play in the street a few years earlier had now taken me across a Continent.

After we returned, Alan Evans wrote; the Expedition was not just about Discovering America, but also about discovering ourselves. I think we all returned with greater self belief, confidence and independence. Anything is possible if you put your mind to it. I often wonder if such an Expedition could be repeated to-day? Would we allow a group of 13-16 year olds to head off on such an arduous adventure? If you think the answer is YES, please let me know because I'd love to be part of it!

ALASTAIR MARTIN   Ex Secretary Ards CC

Cultra Manor 1935

This photograph was taken about 1935 at Cultra Manor, County Down which was the residence of Sir James Kennedy K.C.M.G. and Lady Kennedy (seated centre) who owned the house and land that is now the Ulster Folk Museum.

Sir James Kennedy was invited to become President of Belfast Cycling Club in 1912. He accepted the invitation and held this position until he died. He was President for 26 years. His predecessor was Captain James Craig who was President from 1905 until 1911, but had to retire due to the demands of his political campaign during the 'Home Rule' years. He later became known as Lord Craigavon.

During his years as President, Sir James Kennedy issued an annual invitation to the Club members to visit Cultra Manor and he entertained them with tea and cakes on the lawn. All those present were free to wander around the Estate for the rest of the afternoon.

The person in the photograph standing immediately behind Sir James and Lady Kennedy is the renowned Shafto Kerr who began his racing career in the 1890's. Some of the others present were Herbie Knight (second left) James Blair (third left) Sam Neill (fourth left) Billy Vokes (fifth left) Bill Murray (sixth left) Herbie Neill (fourth right) and Sam Jennings.

Sir James Kennedy died in 1936 and was succeeded by Mr W. S. Caughey who was President until 1969, when he died. 'Billy Caughey' joined the Belfast Cycling Club in the late 1890's and gave a lifetime of service to the club and cycling. 75 years, in fact.

RAB COLLINS

Rebirth of the Star of Down

It was a summer evening as a cyclist overtook me. We exchanged the words "Good Day" as he vanished up the road not knowing our paths would cross again about two miles further along. The gentleman had a slow puncture. I luckily had a pump with me and asked the man to return the pump to my workshop on Monday. I later found out that the gentleman was a Mr. Sam Thompson who owned **The Star of Down Cycle Works** and true to his word on the Monday morning Mr. Thompson returned the pump and asked if I would be interested in some part time work. I agreed as I had been waiting for more work as I was employed by the U.T.A. in Lurgan. Starting as an Apprentice 'spark' on 16th February 1947 I had to cycle to Dromore each morning to catch the 7.15 am bus. As a first year Apprentice I earned 19 shillings per week. After six months of working for Mr. Thompson (now known to me as Sammy) I asked how much it would be to buy a track machine. He said I could work weekends as overtime to pay the machine off. I started to train and as time passed, my training miles increased. Sammy said we would try a sports meeting at Celtic Park. I finished 3rd in a one mile race to Mr. Joe Craig. Sammy was over the moon as was I.

I continued to race and have many a story to tell.

JOHN JESS (Maryland Wheelers)

John Jess: great ability, short career

John Jess, like James McGreevy, came from Leapoughs, Dromore, County Down, even riding a Star of Down bike like his predecessor.

His precocious talent was noted in Olympic year 1948 when he beat one of the Australian team in a 1 mile race at Belfast's Ravenhill sports. They were riding in Belfast in preparation for the Games in London. The defeated Aussie said "This Kid could be world class"

At this meeting the Dublin sports promoter Billy Morton signed Jess to a three-meeting contract at Santry track, all expenses paid. He won almost everything he rode including beating the English champion Lew Pond, who compared him to the great Australian Sid Patterson who won the world sprint and pursuit championships. Another of his victims that day was Irish champion Jim McQuaid.

In 1948 he was N.I. one mile champion and in 1950 Irish ½ mile champion. He rode only one time trial in his short career, a 10 on the Moira Road, in which he clocked 23 mins. 33 secs! The sport of cycling only saw a fraction of him in a career which ended in 1950.

BILLY KIRK

Note: It was known that the great Frank Baird, winner of 65 Irish Golds in his career, went to great lengths in Croke Park, Dublin in 1949 to shake the hand of John Jess.

How Sammy Thompson put Leapoughs on the map

County Down has always been rich in community personalities, nowhere more than in the quiet rural hamlet of Leapoughs, about half way between Dromore and Dromara.

Sammy Thompson was a man who more than any other had made the name Leapoughs known in both sporting and musical circles.

It was in 1925 that Sammy, who had become well known as a cycle rider and was a member of Lurgan Cycle and Athletic Club. He decided not only to build lightweight racing bicycles but also to form the Leapoughs cycle club.

The 'Leapoughs' or 'Thompson' bicycle became widely known in a short time and many of the great riders of the time rode to victory on one of the machines, officially called the **Star of Down.**

Very soon the Leapoughs club boaster of great riders such as Denis Corr, W.J. Crane, Willie Livingstone, Billy Barlow, Harry Fairley, Jack Scott, Fred Jess, Davy Allen, John Greer, Bertie Walsh, Willie John Barlow, Bob Dickson, Bob Kinghan and of course Sammy himself, a frequent winner at events all over the Province.

The monthly meetings of the club were held in the Star of Down Workshop and until well into the 1930's it was rarely that any Provincial cycle race did not contain at least one place winner from the Leapoughs club.

Sadly the Leapoughs club ceased to exist with the advent of World War Two.

Article taken from a very worn newspaper cutting of 1937

Left: Sammy Thompson in 1937

Below: John Jess riding a 'Star of Down' at Wallace Park cycle track, Lisburn 1946.

The 'shirt lifter'

On a Saturday afternoon in 1959 I had completed a 25 mile Time Trial on the Antrim line - in my usual mediocre time. On walking into the shed at the Crown and Shamrock used as a changing facility, George Wilkes had spotted a guy wearing a standard shirt and pulling up his briefs from ankle height.
George walked over and lifted the tail of his shirt and said
"This is what I like about these events - you see all the old familiar faces"
Lots of laughter!

JIM CRAWFORD Ards C C

A tragic day

On the return leg of a 25 miles Time Trial on the Antrim line near Dunsilly, I was waved down by George Wilkes who was in tears. Lying on the road with a mangled bike beside him was a competitor who had collided with an Army 'Champ' jeep. We waited for police and ambulance to arrive and sadly the rider was pronounced dead. His name was John Magill from Whiteabbey. He was a member of Abbey C.C. A tragic day I will never forget.

JIM CRAWFORD   Couriers Road C C then Ards C C

Unruly passengers

It was a Saturday in July and I was travelling to Dublin to compete in the 25 mile T.T. on the Navan Road.
  I was driving the work Morris 'J2' van with some of the Ards guys. About half way en route, Billy Kirk pulled an over ripe banana from his bag and proceeded to eat it. A club member whom I will not name, commented that Billy was a silly ******* for purchasing a rotten banana. This is the only time that I have seen Billy Kirk angry and he was about to 'fill this guy in' inside the moving van! We managed to get the situation cooled down and it was 'all picture and no sound' until we reached the Sunshine B&B on Ormond Quay. I think Billy came second to Peter Crinnion on the Sunday.

JIM CRAWFORD Ards C C

Our wonderful sport

I commenced cycling back in 1950's, riding to Bangor which was a real achievement.

I met up with some lads from the Windsor C.C. and rode out with them for a couple of years, riding in their school T.T. races on the Antrim Line course.

My first win was a 5 mile T.T. with a 'U' turn in the middle of the Antrim Road. Imagine doing this now!

We had good fun in Windsor's club room, at Great Northern Street. It backed onto the railway line.

I tried to ride the rollers and received some nasty burns when I fell off!

1953 Ulster Junior Championships at Roughfort. Tommy Burns won. I was in Windsor CC and we won the team prize. Ian Moore (right with the crash hat and Jack Watson

A favourite ride of mine was up the coast road to Carnlough and back in a day. I would have my 'piece' (sandwich) in my saddlebag and sixpence (2 ½ p) in my pocket. I was not in the YHA yet and would stop at Smiths Restaurant in Carnlough for a pot of tea. Once I was there and the lady came over and advised me not to eat my sandwiches on the premises - for a 13 year old it was a bit of an embarrassment!

I think the Smiths Restaurant sign can still be seen on the wall. It was a great meeting place on a Sunday when there would be 30 to 40 bikes piled up outside.

I did eventually join the NIYHA. I recall going to their offices in Linenhall Street and we were shown how to make our bunk bed. Those days you had to have your own 'sheet bag'. The Hostel supplied two blankets which was never enough in the winter. If the Hostel was full, no extra blankets were available. It was a case of sleeping in a track suit if you had one!

Self catering was the order of the day plus duties next morning, like cleaning the Hostel. I later helped when Hostels like Moneyvart needed a coat of paint.

Talking of Moneyvart, I remember staying one weekend and we were on the third floor and 'Stonewall Jackson' needed to relieve himself. He decided to open the window to save walking down the stairs - it was three flights to the 'Loo'! Little did he realise the warden was doing his rounds checking the building and, you guessed it! He showered the warden! Needless to say he was suspended from Hostelling for three months. My first Hostel weekend was to Silent Valley. Although Cranny Falls and Whitepark Bay were my favourites, Cranny Falls was my number one.

I then joined Northern C.C. to race and hostel with Jack Watson, Jackie Corken (Korky). I remember we always rode 81 fixed. A great bunch! We would meet at the Black Man on Sunday mornings. It was great for me as I lived two minutes away, but I was always last one there. Billy Reilly would take us around roads of Ulster we never knew existed and we had some wonderful drum ups. It was always a competition at the drum ups as to who could brew up first on the open fire. Jack Watson always seemed to win.

I rode a three up T.T.T. with Billy Reilly (can't remember the other rider) It started at Glengormley, went down towards Larne, over Agnew's Hill to Ballymena and back to Glengormley. Now that was some circuit!!

At one time it was also an individual T.T. which would have been very hard. During 1953 I was in the winning team for Windsor C.C. in N.I.C.F. Road Race Junior championships, won by Tommy Burns at Roughfort.

After one of our famous drum ups near Toome we met up with the lads from St. Gabrials C.C. and as you can imagine a burn up started. We were lined out, someone got out of the saddle, a bike came back and touched my wheel and I came down. (I never rode directly behind a wheel again). I was sliding along the road, seeing this wall flying by and counting

Ian Moore, Tour d'Honneur a Rennes 1960
Après sa victoire dans le Prix de l' Economique

six people hitting me square on the back. I lay there thinking: "have I got lock jaw", having just read about it somewhere? So I am laying there moving my jaw. Must have looked like a fish out of water! I managed to ride to Antrim Hospital. I came off the worst. My hands were well cut up. The rest of the lads more bruised than cuts. My good friend Jack Watson stayed with me and we both rode back to Belfast.

Next day, Ronnie Jackson, Northern C.C. turned up at my door. A few other walking wounded from Sunday also turned up and we went to the Pictures. I think it was the Gaumont in Castle Street that we ended up in.

A new year had now started and everyone was preparing for the 1956 Tour of the North. A group of us would meet at Finaghy traffic lights on Saturday morning and head for Dublin. We would stay in the Salvation Army for 7s. and 6d. (about 40p) for Bed and Breakfast. There was also a chain gang out to Banbridge and back, with jumping lorries a favourite trick until one night a lad jumped one lorry. Unfortunately it had a trailer which he did not see and sadly he was killed. That habit stopped.

The season was a big learning curve. The Tour of the North was very hard. I was barely able to walk for about two days! The Dun Laoghaire cycling week was big in the 50's and I went down with Raymond Gregory who owned a bike shop in Gresham Street. Raymond's shop was not far from where I worked in W. G. Baird's the Printers, owned at that time by Belfast Telegraph. His shop was a great meeting place and I would spend many a lunchtime there eating 'Maynards' wine gums.

The winters were always hostelling weekends, good 'craic' and singsongs and hiding parts of each others bikes. I remember once coming back on the Coast Road from Moneyvart in Cushendall. We would play 'Tag' on the bikes. It was so fast and furious at times that we had to stop absolutely exhausted. Hilty Smith was the top at this and I remember we always rode Fixed in the winter as low a gear as possible – 60" was usual. I think because of our use of little gears this is why a lot of 'Vets' are still going. So 'Fixies' is nothing new folks!

Another bonus we had in the 50's was the opening of Wallace Park track in Lisburn. (Come on Maryland Wheelers get it restored)

The opening of the track had Reg Harris and all the Pro tracks stars, including our own Hilty Smith and Jimmy Darragh. The track was open to everyone and you could ride road bikes and some evenings the bunches would be 30 to 40. After a session on the track it would be a lineout back to Belfast with a sprint at Finaghy lights. Once coming back a 'Paris Galabier' bike frame broke on the hill before Finaghy and there were bodies everywhere. Not a pretty sight.

The '57 season started with Handicap events at Dundrod. What a circuit! We would ride up past Tony Meli's fish and chip shop on Springfield Road. Now there was a good rider, Toni. (if only he had had the time to train). We would race and ride home again. During one event we had just caught the limit group and were preparing for the finish whenever this voice shouts out "Let me through. I think I can win!" And knowing who it was, Mervin Cooper, everyone closed the door as we knew he would have, no way, after we had done all the work.

During the '57 Tour of the North in which I crashed on the first day (DNF) I met Dan McGurke of the Glen C.C. and he invited me to join him in London as there was plenty of work and racing. I was beginning to believe I could improve my work prospects in London and racing hopefully too. I also talked with Raymond Vennard who said one could train in London after work with street lights taking you 20 to 25 miles out into the country. Raymond was another good rider from Belfast. He won a stage in the RAS, as did our Tommy Burns. Tommy also won NICF Junior and Senior Championships in the same year. Hats off to Tommy!

I joined a BLRC club to ride more road races. The then NCU (now British cycling) did not encourage road racing, but the BLRC did. To think we had more road races in Ireland and still do, than in England! It was a tough baptism, as most events were 100 miles!

I was home in August and won 1st handicap in Northern C.C. 'Andrews Cup' 100 T.T. down the Antrim Line toward Portrush. Big 'Mo' Donaldson won.

One thing I did miss at first in England was the Hostelling weekends. However some of the East London clubs had 'huts' up near Bishop Stortford that I stayed in in latter years. These were not far removed from Hostels.

During the winter of 57/58 I knew I needed to train hard and see if I was good enough, plus I wanted to make some of my new team mates stop calling me 'Paddy' (I would make a fortune now with my hurt feelings claims).

I had joined Marsh R.C. where the competition was very keen amongst the riders. I won the club championship, broke two hours for 50 mile T.T. (first Irishman to do so). Before I broke the hour for a 25 mile T.T. all on 82 inch fixed wheel.

After the 50 I then rode to Herne Hill track in South London to see Fausto Coppi - everyone's cycling hero at that time. To win the championship you had to ride a 100 mile T.T. and during one I was riding, with about three/four miles to go, I was climbing a hill and a friend passed me up a drink – walking! That's how slow I was going, having blown up big time and still finishing third!

I managed to get home in August and rode the 'Tour of the Glens'. A great event that was. I recall riding up to Cranny Falls Youth Hostel in 1956 on the Friday night after work, then riding the event the next day.

The 1958 Event was won by Seamus Herron, 'Fish' to his friends, yet another outstanding rider in the Northern C.C. I switched clubs in 1959 to ride in a pure road racing team, Zeus R.C. A very strong club in BLRC days. By now everyone was under N.C.U. rules.

I had a bad crash in late March in a race - just when I was making a name for myself in early races. I was immobile for two weeks with a bad ankle injury. The problem was I had been selected to ride the 'Milk Race' for Essex. Once I was able to ride again I had about six weeks to prepare for a 12 day race. Nowadays I would have been worried with the short time, but back then when you are young and keen you just get on with it. I rode at a 2 day 3 stage event in April in Manchester and on the 1st stage I finished in Buxton where I was 2nd to Brian Haskell, who later won King of Mountains in the '59 Milk Race. I eventually finished 3rd overall. It was my final preparation. The best bit of this first day was much to my surprise: My friend Jack Watson was at the finish to greet me. He was now working in England also for the last few months in Coalville and cycled up to Buxton. It was a great surprise indeed.

The first stage of the Milk Race was London to Skegness and I was dropped from the break in the last 10 miles. Bill Bradley won the stage and the race overall. I did manage 4th on this last stage and 9th overall.

Then I rested for two weeks for the Isle of Man International and my first Green Jersey for Ireland. To me it was a hill climb and being my first race since the Milk Race it was quite a shock. Just could not get going and finished 19th. One positive thing at the I.O.M. was our own Shay Eliott. He won the first professional race on the Island and it was a great circuit. Back in Essex on Saturday, the next day I won my first Road Race by 6 mins. So Friday's International must have done me some good!!

I won again on the next two Sundays. Then I came home for the Irish Championships. Big Jim Maguire won (the first Northern Irish Rider to win) What a great race that was! Christie Kimmage was 2nd (Paul's dad) with me 3rd. At this time a lot of controversy was going on as I had been selected to ride the 'Tour of Poland' for England. Now this event started two days after the finish of the 'Tour of Scotland' where I was picked to ride for Ireland. I decided to ride for my country (good thing I did) When I saw the standard later at the World's road race I would have been hammered, but I did have a fantastic race.

The first stage I was 2nd – jumped away from the break in the last few miles. I looked back with 200 yards to go and thought I had won. However a very strong Belgian did a 'Cavendish' and just piped me on the line. I had looked left and he came by on the right! Oops! This was a lesson I remembered. Never think you have won until 'you cross the line'. The second stage to Dumfries I was 2nd again in the pouring rain. At least I became race leader. It would not be until 2004 before I was back in Dumfries again when our daughter and husband were signing a contract for a house they were purchasing in Galloway and we were baby sitting.

On the final stage to Glasgow I won at last from a two man break! Tremendous work in my defence of the leadership by Big Jim Maguire and John Joe McCormick.

Our fourth member in the team was John Lackey. He did not start the last stage. He had a bad crash on the first stage and decided enough was enough. I was very privileged to have three team members and Billy Jebb as Team manager to back me up and advise me with their expert knowledge. Having admired all three and John Lackey throughout their careers, it was an honour to ride and win with them and to be the first Irishman to win an International race.

Next up was the Worlds in Zandvoort, Holland, where I went with great expectations. However we had a training crash. Poor Billy Stewart, our manager, broke his nose and we all had cuts and bruises. The race itself was so fast I never saw the front of the bunch and I had never ridden in an 'Echelon' before. That's when I knew I made the correct decision not to ride the 'Tour of Poland'. On the following day we watched the 'Pros' – Tom Simpson was 4th with Shay Elliott not far away in a chasing group. Never saw so many people at a bike race before!

I travelled to Belgium to ride the 'Tour of Namur'. A 5 day race in an Essex team, while the rest of the Irish lads headed home. Managed to finish about 23rd on G.C. in Namur. Again it was a big learning curve. Came home for Christmas and the N.I.C.F. dinner and had a great few days in Belfast. On the 1st Sunday of 1960 I had an excellent ride round the Little Glen to Carnlough and back with my dear friend Jack Watson and boyhood hero, Geordie Wilkes. A nice start to the New Year. Only sadness was when we returned to Jack's house it was announced on the radio that the Italian cycling legend, Fausto Coppi had died.

By now I had decided to go to France for 1960 and early in February I headed down to Lands End. Saddlebag strapped on for a good 8 days training. A week later after some speed work I won the North Road Hardriders T.T. and set a new course record. A few hard road races, with not very encouraging results, as far as I was concerned.

Arriving in Quimper, Brittany in early April with Jock Wadley, Editor of 'Sporting Cyclist' monthly magazine. He had kindly organized everything via Jean Bobet and also agreed to come with me, as he was going on to report the Paris-Roubaix race. My first race was on 17th April, the French Olympic selection race. I was away in a three man break for about 60 miles but was caught in the last 10 miles and I finished in 16th place, about 1 minute down.

The next day I rode a Criterium and was 6th. A much better result as a team mate from Quimper won the race. One thing I recall on arriving at Quimper Railway Station where we were met by the President of Brittany Cycling. We could not go into town to our Hotel as the French farmers were having a protest regarding the price of potatoes. Imagine an Irishman who loves 'spuds' arriving in the middle of a potato protest! I must say seeing all the police with 'sub machine guns' soon made me realise you don't mess with the French police!

My next race I won by 3 min. and then I was off to Rennes to ride a 4 stage 3 day. The Grand Prix de l'Economique. The first day I finished in the bunch about 40 secs. down. The 2nd stage to St. Malo, I managed to get in an early break and in the last 5 miles broke away with a Frenchman who beat me in the sprint. I was now in the leaders jersey with 2 half stages to go before the last day back to Rennes. Both stages were very fast which kept everything together for the sprinters and made my job easier. After this event I was not given as much freedom in future races.

I did manage to win six more events, but was disappointed with my ride in 'Essor Breton' where the French lads worked me over well and good on 3rd day. I was also disappointed with my ride in the 'Route du France' stage race. I did manage 6th on the first stage. There was a T.T.T. and we all took a hammering. Too many 'egos' in the Irish team! Trying to outdo each other and I was as much at fault as anyone else. We live and learn! I did manage to sign a contract with 'Liberia-Grammont' for 61/62. During the contract I received a bike and clothing, but never got the promised bonuses for wins.

The 'Route du France' was a strange organised event. Half the time we were staying in tents, the rest of the time in hotels. The 'Tour of the North' was better!

During this time I was considering the Olympics in Rome and thinking about what preparation would be needed to race with some degree of involvement. Remembering the standard of the Worlds in 1959, was it worth wasting Federation funds, just to say I went to the Olympics? But it would have been nice for my grandchildren!

I decided to turn semi Professional which enabled me to ride with the 'Pros' and accept start money at all the Criteriums after the Tour de France. With my success and being a foreigner, start money was available and the experience would stand me well for the 1961 season.

The season ended with my journey back to Portsmouth from St. Malo taking two days because of bad weather. To top it all, the boat ended up in Weymouth. I missed the boat train to London and had to stay in a Salvation Army Hostel, which was run by a Belfast man!

The 1961 season started off in the South of France where the 'Liberia Grammont' team meet up for early season training and racing. Our team leader was Henri Anglade, an arrogant Frenchman who had finished 3rd in the 1959 tour. Nobody liked him! I rode a few races and returned to Quimper where I was based once again for the season.

For the next few months nothing seemed to go right. Punctures, crashes and living hand to mouth each week. Going for primes, as they paid up at the end of each race. During this bad patch I was selected to ride 'Le Tour' which was a boost to my morale. (In hindsight, great thing is hindsight) another year or so would have been soon enough! I was hoping my luck would change. I would do a reasonable tour and come out with a few Criterium contracts which were always good money. The 4th stage was my undoing. I was completely smashed and demoralised. Only three of our riders finished. Shay Elliott (who would in a future tour become the first Irishman to wear the yellow jersey in the Tour) Brian Robinson and Ken Laidlaw (Irishman, Englishman and a Scotsman). During August I was coming good at last. I had a couple of wins and was invited to race in Normandy in September by a French rider I had become friendly with in the 'Mid Aut' races in Brittany. His family were keen cyclists and his Dad an ex track cyclist and one of the Normandy region's officials. So the end of the season finished well with my new French friend (still is) winning tour races in

September with my help. They invited me back for 1962 and I decided I would give it one more try, but not go back to France until April. In this way I could save some money, get my health back and look forward to a better season.

During the winter of 61/62 I worked for an Importer of equipment from Italy, building bikes. It was ideal. I could have one day off for training. Again I did my London to Land's End trip as preparation for the new season. It did me more good in 1960 than all the training in the South of France during 1961!
I rode a few early races around London then went up to Liverpool to ride the Merseyside 4 day at Easter. It was a good event, except on 3rd stage I crashed, but managed to finish and I finished again on the final stage with the leaders.
  Now back in France in April I rode a few races and knew my form was coming. Warm weather does wonders! The first objective was the 'Essor Breton' a 4 day where I was hoping for some results. The first stage I won after stripping my 15 Cog in the last five miles after breaking away from a small group.
In the 60's all we had were 14,15,16,18,20 x 46/52 and I was lucky to hold onto my slight lead of 20 secs. gap. Next stage, a T.T., I won with a good minute to spare on the 2nd G.C. rider. I was able to hold onto the Leader's Jersey on the next two stages, with a little help from a few French friends in the bunch. Sweet revenge for 1960's race.
Had a trip back to London and Isle of Man where I rode the 'Pro' race on a great circuit. Not like the International course! Andre Darragade won and I cannot recall where I finished, but I know it was at least two minutes down.
  This short break was good for me and I arrived back in France keen to go again. I was winning on a regular basis now, but needed a really big win to attract a new sponsor for 1963.
There were two big classics in Paris towards the end of September. First one was 'Paris-La Ferte Bernard' where I was caught within sight of the line by Vin Densen who was working for his team mate Jack Andre who won! I was gutted. One thing I remember in this race. I was in a 5/6 man break trying to establish a lead and two of the guys were arguing about the price of a banana. One was out of food! Needless to say we were caught. I did at least win the Criterium the next day in 'La Ferte Bernard'.
The last classic was 'Grand Prix l'Equipe' which was one big circuit around the west of Paris. I got away with about 20 miles to go with another rider who gave up as the bunch was closing in. It was a case of continue as far as I was concerned. I needed a contract for '63. The gaps hovered between 20/30 seconds, but I managed to win by 12 seconds. First foreigner to do so and first time this classic was won in a lone break. This race is now called 'Paris-Tours' for semi Pros and I think its run off the day before the Pro race. This win enabled me to gain a contract with 'Gancia-Urago' for two years.

our wonderful sport

During the first week of 1963, I arrived in the South of France for our first training camp. I thought I had left the snow in England (which lasted for 2 months) but it followed me. For the first time in 40 years it snowed in the South of France. About 10 inches overnight. Luckily it was gone in a week.

We rode all the early races. I was 3rd to Francois Mahé and Raymond Poulidor in 'Gran Prix of Cannes'. I was balked on the last bend by a police outrider. We did not realise how fast we were going! I had taken off in the last few miles, lost my momentum and was caught on the line.

I was 6th in 'Gran Prix St. Raphael' again won from a six man break by Francois Mahé in pouring rain.

The year was busy, too busy. Next was 'Paris-Nice' known as the 'Race to the Sun'! All I saw was rain and wind and it was very cold. Last but one stage was on 'Corsica' and I just blew on the first mountain shortly after the start. Two farmers gave me a lift to the finish in their truck which was an experience in itself – lying down the mountain.

The 'Tour de Sud Est' five day was next up with a stage going out and back over the famous 'Ventoux'. A group of us from various teams had been tailed off on this particular stage and we all looked at each other and did a 'U' turn in the road and rode back to our Hotels. The 'Route de France' was coming up soon, another five day race I had to ride. Our team held the race leaders Jersey. I was with him going over the 'Ballon d' Alsase' (my climbing legs were coming back) but on the descent I was blown into the gutter, hit a water run-off and went flying. The motorbike following thought I was dead! My front wheel which was smashed, was replaced and I was put back on my bike and managed to finish the stage (no laying around like your footballers!)

I did not start the next day. My shoulder was very baldy bruised and I could not move it – still gives me pain when the weather is damp. Four days after I managed to win a race back in Normandy which, little did I know, would be my last win in France. It was a busy year. Next up was riding for my country that the 'Tour de l'Avenir', a two week race. The stages were run the same day as the big 'Tour' only we did 30/40 miles less. It was a nightmare! At the end of every stage we would get on a 'bus' (nothing like to-days coaches) and travel to our overnight stops. The accommodation was in a lot of school dormitories. I was the only Irish rider to finish in Paris. After this race I was just going through the motions, picking up places in events. One incident in the 'Tour de l'Avenir' I recall. On one stage a Portuguese rider had broken away and an Italian attacked to bring him back. Two Portuguese team mates chased him down, road up each side of him and started hitting him with their pumps! (we carried our own pumps and spare tubs then)

Again early 1964 was down in the South of France and racing early season races. The 'Paris-Nice' was again on my programme. On one stage it was so cold everyone got off after five miles and walked to try to warm up. Remember there were no overshoes, knee warmers and clothing which we now take for granted.

Later on the 3rd stage, I could not continue with the cold and wet and ended up in a Bistro with ¾ of the other riders until we were picked up by the 'broom wagon'.

I did manage 6th in Paris-Camembert' at Easter. My French friend was 2nd to our own Shay Elliott. The 'Circuit de Sarthe' and 'Tour de Loiret Cher' were coming soon. I was 4th overall at Sarthe and our team won the overall and team prize at 'Tour de Loiret Cher' with me in 3rd place on G.C. In the first stage I was 2nd behind Guido Reybrouck a Belgian, who in a year or so would win the Green Jersey in the 'Tour'.
Our team rode well to outsmart the Belgians and it was a great way to end my French experience.

I had decided to return to England. I had met my future wife Janet (we have been married 45 years now) and I knew it was time to look to my future in the printing industry. I know I was in good form but I was not prepared to go down another road in the sport. I raced a few events in England, then stopped for a year or so, after getting married.
I was reinstated as an Amateur and started racing again in Essex for Hainault R.C. I won six road races in 1968 and club T.T. championship in 1969. Since then I have become a father of three and have six grandchildren which are the best prizes anyone can have.

I still kept riding all through this period. It kept me fit and sane and I still get that feeling of enjoyment now at 72 years of age as I did back when I started cycling at 12 years old.

So to everyone, keep riding and I hope you enjoy as many memories as I have from OUR WONDERFUL SPORT.

IAN MOORE
West Yorkshire

Bike race and barber shop

The city of Belfast was renowned for men's speciality hair styling in the second half of the twentieth century, due mostly to the brothers Rab and Paddy Maguire in their barbershop at 68 Falls Road.

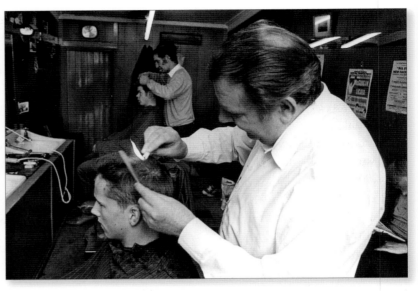

Rab Maguire singes a be-bop in 1983

Setting up in 1952, they were soon undisputed Kings of the Be-bop, striking a special chord with the fight game but catering for all. Politics or religion did not prevent them gaining custom from all over the city, including the Shankill. Policemen from all ranks were regulars until the flare ups of 1969 brought this to a sad end.

In late 1956 Brendan Cardy, a footballer friend and workmate in the aircraft factory urged me to come with him to the shop for a 'crew-cut with singe'. He argued it would suit my cycling better than the hair oil I used, partly in imitation of the great Italian Fausto Coppi.

The demand for the skills of the Maguire's was so great we had to catch the first bus from Newtownards to avoid the long queues to the end of the block. Brendan promised I would be amazed by the characters who used the shop: Teddy boys, Elvis freaks and other exotics mixed with boxers, footballers and athletes of all types.

In 1956 no less than four of their customers represented Ireland at the Olympic Games in Melbourne. They were Belfast's John Caldwell (recently deceased), Freddy Gilroy from West Belfast who won bronze medals, Freddy Teidt and Martin Smith from Dublin who amazingly came to Belfast for their haircuts! The Belfast men won Bronze, Teidt took silver but Smith arrived in Australia overweight and was eliminated. All four became world class professionals, Caldwell and Gilroy taking world titles. They were a famed minority, however, among the great majority of anonymous working class people.

Rab Maguire was interested in my bike racing. He showed knowledge of the sport, mentioning Shay Elliott who was then at the height of his powers on the continent. He said Seamus Herron and Davy Kane of Northern CC were regular customers.

On any visit to the shop listening to conversations between barber and customer could be fascinating. They were more often struck up by Rab, the senior and more talkative brother. Seamen, just off the boat were regular early morning clients, sometimes arriving from romantic sounding climes. Once I heard talk of Valparaiso and Chilean timber. Likewise men just out of gaol often spoke candidly, but sometimes in code, about their experiences.

A seemingly daily caller was a rough-sleeping destitute called Francie who only needed company with perhaps the odd shilling thrown in, but never a haircut. He was of medium height, wore an ankle-length army great coat and was black haired and bearded to the effect that only his eyes, nose and forehead were visible, with an occasional flash of teeth when he grinned.

Little sense could be made of his talk, but the Maguire's established that he came from Ballymena, had suffered shell shock in World war two and was thrown out of his home by his two sisters who found him impossible to live with.

One day I observed him pick up the Irish News and appear to read – a difficult task as the paper was upside down. Rab's intervention in this brought a senseless but strangely logical reply, to the not unkind laughter of the rest of the customers. There was never a hint of mockery in the barbershops treatment of him. One day he was asked why he went down in the sewers. He replied it was 'To get a mouth'. Rab and Paddy interpreted this as meaning 'a mouth to talk to'. Apparently he mostly slept in a tiny shed in McGladderys brick yard on the Springfield Road. Uncommonly he was not a wine or beer drinker and never smelt of alcohol.

Some years later while walking on Royal Avenue I saw Francie stepping out in front of me, the now ragged greatcoat skimming the pavement. In a few strides along the crowded thoroughfare he chanced to meet and pass an attractive woman. Instantly he stepped into a shop doorway and quickly turned his head to view the retreating figure. I had the good fortune, in that fraction of a second, to see a look of almost gleeful appreciation of womanhood on his wild bearded face. It was the last time I saw Francie, surname unknown.

I had my last Maguire crew-cut in April 1957. My wife to be, Mary Fisher, finally admitted she did not like the stubbly look and I was forced to concede.

Paddy and Rab Maguire in their King Street shop in 1983

bike race and barber shop

Almost fifteen years passed before I met Rab Maguire again on the Falls Road one day in 1971. I had hatched a plan to ride a race during the Falls Fleadh under the rules of the National Cycling Association, a body not recognized by the World governing body. If caught I risked suspension from my own cycling organisation (the NICF) so I decided to compete under a false name, or alias. This idea arose from my knowledge that there were hundreds of cyclists in Ireland that I did not know and would possibly never meet. It seemed a deplorable state of affairs and one which should be explained to non-cyclists (or very young cyclists):

In the early 1950's two cycling bodies in Ireland, the CRE in the South and the NICF in the six counties were internationally recognised, thus leaving the nationalist minded NCA out in the cold. They could not compete with the rest of us and international selection was closed to them. It was a recipe for strife which resulted in enmity and recrimination. On a few occasions acts such as throwing of tacks on the road during races were indulged in by both sides.

1971 was a critical year for me. At 34 my best years as a cyclist were past. I was made redundant at the Aircraft factory and was suspected of having kidney disease. It looked like I had no left kidney, or one that didn't work. However, my doctors confidence, "You're to fit", he said, lulled me into thinking it was nothing, especially as I had ridden a 25 in 61 minutes in May of that year. As a consequence I felt like going ahead with the crazy project, almost for the hell of it. It was as if a peculiar fatalism had entered my mind along with unemployment and the threat of illness.

Co-incidentally, of course, West Belfast was having its own critical year; Internment was enacted into law in 9th August 1971 and the Falls Road was in uproar - barricades everywhere and bin lids banging night and day. Despite this I bought a false beard kit in Elliott's of Ann Street and made the organiser of the race, Joe McAloon from Twinbrook, aware of my intentions. Everything was falling into place after weeks of indecision.

On the morning of the race, a late August Saturday, Mary, Brendan (aged 5) and I set off in our Ford Cortina and headed for West Belfast, parking outside the barricades in Castle Street, making our way on foot to race headquarters near St. Peters chapel on the Falls Road. When the race organiser saw me he gave a knowing wink to say all was well. The other officials and riders did not know me, McAloon having agreed to my secrecy. I was about to sign as 'Liam Tuohy', a name chosen for me by an old friend at Shorts, Bobby Delargy, when Joe gave me the name 'Gerard Briggs' which I accepted and simply forgot about 'Tuohy'.

All was set for a completely new experience. Starting at the Falls Baths the course followed the Falls to Leeson Street where it turned left into Raglan Street, leading to Albert Street and back to the Falls, passing the now vacant Maguire's barber shop. The business had moved to Kings Street a few weeks before.

I faced problems in the start area. Rab Maguire was in the crowd and instantly recognised me. I had not used the false beard! Also present was ex-Newtownards Chronicle photographer Farnham Nixon, now a staffer for the Irish News. Luckily he never noticed me hiding in dark glasses behind other riders. A very drunk Rab Maguire however, was quite another matter. He refused to accept my plea that I was not Billy Kirk that day and assumed I did not want to be seen racing with nationalists. The situation became embarrassing until he finally staggered off in a huff. I breathed a sigh and tightened my dark glasses to my face.

The field of about 25 riders were strangers to me, with one exception, the great Shay O'Hanlon, four times winner of the eight-day Ras Tailteann was competing, although I only knew him from press photographs. Only later did other notable riders become known to me: Benny Donnelly, Brian Davey, Davy McLarnon and Brian Holmes from Belfast, Jim McConville from Lurgan and Colm Nulty from County Meath.

The race was on the closing day of the Falls Fleadh of 1971, an integral part of the cultural event. Every pub in the area, but especially, it seemed, 'The Old House' on the corner of Raglan and Albert Street, poured forth a concert of sound: fiddles mingled with guitars, banjos, tin whistles, uillean pipes, bodhrans. Conversation and song in every accent from not only these islands, but also the USA, France, Germany, the Netherlands, Spain and the Basque country.

Once the race got under way the performers spilled out on to the kerbsides bringing their instruments with them, as well as pints of beer and Guinness. They cheered the riders loudly as they swept round 'the Old House' corner on every lap.

The race was 'One hour plus two laps' with the first lap neutralised. At the end of lap two Brian Holmes of St. Agnes CC Belfast attacked strongly, followed quickly by Colm Nulty. The two of them rapidly gained 30 metres. Impetuously I joined them to form a three man breakaway. In the scramble to gain time I found myself gasping for breath for the first 15 minutes, during which I found it hard to take my turn at the front. My partners shouted at me "Do your bit", a sure sign they thought I was 'a fly man'. After about 30 minutes, however, I came round and was able to take my turn strongly, gaining us more time on the bunch. Some of the spectators began to shout "You're going to lap them all!" Very exciting it was especially when we zoomed past the crowd at the Old House, who by this time were going wild and I was getting blurred glimpses of faces, beer glasses and fiddles. The appreciation of the crowd inspired me: I was coming through so strongly I started opening gaps on my companions, smiling to myself when I heard them shout at each other "For f… sake close the gap!"

I later found out that Joe McAloon was panicking in the race directors following car when it appeared that I might escape to win the race. His worry was how could he report Gerard Briggs as winner and not raise questions about his real identity. A dark horse could come third and no one would bat an eyelid.

He need not have worried. My sparkle faded as the race moved into the last ten minutes and we lapped everyone. It was all I could do to stay with Nulty and Holmes as they powered away from the lapped riders.

bike race and barber shop

In the finishing sprint past the Falls Baths, Nulty took the verdict by a length and I finished exhausted about 6 lengths behind in 3rd place.

After the race, sweat still running down our faces, Nulty and Holmes said "You rode well, but who are you?" I answered "Only an old NICF time trialist", but whispered my real name to them.

Only when reading the excellent book 'THE RAS' in 2007 did I learn that Colm Nulty won the event in 1971. Furthermore, some 9 years after racing as Gerard Briggs, when the new arrangements allowed us all to race together, Colm Nulty, among many observers of the sport, was astonished by the strength and speed of my son Lennie, only ten when I rode the Fleadh race. Nulty, from a farming family, generously offered to fund Lennie on the Continent until he signed a professional contract, something which Nulty was sure would happen. Lennie's domestic commitments prevented him from taking up this offer.

After the prize-giving of the Fleadh race, Mary, Brendan and myself retired to 'the Old House', property of Tom Slevin, where we enjoyed the music, song, coffee and a few beers. Except Brendan, who was only five!

I noticed Rab Maguire in the crowd, nearly sober and more sympathetic to me. Seeing me mixing he must have decided I was not a sectarian bigot after all.

We spoke about the old barber shop and its colourful characters, including Francie. I introduced him to Mary and just as we were thinking it was time to go home, Rab invited me to 'come and see the old place for old times sake'.

We strolled around the corner of Albert Street and the Falls, just the two of us, and walked the short distance to the vacant premises where he produced a key to let us in. The place had the musty smell of disuse, but I could tell from the look on his face that it contained important memories for him. To my astonishment there was a juke-box sitting in the corner among a few tiny waiting chairs. He told me it was installed in the mid 1960's by a couple of Falls Road con-men who were, nevertheless, good friends of the Maguires. To show this friendship they gave Rab and Paddy the key to the machine! A juke-box in a barber shop may have been a unique combination at the time.

The barber chairs, mirrors, old fight posters and newspaper cuttings were all gone to King Street, Rab explained, placing his palms from time to time on various relevant parts of the walls.

He told me of a man called Mickey Trudden who had lived upstairs for most of the Maguire tenancy. He was a very quiet and gentle man who suffered from Parkinson's Disease from an early age and lived rent free, compliments of the Maguires. Thinking back I vaguely remembered the clumping footsteps on the stairs and the quiet exit from the shop, despite Rab and Paddys hearty greeting, of a real quiet man.

With hesitation Rab told me how Mickey Trudden had directly witnessed his father's murder in 1921. He was not sure, but said it took place in pre-R.U.C. days at the hands of a special squad of the R.I.C. With even more hesitation, Rab showed me an outside toilet over which Edward Trudden had been held before being shot in the head. Eddie Trudden, an early Belfast member of Sinn Fein had, by Rabs account, begun using the premises for hair cutting and the tradition had continued for over 50 years, in what was originally a two-up, two-down dwelling.

Hoping to relieve the shock to me of these harrowing details, I guess, Rab began to reminisce about his early days as a trainee. Apparently he replied to an advertisement for a barbers trainee placed in the Irish News in 1946 by a man called Esler whose shop was in Donegal Street. There were two applicants and both were given a weeks trial. The man judged in favour of Maguire on the grounds that he was better able to talk to customers – a surprising result when it is understood that the other applicant was Gerry Fitt!

Before I left 68 Falls Road that day in August 1971 Rab gave me one of the little waiting chairs which were forlornly sitting about the barber shop. I still have it, now painted yellow, in a spare bedroom of my Newtownards home.

Driving home with few words for Mary and Brendan, I felt I had gained a new perspective on life, unemployment, the politics of my sport, even my threatening illness on this visit to the Falls Road and the original home of the Kings of the Be-bop.

BILLY KIRK

Footnote:

On 18th January 2010 I visited Paddy Maguire (the surviving member of the great duo) and his wife Ann at their home in the Oldpark Road area of Belfast... The purpose of my visit was to check factuality and gain his approval for what I had written.

He told me of his brother's death in 1992 at 62 years of age.

Possessing an astonishing memory for customers names, occupations and their sports, he remembered Francie clearly and told me about the brickyard on the Springfield Road where he slept.

He corrected certain details regarding the tenant Michael Trudden and confirmed Rab's account of his early days as a trainee. He still does the occasional 'crew cut with singe', mostly for friends and neighbours.

I wish to achknowledge considerable help with this story given to me by the Belfast poet Tom Morgan. An early version had passed hand in hand from a potential sponsor for the book ending up being given to Morgan by Eddie Rafter. He admired it but felt I could improve the grammar and the flow, making contact with me to urge this. Never having met him before I was suprised to find he was a cyclists all down the years. And a great English teacher!

Eddie Richardson - Cyclist and Politician

My father Edward George (Eddie) Richardson was the ninth of eleven children born to James and Kate Richardson of Moybane House, Crossmaglen, Co. Armagh.

He was born on 15th April 1903 and attended Crossmaglen Primary School. In 1929 he married Louisa Murray and had two children, Kitty and myself (Jim).

He held the Ulster Cycling Championship from 1922 to 1929 when he retired due to a knee injury. He won the following races:

- ✧ 1921 he won the one mile race at Reagerstown, Co. Louth.
- ✧ 1922 he won the Cooley Cup and became Ulster Cycling Champion winning the title at Derry.
- ✧ 1923 he won the title again at Rossmore Park, Monaghan and also won the Newry Cup that year.
- ✧ 1924 he won the Governor General Cup in Dublin and took the Ulster Championship at Killaney, in Co. Monaghan
- ✧ 1925 he held his Ulster Championship, this time in Belfast and also won the King and Lee Cup at Kells, Co. Meath and came third in the All Ireland 5 mile Championship.
- ✧ 1926 he retained the Ulster Championship title at Camlough and won the Garda and Bankers Cup in Cavan.
- ✧ 1927 he again won the Championship in Belfast. He won the Garda Cup in Drogheda and the R.U.C. Cup in Derry.
- ✧ 1928 he won the Ulster Championship in Antrim.
- ✧ 1929 he won the Ulster Championship in Derry after which he retired.

He won various other trophies for numerous races during this time and his trophies and medals are in my possession. Moybane House, Crossmaglen where my father was born is retained by myself as a holiday home.

From 1925 to 1928 he was a member of the Armagh GAA County Football team. He entered politics by becoming a County Councillor for Armagh County Council in 1945 which he retained until 1961. In 1958 he was elected Nationalist Member of Parliament at Stormont for South Armagh and continued to represent the Constituency until February 1969.

On at least two occasions he cycled to Stormont from Crossmaglen. A local Balladeer wrote a song about him entitled *The Cycling Champion of Ulster* which was recorded by Margaret Barry and the words of it are as follows and was sung to the air of *The men of the West.*

Eddie died on 29th December 1987 at the age of almost 85 and is buried in St. Patrick's Cemetery, Crossmaglen.

JIM RICHARDSON

The Cycling champion of Ulster

You've heard of the sportsmen of Leinster
Of Connaught and Munster as well,
But you'll find we have good men in Ulster
Quite as famous as history can tell.

When Healy, the Governor presented
A prize to the best in the land
Young Richardson rode out and won it
And brought the prize home to Moybane.

He has conquered from Dublin to Derry
With an ease that would please you to see.
And he reigned the Great Champion of Ulster
Until accident fractured his knee.

On grass-track and cinder they tried him,
While they handicapped lapsed in the rear
But he rode like a hero to victory
And beat all the 'cracks' I declare.

I saw him ride one day at Cavan
When an obstacle got in his way,
His bicycle bounced like an air-ball
And young Eddie was crushed on the clay.

In a moment he sprang to the saddle,
Though the riders had left him behind,
And he tore down the track like an engine
And finished up first in the line.

We are proud of this sporting young fellow
A hero of no small degree
Whose prizes are numbered by hundreds
At his home in Moybane you can see.

Had he been like the lads in the Cities,
With trainers and tracks by the score,
His name would have shone with lustre,
As Champion of Ireland, Im sure.

But he worked at his trade as a brickey
Untiring from dawn until dark,
And he went without practice or training
To wherever the races might start.

He was born with the heart of a sportsman,
Full of courage and power to endure,
And sportsmen shall find a supporter
When they call to young Richardson's door.

This song was sung by Margaret Barry under the Topic records label.

Bronagh Kirk Secy Ards Cycling Club, discovered the above ballad on the Internet and subsequently spoke to the late Margaret Barry's daughter. Her expertise on the computer led us to finding the Dublin barrister James Richardson who filled us in about his father's career.

A berthless night or an ode to slumber

Yes, its humorous and 'tis sad
To gaze on this humanity,
In quest of sleep, O golden sleep
That knows no pride nor vanity

A mother watches o'er her babes
While they in blissful slumber,
Are quite immune to the diesel tune
A couple of decks under.

And here a lass of the merry class
To the postures all around her,
Finds mirth so rare nought can compare
With humanity seeking slumber.

Friends Pat, Big John, Davy and Ken,
Squatting like true Orientals,
Meet some success as they try to rest,
Dreaming of bikes, of home and rentals.

A teenage dame with hair of flame
Men's hearts tore asunder,
Forfeits all for nature's call
In her quest to capture slumber.

Yes, its humorous and 'tis sad
In the lounge of the night-time sailing,
To find that we of the Darwin Tree
Must bow to sleep – no failing.

ELLIOT MATTHEWS   1962

*This poem was written on the Heysham-Belfast ferry after a cyclin
tour of the Lake District in 1962.*

The history of the Derny

*Morris leads
nie Kirk on
the Derny*

The Derny is a bicycle with a small engine fitted to assist in the speed for pacing cyclists – on the track in training and racing. From the time the bicycle was invented in the late eighteen hundreds and early nineteenth century, man's obsession has been: How fast could they go?

Looking back through the years before 1910 many examples are recorded of riders being paced by tandems, over distances far beyond the capabilities of the bikes of that period. It seemed that when the tandem pacers got tired, another tandem would take over.

There is also a report of a contraption that was built, again before 1910 with some sort of an engine on it, but it had proved quite unreliable, never mind the noise. It would just cut out when they were attempting some record or other and they would have to start at the beginning again, resulting maybe in four or five attempts before they would have got to the end and the rider finishing very tired.

Then there is the report of the fastest cyclist of the time 'Mile a Minute Murphy' who covered a mile in less than a minute (over sixty miles an hour) paced by a train. Apparently they laid a board platform between the tracks. I shudder to think what would have happened should he have wavered to the side and touched the rail. It sure required a cool nerve!

In the late 1960's Liam Horner, a Dublin team mate of mine went over to Belgium to ride the World championships and just took a tent with him and set up camp in a suitable site. It so happened that a Belgian gentleman called Herman Nys* came across Liam and decided this was unacceptable preparation for a World championship and made him pack up and come and live in his house for the duration of the event. From that point Herman became a big supporter of Irish cyclists and would turn up at any events that Irish cyclists were involved in. I had the privilege of staying with him and his wife Elsie a few times. He also took a big

Morris Foster and his wife Maureen at the Palace receiving his MBE in 2006.

interest in our domestic scene and would always ask you how so and so was going, even if that rider hadn't been riding in the International teams. When he found out that I came from Glengormley he said to me "That's not far from Larne, isn't it? I was stationed at Carnfunnock Country Park between Larne and Ballygalley as one of the Belgian soldiers during the War and some day I'll return to see it again". Herman was a great friend in fixing us up with accommodation should we be in the Brussels area.

He lived in Villrorde which is on the outskirts of the city. One of Ireland's greatest ever cyclists , Sean Kelly stayed with Hermin at the start of his professional career right up to when he got married and bought a house beside Herman.

Our track racing at Orangefield had been very successful in the Sixties when I was riding and continued in the Seventies when the young riders came along. Like our forefathers, everyone was striving to go faster and one way to increase speed was to train behind pace, be it a car or motor bike. I knew it would be pushing the boat out a bit far by using a motorbike on the track at Orangefield. It would have attracted a lot of attention, probably from the Council so I said to Herman one day "have a look around and see if you could pick us up a second hand Derny". Belgium was totally different than here, as Derny's were used extensively on the track and even the open road where many Belgian riders had their own personal Derny for training. After about a month Herman rang me to say he had found one which belonged to Robert Van Lanker who was a successful Belgian rider of the Sixties and had now retired from racing. We agreed a price and Herman said "I'll take a holiday in Ireland and call and see Liam Horner in Dublin and then come up to Belfast and see yourself and Tom Green who had been over and stayed with Herman and Elsie and had ridden a season of Junior racing. Herman duly arrived at Tom's house in June with the Derny strapped on the roof of his little Citroën car. The Derny had the traditional frame. It was built in the late Forties or early Fifties with the engine sitting vertical above the bottom bracket and central. It had a strengthened frame which would have made it heavier than some of today's Dernys, although I think they are now returning to the traditional style. The engine is around fifty cc and two stroke with two speed gearbox. It also had a fixed gear drive, pedalled by the rider. This was a huge gear with a seventy two tooth chain wheel and a twelve tooth back wheel sprocket giving a gear of one hundred and sixty eight inches. Using the Derny on Orangefield, which is situated pretty high up in East Belfast, we usually had a windy straight with a head wind and the other straight with a tail wind. That meant that the rider could assist the engine unto the headwind and hold it back a little in the tailwind to keep it from running away from the following rider.

We used to use the Derny at the start of the evening's racing where I would just tour around the track and riders would join the line as they felt like it. The rider directly behind the Derny is in the best position and the idea is to sit as close to the back wheel of the Derny as possible to get the most shelter. The riders back in fifth and sixth wheel got a lot of turbulence and didn't last very long if the speed increased just a little. I did a lot of training on an individual basis with Lennie Kirk of the Ards Club, who was just about the best at following the Derny. Irrespective at what speed I travelled at, Lennie could always hold the wheel. With Lennie we always worked in ten lap blocks, increasing the speed in the last five laps up to forty miles an hour where he would have to beat the Derny to the line in the last lap. If he looked to be getting it easy in the sprint, I was always able to tweak the engine in the finishing straight which meant he didn't always beat the Derny to the line. He used to say "I don't think I am going as well today"
I would reply "Never mind, you'll be flying when you get a rest".
I used to take the young riders up behind the Derny on an individual basis and it was good to see how quickly they developed into reasonably good bike riders.

Roll on the day when we may get a new indoor track and modern Dernys to enhance cycling in Northern Ireland.

MORRIS FOSTER

See 'My Friend Henri Scholliers' on page 321.

'Big Mo' in action on the Bath Road, 1964, on the occasion when he broke the 'Four Hour' barrier for 100 miles.

The story of Billy Kerr

Billy Kerr made a huge impact on the Irish cycling scene, particularly during a five season period between 1978 and 1982 when he won all the major honours in Ireland and had some notable international successes too. These included: winning the Tour of the North in 1978, the Sealink International in 1979, the Tour of Ulster in 1980 and 1983, the National all Ireland road race championship in 1982 and the Tour of Ireland also in 1982. He competed in two Commonwealth Games, Edmonton in 1978 and Brisbane in 1982 and also at the Moscow Olympic Games in 1980. However Billy's successes didn't come quickly and he had to apply much hard work and dedication before beginning to reap the rewards.

Billy Kerr with his son Ian in a recent photograph.

I first met Billy Kerr when I joined Ballymena Road Club in 1972 by which time he was beginning to make his mark in time trial events.

Eleven years earlier the first recording of Billy's name had appeared in the Ballymena Road Club results book when, on 19th April 1961, as a 16 year old he recorded 26 mins. 29 secs. for a 10 mile time trial on the Broughshane Road course. Sammy Connor won that night with 24 mins. 15 secs. with Billy's older brother Sammy Kerr second 24.30 and Gordon Caldwell third, 25.04. Such is the enduring nature of the exponents of cycle sport that these three are still active cycling members of Ballymena RC. Billy enjoyed just three seasons as a junior when he was forced to give up the sport because of a bad back. He was able to return after receiving treatment from the then Glentoran physiotherapist, Bobby McGregor who, as Billy puts it, "sorted the problem out". That return came in 1970 after seven years away from cycling and after a couple of seasons, as an average club rider, he started to dominate his own club's results and in 1973 won seven club events. I recall one, fairly modest result which really pleased Billy at the start of the 1973 season. I travelled along with Billy and Jimmy Nesbitt in Jimmy's 'flying' red Mini, bikes on the roof, front wheel and kit bags on the back seat, to the road racing league event at Annaclone. I say 'flying' because Jimmy never seemed to allow enough time to travel to the races and was always speeding. Nevertheless I was lucky enough to hitch a lift that day. The Annaclone event still opens the road racing season in Northern Ireland and on that memorable day, when the entry fee was 20 pence, Billy finished in a lofty sixth position. He was really made up and we were given a blow by blow account of the race as we made our way home.

That was until we ran out of petrol! Nesbit saved the day, however. He took his bike off the roof rack and cycled to the filling station at the roadside café at Ballinderry. It took quite a bit of explaining before the suspicious pump attendant finally loaned Jimmy a can and a gallon of fuel. Once we got the car going again we all called in at the café, where some more fuel was purchased and more importantly, where Nesbitt was concerned, we had tea and cream buns. We didn't leave until Jimmy had devoured several different varieties and had finished watching the Partridge family on the café's TV!

1973 was a watershed for Billy as he finished eighth in the road man's BAR and was second in the second category road man's BAR. This earned him a first category licence for 1974. In time trialing, Billy won the N.I. 100 miles time trial championship (his brother Sammy took the bronze) and finished second in the 50 miles title race. This took him to second place in the NICF time trial's BAR behind Joe Smyth, who had also won the road man's BAR. The Ballymena Road Club team, with Billy in second place, his brother Sammy third and Frankie Robb, seventh won the team medals in the time trials BAR that season.

The following season 1974, he won more or less every Ballymena Road Club time trial he took part in. His first open success came that same season when, as a 29 year old, and on a bike he borrowed from Morris Foster, he won the John Beggs Memorial road race at Dromore.

Billy won the 50 and 100 miles NICF championships in 1974 and was third in the road race title race and was runner up, this time behind Aidan McKeown, in the time trial BAR. In August 1974 Billy rode the Tour of Ireland and finished a lowly 60th.

In 1975 he improved his Tour of Ireland performance to finish 9th and people were starting to take notice. 1975 produced ten open time trial wins and his first Northern Ireland Cycling Federation time trial best all rounder Championship title.

Billy's times in 1975 were 58.34 (25), 2.02.41 (50), and 4.22.10 (100) for a winning average of 24.317 mph. He again won the N.I. 50 and National 100 miles titles and took third in the N.I. road race championship. Billy and those around at the time, remember 1975, if only for one bizarre incident.

Billy was riding in the National (All Ireland) 25 miles time trial championship on the Limavady Road in Londonderry on 3rd May that year and was speeding towards his first ever Irish 25 title when his dentures fell out of his mouth! Now dentures are an expensive piece of kit and being a Ballymena man, Billy didn't want to have to buy replacements. So he pulled up, turned around and gathered up the discarded ivory and continued to race! Amazingly he still managed the bronze medal finishing just 16 seconds slower than the winner, Dubliner, Mick Toolan (Irish Glass CC) who recorded 59.06. Billy's Ballymena Road Club team mate Sammy Connor was second with 59.19 and Billy's time was 59.22. There was some consolation for Ballymena when Sam Gordon, together with Connor and Kerr made up the winning team. Billy wasn't too bothered though and said at the time that the teeth were too dear to leave lying at the side of the road!

Billy attacks during the 1981 tour of Ireland

1976 was even better and saw Billy win his first NICF road race championship, held appropriately at Annaclone, Banbridge where, just three years earlier, his sixth place in the league race had been greeted with such satisfaction. This time Billy lead from start to finish in a magnificent solo effort which gave him a three minutes winning margin. He finished the 1976 season as roadman's best all rounder champion and successfully defended his time trial BAR championship.

In 1977 Billy started to race further afield and he finished 21st in the Tour of Britain, 5th in the Manx International road race, which was held over three laps of the famous T.T. circuit on the Isle of Man. He also rode the Pro-Am Scottish milk race in which he was 26th and at the end of the season he notched up his best result to date with an excellent runner up placing in the Tour of Ireland.

Billy again won the roadman's BAR in 1978 and won the NICF 25, 50 and 100 miles time trial titles and was runner up, again to Aidan McKeown, in the time trial BAR championship. Billy also famously won the Tour of the North stage race over the Easter weekend in 1978 and this was his biggest win up to that time.

In 1978 Billy was a member of the Ireland team for the World Road Race Championships in Nurburgring in Germany. He recalls, "We flew into Dusseldorf on the Monday and when we landed our Manager, Phil O'Brien, after checking if we knew where we were going and instructed us to ride to our hotel which was 80 miles away. We had plenty of time as the race wasn't until the Wednesday, so off we went, all six riders including Stephen Roche and myself. This was a great idea. We all headed off, all clad in our green jerseys. The road had a great surface and was really smooth and we were enjoying the ride but every so often a car would beep its horn and we thought they were just being friendly. Then this car came alongside and the driver instructed us to pull over. He was an off duty policeman who asked us what we were doing. We told him we were over for the World championships and were riding to the Nurburgring. He informed us that there were two things wrong. One was that we were on the Autobahn and the other was that we were going in the wrong direction! He was a great help though and turned us around and told us to follow him until we got on the proper route.

Billy recalls another story while on International duty: "Tony Lally, Pat McQuaid and myself rode on the Ireland team the year that Pat won the Tour of the Cotswolds in the late 70's. It was about 4.00 pm before the race finished and Pat had to stay on for the presentation, so Tony and myself decided to head back towards the hotel. It was late on a Sunday afternoon and there was no one about and the shops were all shut as we rode in through the town. Even so, it probably wasn't a good idea to be riding down a one way street. It seemed okay until a police 'panda car' pulled us over. At this point Lally told me "don't you speak now" (a difficult enough task) and he would do all the talking. The policeman got out of the car, adjusted his cap, the way they do and proceeded to ask us what were we at? Lally responded in Irish and when quizzed further continued to give his answers in Irish. The cop tried a few more questions and was met with the same response, in Irish. I said nothing. The third time the policeman just said "away you go". Frustration had set in!

1979 was the year that Billy had what he considered was his greatest success - victory in the Sealink International stage race, which came immediately after his second Tour of the North victory. "I shouldn't even have ridden the 1979 Tour of the North, as I had been picked to ride for the Irish team in the Sealink which was to start on the Wednesday in Manchester and the Tour of the North only finished on Easter Tuesday. However, John Snodden talked me into riding the Tour that year. I had just won the Tour of Ards and they took me up to Downtown Radio for an interview. Snodden was there and so was the Tour of the North's main sponsor, Bill Franklin. They put me on the spot and asked me was I going to defend my Tour title and I said I would. I won the Tour of the North which finished on the Stranmillis Embankment on the Tuesday afternoon and then it was straight to the airport and we flew to Manchester on the Tuesday night for the start of the Sealink the next day. Peter Crinnion was the manager of the Irish team that year and when I arrived at the team hotel he was attending the managers' meeting. We spoke afterwards and I told him that I had won my race already. He wasn't too pleased but said to keep a low profile for the first couple of days as he wanted me to do a good ride when the race came to Wicklow, as the Olympic selectors would be viewing the race. The race started on Wednesday morning and I found myself in every move that was going and I finished second to a Danish rider. He won again the next day and then it was across to Dun Laoghaire for the Irish stage - around the Wicklow hills, where I took the jersey. Then on Saturday it was back on the boat to Holyhead and the stage which I won at the top of the Great Orme. On the Sunday, during the final stage of the race, I broke my brake cable on the descent of the Horse Shoe Pass. Ollie McQuaid gave me his bike and I got going again. They replaced the cable and I switched back to my own bike for the rest of the stage. I had got away with it and won the race - that's the way it goes. Sometimes its just one of those things, sometimes everything just works out right."

Billy won seventeen road races and time trials in Ireland in 1979 including pushing the NICF time trials BAR through the 25 mph barrier for the first time.

Billy announced that 1980 was to be his final season on the international circuit but he fairly packed in lots of foreign events that year. He rode the five day circuit of the Ardennes and finished fifth. Then was fifteenth in the Sealink and went to Chicago for short circuit racing in May, before tackling the Tour of Britain 'milk race' where he was determined to win a stage. He took a second place in Wales, only being beaten by a Russian and finished 18th overall. Next it was the NCA's Ras Tailteann stage race where he took the lead with four days to go and held on to the end. Billy then travelled to the Moscow Olympics where he represented Ireland and became the first ever cyclist from Northern Ireland to finish the Olympic Games road race. He was 41st from 115 starters. Billy remembers his time in Russia but wasn't too impressed! "Everywhere we went we were accompanied by 'secret police'. We could only train on the Minsk highway and on the circuit which was to be used for the road race. There were soldiers on guard on each side of the road for miles and miles. Each team had an interpreter and a driver but everywhere we went we also had company to keep an eye on us. It was the same when the Russians came to the Tour of Britain. They had police with them to watch them too"

In1981 Billy won all Six Northern Ireland and All Ireland time trials titles at 25, 50 and 100 miles. He set a new NICF BAR average speed of 25.335 mph and had individual records of 21 mins. 43 secs. for 10 miles. 55 mins. 41 secs. for 25. l hr. 56 mins. 25 secs. for 50: and 4 hrs. 8 mins. 37 secs. for the 100 miles distance. The 100 was one record Billy had chased for some time and had never quite managed it until 1981. Morris Foster held the record with 4.8.47 since 1966 so it was quite an achievement when it was finally broken. Remember that Billy recorded those times on a standard road bike. After the Sealink win a journalist commented on the state of Billy's bike. He explained that he just had the one bike and used it for training, racing, club runs, riding to work and going messages!

The same bike was used for the specialist art of time trialing, the only thing Billy changed was to fit a pair of 28 spoked wheels and take off the bottle cage! There were no tri-bars or low profile bikes in those days which makes his time trialing achievements even more remarkable.

Billy had his fair share of mechanical problems. He broke his Raleigh 'Ireland team issue' bike during the Tour of the Glens road race at Carnlough and didn't even realise until the race, which he won by 5 minutes, was

Billy Kerr packing for the 1978 Commonwealth Games

over.

Billy added "the following Saturday I was due in Brighton for the start of the 1981 Tour of Britain. Morris Foster arranged with Barry Witcomb for a replacement frame. He transferred the equipment and I rode the Tour of Britain on the Witcomb and he told me to keep it. The only problem was when I went to ride the 1981 Tour of Ireland and landed down on the Witcomb bike, the Ireland team were supposed to ride Raleigh bikes and I was called in to ride at the last minute and still had the Witcomb. John Beattie, the managing director of Raleigh Ireland was in Clonakilty for the start of the tour and when he saw me riding down the road on the Witcomb he asked where the Raleigh was? I said it had broken and he said he would send me up a replacement the following week. The bikes were made of 753 tubing which was new at the time and I think we were riding them as an experiment and to test them". They certainly were well tested when Billy was on board!

Billy continued "There was another occasion in Holland, during the World championships, when we were riding the team time trial for the Irish team. I thought the bike was handling badly and after the race, when I had a chance to look at it I saw that it was broken near the gear levers on the down tube. That was my CAT International bike which Clifford Davison, Alan Mark and Tom Smyth had given me. There was still the road race to ride and I needed a bike and a local bike shop owner took me into the basement of his shop and told me to pick a frame. He stripped down my broken frame that night and gave me the replacement the next day. Again he let me keep the bike and I rode it for a long time after that".

In 1981 when Billy was asked to ride for Ireland in that Tour of Ireland he knew he would be losing his job in Antrim's Enkalon factory in October. He remembers telling Morris Foster that he would need the equivalent of a weeks pay if he was to take part as his day job would soon be over and the bills needed to be paid. Morris said there would be little chance of that, but six phone calls later Billy agreed to ride and set off for the start in Clonakilty. He reckoned he was badly needed for the Tour because Martin Early and Paul Kimmage were riding for the first time and needed Billy's guidance. Billy did all right though, winning two stages and finished third overall to add to his previous brace of runner up placings.

Billy reconsidered his 'retirement' before the start of the 1982 season. He had been unable to get regular work after the Enkalon factory closed and he said that he would ride that season if he still hadn't got a job and so it was that he embarked on a 'comeback' season. He was unemployed for all of 1982 and was able to concentrate on his racing and training. At that time I rode from Ballymena to my work in Toomebridge several days each week and quite often Billy would catch me as I rode out the Toome Road at 8.00 am. He was at the start of his five hour training ride. He said "When I was working I had to do 8 hours a day. This way I get up early and have my training done by 1.00 pm. - that has to be better than working".

He was part of the winning NI team in the Girvan race that Easter and took 13th overall, despite losing 8 minutes because of a puncture on the opening stage. He was the only member of the Irish team to reach the Blackpool finish of the Milk Race where he was 17th overall.

In mid summer he twice took and lost the yellow jersey in the Ras Tailteann before eventually finishing fifth after having given way to a fellow Irish team member who took the honours. Billy doesn't say much about that one, except that he could and should have won. I think it was the only time Billy had taken a race leaders jersey and not gone on to win the event.

Another win which Billy holds very dear came in the National All Ireland road race championship at Castlebar in August 1982 during that 'comeback' season. Billy explains "I had never finished in the first three in the Irish road race championship. My best was fourth or fifth and I reckoned this was my last chance to win it. The race was held over three big 35 mile laps and I was the last one to get across to the break. I remember that there was a gale force tailwind from Westport on the road to Castlebar. Davy Gardiner was in the break and I instructed Davy to attack before going into Westport and I would get across to him on the hill - that was at the start of the last lap. That worked and Lennie Kirk was already clear, that meant there were three of us from NI out in front, then Lennie got dropped. Coming to the finish I didn't know what to do as I had been trying to win this race for years and there was just Davy and me. We shook hands and we agreed to sprint it out side by side and may the best man win. Lennie got picked up by the chasing group but still won the bunch sprint for third. The same year I finally won the Tour of Ireland and Lennie was second and Davy third. That completed the set – Tour of the North (1978 and 1979) Sealink International (1979), Tour of Ulster (1981 and 1983) Ras Tailteann (1980), Tour of Ireland (1982) Northern Ireland Road Race, All Ireland Road Race (1982) and all the Irish time trial titles, North and South (1981)"

However Billy's biggest regret came in the 1982 Commonwealth Games in Brisbane when, as part of the Northern Ireland team time trial squad, he missed the bronze medal by a mere 29 seconds. He said the team had ridden the final leg of the race beautifully and added "I'm certain we would have got the bronze if I hadn't cracked with 5 kilometres to go".

The 1982 Commonwealth Games road race was a disappointment for Kerr as well. "When I started the road race I decided I wasn't going to do anything until we had done at least 80 miles. Then I broke a spoke in my front wheel with about 40 miles done and had a bad wheel change. As soon as I stopped the Australians put the hammer down. I chased for a lap and an half but never got near them again".

Billy later abandoned the race. I think this was his only "DNF" during International duty. Billy had been disappointed too four years earlier in the 1978 Games in Edmonton. The winner of the road race that year was Australian, Phip Anderson, whom Billy had beaten on the Donegal stage of the 1978 tour of Ireland a few weeks earlier. Anderson later went on to be a hugely successful professional rider and held the famous leader's jersey in the Tour de France. Billy said the power just wouldn't come that day and he finished just over one minute behind Anderson with a group of 17 riders in 22nd place.

Billy raced again in 1983 and he showed true grit in winning the Tour of Ulster that Easter. Davy Gardiner was leading all the competitions – GC, mountains and points when the snow started to fall on the Sunday stage. According to Billy, Davy made the mistake of trying to change his wet gloves for a dry pair. He couldn't get them on and finally had to give in to the conditions and abandoned the race. Billy kept going and won the Tour of Ulster for a second time. That determination shown on a bitterly cold Easter Sunday was typical of the attitude he applier to all the events he took part in during a hugely successful career. 'Never give up' was his motto.

Cycling journalists always enjoyed interviewing Billy and he never disappointed them, always coming up with a witty answer or comment. Once in the Tour of Britain he delighted the press by stopping at a pub at the top of a major climb for a drink. Legend has it that Billy swapped his race cap for a pint and then waited for the peloton to catch up. Billy explained the reality of the occurrence: "it was the 1980 Tour of Britain and the rest day was in Scarborough and we were all in the same hotel. We were sitting around and watching TV. I ordered tea and sandwiches and told the Russian, Sergei Sukhoruchenkov, tomorrow I am going up the road as I need some prize money. He nodded his head and said "you go up the road, I go up and road and then I go further up the road and you go back". Billy added: "So anyway the race started and I was up the road in a five rider break with the two Russians, including Sergei. We were on a climb like Shane's Hill (at Larne) and the two

Russians just cleared off and left us. Then I saw all the locals standing outside the pub and thought we aren't going anywhere with this break! So I jumped off and took a sip of somebody's pint and then joined in again with the race. The next day the newspaper headline was KERR STOPS FOR A PINT. The Russians won everything at the Tour of Britain that year. They were first, second and third and Sergei went on to win the Olympic road race in Moscow.

Billy raced locally until he was 45 and thoroughly enjoyed his twilight years and won many more championship medals and domestic road races, including the Red Hand Trophy, the night after falling off at a gala event around the Ballymena Showgrounds oval.

I acted as assistant Commissaire for a number of seasons on the Tour of the North and during some of those years Billy was, at times, my driver. His knowledge of racing and his ability to read the race and spot the errors made by some of the top challengers was amazing. Even though he wasn't racing himself you could still see the enthusiasm. I feel privileged to have followed Billy's career from his early days as an average club rider to top International. It has given me an interesting insight into our most wonderful sport.

Billy's honours keep coming and in 2006 he, and N.I. football manager, was inducted into the Ballymena Hall of Fame, joining such others as Willie John McBride, Syd Millar, Mary Peters, Maeve and Sean Kyle, Jessica Kurten and David Humphries. Illustrious company indeed. He showed me that to be successful one has to go the extra mile. Billy in reality went the extra mile on a regular basis. He would ride to events, ride the race and ride back home, just for additional training benefits. On club runs he would do more than the rest, too. I remember completing a 90 mile club run from Ballymena to Portrush, then around the coast to Ballycastle, Cushendall and Carnlough. We all then headed for home, all that is, except Billy, who would ride on around the coast road to Larne before completing his days training. He maintained that you needed to do big miles to be able to compete at the highest levels.

He certainly proved that his training methods brought success, nobody would argue with that.

RICHARD WILSON   *Ballymena R.C.*

My friend Henri Scholliers

This story was written by Billy Gordon of 'Gorden Cycles', Hillsborough. It tells the tale of two men, who met absolutely by chance and how they formed a lasting and meaningful relationship down the years.

The year of 1944 was moving on. The World War was on-going for four years and many changes were taking place all over Europe. The Monte Casino battle was raging, the Allies were getting the better of the Germans and their Italian friends, while the struggle in the Far East with the Japs was continuing. My brother Thomas and I would be working hard in the old smith shop – making and repairing agricultural machinery for the farming community. Some evenings we would quit work at a reasonable time, get ourselves washed and tidied up, getting our bicycles out and once astride, cycling the three and a half miles to the town of Lisburn. When we were not out for a serious training spin, Lisburn was a regular venue for us both. Cycling after our work was our life - it was what we took sort of serious.

Cycling was one of the greatest things ever to happen to Thomas and me. We were always enjoying every minute on our bikes and it wasn't just a case of cycling for each others sake – we were in unison, both loving our work and loving our cycling. It also meant we worked together, we cycled together, one always helping the other – that was also our life.

Best wishes to William Gordon

EDDY MERCKX S.A. - N.V.

EDDY MERCKX

s'Herenweg, 11 - 1860 MEISE (Belgium)
Tel. 02/269.62.72 - Fax 32/2/269.93.67

This publicity photograph was presented to Billy Gordon by Eddy Merckx when he visited the factory.

The bicycle was a means of transport used by many people in my early days. Our father cycled and he used an upright bicycle with a back peddling hub brake and a step on the right hand side of the rear axle. He would mount the bicycle by standing behind the machine, with his hand on the handlebars, his right foot on the rear step and with a forward movement, mount the bicycle over the saddle. This was customary with the older generation. At different times he would take off for a long ride around the countryside and he found that very refreshing. I remember the times he did some of these trips, long before I was allowed to even think about attempting to learn how to ride a bicycle. The learning procedure was real fun, not so difficult in my youth as there was virtually no traffic about.

Mother was also a good cyclist. She rode a bicycle which was termed a daisy bell. It was a very upright model with a loop frame. She cycled many miles going around her relations which were many. My mother's connection were many in numbers and she was friendly with them all, giving her a large scope of friends to visit. So you will see my point, cycling was bound to be in my blood and that is one thing in life that I am grateful to both my parents for.

Cycling to places we had never been to before, through towns, villages and the countryside, distance was no object and there was always the chance of meeting other folk, in the same frame of mind. We were always fit, but never finely tuned! Our nature of work and the hours we worked kept us always with rough edges - the fine tuning wasn't all that important. What nicer than after a days work: getting cleaned up and lifting our cycles, getting astride them and the two of us having a good fast run into Lisburn. To hear the tyres humming along the tarmac road was like music to our ears!

In those days Lisburn was a fine market town. It had lots going for it and the people were our neighbours and like us they were friendly. Although the town had many things going that didn't interest us at all. Tommy and I knew many people there and we were always sure of a good crack (a chat). Folk of our age group did frequent the streets of Lisburn and one place in town that did interest Tommy the most was the Picture House in Bow Street. He loved the films and the Gaumont British News. It kept him up to date with the War news. He would go to the Pictures on his own. The films didn't interest me as much, unless it happened to be a good western film, although I liked the news reel. While my brother was at the Pictures I would either go to the cycle track in Wallace Park or wait around until he came out. Sometimes we would have a fish supper wrapped in the Belfast Telegraph before cycling home together.

It was on such a night during the latter part of 1944 while I was waiting outside the Picture House, a young soldier boy came walking up the footpath. Nothing strange about that you might add, for Lisburn is a Garrison town. A large new Army barracks called Thiepval Barracks was just competed before the outbreak of war in 1939. I was standing there holding my bicycle. It was stripped out in racing style just like a thoroughbred horse ready for the track. As this young soldier was passing he paused and came over to me. The bicycle attracted him like a magnet! I knew right away he wasn't English speaking and looking at his shoulder flashes, I knew he was from Belgium and it is the home of many famous cyclists, past and present.

He examined my bicycle from front wheel to the back wheel. He was delighted to have met another cyclist and seemed to be a very bright spirited lad. He looked around my own age and spoke little or no English.

I managed to get him to understand that we should meet again. He was called Henri Scholliers and we

my friend Henri

arranged to see each other on another evening when my brother was at the Pictures. I would use Tommy's bicycle and as Henri liked the style of mine, the idea was we would go out cycling together, getting to know each other. He picked up English quickly and out of this friendly act, little did I think it was to create a life long friendship, secondary to my brother's friendship. I loved Henri like a brother.

We enjoyed each other's company and he was delighted to learn and see more of the countryside. One of our favourite runs was the Ballinderry Road and that, I remember was one of the first words he learned. Henri was learning all the time and each time we met I was learning more about him. He was billeted at Fort Hill House. It was a large house and grounds that stretched along the Low Road in Lisburn. He was there with a contingent of Belgian soldier recruits for army training before returning to Europe, should the war be prolonged. He was proud of the shamrocks on his shoulder flashes. They denoted he had done his army training in Ireland. Fort Hill after the War was over became a Comprehensive School for Girls.

Continuing to meet and go out around the various roads together, my brother was more than generous to lend me his bicycle and making this friendship possible. Henri would visit our house in Hillsborough. Mother would make him very welcome and he would have dinner or what ever was going with us as a family. One Sunday when Henri was visiting my home in Hillsborough we didn't go out cycling after dinner as we usually did. Instead the both of us went for a walk around the village. I was showing him around, pointing out the places of interest. Hillsborough is a very old village steeped in history and as we were walking along the wall of Government Castle grounds. In the distance a local girl was coming toward us. He was able to say "beautiful from far" and when she got past us he continued to say, but "far from beautiful". That saying never left my mind.

On a late summer Saturday evening of 1944 I had arranged to meet my Belgian friend Henri Scholliers, being dressed and ready to cycle down there, when over the street came a local lad called George. He was courting a sweet shop proprietor's daughter. They had come from Belfast after one of the air raids and were known as Evacuees. Their ice cream churn was broken and he was pestering me to fix it. As I was in a hurry I declined to help him at that moment and told him to bring it across on Monday morning and I would do what I could to fix it. He was trying every trick in the book to get me involved and not being rude with him, I listened to him, but still firmly stuck to my guns. The only thing happening was, I was keeping myself back, delaying my departure, knowing as I did, come Monday morning the ice cream churn would be fixed somewhere else. All George was about was to use me, when he couldn't get the job done elsewhere, and I didn't relish being used. I was by this time truly fed up with him and threw my leg over my cycle and pushed off. The delay was to prove funny and yet not so funny. As I was nearing Harry's Road, about a mile from the village, it was getting dusk and the evening light was fading fast. I could see the form of a cyclist approaching in my direction, neither of us had lights. I was travelling very fast and suddenly we collided! The other cyclist and I were on the ground. I was able to get up quickly picking the other cyclist up off the road. And to my utter amazement, it was my own dear Mother! She was returning home from visiting a friend and had a bag of plums and apples hanging on her handlebars. The fruit was scattered all over the ground. I asked her if she was hurt and she assured me she was alright. I gathered up as much of the fruit as possible, saw that her cycle was alright and we both continued on our separate journeys. When I returned home later that night I asked her how she was and had she any ill effects from her fall. I will never forget the look on her face. She said "How did you know that I was knocked down?" She was more amazed when I told her that it was me that had been in collision with her! It took ages for it to sink in and she could hardly believe it. Thank goodness she was alright with no ill effects. We had many a laugh at the funny way it happened.

It proved to me that George was just going to use me, for on Monday morning or any other morning for that matter, the broken part of the ice cream churn didn't come in for repairs. It would have been much better if, in the first place when I told him to bring it over on Monday, I had left him at that point and went on my way. I could then have avoided knocking my Mother off her bicycle.

The war in Europe came to an end on 8th May 1945. Hostilities ceased in the Far East, with Japan throwing in the towel on 15th August the same year. The face of Northern Ireland had changed over the war years. It was an ongoing change. Life was changed forever and the changes that I personally witnessed could fill a volume on its own. This small Province had been the home for many different service personnel and they were soon beginning to disperse. The units were leaving, some on their way home and the Americans were pulling out. My friend Henri along with his fellow countrymen were on their way back home to a liberated Europe and no doubt would be very pleased to be with their families and sweethearts. I would be parting with the comradeship of a friend, but was also glad he was returning safe to his loved ones.

Henri enjoyed his cycling around the surrounding countryside every bit as much as I did. He was a good clean living lad and reasonably fit. Around the month of March 1945 our racing season began and he expressed the wish to ride one of our 25 miles time trials on the exposed Antrim Road course. This road is high above sea level and gets wind from the Belfast Lough. I remember he insisted on riding a 72 inch gear and I couldn't get a 72 inch gear on my cycle for him. All I could achieve was a 68 inch gear. Accessories were impossible to come by during the war time – one had to make the best of what one had. Henri insisted the 68 gear was okay which I thought was a very low gear. He told me it was due to him not being 100% fit. His time for the event was a reasonable 1hr 12mins 41secs. Being a strange road and with a low gear, it was commendable.

The track season was approaching and the better weather was also with us. Lisburn's Wallace Park has long been the home of a cinder cycle track. Not that many cycle meetings are held there, due to the fact the sponsors of the events cannot close the park because of it being a public park. To celebrate the victory in Europe a cycling

my friend Henri

track meeting was to be held in Wallace Park and I asked Henri if he would like to ride in these events.

He was enthusiastic, so I asked the promoting club if they would accept his entry. They said "yes" so all was in order for Henri to compete.

Riding in the half mile and mile events, starting on very low gears, he said he was only warming up to the two mile event which he would ride on a higher gear, we had the necessary accessories at hand to achieve this for him. The changes were made by my brother who was a first class cycle mechanic. The half and one mile events were over and Henri was looking very much forward to the final event. The race was to be run off in four heats and Henri was in the fourth heat.

During the heats an elderly Red Cross nurse came over to speak with me. She had come to realise that Henri was from Belgium. She said she had been friendly with a Belgian soldier in the First World War and was making a cushion cover for him. Before she had the cushion finished for her soldier boy, he was killed in action. She still had the cushion and asked Henri, if she finished it, would he like to have it? I think on the cushion cover she had embroidered the Union and Belgian flags. I've no idea if Henri ever received that cushion cover.

Getting back to that day of the cycle track events, as the four heats were scheduled for the two mile event and during the time of talking to the Red Cross lady, the starter of the event ran the race off in three heats, not four as stated in the programme. Henri was not informed of what was taking place, for he was very much looking forward to this event. It was one of the most unsporting things I have ever come across - especially to a visitor to the country. I personally took it very bad and to heart and was so upset that I resigned from the National Cycling Union and the Road Time Trial Council in protest. They were unapologetic to my friend. When they insulted him they also insulted me. As far as they were concerned for me it was over and out.

I wasn't bothered about resigning from those two cycling bodies. Our cycling didn't suffer in the least. It was enhanced for me and my friends, for an alternative existed in Ireland – the National Cycling Association of Ireland. Their events were more in line with the continental road races, massed start events were run on the open highways. When my brother Thomas and I left our former club, quite a number of our cycling friends followed us. The result of their un-sporting tactics with Henri had backfired on them and the culprit officials were the losers in the long run - losing some of their most important riders.

Both Henri and I agreed to keep in touch with each other and this would be by writing letters. This would be difficult for Henri as he would have to write in English as my Flemish was non existent. It was a joy for me to receive his letters, giving me the various pieces of news. He would tell me about his sweetheart Liliane, send me pictures, newspaper cuttings of cycling events and other things in general. I would reply with some answers to his comments and what was going on in this neck of the woods. One morning in May 1947 the postman delivered a letter from Henri. It was a very interesting one.

Henri had been selected to represent his country Belgium in the Isle of Man International Massed Start cycling event to be held in June over the famous motor cycle T.T. circuit. Teams taking part were from France, Holland, Belgium, Ireland and Great Britain and there was also a team accepted from Northern Ireland. This event was to be a most memorable one for myself, for in the Belgian National Team was a young lad whom I had befriended while he was doing his army training in Northern Ireland.

This was less than two years since Henri had left Northern Ireland and for him to be selected to represent his native country in such an important event in the British cycling calendar was great. I was elated and just over the moon and felt proud that he had done so well, knowing that during his time in Northern Ireland he was able to keep up with some cycling. Although it would be minimal to what he normally would be doing at home in Belgium.

The difficulty in getting to the Isle of Man was posing a problem. The only way of getting there was by boat and they only went every Thursday and that would mean travelling to the Island a week before the event, meeting Henri on the next Thursday the day of the cycling events and not being able to leave the Island till the following Thursday. A stay of two weeks in the Isle of Man would prove impossible for me. I just could not afford to be away from my work for that length of time and the possibility of meeting my friend Henri seemed bleak.

As the time was getting closer to the Isle of Man International Cycling Week, some talk was around cycling circles that some club men were trying to charter a plane to the Island. They would leave in the early morning on the day of the events and return the same day. Now this was very interesting indeed and, moving very fast, I managed to obtain a seat on this aircraft. It operated from Newtownards and the airstrip (before the war) was privately owned by Lord Londonderry. It was the same airstrip upon which Ribbentrop landed for his visits to the pro-Nazi Lord Londonderry at Mount Stewart before the war.

A small plane was in production at Newtownards by Miles Aviation Co. These planes were made from plywood and called the Miles Aeorvan. I was very much looking forward to meeting my friend Henri again and I had never been up in an aircraft before. The joy at meeting my friend outweighed my fear of flying, especially in this plywood crate!

As Newtownards town is twenty one miles from Hillsborough, the only way there was to start off early in the morning on my bicycle. That particular morning in the month of June, the sun was shining brightly when we set off. I was accompanied by my brother Thomas for part of the way – just to ensure that I would have a trouble free ride to Newtownards. That is the kind of care that I received from my brother all through my life.

I had arrived with loads of time to spare. This was to be a new experience for me and I was now having time to think of what I was about to embark on! Thoughts were racing through my mind. I suppose this was a natural reaction. The flight over to the Island was fine and getting over the natural fear of my first flight, I soon settled down still thinking ahead, however. We were approaching the Island and Douglas Airport was

my friend Henri

shrouded in clouds, making landing impossible. The pilot was directed to the Royal Air Force base at Rollingsway. This was high up on the mountain and meant a coach ride into Douglas. This in itself was very good, giving us a chance to see a part of the T.T. Course we otherwise wouldn't have seen. It also gave me less time to find my friend Henri, but I was fortunate to find him in good time before the race.

I was introduced to the Belgian national team, meeting the French team also. The race was won by the Frenchman, Baldasarri in a tight sprint finish. Demulder of the Belgian team was third. I thought sure it was Henri's victory for he was winning the run in to the finish, when suddenly his foot lifted off the pedal. He had taken cramp and this was quickly spotted by Demulder and he immediately sprinted with an extra effort, managing third place. Henri was the Belgian team's number one and he managed seventh place overall. I was ever so pleased Henri had done so well. Travelling back home I felt proud, knowing that some of my fellow travellers has not been so kind to him when he had rode some races in Northern Ireland during his stay there. His performance that day was a great boost for me. I felt ten foot tall!

Back at the hotel where the Belgian team was staying one of Henri's team mates was feeling under the weather. He had to retire from the race early. He was sad and couldn't speak English so I asked Henri what his trouble was. Henri told me that he had got a nasty tyre burn on the back of his leg and was forced to retire. Some rider had come too close to him. It wasn't the tyre burn that was bothering him for these boys are a tough breed. His father told him before leaving Belgium, if he didn't do well in the race he was to give up cycling in the competitive sense, as it didn't fit into the plans he had for him. He was sobbing at not making more of his chances, with Henri saying he had come so far for so little.

Shortly after that we said our goodbyes - that was our last meeting for some time. I hurried to meet up with my fellow travellers for the return flight to Northern Ireland. The flight from the Isle of Man was going fine until we reached Strangford Lough, when suddenly the aircraft gave a shudder and seemed to loose height. I was scared I admit and I thought all was lost and was ready to sing Abide with Me. Just as suddenly all was right again. It was only for moments but it seemed an eternity. Enquiring later what had happened I was told the plane had hit an air pocket. I was ignorant of the fact. That is really what puts the fear into one, to be ill informed or not informed at all. The aircraft landed safely and we were on firm ground again. I picked up my bicycle from the parking lot, and started the homeward journey. On my way up the Lisburn Road I made a stop at Marlborough Park to pay a visit to my girl friend, Mary Lewis and let her know that I had returned safely. Also to tell her of my little experience. It was an excuse to stop by and see her!

I learned quite a lot from sporting experiences and it is only a few that reach top flight. One has to be dedicated to remain there. But the few that reaches the top are not necessarily the true sportsman or sportswoman. There are the runners up in every event and the also ran's. Some of these people are amongst the finest of all sports persons. Sport was as I had always saw it: about enjoying ones self and that seems to be enjoyed down the ranks when no pressure is on and that give me a philosophy - one shouldn't be in sport for what one can get out of it but should be in sport for what one can put into it. That to me is the true sports person. Only three can share the top honours – all the rest are also ran's.

After the Isle of Man meeting with my friend Henri, as before we both kept in touch by letter writing. It was as much of a joy to write to him as it was a joy to receive a letter from him. He must have struggled with his English, but it was no trouble for me to follow his line of thought. He would send me cycling clippings from Belgian sporting papers, keeping me up with the latest news. During this period of correspondence Henri told me how he signed a professional contract in 1949 for the Groene Leeuw team, a big Belgian firm of Bicycle manufacturers.

As a domestique he rode well for the team leaders, getting many good placings. However, his career came to an end in a sad way: One day in 1951 his team manager gave him a package of race food just before an important event. As it happened he had a convincing win, but when he turned around and came back to the team manager expecting congratulations and a hug, instead the man was extremely angry! He accused Henri of taking a stimulant instead of the food he had been given. The ensuing disagreement was so bitter Henri realised he was not supposed to win that day and that the background to the row was almost certainly the involvement of bookmakers in the sport. Disillusioned, he retired from professional cycling, continuing, however, to cycle for pleasure. He married Liliane and in due course they had two bonnie children. Henri was a proud and loving father always speaking highly of his wife and children. That made me feel extra proud of him too.

In 1988 my wife Mary and I went to visit daughter Glynis and family in Germany and it was only after we had left home that I discovered I had forgotten Henri's address in Belgium. It was his phone number in particular I had forgotten to bring with me for his address was stamped in my mind like carved in stone, for I had written it so many times since 1946.

When we arrived in Germany and had tried several ways to obtain Henri's phone number with no success, until Mary in her usual business manager like style, went into the Post Office using her knowledge of German to be understood, she eventually got the phone number. Being late on into our holiday when I phoned Henri he enquired where I was and when was I coming to see him. I informed him that we would be travelling to Belgium the next Saturday for we were due to leave for the return journey home to Northern Ireland the following Saturday.

A long and eventful journey through Germany and Holland led us to the town of Grembergen. It was not quite our destination and a visit to the local police station was necessary. A gentleman came to the rescue. He said to follow him and he took us almost to Henri's door. It was quite a reunion.

My family, including Mary, returned to Germany. Mary would have stayed with me but had decided it was best if Henri and I spent a few days by ourselves.

Sunday morning came and we were all up by 9.00 a.m., had breakfast then off for a walk with his yellow Labrador. We went through his vegetable allotment. This is the first time that I had seen a Colorado beetle. It was a pretty coloured beetle, it's a pity it is a harmful little devil. On the way back, Henri asked me would I like to see a Professional cycle race. As we could only go to one race, he told me he'd picked out one from around twenty races taking place that day. This one was the most likely one to have the best Professionals riding in it. It wouldn't have the top Pro's as they were competing that day in England in the Wincanton Road Race, which included the Worlds top riders. Ireland's Sean Kelly came second.

Henri took me on a run out to show me where he was born at Appels, near Dendermonde. Also the little rivers and waterways where he had played as a boy. It was nostalgic for him. We returned to Dendermonde and walked around the square admiring the architecture of the lovely old tall buildings. We moved on and Henri explained that we were now in an old part of Belgium. Built around the early 1600's and was the home of widows, complete with its own private Chapel. It was at that point that I said to Henri that I was surprised that he had not gone to Mass earlier in the morning. To which he replied that he was a non practising Catholic. I did ask him for some of his reasons, for I was more than interested to know a little more why that was so? He said to me that a Priest could be living beside him and could be committing worse sins than he (Henri) was, so he said how could the Priest give absolution of sins? That was the most honest thing I have ever heard during my life time about the Church, from any Catholic. For the forgiveness of Sins there is only one Mediator between God and Man and that is the Lord Jesus and in my heart I believe Henri knew that.

The next morning we were up early, the dog had his usual morning walk and during the walk Henri said he had a surprise for me. He didn't give me any more details than that, as I was his guest. He laid out the time etc. I just did what I was told. After all it was to be a surprise. Once on board his lovely kept red Toyota car, he was heading for Brussels. We travelled up the road for a few miles. Henry was giving me a commentary on the way when suddenly I noticed a sign pointing to the left to which I said "there's a sign saying EDDY MERCKX."

At the junction Henri turned left. He passed no remark thinking that I had stumbled on his surprise, but I hadn't! He still kept the chat going till we arrived at the neat little village of Meise. Stopping the car and parking it, and walking back up the road a few steps, Henri said this was the surprise he had for me. There before us was a lovely large, low brick building with the name across the buildings front: EDDY MERCKX in big letters. In the short time available to Henri, he had arranged that I could visit the Cycle Factory of this most celebrated of Belgium's cycling Sons.

It was surely a pleasure for me to be invited to visit this Factory. We were greeted by one of Eddie's managers – a former six day rider from West Germany. He had to leave us to answer the telephone, when in came the man himself – Eddy. Henri introduced him to me, we had a brief exchange and it was indeed a very big moment for me to meet a former three times World Champion and five times winner of the Tour de France, amongst a host of other successes. There are not many professional cyclists in the world that one could meet with such an impressive a record. Henri got me a catalogue written in English. The frame building unit was very interesting for me. Leaving the factory and continuing on our way toward Brussels, Henri said he'd forgotten to get a signed autographed photo of the maestro himself. He promised he would get one for me and send it to me at a later date. This he did and I treasure that photo very much. I gave it on loan to my little granddaughter, Faith Gordon when she was doing a project on cycling during her time at Primary School. It is not every child that can boast their grandfather was a cycle frame builder. When finished she promptly returned it to me.

Henri had yet another surprise in store for me. We were going to see the home of Sean Kelly. Henri made inquires if we were in the right street. Suddenly a man came striding across saying in Flemish "who wants to know?" Henri explained that we had just come from seeing and meeting Eddy Merckx at his factory and that I, his friend from Ireland would be delighted to meet Sean Kelly, if he were at home. The man asked Henri how we had met each other and Henri explained that we had met during the Second World War while he was stationed in Lisburn. The man went on to say that he knew Lisburn well as he was also stationed in Northern Ireland with the Belgian Army. He was based on the Antrim Coast.* He also explained the reason why he asked Henri who wants to know where Kelly lived. He told us that a few gangs of burglars from near Brussels were operating in the area and people had to be careful who they gave information to. We followed him as he drove a few streets further on to Sean Kelly's house. We met Lawrence Roche, brother of Stephen Roche. Stephen who had won the Giro-de-Italia, the Tour-de-France and the World Championship – all three races in the one season. Quite a major feat by any standard. His girlfriend told us that Lawrence was riding for the Carrera team, whose top man was Claudio Chiappucci, and was a close second overall to Greg Lemond in the 1990 Tour de France. I had a long chat with Laurence. He knew our cycle frames well but he and I had never met. They asked Henri what refreshment would we like? I said "Tea". He started to laugh, maybe he expected me to say whisky or some other alcoholic beverage. He disappeared into the dwelling, returning still smiling, holding a bottle of whisky. On the label was a picture of Sean Kelly. The whisky was specially made as a present from the Paddy Whisky Co.

Laurence showed us inside the house. It was a very large room, no windows in the walls, light was coming from domes in the roof. There, lining the walls were row upon row of cycling jerseys in all the colours of the rainbow. Mussete bags and loads of trophies - small and large cups, the Tour of Spain Trophy which must have been a metre high! Henri and I just stood in amazement at so many trophies all assembled and won by one man – Sean Kelly.

We were told that this collection was only part of his winnings and when Sean came to the Continent he lived in with this family.

We came away and Henri told me how delighted he was to see the trophies. After Eddy Merckx, Sean Kelly was his second cycling hero.

On returning to Henri's home we found Liliane had prepared a lovely spread for us. My short stay was drawing to a close. That evening Henri's family came and we talked till late. I had a magnificent short time with Henri and his family, which I will cherish for the rest of my life.

There was a time in our friendship when we had lost contact and time drifted by but he was often in my thoughts. Suddenly we were reconnected and it remained that way until only one of us was left. Although I have never quite accepted the fact that Henri is gone, I had spoken to his daughter Agnes by phone, but could never bring myself to write the family expressing my sympathy for the loss of a husband, a father and a grandfather. If I had done that I was admitting Henri was no longer with us, so I blocked that part out of my mind. I just held on thinking he was still with us. That may sound foolish to anyone that may read this, but having lost my brother who was my best friend and this was a reality I had to live with, I used the distance between Henri and myself to block out the passing of another best friend, into believing he was still around and that gave me a bearable feeling to get by on.

BILLY GORDON

EDITORS NOTE

This was Herman Nys who was stationed at Carnfunnock, near Larne and is described by Morris Foster in 'The History of the Derny' on page 316.

Seamus Herron Cyclist

I am honoured to be asked to contribute to this publication.

My early recollections of living in Belfast are greatly influenced by the outbreak of World War 2. No – I'm not going to do an 'Uncle Albert'!

I remember my Mother and us kids being huddled together under the stairs in our home in Thompson Street as we listened to the bombs dropping around East Belfast. We lived just 50 yards from the river Lagan and I believe the German pilots used the Lagan as a guide to the shipyards etc.

I'll fill the cup Dad!

Seamus Herron of Ballybay Park, Corcrain, had no worries about filling the cup which he collected on Tuesday by winning the 1000 metres all-Ireland cycling championship. He beat Gerry Kinsella of Dublin, holder of the title for the past two years. Mr. Herron's baby son Michael filled the cup.   T3132

My father James worked in the shipyard as a crane driver and at night he was an A.R.P (Air Raid Precautions) Warden, riding about on his big Raleigh bicycle checking that all the lights were out and windows covered in black. He called in every so often to see that we were okay.

Because of our close proximity to the Lagan we were advised that we should evacuate. I remember the long walk we had early one morning from our home to the railway station on the Shore Road. We eventually ended up at Ballycastle where, after a few days, we were housed with a farming family called Hunter, living on the road to Fair Head. After sharing the Hunter family home for a while, we were housed in a cottage at Fair Head – right at the end of Ireland. I believe it is now owned by the National Trust.

Cycling from Belfast to Fair Head after work every Friday had a great influence on me eventually adopting cycling as a sport. He would arrive at Fair Head in the early hours of Saturday morning and leave on Sunday afternoon on his old faithful Raleigh Roadster. My Dad was one tough guy. He never took up racing, but had he done so, his stamina would never have been called into question.

When I was about 8 years old we moved from Fair Head to Teconnaught – a little town land between Ballynahinch and Downpatrick. We had a great time there. I still have the Roll Call from the school we attended which identifies us as evacuees. My Father was able to visit us on his bike during the week and at weekends.

Back in Belfast and now 11 years old, I had to learn to ride a bike. I can remember falling off a lot, much to the amusement of my new found friends. As soon as I was able to stay upright, I was off up the Saintfield Road and the countryside.

Seamus Herron

At school at St. Matthews, like most lads, I had a go at Boxing. I was shaping up well until I was entered in an Inter Club match against the Shankill Road Boys Club and matched against a stocky lad called Bush. You don't forget a name when someone punches the daylights out of you for 3 rounds!

During the fight our trainer, J. B. Brady was shouting: "On your bike, Herron". On your bike in boxing terms means to back pedal. I met JB many years later and he said "Young Herron, do you remember that night in the Shankill Road Boys Club when I told you to get on your bike? Well, that was the best advice you ever had".

I agreed with him. I left school at age 14 years and my first job was as a delivery boy for a wholesale chemist in King Street. To my delight they gave me a box trike which I would load up and deliver orders to chemists all over Belfast. I had a few scrapes with that trike. I can remember creating havoc by mounting the footpath and scattering the queue outside the Ritz Cinema and being told by a policeman "You are not supposed to ride that thing so fast – and NOT on the pavement". I think he reported me to my employer and that was the beginning of the end of that job.

Next up I got a job which was supposed to lead to an apprenticeship in a print shop in King Street Mews. I hated being indoors and the only good thing I remember about that job was that I got to use an Arab Printing Machine, which you had to pedal. I spent a lot of time printing dance tickets and programmes for various events. I did get outdoors occasionally to take work to the bookbinders in North Street – on a hand cart. And, would you believe it, on one such trip, I got stuck in the tram tracks in Castle Street and was helped out by the same policeman from The Ritz who just happened to be on points duty. I cannot put into print what he said – he was not pleased.

By this time I had bought myself a Raleigh Lenton from George Stone in Cromac Square. It had a Dynamo Hub, Stormy Archer Gears etc. On a trip out on the Antrim Road I came across a time trial starting from the 6th Milestone. I carried on up the Antrim Road and ended up at the top of Antrim town where I met a gentleman called Billy Blair from Sugarfield Street, Shankill Road. He was a very special kind of man, who invited me to help him hand up drinks and food to the riders as they raced back to Glengormley.

This became a regular fixture, Billy Blair and I at the hill out of Antrim, handing up drinks etc. to the Knights of the Road – P. J. McNeilly, Gordon Reid, George Wilkes, Billy Dowds, Tom Smyth, Davy McNutt, John Harvey and Eddie McArdle, to name but a few.

Billy Blair invited me to join the Kings Moss CC meeting at the Pig and Whistle in Templepatrick on Monday nights. I became a member, I believe in 1950. After some time I joined the Northern C.C. I think I was influenced by their interest in road racing. Following on from my job in the printing firm, I started to serve my time as a bricklayer. This was the life for me, outdoors in the fresh air and travelling from job to job on the bike. Best of all, as an apprentice in the building trade in those days, part of your job was to make the tea and fetch things from the shops. With rationing of everything, cigarettes were very hard to come by. Shops would only let you have 5 Woodbine or Park Drive. My Raleigh Lenton earned its keep when I built up a cig run whilst working at Flush Park estate between the Cregagh Road and Rosetta. After a couple of hours I returned to the site with my saddle bag full of cigs. I was the best pair Nipper ever! On Friday nights the builders were queuing up to give me their tanners and all the time I was getting faster and going further in my search for cigs. Well, sadly that gravy train had to stop and I got down to being a bricklayer.

Having seen my heroes of the road with Billy Blair, I had to have a go at racing. My first race was a 10 mile T.T. I only managed 29-23. I was very disappointed until my Father came home from work and said that Joe Craig, a top rider at the time said "That was a great ride on a Raleigh Lenton Dyno Hub and all".

I can't recall the year: it must have been early 50's when I made my family run to the Albert Bridge to see my hero, Geordie Wilkes, pass by in the Plaza Grand Prix. Little did I know then, that when I won my first road race, The Tour of the Mournes in 1955, Geordie would be second. Geordie brought a lot to cycling. His influence on young riders of that era should never be forgotten. The satisfaction of being a bike rider is all the reward you need and the friends you meet make it all the more fulfilling.

I spent many hours with my Father in George Stone's Workshop in Cromac Square. I watched George build my first racing bike, a Stone Special. It was a little heavy but ahead of its time – 74% parallel with straight forks and 11" bottom bracket. He said it would be just right for a sprinter. Maybe he knew something.

I handed my Lenton down to my Dad and we put together a bike for my older brother Liam. We went on touring and camping holidays round Ireland, and crossed over to Wales. My brother was a natural, he could just go for hundreds of miles without any preparation, but football was his first love. He played for Irish league teams like Ballymena and Bangor in the 1950's and ended his playing days at Altringham in Manchester. He once rode to Dundalk with me where I rode in the All Ireland 200 kilometre road race in early 1950's. It was won by the great Shay Elliott and as we rode back to Belfast my brother said "I must do that more often" - and he did. He regularly went down to Dundalk bringing back lots of things we couldn't get in the North in those days.

I along with most riders in the 1950's had to ride to get to races no matter how far away they were. We would get a group together, ride to Dublin on Saturday and race Sunday morning in Pheonix Park and then back to Belfast on Sunday afternoon. It certainly made bricklaying on Monday morning a little bit trying.

Then came the time when some of our great supporters like John Snodden and W.L. Smyth would hire large cars and transport us South in the early season. Then of course, that became too easy and lots of these trips became social outings. I can recall John Snodden, the most willing and helpful person you could ever meet, collecting us to go to Dublin. The last collection was Frankie Thompson. When we pulled up in Devonshire Street, Frankie's mother would wheel his bike out for someone to put it on the roof rack and then Frankie would appear dressed to kill in suit, white shirt and tie.

Talking of Frankie reminds me of a time at Orangefield Track when there was a massive pile up and Frankie having broken his arm in a serious fall in France – and been warned not to break it again – put his hands behind him and ran into the fence full face. What a crash that was! It made the headlines in the papers and at the following track meeting we had several photographers present expecting the same again. The evening following the crash, Frankie and I had a date with two girls, one of them being my now wife, Anne. When we told them we were in a crash they thought we meant a car crash as we were bandaged and plastered everywhere.

Another memory I have of crashing was a stage of the Tour of the North, when almost the entire bunch crashed because of ice or mud on the road near Cookstown. I borrowed a bike from some lad from Dublin who said he couldn't go on. At least I believe that's when he said. When I finished on the Stranmillis Embankment I got my own bike back, but to this day I don't know whose bike I finished on.

Cycling throws up many adventures which is one of the joys of the sport. My life long pal, Michael Horgan and I , having been in Amsterdam for the World's Track Championships in 1959 decided to see a little of Holland, Belgium and France on the way home Quite some journey on track bikes, fixed wheel, no brakes and our baggage strapped to the handle bars! On one occasion we got caught up in a Belgian Road Race, much to the amusement of the riders. We stayed in the bunch for some time. Micky even suggested I should try for one of the sprints. We eventually ended up in Dunkirk where an obliging French farmer allowed us to occupy his barn for a few days until we could get enough funds to get us home. Michael even tried to get me some building work. He was good like that!

Last but not least, I would like to thank all the people who helped make my cycling journey so enjoyable. The many people who gave up their time willingly so that we, sometimes very selfishly, could achieve our ambitions. People like Tommy Givan, W. L. Smyth, Stanley Martin, Tommy Taylor, Peter Woods, Billy Stewart and of course John Snodden to whom I owe a lot. Many like John, are no longer with us, but they left a legacy never to be forgotten.

What little cycling I do now is in the Summer around the Dordogne Region in France where I have a holiday home. I trundle along the traffic free lanes and think of the old days of joys and disappointments, of what was achieved and what might have been. Above all I think of how lucky I am to be still doing what I love best of all – getting the pedals round and breathing in the fresh air. I hope many of the friends I met in my life in cycling are well enough to still climb on that old piece of iron we call the bike.

SEAMUS HERRON

My 100 mile debut

Larne Cycling Club was reformed in 1958 and affiliated to the Northern Ireland Cycling Federation.

Our first President was William 'Tosher' Burns, an Official of the well respected Ballyclare based Kings Moss Cycling Club. The original Larne Club had been established in the early 1950's but limited its activities to club runs and club Time Trials.

One of the senior members of the local Boy Scout Troop where I held the proud rank of Patrol Leader of Wolf Patrol, was a keen cyclist and would turn up on Scout nights, when not in uniform, in his heavy knitted green cycling jersey with its thick red band around the middle. He rode a Viking machine. We impressionable young men would all cluster around Dan as he arrived at the Scout hut. We stood astride the crossbar of his Viking and recounted his successes in the old Larne club's 10 or 25 mile time trials along the famous Antrim Coast Road.

Winner of the 1959 Andrews Cup 100 mile time trial.

Winner Billy Stewart - Northern CC (centre), being congratulated by Sammy Kerr from Ballymena (left), and John Magill - Larne CC who finished second.

Whilst we all enjoyed 'the Scouts' a number of us, attracted possibly by the thoughts of wearing our own heavy knitted green jersey with its broad red band, decided that we would like to extend our horizons and take up this new sport.

My first problem was a simple one – I didn't have a bicycle nor did my father nor any of my brothers. There was only one bicycle outlet in Larne, a garage, almost opposite the house where Isabel Woods, a legend in Irish cycling, was born. Various frame sizes were available but all in the same species of 'sit up and beg' bicycles, in black paintwork and each with a sturdy Brooks leather saddle with coil spring suspension for maximum rider comfort. Unlike today, in the 1950's young men seldom ventured outside their own town to shop for their

my 100 mile debut

needs, so my budding career as a cyclist was put on hold. That is until one day when I was 'doing a message' for my mother at the local Co-op, I walked past a newly opened shop and there in the window was a vision to behold! A gleaming Pillar box red coloured Armstrong Sovereign with turned-down handle bars, shiny steel rims and a saddle bag – just what I wanted. At £26 and 10 shillings it was way beyond my means, but this was the era of Hire Purchase and Green Shield stamps. So with my father as Guarantor, I was soon licking and sticking. 1958 was a wonderfully happy year on the bike as we discovered the joys of long club runs to such places as Ballycastle and Portrush. We would stop off in the woods near Carnlough on our return journey home to brew-up in our tin cans using water drawn from the stream rushing through the woods on its way to the shore.

What excitement there was when the newly formed Larne CC held its first 10 mile Time Trial on a Tuesday evening in April along the Antrim Coast Road. No one knew what to expect as none of the 12 entrants had ever 'raced' before. With no guidance given or sought on how to prepare ourselves or our bikes for a time trial, a strange assortment of men and machines faced the Timekeeper. With no proper bike shop in Larne, football shorts were the rig of the day and 27inch wired-on tyres on steel rims were blown up rock hard – there wasn't a tubular in sight. Virtually everyone, including myself, favoured the Reg Harris look – low-down handlebars and high-up saddle – if it was good enough for Reg, it was good enough…..

No one bothered to warm up as we had all ridden to the start, either from home or straight from work. 'Warm-up' just wasn't in our vocabulary. I was one of the last to be pushed-off and with head down sprinted off along the Coast Road. By the time I reached The Black Arch, a well-known landmark outside Larne and less than a mile from the start, I was gasping for air and my lungs were bursting. No one had told me that Reg Harris didn't ride 10 and 25 mile time trials and I soon found out why. However with my minute-man visible in the far distance I tried to compose myself and started the chase.

I was pleasantly surprised to win that first event and all the other Larne club time trials that I entered during that 1958 season. However our times were slow but we were comforted by our President who informed us that we shouldn't expect fast times on our course, as there was a lot of Ozone in the sea air. He knew about such things as he was a big wheel in the St. John's Ambulance Brigade. It obviously followed that there couldn't have been the same amount of Ozone in the coastal air around the County Down shores where John Fennel and Billy Kirk were regularly beating the hour.

When the season ended we continued to enjoy club runs in all weathers. Going out on the bike became addictive even on the darkest winter evenings as we began our preparation for the 1959 racing season. After the club's Easter tour to Letterkenny and back, the season opened for me with participation in my first Open event on the Antrim Line, a four-up 25 mile Team Time Trial. I was part of a composite team along with a

John Magill in Derby Wheelers strip during the Burton and District Cycling Association 100 mile Time Trial in 1960. John was beaten by 3 seconds into second place by winner Vin Denson, a well-known British Professional cyclist from that era.

Awaiting the off at the four-up 25 mile team time trial on the Antrim Line. will recognise the Timekeeper, Tommy Taylor and John Magill is third from the left.

club colleague and two riders from Kings Moss Cycling Club, Ivan Beggs of the Moss being the most experienced rider of the four. We finished way down the field but the atmosphere surrounding such an event was intoxicating and standing for the first time alongside riders from clubs like Cyprus CC, East Tyrone CC, Old Bleach CC, Northern CC, Windsor CC, Ballymena Road Club and Maryland Wheelers gave me such a thrill and I was truly hooked.

As the season progressed I rode all the club events ranging from 10 to 50 miles and entered all the Open Time Trials on the Glengormley/Antrim course which seemed to be the course most favoured by event promoters. Although winning club events, I was well and truly put in my place when riding the early season Open events. The spoils were usually shared by the 'fast men' of that era, including Billy Kirk, John Fennel, Tommy Talbot, Bobby Talbot, Billy Hudson, Maurice Donaldson, Sammy Kerr and Sammy Connor. Morris Foster was having time-out from cycling and Billy Dowds had retired, otherwise I would have been even further down the results sheet.

my 100 mile debut

By mid summer the longer distance Open events started and first on the calendar was the Northern Ireland 100 Mile Time Trial Championship. I had never ridden a 100 mile time trial before, but decided to enter. The Saturday was warm, sunny and there was little wind – a lovely summer's day. As usual I rode my Armstrong Sovereign from Larne to the start and was soon aware that I was within reach of event headquarters near Glengormley as the air was laden with the aroma of embrocation and Sloane's liniment.

I had only one objective for my first 100 – to finish in time to allow me to get to the 'second house of the pictures' at the Regal Cinema in Larne which was showing an Errol Flynn adventurous block buster about pirates on the high seas. One hundred miles was a long way and a step into the unknown. Some concerned team mates suggested that I should take my saddle bags with a flask and some brown bread and date sandwiches. I toyed with the idea but decided against it.

The perceived wisdom of the age said that to ride a 100 you should start steadily and keep something in reserve for the second half of the race. Since I had no real speed in my legs I thought that if I started off slowly I would end up very slowly. So I set off from timekeeper Tommy Taylor the only way I knew how – to go as fast as I could for as long as I could.

The early part of the race was uneventful but there were obviously a few lads who were holding something in reserve for part 2, as I caught and passed a few riders which for me in an Open event was completely unheard of. However, as I returned from the Antrim leg somewhere near Corr's Corner, there was a rhythmic tapping sound from the rear of the bike. I looked back and discovered that a spoke had broken in my rear wheel. I stopped as quickly as a fixed wheel and a front brake would allow me and found that the spoke had broken at the wheel hub end and thus I had to unscrew it at the nipple end which seemed to take an eternity. In two plus years of ownership, this was the first 'mechanical' I had ever suffered with my trusty Armstrong Sovereign. With a lighter bike but a wobbly back wheel I remounted to head off on the leg to Larne.

As I approached the Village of Glynn I was pleased to see that the good villagers still retained the Continental practice of writing the name of their favourite rider on the road. His name was William and he must have been highly regarded by the villagers as they had nicknamed him King. Furthermore they had even painted his start number on the road – 1690. Since I was number 31 he would obviously have started well down the field and was unlikely to catch me. Was it Billy Campbell of Maryland Wheelers or perhaps Billy Stewart of Northern CC they supported? I never did find out.

Coming into Larne I caught sight of a familiar figure by the roadside. With one hand in his pocket and the other lightly cradling a Gallagher's Blue between his second and third fingers, my father had broken with years of tradition. Every Saturday afternoon he would have been glued to the radio at this time on a Saturday, listening to Sports Report to see if his 8 draws on Vernon's pools had come up. In winter it was the English and Scottish league results and in summer the Australian Pools which was going to change the family fortunes.

It was a lovely gesture on his part to come out and cheer me on when he had other priorities.

On the way back from the Larne turn I was starting the climb of the 'Bla Hole' above Whitehead when I caught up with Jack Watson of Northern CC. I didn't know Jack so there was not much conversation between us as I passed him. Jack however had other ideas and must have wanted to get better acquainted as this mop of blonde hair kept appearing at my right shoulder. I just couldn't seem to get away from Jack who was a very gutsy rider, so I searched my bike frantically for something to hit him with. Then I remembered that I had left my pump in my saddle bag. I knew then that I had made a mistake in deciding not to take the saddle bag – so much for the Scout's motto 'Be Prepared'. However patience and persistence paid off and as we neared the top of the Bla Hole, I eased away from Jack. The following season Jack and I met up in the East Midlands to where we had made our separate ways to take up new jobs. Jack was riding for the well known Leicestershire club Coalville Wheelers, and I had joined Derby Wheelers.

The finish was somewhere near Rathcoole, on the Shore Road going into Belfast. As I approached the finish I closed in on Billy Stewart, Northern CC. Tommy Taylor on the finish line was in sight and Billy was determined to get there before me so he gets out of the saddle and goes for it. I hadn't come all this way on a wobbly back wheel to get beaten in a sprint and Reg would have been proud of me as I got there by half a wheel. (Billy got his own back when he beat me and Sammy Kerr into second and third places in the Andrews Cup 100 some weeks later).

There were raised eyebrows and re-checking of watches and figures when this unknown from Larne had returned the fastest time in the championship so far. The real stars including Tom Allingham, Sammy Kerr and Bobby Talbot had yet to finish so I had no great expectations of the outcome. With only Tom Allingham to finish no one had bettered my time, so when Tom crossed the line I was anxious to catch Tommy Taylor's eye. He confirmed that I had beaten Tom's time and that I was Northern Ireland champion at my first attempt at the distance.

After the race I was sitting under a tree on the Shore Road when I was approached by Stanley Martin. Stanley wrote occasional articles on cycling for 'Ireland's Saturday Night' and other newspapers and asked if he could have a few words. He was kind enough to write a nice article about my performance, but was not going to let the facts get in the way of a good story. Monday morning's Belfast Newsletter article carried the headline 18 YEAR OLD WONDER BOY WINS NORTHERN IRELAND CHAMPIONSHIP. In fact I had just turned 21. Riding home to Larne that evening, lost in my own thoughts, I was caught up by Charlie Meban, a very useful roadman from Kings Moss CC. Charlie had been at the finish line and knew that I had won the championship. As we neared a garage at Whitehead, Charlie offered to buy me an ice cream to celebrate. As we sat at the roadside in the warm sun's dying rays it slowly dawned on me that I would never find out what daring adventures Errol would get up to on the high seas that evening.

my 100 mile debut

Happily for me that first Open win proved not to be a fluke and as the season progressed I was fortunate enough to win the All Ireland 100 mile Time Trial Championship, the Northern Ireland 12 Hour Championship and the All Ireland 12 Hour Championship all within a few weeks of each other and all on my trusty Armstrong Sovereign. I finished off the season winning the Northern Ireland Best All Rounder competition.

Sitting under another tree after the last of my championship wins, Stanley Martin suggested to me that it might be something of a record for someone to win all four long distance championships in his first season of Open competition. I never did find out if it was.

I never had the pleasure of personally receiving any of my championship trophies. Although I went along to the Prize Presentation evening, the dinner took so long to complete that I had to leave the hall before the presentations started. I needed to catch the Belfast-Heysham Steamship that evening as I was due to take up a new job in Derby in under 36 hours time.

Riding for Derby Wheelers, where I had as team mates, Derek Woodings, winner of the British National 100 mile Title and Mick Potts, winner of the British National 24 hour title, I improved my times considerably, but nothing again ever matched the feeling of happiness, contentment and well-being as on that Saturday in June when I won my first 100 on home roads.

JOHN D MAGILL

Sadly John Magill passed away in July 2010.

Personal best

As the youngest of five children in a sporting family, I grew up hearing talk of 'personal bests' and racing exploits from an early age.

I recall my sister Diane who was a good swimmer and my brother Leonard comparing their performances. It couldn't really be done, but Leonard would argue that his personal best for a ten miles time trial was better than Diane's best for a 100 metre freestyle!

Diane became an Irish Champion in the pool and later was the first Ladies Irish Triathlon Champion. Leonard's performances on the bike are legendary: ranging from Irish Sprint Champion on the Track to Long Road race and Stage race wins. He also represented Northern Ireland at two Commonwealth Games and more recently won the National Veterans Road Race title. My other brothers, Clifford and Billy also did some cycling in their youth. I remember being in the car with my Mum and Dad while they followed him training on the Portaferry Road. He was a strong rider and did some good rides in his early teens, but he didn't continue. Billy did a few time trials at a young age. I remember Mum and Dad joking that he only tried hard when he saw someone watching him! Maybe my Mum had 'overdressed' him as I've seen a photograph of him on the bike wearing a shirt and bow-tie!

My turn had come and in the summer of 1976 I did my first 10 mile time trial on the Portaferry Road. It was organised by my Dad, Billy and Bobby Adair, who had kept the Ards Club going during some lean years in the 1970's. It was a warm July evening and I did the race on my new single geared Dawes Vindec. Leonard was fastest with a 24 minute ride and I did 34.10. I was almost 10 years old and the youngest rider. My Mum Mary was down watching and I asked her what her best '10' was? 28.21 was her 'personal best'. So that became my target!

In 1977 I didn't do any time trials but I did the novice race at the Town Centre racing which was always part of the Borough's Civic week. Leonard was 16 by now and had just won the 'ESCA' Youth International stage race in Yorkshire, England. It was also Queen's Silver Jubilee and a big crowd cheered Leonard to a memorable win in the main race, after he 'lapped' the entire bunch.

The next year, 1978 my Dad asked me to tell every novice at the Town Centre race that the Ards Club would be holding 5 and 10 mile time trials on Wednesday nights on the Portaferry Road. The first night of these was very well attended and there was a great 'buzz' about there being such a lot of new young riders competing. This was the start of a boom period for Ards CC. Among the new recruits were: Alastair Martin who would later be Club Secretary for 17 years and an Olympic Games representative. Anthony Mitchell, a prolific junior winner and now the Tour of the North Race Director. Stephen Dunn, the first of the well known Dunn family to make an impact. Gary Morrow and Ralph Fowler. My dad said that all these guys had been 'bitten by the bug'. They couldn't get enough of the bike!

Other members at the time included: Billy Hudson, an ex. Cyprus man who had won many '25' titles, Mike

McConaghy, who was later Sponsor and Chairman of the club. Jimmy Thompson, Larry Parker, Ron Martin (Alastair's dad) and Hugh Mitchell (Anthony's dad).

With the regular club races and runs I started to 'catch up' with my Mum's personal best for a 10! I passed the mark in a club '10' on the Portaferry Road on 9th August 1978.

The result was: 1st (A Mitchell 27.22) 2nd (Brendan Kirk 28.15) 3rd (Gary Morrow, 28.43) 4th (Hugh Mitchell 29.05) 5th (Stephen Dunn 29.11) 6th (Colin McGivern 30.04) 7th (Alastair Martin 32.06)

"You're faster than your mummy now!" my Dad said. It was to be some years before I got close to my Dad's personal best as he was a Northern Ireland Competition record holder for 25 miles! Now he has amazingly raced ahead of me again as in 2006 he set a new personal best of 57.59 for 25 miles!

BRENDAN KIRK

A Great Rivalry

Around the turn of the century (what a momentous phrase!) I began to hear reports of Cormac McCann (a man of my own age) doing '10's' in under 24 mins. and 25's in 61 mins. I said to myself, just like the character in 'the boys from the Blackstuff' "I could do that"!

In 2001 after a few months of harder cycling I got down to 23 mins. 49 secs. for a 10 and a great rivalry was born. Gradually we both got down to about 60 ½ minutes for 25's and there were many discussions of what was possible for an oldie. Now and again my rival would talk of breaking the hour for 25 and I found myself saying under my breath "come on Cormac, get real". However, proving that dreams and aspirations are very important to us all, in 2003 Cormac clocked 58 mins. 2 sec. on the Moira-Nutts Corner course!

I did not ride well that evening and returned a 63 minute time, but I remember thinking "I *hope* I can do that".

Three years later on the faster Ballymena course I did a new personal best '25' of 57 mins. 59 secs. which brought tears to my eyes as it eclipsed a N.I. record I set in 1955.

The rivalry that produced these results continues today.

BILLY KIRK

The Story of the Turnip

*Twenty years ago (1989) when
we were all a lot younger, even more keen to
enjoy a good days biking, a group of 10
riders set off from Dunmurry.*

We didn't have great ambitions as to get in too many miles. It was an early summer's day as we set off into the County Down countryside. We travelled down through Ballynahinch and on 'Vinty's' beckoning we decided to follow him (Vincent Tubridy) up some of his 'wee roads'. After approximately three hours we arrived in Newcastle and headed for the Strand Café for the traditional coffee and scones. During the well earned rest and 'fill up' we discussed where to go next. It was decided to head round to Kilkeel, but when we reached Attical, it was decided Kilkeel would be a bridge too far. So we headed up the Silent Valley. After the climb up to the Dam, it was a well earned free wheel off the mountain. We headed down to Hilltown, then on to Castlewellan. By this time we were all starting to make sure the face masks were firmly attached. As we got to the bottom of the hill out of the town we turned left, heading back to Dunmurry. Through the Spa Road - this road is hard enough when you are fresh, but after approximately 6 hours the space age technology for sticking the face masks is called for!

As we rode by the Golf club and crested the last of the hills and onto the road for Lisburn, we happened to notice that one of our riders was missing! To put it this way, as 'Morale' Davy McCall would do, let's go back and give him another chance to get dropped!

So we all turned around and came up to an abandoned bike by a lane. We happened to ride down this lane and what we witnessed was the rider, sitting in this field. He had a set of 'Blumels' tyre levers – back then there was none of the toy plastic tyre levers, but the metal ones, and there he was - getting 'stuck into' this turnip.

The only words we got from him was "I was famished and couldn't go any further."

Hence comes the legend of the 'Turnip'. For years after this he was affectionately known in cycling circles as 'turnip'.

Footnote: Be careful when you are out cycling you don't want to create a legend!

JOE SMYTH

Eddie Cassidy

This book could not have been printed without acknowledging the contribution and long service which Eddie Cassidy gave to cycling in Northern Ireland.

He had a cycle shop in Cromac Street, Belfast which was a Mecca for general and especially Club cyclists who regularly visited his shop for spare parts or the latest improvements in cycling accessories - and more importantly, advice on bikes, gears and cycling in general.

Eddie was very much more than just a cycle dealer. He was involved in many aspects of the sport and pastime, although I cannot recall or find any record of him taking part in the competitive side, such as racing. He was much in evidence as a Timekeeper and was always a familiar figure at the start of the time trial races against the clock.

His allegiance was to the Cyclist Touring Club and he was affiliated to the Belfast CC and also the North Belfast Temperance Club. Many of the members of those two clubs cycled together and were also attached to the C.T.C. and often held joint club runs in the 1920's and 1930's.

He was one of the main people who lobbied the Cycling Touring Club Headquarters in London, which was the controlling authority for Touring cycling in Britain and they gained local recognition from them to establish the Northern Ireland District Association of the Cycling Tourist Club in March 1928. Eddie became the local representative and he would have been informed of any changes in the Government laws regarding cycling by the central body in London.

Eddie wrote a number of articles of advice on such matters as forming a cycling club for any groups of interested cyclists wishing to do so. He also advised them on the proper way to conduct cycling club meetings and how to register with the controlling bodies and the appropriate committees.

He gave advice on planning and organizing record attempts in which he was greatly involved in as a Timekeeper, as well as an Official Observer to see that regulations were adhered to.

He was also known to mark out starting and turning points in time trials races from 10 miles to 12 and 24 hour races, by measuring them out with his revolution counter which he would have lent to clubs for measuring out club race distances.

He recalled an occasion while checking the mileage of the route for a twelve hour time trial event in which he discovered a two mile error which was probably caused by some minor road alignment as roads were being improved. This was rectified by altering the start and turning points. Another civic duty he took great interest in was the school cycling proficiency tests that were held in the school playgrounds and Eddie would attend as an Observer and Adviser. When the competitive season came to an end, Eddie was usually an invited guest to various club annual prize presentation dinners and would invariably be called on to reply to a toast to the visitors, or to propose a toast to the prize winners. When congratulating the champions he would remind them that they were looked up to by the young members of the club, who hoped to be champions one day too.

He asked them to accept their awards with modesty and their losses with grace and remember the "also-rans", because if there were no losers there would be no champions, and also not to forget to thank the club officials for making the events possible for them to compete in.

Eddie's shop eventually closed, probably due to his retirement, but that part of Cromac Street became a one way thoroughfare and some re-development took place shortly afterwards.

Eddie probably had other interests which I have not known, but he devoted a large part of his life to cycling and the welfare of cyclists because he was an ardent cyclist himself. He was always available to fulfil his obligations and his reward was the self satisfaction of a job very well done.

RAB COLLINS

Eddie Cassidy's advert from 1935.

Almost stranded

It was in the 'Twelfth Fortnight' as it was called in those days that three of us – all C.T.C. members – decided to go on a cycling camping holiday to the West of Ireland. All went well until one day looking for a nice spot for lunch we spotted this nice little hillock approached over a little stretch of sand. Nice and firm and easily rideable even with heavy camping loads. On the other side, Primus stoves (everyone had them in those days) were produced and a pleasant meal was enjoyed in the sunshine.

After this I walked up the slight hill to view the route ahead and discovered to my horror that this was not part of the mainland but was a little island (of which there are many off the Mayo coastline) I rushed back to the others to tell them, and at the same time the tide came rushing around our side! Never did a meal come to such an abrupt end and we started off, but literally within minutes the tide was round our feet (and wheels.) Luckily there was a sand hump towards the middle where the tide had not yet reached. However we were trapped with the tide rushing around us fore and aft! There was one farmhouse in sight on the mainland. By shouting and waving we attracted attention and to our relief we saw the farmer set off in his little boat, making slow progress with the very strong tide. He reached us but with a small row boat and a strong current he could take only two of us at a time. As befits the captain of a ship, I opted to wait and by the time I was rescued the water was round the bottom bracket of my machine (not recommended)

The moral of this story is – before you stop for lunch make sure you have an escape route.

Or a lifeboat!!

BILLY McCORMICK

1948 N.I. B.A.R. results table

Place	Name	Club	25 miles Time			50 miles Time			100 miles Time			Average Speed (mph)
			H	**M**	**S**	**H**	**M**	**S**	**H**	**M**	**S**	
1	J Harvey	Cyprus	1	03	21	2	09	55	4	42	40	22.665
2	I Matier	Belfast	1	05	37	2	12	17	4	39	03	22.347
3	T Forde	King's Moss	1	04	00	2	10	41	4	57	31	22.183
4	G O'Neill	Cyprus	1	05	48	2	14	38	4	48	23	21.961
5	W Mills	Cyprus	1	06	44	2	15	12	4	45	43	21.889
6	A McIlhagga	Maryland	1	06	06	2	13	30	4	56	11	21.807
7	G Wilkes	Windsor	1	06	18	2	16	51	5	00	44	21.499
8	R Hill	Cyprus	1	05	52	2	16	42	5	08	37	21.386
9	W McClean	King's Moss	1	08	05	2	18	09	4	54	35	21.372
10	W Pike	Windsor	1	08	28	2	23	57	5	05	40	20.792
11	S Haveron	Windsor	1	11	28	2	18	21	5	13	47	20.598
12	W Campbell	Mayland	1	09	36	2	18	21	5	23	32	20.593
13	S Lunney	Belfast	1	09	28	2	20	23	5	20	21	20.564
14	J Hutchinson	Maryland	1	13	12	2	19	37	5	06	04	20.527
15	A Granville	Cyprus	1	11	24	2	21	27	5	12	32	20.471
16	W Rea	Belfast	1	08	34	2	23	00	5	23	42	20.460
17	A Brown	E Ulster	1	10	19	2	19	32	5	32	45	20.288
18	G Gilroy	Maryland	1	10	14	2	23	01	5	28	05	20.207
19	R McKnight	Belfast	1	10	54	2	28	08	5	20	00	20.053
20	T Anderson	Cyprus	1	12	14	2	31	43	5	13	34	19.891
21	J Shiels	Cyprus	1	14	43	2	26	50	5	22	17	19.708
22	W Gray	Maryland	1	14	03	2	31	58	5	25	20	19.480
23	R Moore	Northern	1	12	39	2	46	36	5	12	50	19.244

The title inside the table reads: **1948 N.I. B.A.R. article to comeesult**

1st Team   Cyprus
2nd Team   Belfast
3rd Team   Maryland

Smyths hotel, Carnlough 1949

The Hotel mentioned in so many of our stories.
Photograph by Bill Jebb, Kings Moss C.C.

Ballymena's Olympic cyclist, Billy Kerr, with some of the competitors who will be taking part in the Co-operation North Maracycle.

1600 ready to pedal off in Europe's first maracycle

MORE than 1,600 cyclists are under starters orders for Europe's first ever maracycle, which sets off simultaneously from Belfast and Dublin tomorrow.

The organisers, Co-operation North, are delighted with the entry and today the participants were tuning up for the 206 mile run which starts from the City Hall in Belfast, and Dublin's Mansion House at 8.00 a.m.

Last weekend more than 60 cyclists warmed up for the main event by completing an 80-mile training jaunt from Belfast to Newcastle and back via Banbridge.

The aim is for the entrants to cycle the 103 miles from Belfast and Dublin to the opposite city, spend the night there and cycle back the following day.

Belfast's Lord Mayor, Councillor Alfie Ferguson, will send the local cyclists on their way tomorrow, while his Dublin counterpart will signal the off to the Southern participants.

A number of blind cyclists will be attempting the maracycle, including Drew Cochrane, from Ballymena, Tomy White, from Drumcondra, and Ballymena's Mr. O. Ross who will all be partnered on a tandem for the event.

Mr. Bill Kirk, from the Northern Ireland Tourist Board, is undertaking the maracycle with his son, Brendan, and daughter, Diane.

The oldest entrant is Fr. Fergus O'Higgins, parish chaplain, North William Street, Dublin. He is 74 and has seen Ireland, Scandanavia, and the Middle-East on his bike.

From Cookstown comes Northern Ireland's oldest entrant, 72-year-old Cyril Henry, who has cycled across America twice.

An Olympic cyclist, Billy Kerr, and several husband and wife teams are also in the field.

Everyone who completes the maracycle will get a special certificate, and the event will help raise money for more than 100 charities.

Touring in the Carlingford / O'Meath mountains

This photograph, near Flagstaff, was taken in 1946 by Billy Jebb, Kings Moss C.C.
Left: Al Anderson and Bobby Molloy from the Shankill Road

Tommy Givan

The famous gathering place at Newtownards Town Hall Door. Photograph taken in 1950's. Left to right: Philip Smith, Bobby McKee, Eddie Hanna, Ivan Patterson Gordon Gillespie.

All members of Ards Cycling Club

Tommy Givan was born to a moderately well off family in Kensington Avenue in the Bloomfield Road area of East Belfast on 23rd March 1920. His father's grocery business was based at first at their home but he progressed later to become established in grocery and cooked meats at Lord Street, off the Albert Bridge Road. Tommy's childhood was happy and he grew into a healthy teenager. His first 'serious' cycling was on a carrier bicycle delivering goods for his father. One day he was stopped by a policeman on the Queens Bridge. The constable judged the bicycle to be overloaded and inquired of Tommy what employer has sent him out with such a burden. His reply that it was his father drew a response something like "tell him not to work you so severely in future!" His exertions during those years, however, almost certainly contributed to his great strength and stamina in later years.

His first bicycle race was a Maryland Wheelers 20 miles time trial. It was early season 1937 on a restricted gear, as was the custom then. He was 17 years old and came just 3 seconds behind the winner, but easily won first handicap prize. Observers said his time of 56 mins. 37 secs. showed great promise. Indeed he was soon a prolific winner of club events and (later) open races. His all round ability gained success on both road and track.

Tommy Givan

Tommy and his club mate George Beattie gained variety in their racing by tandem riding. They set new N.I. records for 50 and 100 miles in 1939, clocking 1 hr. 56 mins. 3 secs. and 4 hrs. 7 mins. 54 secs. respectively – as well as Belfast to Dublin in 4 hrs. 18 mins. 58 secs.

The Givans were evacuated from Belfast to Newtownards in 1941 to escape the German bombing. Their temporary home was a farmhouse on the Bangor Road just a bit above the North Road junction. They lived there until 1943, keeping livestock, including pigs. Not long after arriving in Newtownards Tommy struck up with a girlfriend – May Wilson from Mill Street – now a widow named Caughers. In those days it was a custom for cyclists to gather around the town hall door where bicycles were often parked ten deep on both sides of the door! The crack was always great (tells May Wilson) and the lively young people used to step over to Charlotte Herron's, a fruit and vegetable and fish and chip shop on the East side of Conway Square, to get refreshments either in the form of a fish supper (wrapped in newspaper) or an ice cream cone or 'slider'.

Charlie Henderson, later to found Ards Cycling club was prominent among those who kept the crack on the boil. Everyone, of course carrying an awareness of the World War, but determined to keep their spirits up. May Wilson tells how Givan, always immaculately dressed, used to take her to the pictures. The town had two cinemas – the Ritz and the Regent. One night he took her to the Ritz, the grander of the two, to see 'The Oklahoma Kid' with Cagney and Bogart. Although he was as well dressed as usual, there was a bit of a smell in the air – eventually traced to his shoes. He had been working with the pigs and had failed to completely get rid of their smell. May said she would not go to the pictures with him ever again, but this did not happen and they had many a laugh about the incident. Tommy's sister Betty also met a boyfriend at the town hall gatherings – he was Geddis Amberson from Pound Street who became a prominent builder in the town.

Givan won his first N.I. track championship at the time (1941) – the 1000 yards – adding the mile in 1942, which he retained in 1943 as well as adding the 5 to his tally. In fact he won the mile championship on four years out of five at Short and Harland's sports at Celtic Park. Unstoppable on his 'Stone Special' track bike, he again became 1000 yards champion in 1944, as well as taking the two mile title, often battling his good friend and rival, Charlie Henderson at Castlereagh Park.

In 1944 when the Ards club was founded, Givan's closeness to the town and friendship with Henderson led to his timing all their events for their first year.

I well remember my father taking me to Castlereagh Park one evening in 1945 and saying "You will see a great race between Charlie Henderson and Tommy Givan".

It would be one of the last race meetings on the cinder track. A brick wall was soon to be built around the perimeter making it unsafe for bicycle racing. I was 8 years old but I vividly remember seeing the riders cross the finish line only as silhouettes, an effect due to our position in the crowd and the evening sun setting over Scrabo. I think Tommy Givan was the winner.

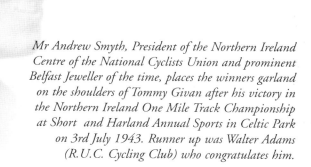

*Mr Andrew Smyth, President of the Northern Ireland
Centre of the National Cyclists Union and prominent
Belfast Jeweller of the time, places the winners garland
on the shoulders of Tommy Givan after his victory in
the Northern Ireland One Mile Track Championship
at Short and Harland Annual Sports in Celtic Park
on 3rd July 1943. Runner up was Walter Adams
(R.U.C. Cycling Club) who congratulates him.*

Givan won the first N.I. Mass start championship at Bangor's Castle Park in 1945, beating Lurgan's Billy Dowds in a close two-man sprint – the rest of the field left well behind.

Givan and Dowds won 'all round them' at this time and had the honour of being selected to ride for G.B. in the International London-to-Paris road race in 1946 and 1947, in which they both performed well.

On 6th November 1946 Tommy married Girly Cairns (not the name on her birth certificate but the one she 'got' all her life). She was the sister of Billy Cairns who was N.I. 25 mile record holder in 1948 with 1 hr. 1 min.37 secs. Girly was an advanced and accomplished ballroom dancer but despite the contrast of lifestyles, they discovered the secret of a lasting relationship. In time they had four children: Wilson, Jennifer, Ena and Harry.

Givans time trial ability could not be dismissed as two events in 1945 showed: On 26th May he won the Maryland 50 beating the renowned Dowds by over 2 minutes.

Then on 3rd June he won the Dublin to Belfast in 4 hrs. 49 mins. 46 secs. taking over 13 minutes out of the Lurgan man.

However, his greatest win in Mass start racing (now simply called road racing) was at Ards Airport in 1950. He beat Kings Moss C.C.'s Charlie Montgomery, again in a two-up sprint, to take the N.I. championship at an age (30) when you were thought to be past your best.

Tommy was a thinking cyclist and would have loved a 'go' at Irish championships, but there was no cross-

Tommy Givan

border racing then, partly because of Irish neutrality in the war.

Possibly as a result of thoughts about Irish championships, he controversially advocated, in the November 1944 issue of 'The Official Circular' that N.I. cyclists should affiliate to the National Cycling Association – a body with Nationalist leanings. His main argument was there seemed little return on all the fees paid, not only to the England based N.C.U. but also to a separate time trial body, the R.T.T.C. Needless to say, his suggestion raised some steam in succeeding issues of the magazine, these being reply and counter reply for months.

Tommy character is best shown by the interest he took in others. I once came to his cycle shed at his home in Orby Parade and was advised to fit a longer handlebar stem – finally being given a lovely Italian Cinelli – for which he would not accept money. I also remember him actually running over to me after a hotly contested '5' at Wallace Park back in 1955. He had appreciative laughter in his eyes for my contribution to the speed of the race – in which I did not even get placed!

Tommy and Girly's children grew up strong and healthy just like themselves. The boys, Wilson and Harry went into the cooked meats business in Lord Street, which has since moved to Prince Regent Road. Jennifer became a teacher, but her big claim to fame was her ability on the hockey pitch, on which she gained International selection for both Ireland and G.B. She now teaches at Bloomfield Collegiate. Ena is a senior manager in the Early Years educational organisation.

Tommy Givan continued cycling right up to his death in a cycling accident on 15th September 1981, aged 61. Right through the 40's and 50's he trained hard, rode veterans time trials and track races at Orangefield, where the track is now named after him, there being a memorial stone to him on the site.

The County Meath sprinter Eddie Dunne often stayed with the Givans on his visits to compete at Orangefield. He fondly remembers the great hospitality he received from the family

The accident happened on the Old Saintfield Road at 7.00 pm. but Tommy died at 11.00 pm in hospital. He had been in the company of his six friends and training partners among whom were John Harvey of Cyprus C.C. and Maurice McNally of Maryland Wheelers and Willie Reilly of Northern C.C.

His wife Girly outlived Tommy by 27 years. She died in June 2008.

Many in the Northern Ireland cycling community, including Eddie Dunne regret that we did not learn of this until after the funeral.

BILLY KIRK

Tommy Givan

Tommy Givan (left) races John Jess at Wallace Park.

Smithfield in flames

From the archives: *Smithfield in flames*

On the morning of May 7, 1974, one of Belfast's best known landmarks was a smoking ruin.

Incendiary bombs had reduced the 200-year-old Smithfield market to ashes.

The old buildings were mostly made of wood and the flames caught hold quickly.

All the fire service could do was prevent the blaze from spreading.

When dawn broke and the smoke began to clear, traders, who had lost everything, began to talk of rebuilding the market and restoring their ruined businesses. No-one typified the 'business as usual' character of the time more than bicycle retailer Jimmy McGarvey.

Within 24 hours of the massive blaze, Jimmy resumed business in a converted dormobile van parked outside the smoking rubble of shop. "This is to show we intend to remain in business in Smithfield, despite the tragedy of yesterday," he said.

Jimmy had been trading at Smithfield since 1950 and his family's business connections with the market stretched back even further to 1900.

Jimmy wasn't the only trader to call for the immediate rebuilding of Smithfield. One of the area's best known traders, Joseph Kavanagh, said: "All morning people have been asking, appealing and demanding that we get together and rebuild the market. It will never be the same again, but we must do our best to preserve as much of the character of the place as possible."

Below are some pictures from our archives.

— PAUL CARSON

This article, dated 30th Jan 2010 was taken from Belfast Telegraph's FROM THE ARCHIVES.

Bicycle retailer Jimmy McGarvey epitomises the 'business as usual' spirit by offering what remains of his stock for sale on the street outside his burnt-out premises. 9/5/1974

Club badges

It was the custom of most cycling clubs in the past to have club badges made to their own design. They would have been worn on club runs and at Annual General Meetings as well as special cycling occasions. The badges would have been displayed on the lapel of the cycling jacket or on the front of skull caps that were worn by members in years prior to the 1914 World War.

As well as the few that are shown, quite a lot of other well known clubs wore their own club badges and I am sure there are hundreds still lying forgotten in the drawers or cupboards and cabinets of parents and grandparents around the Province, who were members of a cycling club.

club badges

Many of the earlier ones could be very valuable as they were cast from a die which would be sculpted to the design that was submitted. They could be bronze or solid sliver and even gold and some were enamelled in two or three colours for presentation purposes.

In the past, solid gold and silver medals were awarded as prizes in some events which would have been proudly displayed on the gold Albert watch chain of the recipient. With the passage of time many of the dies for producing these badges and medals ended up being lost or displaced by the makers and it would be expensive to replace them today.

When I was Secretary of the Belfast Cycling Club in 1949, it was decided to make inquiries about having some additional badges made. Our badge was probably made before the 1914 World War. The Company that was alleged to have the original die was the well known firm of Riddles of Ann Street, Belfast who, when approached could find no trace of it as they suffered some bomb damage during the Belfast Blitz in 1942. The Company is no longer in existence and the area has since been redeveloped.

As an alternative to the aforementioned badges, some Clubs and Associations had their designs pressed into sheet metal and enamelled. Others like my own club had our badge embroidered on cloth with a felt backing that was displayed on the breast pocket of a blazer jacket or club jersey.

Any reader who may be able to locate any of the solid gold and silver badges, or medals within their family circle would be most fortunate – especially if they inherit them. And with a bit of luck they might even get a gold Albert and watch chain to accompany them!

Good hunting.

RAB COLLINS

Harry Lane

He was one of the most stylish time trailists in the early to mid 50's. In 1951 he set the 50 mile road record association with a time of 1 hr 53 mins 52 secs. He was married to Rose Rainey who was a great track rider.

Harry Lane on the Antrim Road in early season

Sketch by Rab Collins

⇥ Lap Scoring Card. ⇤

Competitor's No.

81									
80	79	78	77	76	75	74	73	72	71
70	69	68	67.	66	65	64	63	62	61
60	59	58	57	56	55	54	53	52	51
50	49	48	47	46	45	44	43	42	41
40	39	38	37	36	35	34	33	32	31
30	29	28	27	26	25	24	23	22	21
20	19	18	17	16	15	14	13	12	11
10	9	8	7	6	5	4	3	2	1

Lap Winners Nos. 40 J McCartney 36 Laps

Finish = Time 1. 9. 15
                Hr. Mts. Sec.

Order of Finish Nos. 39. J Stewart 1st
40 J McCartney 2nd
15. C Gibson 3rd
2. S Neill 4th

IRISM ROAD CLUB,
NORTHERN BRANCH

25 Miles Championship
of Ulster

AND INTER-TEAM RACE.

AT CELTIC PARK, BELFAST,

— ON —

Saturday, 8th September, 1923

STARTING 3-30 P.M.

Programmes   ::   3d. each.

Macarthur & Co., Ltd., Belfast

Officials.

President ... Mr. J. Manson

Vice-Presidents :

Messrs. Rt. Hon. Thos. Moles, M.P.; W. H. Alexander, J.P.; Isaac Baxter, Elias Jones, A. H. Ward, W. A. Dale, A. Lorimer, W. J. Davidson, W. J. Chambers, A. Ross, H. M. Jackson, R. M'Lardy, M. Stevenson, P. M'Kenna, J. Stewart, G. Henderson, W. Andrews, C. Montgomery, S. Cochrane.

Committee :

Messrs. F. Guy, Chairman; S. Kerr, J. Kerr, O. Jackson, J. Ross, T. Watson, G. Stewart, H. Knight, J. M'Kee.

Hon. Secretary :
H. Neill

Trustees :
F. Guy, J. A. Ross

Judges :

Messrs. Rt. Hon. T. Moles, M.P.; W. H. Alexander, J.P.; R. Barr, T. J. Millin, Isaac Baxter, J. Manson, W. J. Chambers, J. Lynch, E. Jones, C. Montgomery, W. Andrews, S. Kerr, F. Guy.

Timekeepers :

Messrs. A. H. Ward, J. Kerr, J. Murphy, D. M. M'Keag, T. M'Keag, R. M'Lardy, N. Brown, J. Fisher, W. F. Osborne.

Lap Scorers :

Messrs. W. Mol, J. Stevenson, J. Ross, S. Hutchinson, J. B. Stewart, J. Vance, J. Ross, S. Cochrane, A. Lorimer, W. Dugan, F. Bradford, W. Corry, H. M'Comb, W. Lapping, W. Caughey, W. White, S. Jennings, W. Oxley, P. S. Hall, J. Boyd, J. M'Master, G. Magahy, W. Hayes, W. Maitland, L. Mills, W. Bowden, J. Mackemson, N. M'Kibbin, A. Smyth, H. Longmore, A. Stevenson, S. Maxwell, A. M'Lardy, O. Jackson, W. Whiteside, W. Boyd, J. Watson, A. Finlay, J. Belshaw, W. Wilson, J. Kerr, G. Bowman, S. M'Connell, J. Moore, W. Kerr, G. Gibson, J. M'Quaid, J. Cull, T. Murphy, R. Ferris, S. Campbell, A. M'Auley, A. V. Bradley

Field Stewards :
J. Ross, A. Ross, R. Purdy, A. M'Cully

Starter :
J. W. Jefferson

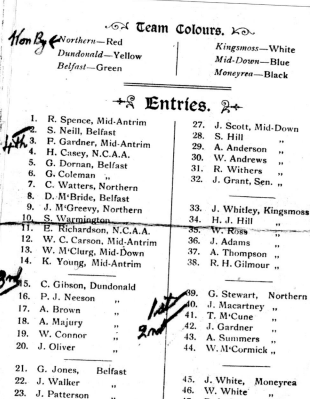

Team Colours.

Northern—Red
Dundonald—Yellow
Belfast—Green

Kingsmoss—White
Mid-Down—Blue
Moneyrea—Black

Entries.

1. R. Spence, Mid-Antrim
2. S. Neill, Belfast
3. P. Gardner, Mid-Antrim
4. H. Casey, N.C.A.A.
5. G. Dornan, Belfast
6. G. Coleman ,,
7. C. Watters, Northern
8. D. M'Bride, Belfast
9. J. M'Greevy, Northern
10. S. Warmington
11. E. Richardson, N.C.A.A.
12. W. C. Carson, Mid-Antrim
13. W. M'Clurg, Mid-Down
14. K. Young, Mid-Antrim
15. C. Gibson, Dundonald
16. P. J. Neeson ,,
17. A. Brown ,,
18. A. Majury ,,
19. W. Connor ,,
20. J. Oliver ,,

21. G. Jones, Belfast
22. J. Walker ,,
23. J. Patterson ,,
24. J. M'Kee ,,
25. J. M'Mahon ,,
26. H. Knight, ,,

27. J. Scott, Mid-Down
28. S. Hill ,,
29. A. Anderson ,,
30. W. Andrews ,,
31. R. Withers ,,
32. J. Grant, Sen. ,,

33. J. Whitley, Kingsmoss
34. H. J. Hill ,,
35. W. Ross ,,
36. J. Adams ,,
37. A. Thompson ,,
38. R. H. Gilmour ,,

39. G. Stewart, Northern
40. J. Macartney ,,
41. T. M'Cune ,,
42. J. Gardner ,,
43. A. Summers ,,
44. W. M'Cormick ,,

45. J. White, Moneyrea
46. W. White ,,
47. D. Ireland ,,
48. G. Spiers ,,
49. J. Headly ,,
50. T. Hogg ,,

Ex.Councillor Scott, Shafto Kerr and a young George Stewart
Shafto's rig became standard wear for cyclists

Potatoes for Mongolia

Some years ago Cyril Morrison one time member of Belfast CC attended a Water Colour class and befriended a man from Castlederg, Paddy Masterson.

Although Paddy was a Roman Catholic he was more than interested in Buddhism and talked about becoming a monk. Cyril and Paddy shared many conversations on the Buddhist teachings. Paddy would have loved if Cyril could have journeyed on this road with him and although there were many of their beliefs that Cyril could have accepted there were some teachings that he could not accept or ever agree with. However their friendship grew and lasted. Eventually Paddy fulfilled his desires and became a monk and Cyril and Nan were special guests at his Ordination in Jampa Ling Buddhist Centre. Their circle of Buddhist friends in Ireland steadily grew over the years and here Cyril takes up the story (on a theme of 'where are they now?') editors note:

The Panchen Lama is one of the Dalai Lamas' (of Tibet) top Monks. He was responsible for re-establishing Buddhism in Mongolia after the fall of atheistic Communism. The Panchen Lama began by teaching the local people to grow vegetables to feed themselves. After some time his potato crop failed and I was responsible for finding out what type of potato would grow successfully in Mongolia where winter temperatures can be 40 degrees below. I asked my cousin's son who worked in potato research for his advice. He recommended a hardy potato grown mostly in Donegal. These seed potatoes were sent out to the villages and were buried inside their houses (Yurts) under the floors to keep them warm for the spring planting. In due course we sent out new seed potatoes which grew successfully in Mongolia and to the best of my knowledge the crop continues to flourish each year.

The Panchen Lama also founded a Home for Orphan children in Mongolia. So much is happening in that part of the world with vital support from Monks and friends at home.

CYRIL MORRISON

Cyril Morrison and Ven. Lama Panchen Otrul Rinpoche
Photograph taken at Jampa Ling,
The Buddhist Centre in County Cavan

N.I.C.F. officials at the Windsor CC clubrooms

A group of Windsor C.C. cyclists taken at the clubrooms at Great Northern Street Belfast
Looking at the group, left to right:
Jimmy Trimble, Peter Woods, Paddy McAteer, Raymond Moore, Frank O'Brien (lighting up) ? hidden
behind Alex Dickson, Elliot Matthews, ? , Jack Watson, Norman McKeown,
Roy Erskine and Billy Jebb.

Isle of Man winners, 1952

*Shay Elliott and Noel Tully of Dublin Wheelers with their winners sashes for the Mannin Veg (1 Lap)
and Viking trophy (2 laps) races in the Isle of Man in 1952.*

*Elliott's win in the Mannin Veg ushered in a great International career.
On the left is Kay Nolan who later married an African nobleman and lived in Africa since the mid Fifties.
Right is Marie Lyons, sister of Nan, a prominent member of the organising committee of the
Dun Laoghaire Cycling week who later married Con Enright.*

Photo courtesy of Con Enright.

Minerstown Youth Hostel

Minerstown Youth Hostel, situated between Tyrella and Killough, Co. Down
Photo taken in 1946 by Bill Jebb, Kings Moss C.C.

Mass-start Championship at Ards Airport, 1949

On the start line of the 1949 Northern Ireland Mass start championship at Ards Airport.
Naming who we can:
First left is Aubrey Brown, East Ulster Road Club. Billy Henry, Ballymena (almost hidden) second left is
not known. Albert Ewart, Maryland Wheelers.
Walter Mills, Cyprus C.C. (just his head)
Then second from right: George Wilkes, Windsor C.C. who won at the venue in 1952. right: Stanley
Thompson, Banbridge C.C., the winner on this occasion.
Behind Thompson (looking out of photograph) Gordon Reid, Cyprus C.C.
Then right beside him Jackie Fee (head only) Cyprus C.C.

Shortly after the start.
Left to right where possible: Tommy Givan, Maryland Wheelers.
Elliot Matthews, East Ulster. George Wilkes, Windsor C.C.
Billy Henry, Ballymena R.C. Stanley Thompson, Banbridge CC.
Albert Ewart, Maryland Wheelers. Aubrey Brown, East Ulster.

Tudor Cinema, Comber, 1997

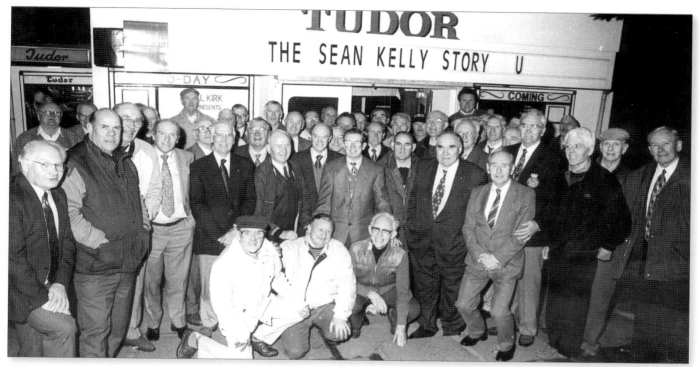

The first reunion of cyclists was a film show of the Sean Kelly Story at the Tudor Cinema in Drumkirk Road, Comber.
Those present, moving from left to right:

Stanley Thompson from Seapatrick. John Jess, Ballynahinch.
Maurice Donaldson, Bangor. Morris Foster, Glengormley.
George Wilkes, Dundonald. Stanley Connolly, Newtownabbey.
Bill Jebb, Ballyclare. Jackie McCord, Newtownards. Billy Stewart, Belfast.
Tom Smyth, Bellaghy. Gordon Reid, Belfast. Gary McGrath, Belfast.
Billy Campbell, Belfast. John Harvey, Belfast. Charlie Henderson, Newtownards. Billy Boal, Newtownards.
Willie Reilly, Belfast. Tommy Talbot, Antrim.
Jim McBride, Belfast. Charlie Gardiner, Lurgan. Jim Lavery, Bangor.
Billy Dowds, Lurgan. Tommy Taylor, Belfast. R. McGreechan, Newtownards.
Joe Hadden, Belfast. Tommy Moore, Belfast. Alex Dickson, Comber.
Davy McNutt, Glengormley. Billy Williams, Newtownards. Raymond Carroll, Belfast, Marshall McAdam, Belfast.
Jimmy McCormick, Holywood.
Front: Bobby Conn, Bangor. Joe Craig, Bangor. Cyril Henry, Cookstown.

Clancy's C.T.C. Hotel, Killarney

Back row: Mr. Clancy, far right.
His daughter is between two N.I. Cyclists Bill Jebb (left), of Kings Moss C.C.
and Andy Goodall (right) of Northern C.C.
Front row: Unknown.
Photo taken with Bill Jebb's camera in 1947.

Maurice Donaldson and friends

Left to right:
Maurice Donaldson, Maryland Wheelers, Billy Stewart, Maryland Wheelers,
Billy Dowds, South Lurgan R.C.   Jimmy McCormick N.I.C.F. Registrar/Secretary

Eddie McArdle and friends
Bobby Conn and George Gilroy

Eddie McArdle who set Irish End to End record in 1953 with Bobby Conn ex. Maryland Wheelers and George Gilroy, Windsor C.C. at a Belfast City centre professional race in the early 1990's

Destination - Land's End to John O' Groats

A Group of North Down cyclists prepare to leave Conway Square, Newtownards to travel to England to ride from Lands End to John O'Groats in 1986. They raised a substantial sum of money for Newtownards Combat Cancer Group of the Ulster Cancer Foundation.

Here they are pictured with Chairman, Craig Wallace
Left to right: Malcolm Kerr, Saintfield,   Bobby Conn, Bangor,   Bobby Adair, Newtownards,
Stanley Roy, Newtownards,   Jim Cunningham, Comber,   Sandy Burns, Gilnahirk.

"Whereabouts" is that rider BY JACK WATSON

Any one who has an interest in sport will be well aware of the controversy which is aroused when the question of a riders whereabouts is mentioned. In fact some athletes have gone as far as the courts as they feel that it impinges on their civil rights. To date the courts have upheld the rights of the various agencies to implement the athlete's whereabouts conditions as contained within the WADA (World Anti Doping Agency) Code.

But what actually is it and why is it arousing so much controversy in athletic circles?

Basically most of the sporting National Governing Bodies (NGBs) and International Governing Bodies (IGBs) are obliged under the WADA code to identify a Registered Testing Pool (RTP) of their High Performance (HP) Athletes. Within Ireland, Cycling Ireland's (CI) Anti Doping Officer, currently Declan Byrne, will, in conjunction with the High Performance Director, currently Phil Leigh, identify the athletes who will be registered with the Irish Sports Council (ISC) Anti Doping Units. These are the members of the CI RTP. This list will contain all riders who are receiving Sport's Council (SC), either Irish or Northern Irish, funding. This includes Para-cyclists as well as able bodied riders and includes both genders. In addition to which there would be other HP riders who for various reasons do not satisfy carding criteria but are considered as potential international riders. Because of the diversity of HP cycling i.e. road, track, cross country mountain biking, down hill mountain biking, marathon mountain biking, BMX, para-cycling in all it's various disciplines etc, and bear in mind that most of these disciplines are double gender, then it is obvious that the cycling RTP is probably one of the largest within the Irish Sports Council's RTP system.

Members of the RTP will be advised by the ISC of their responsibility within the system and they will be advised of the four quarterly dates before which they must submit their Whereabouts Forms for the next three months. This can be done manually or on line and of course the latter method is becoming more the norm. In addition to where these riders anticipate they will be over the next three months they MUST give a one hour envelope and a location as to where they will be within this one hour period and this is for every day of the quarter. This is where they can be tested Out of Competition (OOCT). Of course they can be tested at any other time of the day but if they are not found at the location indicated on their Whereabouts Form it is not treated in the same way as them not being available within the one hour time slot.

If a rider does not submit their whereabouts form by the required date or if the rider is not at the location or at the time of their one hour slot this is regarded as a "hit" and three hits in a rolling 18 month period will be treated as an Anti Doping rule violation and render the athlete liable for a period of suspension.

If a rider becomes aware that they will not be at the location specified on their whereabouts return then a text message must be sent to a mobile phone situated in the office of the ISC Anti Doping Unit. A Doping Control Officer (DCO) if going out to perform an OOCT must access the ISC computer system at the last possible moment to check if there has been any change to the riders information.

So there you have it, the Whereabouts System as it applies to the Irish High Performance squads.

Shay Elliott - Irelands first professional

A career on the international stage ignited for Shay Elliott when he gained prominence by winning the Mannin Veg in the Isle of Man in 1952. In those days, the Island was a Mecca for racing cyclists.

The following year he was selected to ride the Manx international – 3 laps of the 37.5 mile mountain circuit. He finished fourth, but was the moral victor. Les Wilmott was ahead of three riders, one of whom was Elliott. On the descent of the mountain for the last time, Shay decided to go for broke. Leaving the others he was closing in on Wilmott when he crashed on a bad bend. By the time he remounted his bike, the chasers had passed the distraught Dubliner.

Cometh the hour, cometh the man and the An Tostal Tour of Ireland was another defining moment in his career. He finished second, winning the Cork-Killarney stage and the King of the Mountains. The KOH title was an earth moving experience for Shay and he would move into a select league of cyclists. The prize was a trip to the Simplex Training camp in Monte Carlo. Rather than return to his native land, Shay decided that he would race in France. As luck would have it, he was invited by Paul Wiegant to join the famous ACBB club in Paris. (The same club that Stephen Roche would join in 1980).

Within a short time of making his debut for the Parisienne outfit, the young Elliott won the Paris-Evreux. This was a famous amateur classic which invariably was a stepping stone to greater things, i.e. a professional contract.

The 1955 season was a good one for Shay. On his Helyett bike and representing ACCB he was by a mile the 'outstanding French amateur of the season' clocking up a number of wins, including the Grand Prix de Boulogne in the western suburbs of the city. He won the first stage of the Route de France. Again lady luck was not on his side. Subsequently he crashed out of the event, but now the Dubliner was causing ripples in various publications, both on the sports and news pages of the day.

Although a few cycle firms were still fighting a rear guard action and financing their own teams, most realised that extra sponsorship would have to be brought to bear if they were to stay in the peloton. Shay's arrival on the scene gave a fillip for a grocery chain named Felix Potin to link up. The chain had been on the verge of launching their own outfit, but both the bike company and the chain of grocery stores worked well in tandem. 1955 was a good season and a Pro Contract for '56 was inevitable because he was doing the business on the bike.

It was between '55 and '56 seasons that the former St. Brendan's Cycling Club member in Donnybrook, Dublin (which he joined in 1950) was beginning to bear the fruits of success in France. Shay was proving to one and all that he pressed all the right buttons, first as an amateur and in his first season as a professional. Also he was single minded and rather than travel back home in the off season, he stayed in France that winter. He maintained his fitness by turning to track racing at the Paris Vel' d'Hiv. He was a regular at the track and on one occasion he took his first lap in an Italian pursuit and had the time keepers checking each other as to the remarkable time he set. He clocked 15 seconds for a flying start 250 metres, or in layman's terms, .4 seconds slower than sprinters of the day, Reg Harris and Van Vliet. On a similar sized track, the Saint Etienne, during a tough afternoon of competition, including an omnium, sprints and points event, he also won two separate 4 kms pursuits in just 5 mins and 4 secs and 5 mins 1 secs (All of 54 years ago).

The showing by the young Irishman, made his tutor and manager Paul Wiegant look at possible new horizons. Paul brought Shay to Brussels in November '56 to attack the World 1,000 metres flying start record which would be the curtain raiser for the six day event.

Again lady luck deserted Shay as they arrived when the meet had started. Hence he was not afforded the opportunity to warm up. So, it was straight onto the boards for the attempt. He needed to get his gearing 48 by 14 in shape, but with 235 metres a lap and therefore only fractionally smaller than his 250 metres home track in Paris. The old Brussels Palais des Sports was different in shape, all bends and little straight which took ill afforded time getting the hang of.

For once the Elliott attempt was not stylish which had been seen on those boards, but because of the circumstances, the general consensus, was his effort was appreciated by the crowd in the Velodrome. He had difficulty in holding the line, wobbled a lot, yet still finished in a time of one minute and six seconds, or .4 of a second faster than the local hero, Belgian, Van Oostende. In the auditorium that evening was one Cyril Peacock who, the previous year had been world sprint champion.

"Young Elliott must have exceptional class for a road man," he said. "A kilometre flying start is a sprinter's event, but I'm pretty sure I could not do a 1.6 at Brussels and I know the track well...."

Now the young man from the St. Brendan's Club in Dublin was getting advice from his colleagues and advisers that all too often the cyclist who has an outstanding amateur career in his first season, ends up a total flop when venturing into the professional ranks. But the 'bould' Seamus had upstaged the pundits and proved to be the exception.

The 1956 season as a professional for the young Elliott started in North Africa. His first event in Oran was not covered in glory as he punctured early on and retired. It was all change the following week at the Grand Prix de l'Echo Alger. He took the event by the scruff of the neck and blasted away from the main pack with two compatriots. The race finished on a cement track where he comfortably out-sprinted his breakaway companions. The margin over the next man home was all of four minutes. Interestingly the runner up was none other than the champion of France of 1955, Andre Darrigade wearing the distinctive 'Champion of France' jersey. Darrigade had been a sprinter in early days, winning the Prix Medaille competition from Toni Maspes, an Italian who went on to win seven world sprint titles.

Eight days later, Shay was making the headlines when he won the Grand Prix Catox at Marseilles. Later he was in action in a six day event with high placing on each stage. Going into the final stage he was placed 3rd on the standings, but a crash saw his chances nose dive and he finished 20 minutes in arrears.

For the remainder of the season he was always to the fore and getting plenty of column inches in the newspapers on both sides of the Irish Sea and beyond.

For eleven years he was to remain as one of the brightest lights in the peloton. He on many occasions threatened to win many of the great single day 'classics' but unfortunately often came up short on luck. In the Paris Brussels 'classic' he had the race at his mercy, but his front forks broke with a couple of kilometres to go. In those days, a change of machine was out of the question from his following team car, but he was allowed to borrow a bike from a local stranger (priest/curate). In the Paris Roubaix he entered the velodrome with a marginal lead, but his saddle broke. Two 'classics' at his mercy and the luck of the Irish deserts him.

But it was not all doom and gloom for the Dubliner. Soon after his debut for the Potin team Shay was joined by none other than Jacques Anquetil. For the next six years a close bond existed with Anquetil. Shay was a team mate and not a back up man for the Frenchman who graced many a stage. Shay won stages in all the grand tours, Italy, France and Spain. His stage win in the Tour de France in Roubaix was extra special as he took over as race leader of the Tour itself, keeping the yellow jersey for three days. A great moment in the life of the Dubliner, but it also signalled that the sport was being recognised in this island. But the irony of the stage win into Roubaix was inextricably linked to his great friend and team mate, Jean Stablinski.

You have to roll the clock back to the World championships the year before. In September at the Worlds, it was Shay who sacrificed his chance of the rainbow jersey of becoming champion, allowing Stablinski to move ahead to win the event with Shay in second place. The irony of it was that both were representing their country, France versus Ireland.

But the friendship went deeper with Stablinski. The Frenchman was godfather to Pascal Elliott. Shay had met his wife at the start of the 1959 tour which co-incidentally he rode on an international team.

Like many a relationship it faltered on the rocks. It was in dramatic fashion and it was the 1965 Paris-Luxembourg that the ship floundered. In his life time on the bike, Shay was again on the cusp of an outright win and strangely the race organiser was Jean Bobet.

The last day of the event started with the Dubliner in the distinctive tunic of race leader. As they say it was a gimme for Elliott, but his plan went off the tracks. Rumour has it that Stablinski and Anquetil stuck a deal which marooned Elliott. He finished fourth and was totally distraught. As you can appreciate the French press carried the story for days and days. Each time they thought they had answers they were again in a cul-de-sac. The consensus was that the Irishman had been duped by the eventual winner.

The following year, Shay left the Anquetil and Stabinski team and joined Mercier. It also uprooted the family from the comfortable surroundings of east Paris to Loctudy in South West Brittany. He also purchased a hotel. Both the move and the hotel were the beginning of the end of an illustrious career in the sport.

Shay Elliott

Shay returned to Dublin where he opened a panel beating shop. He always maintained his interest in the sport and accompanied the Bray Wheelers on many of their club runs during the off season. It was interesting that the President of the Bray Wheelers, Joe Loughman who many years before had invited the young Elliott out to Shankill, Co. Dublin to speak to the Bray lads who were embarking on the road scene. Joe moved in the committee stages to call the Tour of Wicklow the Shay Elliott Trophy. So thankfully before Shay went to the peloton in the sky, he was being honoured in life, not in death as is the normal scene in Ireland and afar.

Back home and running a successful business, thoughts turned to racing again!

In 1970 he took the plunge and went in at the deep end. He lined up for the London Holyhead event. It was his first competitive race in four years and typically it was in at the deep end. It was a 260 mile race which must have been daunting to a man who graced the European scene for over a decade.

Shay had raced the event before, finishing second to Tommy Simpson and was literally beaten by the width of a tyre. But there was no fairy tale ending with Shay finishing 30 minutes down on the eventual winner, Sid Barras, but it still was a heroic effort.

It has to be said that the Elliott from Crumlin where his father had a garage set the bar for those who followed in his footsteps or should I say on his wheel. He took on the might of cycling in their own back yard and was an equal, if not better than those around him.

Like any youngster growing up who had aspirations to be a cyclist, well, Shay was at the head of affairs when it came to European diplomacy on the roads.

TOMMY CAMPBELL

Hold on?

During the July Holidays of 1978, I went to Bobby Adair's house to go out on a bike ride. The Ards club was based at Bobby's back then, as club runs would meet there and meetings would be held there. Bobby was the club President and his daughter Alison was the Treasurer. Bobby's wife Bella made sure everyone had a cup of tea or coffee! His son Robert was a good roadman, winning the Irish Junior Road title in the late 1960's. My brother Lenny did a lot of his early cycling with Bobby and I did the same five or six years later.

Lenny would later marry Alison, so the Adairs and the Kirks were closely linked over the years.

Bobby was also known as 'Bantie' as he was a Bantam Weight boxing champion in his younger days in the Navy. He was a well known builder, but his real love was the bike and he was responsible for bringing a lot of youngsters into the sport.

That day in July 1978, Bobby and I decided that we would ride to Castlewellan. That's about 35 miles from Ards, but he said not to worry because Bella and his daughter Eileen were going in the car so we could get a lift back home if we wanted!

On the ride there we were going well and every now and then Bobby would ask if I was alright? The previous winter I had been diagnosed Diabetic so he was keeping his eye on me. On one of the hills I dropped back a bit. He turned and said "Just hang on son till we get over this". I took him a bit too literally and grabbed a hold of his seat pin!

He wasn't long telling me exactly what he did mean! When we arrived at Castlewellan Forest Park he told Bella about it all and we had a good laugh about it. Thinking back I was a bit embarrassed at the time, but it was all part of the learning curve! We enjoyed a picnic and then the bikes were put on the roof rack!

BRENDAN KIRK

The bike...... for business, for pleasure

In the year 1890 my father, Isaac Matus then aged 20, was successfully smuggled out of a town called Zager in Lithuania (then under Tsarist rule) to escape the tyranny that was being unleashed in Tsarist Russia against the Jews. They were being killed, their homes and businesses and Synagogues destroyed.

This was orchestrated by the Anti-Jewish 'Black Hundreds' who worked closely with the Tsarist secret police and were later responsible in the 1920's for bringing the forged document 'The Protocols of the learned Elders of Zion' to the U.S.A. where Henry Ford was convinced of their truth and became Hitler's biggest sponsor outside Germany, earning the Iron Cross in 1934.

The attacks on Russian Jews came to be known as the Pogroms and were rampant under the Tsars rule from about 1860 to the early 1900's. However, thousands were successful in getting out of the country and making their way to the west, mostly to the U.K. and U.S.A. My father was smuggled over the Lithuanian - Polish border inside a cock of hay on a horse drawn cart and eventually arrived in Lurgan, where he was apprenticed to a credit draper. Later in 1896 he set up his own credit drapery business in Lurgan.

My mother's father and mother also escaped the Pogroms in the Ukraine and arrived in Halifax, England, later to settle in Belfast where she met and married my father. I was the youngest of a family of six, all reared in Lurgan. When my two elder brothers became 15 years old, father helped them to purchase Raleigh bicycles (costing £7.19.6) fitted with Sturmey Archer 3 sped hub gears and generous sized carriers front and back. These were loaded with drapery and fancy goods to be pedalled around the Lurgan – Portadown – Lisburn areas and hopefully establish credit customers to be serviced on a regular basis. They would have cycled about 20 miles every working day in all weathers. Hard work when you consider the weight of the bike plus the loaded carriers and country pot-holed roads. After about 5 to 6 years of this hard labour they got life a bit easier by purchasing their first cars.

Against my father's wishes, but with the support of my mother, I decided not to go into the business and followed a career in engineering instead, serving my apprenticeship in two Lurgan factories and finally serving over 40 years in the Sirocco Engineering Works drawing office in Belfast.

Unlike my brothers, most of my cycling was for pleasure with an emphasis on touring. My other interest – photography – went hand in hand with cycling. I enjoyed a bit of racing as well, mostly time trials. Not being a real fast man, at least in a time trial you had the urge to beat your own best time.

Even in club races it was hard to get a win when you had a man called Dowds passing you as if he had a secret motor attached to his bike!

Christmas 'Ten'

The Ards CC Christmas '10' of 1995. Timekeepers are Ron Martin and (right) the late John O'Sullivan who was club treasurer for almost two decades. He served faithfully even after his children returned from the sport in the 1980's. About to start is Bronagh Kirk, current club secretary. (See also page 244).

My first club, of which I was a founder member along with W.J. Dowds and a few other cyclists was South Lurgan CC. However, on moving to Belfast in 1955 I joined the East Ulster Road Club which had a membership connection with the N.I. branch of the Cyclists Touring Club.

My favourite cycling memories:

1950 Riding from John O'Groats to Lands End with pal David Alexander (head wind most of the way) Total miles cycled approx. 1200 in just over 9 days.

1952 Tour of the French - Swiss Alps during the period of the Tour de France which the great Fausto Coppi won and getting the feel and atmosphere by riding the great passes.

1953 Winning lst Handicap in the all-Ireland 50 miles championship on the Navan Road which Dowds won in 2 hrs. 2 mins. 49 secs.

I am sure we cyclists all agree there is no better sport than cycling and the friendship that is always present when cyclist meets cyclist.

ELLIOT MATTHEWS

Bellaghy's famous cyclist

Tommy Smyth from Bellaghy was a member of Kings Moss between 1939 and 1955 and he gained many club successes. His undisputed golden era extended through the 1953 to 1955 seasons when he gained Northern Irish and Irish 10, 25, 50, 100 mile and 12 hour honours.

His most celebrated achievements however took place on a tandem. He was partnered by Paddy McNeilly. The pair set a variety of records, including: Belfast-Enniskillen, Belfast-Londonderry-Belfast and the most famous of all – Mizen Head in Co. Cork to Fair Head, Co. Antrim. They covered 389 miles in 19 hrs and 23 mins.

He remained deeply involved in cycling long after retiring from competition.

He was both respected and renowned for active support of N.I. cycling. This culminated in becoming Vice President of Ballymena Road Club and lending his name to the Tommy Smyth Cup.

To his family he personified all that's good in Irish cycling. He loved friendly conversation, regardless of your credentials. From Sunday afternoon cyclists to prolific racers, Tommy always found a pleasant and encouraging word, expressed in his own unassuming way.

He died in May 2003 aged 82 years. His legacy within cycling had extended back some 70 years.

Taken from Cicli Sport Website.
MARK GREER
Cicli Sport contributor

The Tandemists are Tom Smyth (rear) and Paddy McNeilly (front), held by Frank McKeown of Kings Moss C.C. Tommy Taylor strikes his characteristic pose as time keeper at the GPO in Belfast's Royal Avenue 1953. The two men were about to attack the Belfast-Derry record.

How I started cycling

I left school aged fourteen years. I took a job as a messenger boy, delivering meat and groceries on a bike that had a small wheel and a large basket on the front.

I was on the go most of the day and a lot of the calls were up hills, so I soon got cycle fit. In those days Apprenticeships only started at sixteen years, so I had two years from 1949 riding this bike.

One of the butchers in the shop was a keen cyclist and encouraged me to take it up. He was a member of the Northern and told me to see two senior men namely, Mr. Jack Watson and Mr S. Vance as they were starting a Juniors Club. So I joined up.

I saved a few quid and bought an old semi-sports bike which I cleaned up and painted. The first Sunday we went out there was only five of us on basic, non-racing bikes, trouser clips and no cycling shoes.

This figure soon increased to twelve and more. The fun was good. Some were students, apprentices etc. so we were financially strapped most of the time. One Sunday we set off towards Ballymena and The Glens. We had a drum up near Ballymena. The two senior men had to go home early so they left us at Ballymena. We young lads went on towards The Glens. We came back by the Coast. Everything was fine until after Larne when we all in turn started to feel tired, weak and very hungry. Between us we dug up a few bob, stopped at a wee shop attached to a house. The woman could only sell us a few batch loaves. No butter etc. as it was all on ration. We were all glad to get anything to eat as we were too weak to proceed any further. We divided up the loaves and wolfed them down. We rested for a while, felt a lot better and we learned later that we all had 'the hunger knock'

In the early 50's I took part in a two day Massed Start from Belfast to Dublin. We left the Kings Hall on a very wet Saturday morning. When we finished at Whitehall, Dublin it was still lashing. No arrangements had been made for changing. We spotted some houses were being built near hand, so we were glad to use them even though we got covered in cement, dust etc. Then we were advised to find accommodation as none had been booked for us. The only place some of us could afford was one room in an old Guest House at the back of O'Connell Street. Five of us in one room (We did not get much sleep, but the craic was good!)

The race was run by the N.C.A.

THOMAS BURNS

P.S. Among Tommy Burns' many achievements, he won both the Junior and Senior Road Championships of N.I. in 1953. Subsequent to this a rule was passed by the N.I.C.F. prohibiting young riders from competing in both championships in the one year. The probable reason for this was to prevent the young from over exerting themselves.

A special rocking horse *from BILLY GORDON's Journal*

Forty years or more ago, my brother Thomas and I had the notion of making a wooden rocking horse. It was one of the many things we had talked about tackling, many have been long forgotten and now and then, some would slip back into my thoughts and mind.

Some may seem foolish and some would have been fun. The rocking horse was always lurking there in the back of my mind. The horse always fascinated my brother and I. As time went by the rocking horse has saw a great revival. Nearly all the woodworking magazines often carry articles on the project from different makers. So in the year 1997, the prospect of trying my hand at making a horse began haunting my mind again. So much so, that I had to try to carry it out to a conclusion and I ventured into the unknown.

I went to Jeffery Wilson's – halfway between Hillsborough and Dromore. (known nowadays as Wilson's Yard) His business is selling reclaimed timber and artefacts for the building trade. I was able to purchase from him a second hand yellow pine beam. It had held up a factory roof for a hundred or a hundred and fifty years or more. The beam was 14 feet in length, 14 inches deep and 11 inches wide. It was real lovely wood. The shavings were like silk! Kenneth, my son took the beam by car trailer to a man near Katesbridge. This gentleman had a saw mill and he was able to cut my beam into suitable planks with his circular saw. In the meantime I had drawn out the plans for my rocking horse on light cardboard, transferring that unto a sheet of hardboard, cutting out the templates and dressing the edges so that when I took the sawn material to the Lisburn Technical night class, I was able to saw the planks to the required size and plane to the right thickness needed. At the classes I befriended a man called Alan Howarth. He too had a great love for woodwork. Incidentally Alan's Father-in-law was Leslie Mehrten who was a member of Belfast CC and Leslie and Bill Murray were long time friends.

Using my previously cut out templates, I was able to mark out the component parts, sawing them out on the circular or band saw. When I was at Katesbridge I was able to purchase a plank of beech wood. This was to be used for the horse's legs as the yellow pine would be too soft. The legs need to be hardwood to be able to take the strain. The beech plank was planed to a thickness of 2 inches. The template used to mark out the legs was then cut out on the band saw. The various pieces were prepared to be assembled. You have to make a dry fit of all the pieces so that when you start to glue up, the whole project comes together. No alternations will be needed for at this point the whole process would be in a rather sticky mess.

The upper middle and lower body blocks, put together, form like a square block. The head and neck being already fixed to the upper body block, because it can be screwed and dowelled from the bottom side, the middle body block is hollow inside and just as the Victorian rocking horse makers had done previously, I inserted a copy of the Sunday Times, some of our cycle frame transfers, photographs and a letter setting out who I was and the purpose for making the horse. Also my age and general information, for who knows, nothing lasts for ever and if the rocking horse ever comes apart, the finder will have a little history to ponder over. Some makers insert a letter below the saddle as this is the first part to be replaced. My horse will have to disintegrate before my identity is known!

When the bits and pieces are all glued and screwed together, it is not a pretty sight and far from looking like a rocking horse. I could imagine many people would ask themselves why on earth did I ever attempt this! For the mind would boggle at this ugly thing, with all the protruding square edges. Various methods can be used to carve away the surplus timber and dear knows there is surplus aplenty. But one should not be despaired as you take the square edges down to the glue lines. The shape of the horse just transforms before your eyes. It inspired you to cut and cut, for now you see it all happening! It is in the refining points that makes or breaks the project. If you are not in form, you simply, like all other work, walk away and leave it be. Everything has it's on and off days.

The old Victorians would at certain stages and having all the bits clued together, leave the job sitting for up to six months. Serving two purposes: the timber would have time to settle down and any cracks that appeared could be filled in and painted over as a finished article. The other advantage would be to work on them at slack periods. There is a time to work and a time to sleep. Everything in it's proper order. In my case that would not have been necessary for the wood I was working on was cut and had ceased growing as a living thing of beauty. That tree must have been cut down a century before I was born. In fact it could have been made into the beam of wood I had bought long before my Grandfather was born in 1840. The yellow pine that my horse was being made off was moisture free and as stable as a rock, meaning that I could have worked right through the entire project without leaving it to settle down.

a special rocking horse

Nevertheless I had no need to rush, as no deadlines were to be met. The entire project was to work it out of my system. I was creating a masterpiece under no hassle. When it was glued up and partly carved, it was put behind our spiral stairway and there it sat for a few months until the urge came on me to get it completed. When I finally got back to my final carving, Mary had discarded a two skin sheep rug. It was lying in the garage so I rolled it up and put it in a strong plastic bag. With a piece of carpet on the garage floor, this rug was ideal for putting the horse on its side. It was then easy to gouge, spoke shave and surform the surplus wood away. The idea was to take so much off, then turn it over, repeating the same on the other side. That way it kept a balance and from time to time it is necessary to stand the horse on its legs and eyeball it. This rule I've always worked on. If it pleases the eye it must be right. I apply this rule to all objects.

After many hours of labour and love, I had reached the final shape. Hours and hours of sandpapering were to follow, my eyes continuing to follow the lines and contours. Little adjustments would be made as my eye picked them up, but the time was reached for applying the finish. This would consist of all the fiddly bits. Eyes had to be fixed in with epoxy resin, a two part mixture. After the eyes were pushed into place they were left to dry for a period. The track was cut to receive the mane, the hole drilled for the tail. This was real horse hair purchased from England.

The horse was now ready to be painted. I had never had any doubt that the colour of my rocking horse was to be dapple grey. The first step was to prepare the rabbit skin glue. This was put into a bowl, placed inside a larger bowl with hot water and heated on the cooker ring. When melted, the glue was set aside to cool overnight. In the morning the glue could be cut with a knife and then a portion was warmed up in another pot. When in liquid form the warm glue was then brushed all over the horse. Two or more coats were applied and this process was called sizing.

The next step was to heat the remainder of the glue, stirring in a very fine powder called gilders whitening. This had to be carefully done and brought to the right consistency. As many as six coats are applied to the horse. This can be done in quick successive coats, thus building up a good solid base. When it was dry (after being left for five or six days), the horse can be sandpapered. Any flaws that show up can be touched up. Only when all the flaws and marks have disappeared are you left with a wonderful base to apply the colour.

The first coat of white acrylic with a hint of ultramarine blue was applied. Two coats are brushed all over. You may wonder why blue? Well, all grey horses or mostly all, have a blue hue coming through. The next coats are white acrylic tinged with Payne's grey. It looked perfect and was pleasant to the eye. I was getting excited and pleased that the end and the finished article was in sight. Isn't that what sells the product? An old customer of ours, Jimmy Gregg, always maintained that I have the knack of putting the finishing touches to our work. I hope I just tried my best, but that is how he saw it. So far so good.

I was now ready for the dappling and shading which in my minds eye was just a matter of form - mixing some more of the Payne's grey to achieve a slightly darker hue than the body of the horse. So the paint was now ready to apply. But alas what a nightmare!

It looked like nothing on earth! I quickly painted over the whole horse and it was now light grey again, as it takes only a short time for the acrylic to dry. I tried again, but to no avail! Back to all grey once again. I just packed it in and walked away. It was beginning to cross my mind that I had met my waterloo, or to coin another phrase, my Beecher's Brook, that famous water jump at the Grand National where so many gallant horses fall.

Mary tried her hand, thinking it looked a simple task, but that did not work and was covered over too. It became more or less a joke, but I am honest when I say it looked like having me beaten. Meanwhile I was working at my Grandfather clock, also nearing completion and during that period I met a chap I had known for years and I mentioned to him about woodturning and he gave me the telephone number of Tommy Yarr who lived outside Lisburn.

I gave Mr. Yarr a ring and met up with him. During conversation about the Grandfather clock, the rocking horse was mentioned and he told me about this chap in Dromore who made rocking horses. As the conversation developed this guy turned out to be Barry McIlwrath, whom I happened to know many years ago. On getting back home I looked his number up and giving him a ring, he invited me to his house. Mary and I went up the next day.

Barry gave me a preview and he also described how this dappling was done and showed me one of his finished rocking horses. This was the tonic that I needed, for straight home we came, into the garage, got the stencil brush and paint going and hey presto! After some time the horse had got his dappling and shading with a little red paint here and there. I mixed some varnish, burnt umber and yellow ochre and applying this all over the horse, wiping most off with clean rags. This gave an aged look to the project. The hooves were painted black. The following day a good coat of satin varnish was applied. When this was dry the horse was ready to receive its tail and mane and the saddle and bridle were fitted.

Now the horse was completed and it gave me a degree of satisfaction. A very pleasing job indeed. The horse was then mounted onto a stand. This was made from pitch pine floor joists. My brother Thomas had purchased these joists many years ago when a factory was demolished at the end of the Motorway (M1) at the start of the new West Link to make way for the new Nurses Home at the Royal Victoria Hospital.

The stand was finished in its natural colour with three coats of yacht varnish applied. The completed horse and stand was then brought into the house and stabled in the hallway, then handed over to its first owner, Mary Gordon. She calls her horse Silver after the children's much loved Connemara pony. It is very much admired and probably will be for years to come. It has given me many hours of enjoyment – in the thinking out and the making, and bringing it to a final conclusion.

A journey to Fair Head

There are three friends all of whom have been connected with cycling for a long period. One reported on cycling, another photographed the sport and the third was a real cyclist. They were: Jim Gore of the Newsletter, Jim Lavery, photographer and Morris Foster.

The tale began when a remark was made concerning Fair Head, the most northerly and highest point in Ireland. The 'real cyclist' divulged when they were together, that it was ages since he had been there, so a journey was planned.

Of the three, one had never been there, another had been there taking photographs and the third on an occasion had travelled 386 miles to get there. So one fine day in 2009 the three ventured out by car and arriving in Ballycastle, visited a homely café and fed themselves on tea and home made scones, the size of a plate, to sustain themselves for the venture ahead.

It was their intention just to have a day out together, dressed not in their Sunday best, but near enough to it. Onward they went until they came to National Trust cottages within sight of Fair Head. The idea then was to just have a look around and continue the day out. However, inquisitiveness got the better of the three and on seeing a National Trust sign and reading the content, the adventurous three decided to climb to Fair Head itself. The sign depicted a designated path which was marked by 3 foot circular yellow rings, said to be displayed on large rocks. The rocks, never mind the yellow circles could not be found, but this did not deter the valiant three. I should say here no drink except tea had been consumed. Anyway the journey to the top began, climbing over barbed wire fences, snagging our clothing, stepping into gutter and bog holes, which led to being up to the ankles in water and left with squelching footwear. Eventually the summit was made and Fair Head was conquered. The view was terrific across the Irish Sea to Rathlin Island and beyond to parts of Scotland. What goes up must come down, so the descent began and the adventurers were on their posteriors more than once, before making it to the cottages. They even found the rocks and yellow circles.

Having climbed Fair Head, next stop was Murlough bay. Anyone who has been there would know the downhill descent, which is like climbing down Slieve Donard and as said earlier, mode of travel was by car and one of the three got 'the willies' but calmed down when we got to the bottom. A walk on the beach brought forth the suggestion that Torr Head should be the next trek. On reaching there, the winding path to the Marconi wireless mast was climbed. Not having eaten since the large scones in Ballycastle, the three were feeling peckish and it was decided to dine in Cushendun. On getting there, soup and sandwiches were eagerly devoured, satisfying the hunger brought about by the exercise. Whilst there, a telephone call was received from a cycling colleague, enquiring where they were and what they were doing. When the exploits were explained, the colleague aptly said "So it was the last of the summer wine, day out. Tell me this who was it?" which was followed by a fit of laughter.

In all it was an enjoyable day out which will hold memories for those involved.

JIMMY LAVERY

If John Wayne and Maureen O'Hara can ride a tandem, then so can we!

Why did we buy a tandem? Maybe we were inspired by this scene in "The Quiet Man" where the stars rode the ugliest tandem in captivity. At the time of purchase Ian was 50, and had always ridden bikes; Janet, who seems much younger, had always avoided bikes. We had hired a tandem in France on holiday, and found that, despite their disparate cycling experience and physical strength, man and woman can travel at the same speed, and maintain a conversation without too much difficulty. We liked the green dream of holidays without a carbon footprint.

We bought our first tandem in February 1997 from Craig Cycles, Limavady for only £200. They had it outside the shop chained to a lamppost as an advertisement for their business. It is a Fothergill custom-built in 1954 for indoor banked track racing with 2 men. The space for the stoker is very tight, even with a woman on board. It has history, Mo Molan used it to open part of cycle route 93 on the North Coast; George Jones used it for some sponsored run. We have changed many of the bits, the captain now has a leather Brooks saddle, and the lady stoker has a Gel saddle. Why had we not bought a modern Dawes? Because they are huge and heavy and feel like 2 bikes welded together. Our Fothergill felt like a greyhound in comparison. Eventually we wore that bike out. We found it a good home and bought a 2nd hand 1970's Peugeot, which was slightly heavier and longer, but still a very comfortable bike.

The idea of cycling round the coast of Ireland was a natural follow-up to our having completed the Ulster Way. As we rode the tandem over the first few months we had great issues and practicalities to discuss. The Captain talks to fresh air, and the stoker faces a rigid back. We agreed not to ride long trips living out of panniers. Instead we would stay in good hotels or B & Bs, or go self-catering. From these bases we would drive to a different start point each day, and then ride a circle of between 40 and 70 miles, returning to the car in time to get home and showered for a good meal wearing conventional clothes, anything but Lycra!

The bike fitted well on the Golf's roof rack with a modified bike carrier. However, it was not that easy to lift the bike up. People have commented that it looked like a farm gate when it was on the roof! We also had a MGB and on it the bike was delicately balanced on the boot rack. One of our earlier discussions was whether or not to tie a red flag to the back of it, as it overhung the car bumper by a good 3 feet. Now we buy estate cars with plenty of room inside for the bike.

Highlights and lowlights of our adventures can get confused, and are often the same story. The fastest speed we achieved was 50mph on a downhill section. Then we saw the halt sign. The steel rim got so hot under braking that we could smell burning rubber. We thought it was the brake shoes. Wrong! It was the edges of the tyre melting with the heat and partially welding itself to the rim! When we got our daily puncture we had to rip the tyre from the rim.

Food and drink features in our trips. We had some excellent lunches in the very best hotels and restaurants. However, lunch more than once was in a wee pub where the owner's wife made us tomato sandwiches in hand cut bread. Why tomato? It was all she had in her kitchen. In one pub the choice of drink was either Guinness or Jameson's whiskey, nothing else.

Everyone wants to talk to cyclists who are standing by their tandem. Everyone has a joke or a story. Unfortunately there are a very limited number of jokes; none worthy of repetition.

One day we went to Rush to try and catch a train back to Bettystown, where we had started. Ian went into the tiny station to see if any trains stopped there and if we could get tickets. The sign said "No Bikes". There was a man in the ticket office! "Hi" said our hero. "Are there any trains from here to Bettystown?" "Ah Jesus, you'll have to run. It's coming in 1 minute. How many tickets do you need?" "2 and what about the bike?" "Ah Jesus we don't take bikes. I can't give you a ticket for the bike. The guard will put you off if he sees you. That will be 4 Euros for the 2 of you please." "But what about the bike?" "Leave it against the wall and when the doors open run on with it. He may not see you. He might put you off at the next station."

We followed the instructions to the letter, including a sprint for Ian over the railway footbridge. The train was on time. We never saw the guard, indeed there was only 1 other passenger on a 6 carriage train. We got home. A happy ending.

IAN AND JANET BELL, Captain and Stoker.

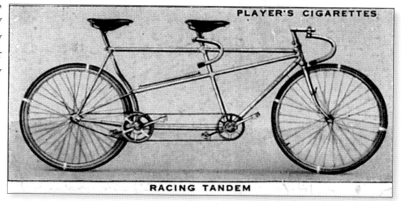

PLAYER'S CIGARETTES

RACING TANDEM

Everything in moderation!

The Motto of the old Cyprus CC was
'Moderation in everything'

Vincent O'Brien has a wee tiple at Cappa, near Kilrush, County Clare in
1952, assisted by Alex Dickson and Marshall McAdam.

Bicycle polo (revival)

In June 1945 Mr H. Gregg and a group of past players along with other interested cyclists met at No.2 Sandy Row Belfast just after the War ended, to organize the sport of bicycle polo. The result was an Annual General Meeting was arranged for a later date in the same premises. This was very well supported.

The meeting was presided over by John Lynn and those present were:
J.Stanfield, W.J. Millar, J. Carton, A. Gregg, H. Moore, B. Hutchinson, S. Burnside, R. Killen, T. Reid, H.O'Neill, R.Winter, H.Smyth, J. Craig, D. Dougan, C. Cranston, V.Smyth, W. Mullan, J. Watson, W. Nelson, W. Patterson W.McKeown and J. McCay.

An election of Officers was conducted and Mr. J. Carton was elected as Chairman. John Lynn became Vice Chairman and the Treasurer was A.Gregg.

Secretary was W. Mullan, Press Secretary, J. Lynn.

Assistant Press Secretary: B Hutchinson. Auditors: J. Watson and W. Nelson.

Committee: J. Carton, A.Gregg, W.Mullan, G.Piddington, H.Close H.Moore and J.Millar.

Referees: W. Mullan, J. McCay, W. Nelson, C.Cranston , A.Gregg, T.Reid, R.Winter, J. Watson, H. Close.

Following the Elections a number of teams were formed to create a league and the membership was five shillings a year. They received permission to play their matches at Gibson Park on the Cregagh Road, Belfast, the Co-op playing fields on Castlereagh Road, Belfast and Dunmurry Hockey grounds.

The advice to new members was that any old machine would do to start with, but it is best to fit straight front forks and flat narrow handlebars, remove all brakes, wing nuts, toe clips and any similar projections. The ideal wheelbase should be 40 inches or under with ample clearance between the front and rear wheels as the ball should be able to pass between them. The usual gear is 39 inches which is obtained by fitting a 36 tooth chain wheel and a 24 tooth sprocket with 26 inch diameter wheels, fitted with heavy spokes.

It is also advisable to wear a helmet, gloves on your hands, felt pads on knees, shin pads on legs, with pads on ankles or boots. Bicycle polo is not regarded as dangerous but if you are unfortunate to receive a blow from a ball, mallet or bike, you could be incapacitated for a while and the precautions mentioned would help to prevent an injury.

When playing on hard, fast grounds it is advisable to wear two long sleeved jerseys and two pair of shorts. At the start of a game the four members of each team line up on their respective goal line and the ball is placed in the centre of the field.

When the Referee starts the game, one player of each team on the left hand side of the goal line sprints straight for

bicycle polo (revival)

NORTHERN IRELAND BICYCLE POLO TEAMS

" TIGERS "
W. MULLAN
  (trainer)
B. HUTCHINSON
W. McKEOWN
R. KILLEN
C. CRANTSON

" YORKS "
G. PIDDINGTON
  (trainer)
W. PATTERSON
H. SMYTH
D. DUGAN

" WRENS "
J. STANFIELD
  (trainer)
J. WATSON
J. McCAY
R. DOUGAN

" RANGERS "
A. SMYTH
  (trainer)
H. MOORE
R. WINTER
W. MURRAY

" FOUR ACES "
V. SMITH
  (trainer)
J. MILLAR
W. KELLY
S. BURNSIDE

" HAYPARK "
A. GREGG
  (trainer)
H. CLOSE
J. CRAIG
H. O'NEILL

*Northern Irela[...]
Bicylce Polo
Teams*

Matches and practices : Mondays and Wednes days at Dunmurry Hockey Ground, 8 o'clock.

the ball. This process is repeated after each goal is scored and at the start of each chukka.
The game consists of six chukkas and each lasts 15 minutes and there must not be more than six players in each team.
The usual positions on the field of play are: a sure hard hitter as a back and a half back that can tackle and has a
quick recovery rate and two fast players as right and left forwards.
  The offside rule is the same as football and the corner hits are taken from the side lines – the ball being rolled into
the centre of the field by the Linesman at the point where the ball went out and parallel with the goal line. In the
case of a penalty being awarded the offending team line up clear of the goal posts and must not move until the ball
is struck. A penalty is given when a player deliberately obstructs a player in the opposing team, or dangerous play etc.
and the incident must take place within the 25 yard line. The art of dribbling and ball control etc. are only obtained
with practice. The novice should start by hitting the ball with the side of the mallet and will find through time that
he will be able to hit the ball hard and clean at speed and be also able to dribble with ease.

A League was duly created involving six teams of four players in each which was an opportunity for those taking part to develop their skills and provide another entertaining side to the sport of cycling. As the weeks went by the game began to attract more spectators and the players became more proficient.

On 15th December 1945 the Northern Ireland Bicycle Polo Association organized a Reception in the Windsor Café Belfast to welcome Mr. Albert Lusty and Mr. George Brake who were the President and Secretary of the Bicycle Polo Association of Great Britain. This event was well supported by the local District Association and they were given a warm welcome by the Chairman: Mr. J. Carton.

Polo Players: Left To Right: W. Mullan   B. Hutchinson (4th Left)   Jim Sharp (6th Left)

bicycle polo (revival)

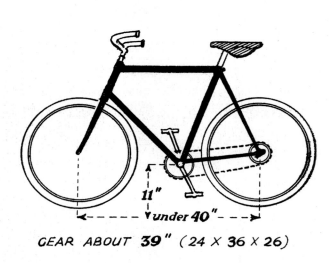

11"

under 40"

GEAR ABOUT 39" (24 X 36 X 26)

A suitable Polo Machine

Mr. Lusty in his reply stated that the policy of the Association was to encourage everyone to play Polo - irrespective of whether they were attached or not to a Polo Association.

Mr. Brake stressed the point that they did not wish to Affiliate to the N.C.U. or the R.T.T.C. and would not brook interference in any way and he went on to outline the plans of the B.P.A. The Association was founded in 1930 at Croydon which is the spiritual home of bicycle Polo and the game was originally introduced by a man named Mr. R.J.Mecredy in 1899.

Ninety per cent of English International teams were drawn from the Croydon area, where the Council have provided sports grounds and granted funds, equipment etc.

England, Scotland and Wales have formed clubs to have International competition and the object of their visit was to assist in the formation of a club to represent Polo players in both North and South which would select International teams to represent Ireland as a whole.

The following day the Inaugural Meeting of the Irish Polo Club was held in Dundalk with representatives of the North and South of Ireland, also Mr. Lusty and Mr. Brake who outlined the scheme for the formation of clubs to select teams to represent their respective countries. The control of the sport would remain vested in each of the Leagues of Northern Ireland the Eire and the name of the Club would be 'The Irish Polo Club' The meeting continued on to formulate a set of Rules to govern both parties, which included the colours: Green jerseys, white shorts and green and white striped stockings.

Future Annual General Meetings would be held in September alternatively in Belfast and Dublin.

The sport of Polo continued to grow as more individual clubs began to form their own teams which made the League much more competitive and some went on to take part in representative matches with other Leagues. The sport continued into the sixties and I can't recall it being played since then.

RAB COLLINS

Doping control in cycle racing

The standards relating to all aspects of doping control within sport which naturally includes our own sport of cycling are established on an annual basis by the World Anti Doping Agency (WADA). Amongst the standards which they set are *The Prohibited List*, which lists the substances and methods prohibited in and out of competition. *The Standard for Testing*, which refers to the testing procedure and the list of Accredited Laboratories.

Persons involved in testing were very optimistic that when WADA was established, and this is primarily funded by the various governments and sporting organisations world wide who subscribe to this, that everything would be standardised which would ease the strain both on testers and athletes but this was not to be the case. The end result is the same in that the athletes urine sample is divided over an "A" and "B" bottle and sealed for transport to the accredited laboratory. How the end result happens is slightly different with different paperwork to be completed, depending on which agency is

Jack Watson

carrying out the testing procedure. Some agencies insist on filling the "A" sample bottle first whilst others insist on the "B" sample bottle first. Some work to a 24 hour clock, some to a 12 hour clock. Some insist that the athlete fills out the medication list others that the athlete dictates this to the Doping Control Officer (DCO) for completion. And in respect of a partial sample, i.e.less than the minimum (90 Mls of urine), there is a method of sealing this but in fact for the three agencies which I test for the partial sealing methods are all different. So, for example, a High Performance Irish rider could in the period of a week be faced with testing by the Irish Sports Council (ISC) in an Out of Competition Test (OOCT) situation, then go abroad the next day to ride an event on the International Cycling Union (UCI) calendar and be tested under the UCI testing procedures, and that same weekend go to England and be tested under UK Anti Doping procedures. All the procedures and paperwork will be different but yet the rider has to certify on each form which he signs that he is satisfied with the testing procedures - bearing in mind that whilst a rider is in the Doping Control Station (DCS) he is usually quite tense and in some cases even stressed.

Not to run through the entire testing procedure in full detail but to simply give the reader an overview of the various steps once a rider has been selected for testing. Normally the winner and two randoms are selected in a single day race, with the race leader included in the case of a stage race.

doping control in cycle racing

It should be noted that the rider has certain rights but all these must be conducted in the presence of a chaperone i.e..a person, of the same sex, appointed to accompany the rider from notification of his selection to his appearance in the DCS. Riders are encouraged to go immediately to the DCS but they have the right to:

◆ Locate and bring a team attendant with them.
◆ Locate and bring an interpreter with them.
◆ Go to their kitbag to locate a method of photo identification. In cycling this is the riders licence but may be a drivers licence, passport etc.
◆ Carry out a warm down.
◆ Attend the prize presentation.
◆ Attend a press conference.
◆ If in a track situation compete in another event.
◆ Demand to see the DCO or the Chaperone's identity.

Once the rider signs in to the DCS he is only allowed to leave under the authority of the DCO for a specific reason and provided there is a chaperone available to accompany and observe him at all times.

Within the DCS the rider must select his drink from at least three bottles of sealed water, and he must not have it handed to him by any of the doping control staff.

When ready to provide a sample he must have a choice of at least three sealed collection vessels and he must satisfy himself that this has not been tampered with otherwise he can refuse to accept it.

He will be accompanied to the toilet by a member of the doping staff and this can be the DCO, the chaperone or, in the case of a UCI event, a doctor or a female nurse for a female rider. Again a slight change in procedures depending on the agency carrying out the testing.

Unless the rider has a disability there will only be the rider and the observer (DCO, doctor, nurse or chaperone) in the actual toilet when the sample is being given. I would mention at this stage that there are different procedures if the rider is a junior or is a rider with a disability.

Again at this stage there are slight differences in that some agencies insist that the rider washes his hands with soap, some do not allow soap as it can be used to contaminate the sample, some insist on the use of rubber gloves whilst some give the rider an option and indeed some insist on hand washing as well as rubber gloves.

In order to ensure the urine comes from the right place the standard term used is that the rider must be completely naked from nipples to knees and if a piece of clothing with long sleeves is worn then the sleeves must be rolled up. Most readers will be aware of the case in cycling where a very famous rider had a rubber ball filled with urine hidden under his arm pit with a tube leading down his back from this and under his crotch. The method of observation used now should prevent this sort of thing. In fact in the toilets used at the Athens

Olympic Velodrome for testing there are mirrors on all four walls so that whilst the observer is watching diligently as to where the urine is coming from he has also an unobstructed view all around of the rider's lower torso.

Once the rider produces the required urine sample consisting of a minimum of 90 mls and a maximum of 170 mls he seals the collection vessel and returns to the administration room of the DCS. There are established procedures in the event of less than 90 mls being produced regarding the sealing of a partial sample but I will not go into these.

The rider then must have a minimum of three kits to chose from and again this choice must be made by the rider alone and at no stage until the procedure is complete should anyone other than the rider touch the kit or its contents until the final sealing of the sample is completed. There is a series of numbers on the outer box of the kit and the two bottles, an "A" and "B" bottle contained therein and the rider and DCO must verify that all these numbers are identical before proceeding to break the seals surrounding the caps on the bottles.

The rider is then taken through a procedure of splitting the sample over the two bottles ensuring that there is a minimum of 60 mls in the "A" bottle and a minimum of 30 mls in the "B" bottle.

The bottles are then sealed with a locking cap system before being placed in plastic sealed bags, transport authority requirement, and placed in the protective polystyrene box which they came in and which completes the kit.

Every stage of the procedure is detailed on the appropriate paperwork with the time of each stage of the procedure recorded. Details of all prescription and non prescription medication taken by the rider over a past period of time is recorded. Again, here there is a variation in this period of time when the medication had been taken, between the various agencies. The rider is also obliged to give the name of his coach and doctor. There is also a test taken on the specific gravity of the sample and if this does not fall within a predetermined value a second sample will be requested and the whole procedure starts over again.

The paperwork accompanying the sample to the lab is completely anonymous and the sample is only identified by the numbers which are on the bottles and it is only when the result related to the bottle number is sent to the relevant agency that this can be married up with the rider's name. The results are also forwarded to WADA which has it's headquarters in Canada.

When the samples arrive at the lab the analysis is done on the "A" bottle containing the minimum of 60 mls. There is enough urine here to allow the lab to perform a second analysis in the event of a non negative result being obtained. If the result is non negative the rider has the right to be in attendance at the opening and the analysis of the "B" sample.

The whole question of the selection of riders for testing is now becoming more selective and the buzz phrase is now "intelligence testing," and this in no way refers to our old 11+ scenario. More and more credibility is being given to riders suddenly getting abnormal results, rumours which may be circulating within sport relating to someone using something, reports from border agencies etc etc. But of course in cycling the Biological Passport has played a major part in cleaning up cycling to a level never previously seen. It is a complete subject in it's own right but I will just cover the concept somewhat briefly.

The riders included in the Biological Passport are the Pro Tour Teams and those Professional Continental Teams with a UCI wild card. These teams fulfil certain obligations as set by the UCI and as such are eligible for consideration for selection to Pro Tour events. The most recent figures indicated 18 Pro Tour Teams, 16 Professional Continental Teams giving a total of 852 riders. The testing target under the Passport system is 6 blood and 3 urine tests per year per rider. It should be noted that successful riders can receive a lot more than 3 urine tests but these are a minimum required to ensure the correct profile parameters are obtained.

The breakdown on tests carried out on behalf of the UCI in respect of the Biological Passport system in 2009 were as follows,

blood testing	6766
urine testing	3837
Total	**10,603**

It goes without saying that the cost of all this is astronomical, in fact in excess of €5,000,000 per year and this is funded by contributions from the UCI, the teams, a percentage of prize funds and contributions from National Federations. This is administered by the UCI Cycling Anti Doping Foundation chaired by the UCI President Mr. Pat McQuaid.

Just as a small aside to the Biological Passport in that up until the introduction of this if a rider was subjected to a blood test in the morning of an event and the on-site laboratory test showed he had a haemocrit level in excess of 50% his licence was immediately taken off him for health reasons and he was not allowed to compete for 14 days. This method did not identify the rider who perhaps had a natural level in the region of 40% but with the use of an experienced doctor had taken the necessary banned substance to bring his level to 49% or the rider who possibly had a natural level in excess of 50%. Now with the Passport system this forms a medical profile of the rider and anything untoward in his profile can be studied by a panel of suitably qualified specialists and a decision made as to further tests or a decision made to declare a case against the rider. It can also trigger the need to target the rider for urine testing to actually identify that the rider has in fact been using banned substances.

All the above tests can be carried out both in and out of competition and as such all the riders involved are

Madrid 2005

on a strict Whereabouts System (see separate article) All the information relative to each rider re his whereabouts, testing, results etc is entered electronically in a world wide system known within the Anti Doping world as ADAMS (Anti Doping Administration & Management System). This is rigorously controlled by a very tight password system to allow access only to those who need access and only to those parts of ADAMS that they need to access.

Testing at times can throw up the odd humorous situation and the following is one such situation I found myself in last year. The rider who had been a random selection was Russian and his only other language was Spanish. The Doping Control Station was a very luxurious mobile home and the transfer from the stage finish to the hotel was a 4 hour drive on a Friday evening. The rider was unable to give a sample and after approximately an hour and a half the team manager was becoming quite frustrated as all the rest of the team were still hanging about with this long transfer in front of them. I then suggested that the rider and I should travel in the mobile home with the doctor travelling in our car behind which would satisfy the requirements for the rider to be chaperoned as I would be with him at all times. The driver of the mobile home was in agreement with this and of course the manager was more than pleased with my solution. I decided to wait for another hour before we moved off and by this time the rider had made himself completely at home and climbed into the bed in the mobile home. Catastrophe then struck when the driver decided to check the insurance and found that he could not drive with people in the back of the mobile home. I then decided that the rider should travel in the passenger seat of our car with me in the back seat fulfilling the chaperone requirement and the doctor would drive. Just one snag in that none of us, that is the doctor, mobile home driver or I could speak either Russian or Spanish. Pigeon English did not work on the rider or possibly he didn't wish to move from his comfortable bed.

Suddenly the doctor had an idea. He had a colleague who was in Madrid and spoke fluent Spanish, (talk about phoning a friend!). Lucky enough he was at home when the doctor rang and he gave him the message which he was to tell the rider. Reluctantly the rider climbed out of bed put on his shoes and got into the front seat of the car. We had been driving for some time when the rider indicated that he was now ready to give his sample. As we were in a Friday night traffic jam there was nothing we could do so we decided that we should carry on until we found a service station. Again it was a matter of the doctor phoning his friend to have him explain to the rider our intentions.

After some time we came upon an old fashioned service station with a single toilet outside the shop and as such we pulled in and stopped. The rider selected his collection vessel from the equipment which I had in the back of the car and the rider and doctor headed for the toilet. At that moment a car drove into the parking area and the male driver was confronted with the sight of two males heading into the single gents toilet and closing the door behind them. I will let you form your own opinion of what must have been going through his head, more so when they came out a couple of minutes later with the rider carrying a see-through container containing a light gold coloured liquid. He continued to stare in shock as the rider selected his sampling kit and started to pour his urine sample into the "A" and "B" containers. I was sure his opinion must have changed from his first observation of the two males going into a single toilet to seeing them split the sample. I was sure he would now be thinking that he had come across drug dealers at work. He continued to stare until we had completed the procedures and vacated the car park. He must have had some stories to tell his cronies in the pub that evening. I was sure that he would contact the police but anyway we eventually arrived at our hotel and I felt completely satisfied that the sampling had been successfully completed within the regulations.

JACK WATSON
Doping Control Officer

Union Cycliste Internationale
UK Anti Doping
Irish Sports Council

Hon. Secretary of Cycling Ireland

Jack was awarded the International Cycling Union's Gold Merit Award at the Congress in Hamilton, Ontario for his work for National and International Cycling. There are only four holders of this in the UK and Ireland.

Jack with his wife Rea.

Have bike will travel

In April/May each year I cycle to Kenmare in County Kerry to visit my brother.

It's a 630 mile return trip, approximately. Last year my journey took four days each way and I had a five day stay with my brother.

My bicycle is a Thorn, 14 speed Hub Gear and I tow a Bob yak trailer. I make a list of what to take - my gas cooker, tea and coffee I count essential kit.

I set off in the morning around 7.30 am. to avoid the heavy traffic around Lisburn and head down the A1 to Newry. Near Newry on the A1, I turn right on the bypass and start climbing. At the top of the hill on the south side of Newry, I take the cycle path and this takes me to the old Dublin Road and then on to Dundalk. I have always managed to get dry weather and the wind on my back.

I would call in the village of Ardee for a pub meal and a glass of Guinness. Refuelled I would head for the neat little town of Kells (still on N52) and on to Mullingar where I would stop for Bed and Breakfast and a good night's rest.

The following day I would head for Birr, Borriskane, Nenagh and finally Limerick. On the third day I would travel the 70 mile stretch down the N21 to Killarney where I would stay overnight and enjoy a walk around the town. Day four would take me on the scenic route by the Lakes towards Cork and on to Kenmare.

My brother's home is four miles away up a hill, past an old, unused building which had been a Workhouse during the famine years. This building is always my landmark for making a right turn. There are lots of little gravel roads in the area and my brother lives three miles along one of those roads. The road (which was used by Rally cars) was full of potholes, so I walked the last 3 miles as it was getting dark and impossible to see the potholes. The warm welcome from my brother made it all very worth while.

I stayed for five days last year and during that time I parked the bicycle and went visiting and sight seeing in the car.

I returned to Lisburn by the reverse route, tired but pleased to have completed the 630 miles and hopefully in another couple of weeks I shall travel again to Kenmare.

This time by a different route.

I manage to cycle as often as I can during the week and each Sunday I cycle to church. My cycling has brought me much pleasure in life and I thank God for my health and strength to keep the wheels turning.

OLIVER WEIR
Lisburn

The origin of the bicycle

While reading a book called: **The Art and Pastime of Cycling** *which was printed and published in 1890 by R.J. Mecredy and A.J. Wilson on the history of the bicycle it stated that the first machine to travel without horses was designed by a Mr. Ovenden in 1761 on which the passenger did the steering while a footman provided the motive power and travelled about six miles per hour and by extra exertion of the footman, it could reach nine or ten miles per hour.*

The Hobby-Horse made its appearance in Paris in 1808 which consisted of two equal sized wheels with a wooden bar connecting them and a seat placed in the middle. It was propelled along by the rider striking the ground alternately with each foot in a walking motion. The one drawback of this design was it had no means of turning.

In 1818 a German named Baron Von Drais improved it and patented it in England and it was known as the 'Draisena' or 'Dandy Horse'. Baron Von Drais was a gentleman at the Court of the Grand Duke of Baden. The 'Dandy Horse' attracted much attention and it was said to be a beneficial exercise for people in the parks and for those who have the opportunity to travel on level roads and they could propel themselves along at a rate of eight or ten miles per hour. In one account it was said to be possible to travel fifty miles in a day.

A man named Gavin Dalzell who was born in 1811 and died in 1863 in Lanarkshire, Scotland designed a machine about 1840 that was the first one to have fixed cranks fitted to the rear wheel. At a later date a Mr. Pierre Lallement fitted cranks to the front wheel of a 'Hobby Horse' which then became known as 'The Boneshaker'. Pierre Lallement was employed as a mechanic by Mr.M.Micheaux who was regarded as the inventor about 1864.

Mr. Micheaux exhibited the 'Boneshaker' at the Paris Exhibition in 1885. The Boneshaker was very popular and their numbers multiplied in England and Ireland.

The trend in design changed to the 'Penny Farthing' style and was introduced into England by a Mr. Turner from Paris in 1869 and as more makers began to build them, the competition created a lot of improvements in wheels, tyres, spokes, bearings, brakes and saddles.

One Maker in London named James Sparrow paid the expenses of four riders who travelled from London to John O'Groats in fifteen days to popularise the machine in 1873. I presume this was the beginning of place to place record breaking as we know it today.

On the early machines they had only one brake which was used on the small rear wheel and it was very unreliable as it was operated by a length of cord from the handlebars which was liable to break at a critical moment. The brake was then transferred to the large front wheel which consisted of a spoon shaped piece of metal that was applied on the tyre by a brake lever on the handlebar. This was not very successful either as the wheel was rarely true and therefore the brake shoe would only make contact at certain points during the revolution of the wheel and the rider was in danger of being thrown over the front of the machine.

The next very important improvement was the bearings. The early ones were either parallel and cone bearings which were replaced by roller bearings but the ball bearings made all the previous ones redundant from about 1878.

Well known names of makers such as Rudge, Humber, Coventry and Phillips began to emerge in the development of the 'Safety' bicycle in the 1880's and which was the original design of todays bicycle and many manufacturing companies have built variations of it up to the present day.

In the early days of the 'Penny Farthing' bicycles, one had to receive a lot of instruction to learn how to ride one of these velocipedes which was an entirely new mode of travel. It was not easy at a time when allowance must be made for the quality of the roads in the 1880's. If one wished to learn there was a number of cycle agents where they could go to. They kept 'learner' bicycles for that purpose and were given general instructions in the art of balance.

The lessons usually took place on a road which had a downward slope and the learner would place their left foot on the step on the frame, just above the rear wheel and push the bicycle forward with their right foot, then lift it up quickly onto the step to learn how to balance. When they had mastered that, the next stage was to practice getting onto the saddle and both feet on the pedals. It would have been quite an achievement when you consider you would be sitting about five feet above ground! According to reports it would take about a week to six weeks to accomplish the art – depending on the ability of the individual.

The advice to all learners was "that they should practise 'legs over the handlebars' as this was useful if in trouble going downhill or on a rough road as riders have been known to escape serious injury by throwing their legs over the handlebars and alighting on their feet!

Never jerk your knees out at the beginning of each stroke of the pedals as this has an ugly appearance and is a waste of a considerable amount of power which was better used for forward propulsion. The knees should travel up and down without any lateral motion. The mouth should be kept shut as the nose is the proper organ to breathe through because it has blood vessels which warm any incoming air, also it has hairs to catch any dust or germs of infection. By breathing through the nose it reduces the danger of contracting lung disease. To ride with an open mouth gives one an idiotic appearance, and is apt to cause severe cold or neuralgia especially in winter.

A day may come when your ordinary machine will get beyond your control on a downward hill, then stick to your saddle, keep cool and assist your brake by back pedalling and try to jump off the back of the machine, using the step. If however you wait too long and feel unable to dismount due to the speed, then steer for the nearest hedge or hawthorn bush and as you approach it, throw your legs over the handlebars. You are sure to be hurt, but you may escape with minor scrapes and bruises. If there is no hedge or bush then throw your legs over the handlebars and pull the brake hard on. You will shoot forward over the front wheel and land on your feet, then run as fast as you are able, because your bicycle will be in hot pursuit and if it hits you it may severely injure you.

Another great danger is overhanging branches. If they are not too low the rider may avoid them by bending down over the handles and keeping a firm grip to steer the bicycle in a straight line under them. If in doubt dismount and walk, as a branch might hit you on the head and sweep you off the saddle.
There was one case when a very tall rider tried to pass under a low branch with his head right down on the handles and a jagged branch passed under his coat collar and out the back and he was lifted clean off the saddle and suspended in the air for a few moments.

Always watch out for donkeys because they are a great source of danger as they rarely get out of your way and as you approach them they will turn their tail towards you and upset you.
Horses should be given more consideration and take care not to pass them at a fast speed. Especially when meeting one that shows signs of restlessness. So ride slowly and pass it as far as the width of the road permits. Also the rider should even stop if requested to by the driver. When passing a horse which is going in the same direction as you, do not take the ground in front of the horse until you are at least ten yards ahead of it.
The bicycle should have an alarm to warn pedestrians of your approach so they dont step off the pavement onto the roadway. There are bells that ring continuously which can be a nuisance, so the gong is much better as it can be activated by the fore finger".

Today we are fortunate to be free of some of those elements of danger and not have to perform acrobatic feats to avoid them.

The book continues on by giving advice about every aspect of bikes and cycling from maintenance of the cycles to touring, camping, racing. Also appropriate clothing for ladies and gents.
Cycling Institutions then began to come into being as far back at 1877 such as the Bicycle Union. Then the National Cycling Union in 1883, followed by the Cycling Touring Club which was inaugurated in Harrowgate in 1878 and the membership grew rapidly under the Secretaryship of Walter D.Welford and Mr.E.R.Shipton who was the Editor of the monthly circular. It became the largest club in existence with a membership of over 20,000.

Before bringing this story to a close it would be unfair not to mention that Mr. R.J.Mecredy who was one of the Authors and Publishers of the book was a no mean cyclist himself. He held World Grass records for 2 miles, (5 mins.52 secs.) 3 miles (8 mins. 51 secs.) 4 miles (11 mins.49 secs.) and 5 miles (14 mins.41 secs) in the 1890's.

He held the Irish Path record for 4 miles (11 mins. 54 secs.) also the 1 mile tricycle record in 2mins. 44 secs. His times riding a safety cycle were 20 miles (1 hr.16 mins.30 secs.) 25 miles (1hr. 35 mins. 26 secs.) 30 miles (1hr. 56 mins.15 secs.) 40 miles (2hrs. 36 mins.27 secs.)
50 miles (3hrs.18 mins. 20 secs.)
As well as all that he introduced the sport of bicycle Polo to England in 1899 and was selected to ride for the Irish team at the 1912 Olympics in Stockholm.

RAB COLLINS

(Extracted from:
The Art and Pastime of Cycling by R. J. Mecredy &
A. J. Wilson, 1895) which was loaned to us by
Austin McNally of North Down Cycling Club.

Photo of Irish Olympic Team in 1912

L-R: R. J. Mecredy, B.J. Doyle, M. Walsh
(on top), M. Walker, F. Guy
and J. Walker (seated).

The McGreevys' of Leapoughs

James McGreevy was the founder of a veritable cycling dynasty in the Dromore area of County Down.

Born on 13th December 1915 at Annaclone Parish, his family moved in a series of small flits to the Townland of Leapoughs in or around 1929.

Sam Thompson the maker of 'Star of Down' bicycle frames lived there and a long tradition of cycle sport existed in the area. It was not long before James began touring the countryside on old ramshackles at first, but later on a Star of Down with 20 inch frame, 40 inch wheelbase and the steep angles for which Thompson was famed.

Co-incidentally a grass track expert called William James Crane lived at Leapoughs. When young McGreevy showed an interest, Crane coached him in the various techniques of track racing, such as fast starting and the correct choice of gear ratio. A number of enthusiasts travelled the short distance to the Holm Factory (main business weaving and fabrics) on the Lurgan Road, Dromore, where the firm offered the use of their sports field for grass track training. James McGreevy eventually gained a reputation for being able to rapidly 'pull in the limit men' in handicap racing with great acceleration and fast pedalling.

One of his first races was a long established road race at Dromore. It was known as 'The Easter Six' and covered one lap of a six mile circuit. In his own words "at his first attempt he was an also ran". However the next year he came 2nd to win the fruit bowl shown in the photograph. The winner was Willie Burton and the year 1932.

He made great progress, racing all over South Down against the best competitors. He mentions the name 'Poppy' McKeown from Bessbrook and tells that "he beat me more than I beat him". Among his encounters was the great Frank Baird who he raced against at Shrigley, near Killyleagh, on a banked red shale track. Dubliner Baird in an illustrious career won a record 64 Irish gold medals. McGreevy also met B.J.Donnelly at Shrigley in 1937. This man went to England in 1936 and won the British 5 miles grass championship. Surprising for an N.C.A. man.

James McGreevy tells of riding against the Gordon brothers of Hillsborough who later became frame builders. He vividly remembers riding at Wallace Park track shortly after it was built. He also rode at Croke Park in Dublin and says it was always "dead up the stand straight".

His greatest claim to fame, however, was winning the Ulster ¾ mile grass championship at Annaclone in 1938, beating none other than Jim McQuaid from Dungannon to win the chiming clock shown in the photograph. McQuaid, of course, moved with his brother Paddy to Dublin in 1945 and the rest is history! They founded the cycling dynasty to end them all, the culmination of which is that Jim's son Pat is current President of the Union Cycliste Internationale and lives in Switzerland.

1938 was McGreevys last year of competition. Wartime put such demands on his business of Agricultural contractor that he had no time for sport. However, he tells of his brother Mick who had great ability but did not give a damn about training, technique or anything else. He says a win for Mick (under his tuition) gave him as much pleasure as winning himself.

James McGreevy married Roseleen McPolin in 1948. They had five sons and two daughters. The sons are: Peadar, Brendan, Seamus, Malachy and Sean. Sadly Sean was killed in 1972 while reigning Ulster schoolboy champion. The Sean McGreevy Memorial race, run by Banbridge CC is in his memory.

All the sons are successful in their various occupations, with Malachy the highest achiever as Manager of Northern Ireland Railways/Translink. The daughters are not to be outshone: Bernadette, is head of one of the largest comprehensive schools in Hertfordshire with 91 teachers responsible to her. Its reputation is apparently so high and its results so good that the Prime Minister and Prince Charles have visited, perhaps to discover its secret? The youngest daughter, Roseleen, is married to the Dromore publican, David Mulholland.

James McGreevy now lives on Ballymacormick Road, Dromore. He is as bright and sharp as a new pin at 94 and remembers in detail those golden days before the War. His wife Roseleen suffers a degree of memory loss, but is still at home.

James can still drive "but doesn't bother". In 2000 he was made chief of the International McGreevy clan at a great gathering in County Cavan, a position he held for four years with pride.

BILLY KIRK

James McGreevy with his clock and rose bowl

Northern Irelands greatest cycling journalist ever

The greatest cycling journalist ever to grace the pages of the Belfast Telegraph or Ireland's Saturday Night was **STANLEY MARTIN** from Premier Drive on the Shore Road, Belfast.
He was a lifetime member of Northern C.C. and served on the Board of Crusaders football club for years.
He is seen here in characteristic attitude with notebook and pen in hand in the company of his wife, Agnes.
He was born 1918 and died 1990. Agnes died not long afterwards.
The photo also shows Dave Kane (in the Castelli sport top) and was taken at a race somewhere in County Down by Ards CC's Bobby (Bantie) Adair.

It could only happen in Ireland

In the 1960's Joe Smyth and myself were on the N.I.C.F. Team in the Wicklow 3 Day. We were both in good form with Joe winning the first stage from a 4 man breakaway.

I was in the winning break on Day 2 with five miles to go, I left the group and went out front on my own. The Finish was in Wicklow Town and the judges from the last prime went past me coming to the Finish. I turned the corner and over the bridge into Wicklow. The judges were there with the chequered flag. I went over the line, hands in the air for the win. I turned in the road and stood beside the Judges to see who would be second. The bunch turned the corner and went straight past! I could not believe it! Half a mile around the next corner there was another finishing line with another chequered flag. The Judges in the car were not told where the Finish was! So instead of me being in Yellow by minutes I was declared joint winner with Pete Mathews who won the second finish. Our times were equal, but all ended well. I caught him in the Time Trial stage and won overall with Joe Smyth second overall and we won the Team prize. Also I got the King of the Hills.

DAVE KANE   NORTHERN C.C.

Bicycle history

The oldest competitive bicycle that I'm familiar with is my grandfather's

1930's tandem which holds the Irish end to end record.

The frame was made of 531 Reynolds tubing, the same tubing that would have been used in the famous Norton racing motorcycles. The rims were made of aluminium but the rest of the components including the handlebars, stem & chainset were made of chrome plated steel. The racing bicycle continued to evolve with more of the components being made of aluminium, by the early 1970's my father was importing Pinarello bicycles, their frames made of Columbus Chromo. tubing & equipped exclusively with Campagnola of Italy.

In the 1980's a new company came alone, the then small Shimano began to revolutionise cycle components, with the development of such things as index shifting & handlebar controlled gear & brake levers (STI), leaving European companies like Campag, Mavic & Simplex in their wake. The 80's also saw clipless pedals come on the market. Although earlier attempts were made it was Look who developed the system we are all familiar with today, derived from skiing and making for a more efficient pedal stroke.

Through the 90's manufactures sought to make lighter & stiffer machinery changing from steel to aluminium and eventually to carbon fibre. By the early 21st century all top competitive bicycle frames were made from carbon with more & more of the components being made of the same.

Recently a very interesting change has occurred in high end cycle components, what could be a case of history repeating itself. The American company Sram has rivalled the Japanese Shimano, developing a double tap gear lever making the shift quicker & the mechanism significantly lighter.

After the frame the wheel is the most important part of a bicycle, Mavic is still a market leader but yet again we see an American company, this time Zipp who have focused on building top end competition wheels, where we see the use of carbon fibre again & now wind tunnel testing for aerodynamics to achieve maximum economy and speed.

Today in the shop we sell Specialized bicycles from Morgan Hill California, as consumer awareness for the brand Specialized continues to expand, its reputation for design & innovation grows from strength to strength. It takes a certain kind of passion & belief to achieve what Specialized are today & for us at Cicli Sport to be part of what is quite simply the best bike brand in world is something special (pun not intended) & helps drive us to reach our own goals as a retailer.

At present from what I believe no manufacturer is investing in cycle research as much as Specialized who are now the world leader in bicycle development both on & off road. Some of the most interesting innovation is shoe development with Dr Andy Pruitt together with the development of the Sportive bicycle. For those not familiar with this concept Specialized took the Tarmac, their race bike, & added an element of comfort to the mix with minimal compromise to performance. Designed for endurance racing it is also ideal for anyone looking for a racing bike who isn't going to race it.

So what does the future hold? None of us know the answer but thanks to our Taiwanese/American friends I'd say someone somewhere has something exciting up their sleeve but the next step for our business will be computerized bike fit.

JONATHAN SMYTH

Yellow Arrows

The modern day cycling fraternity is alive and well in Larne in the form of the 'Yellow Arrows'. This loose band of former rugby players from Larne Rugby Club has been plying the Coast road and Antrim hills for 13 years now. Each year we partake in a special trip away to pastures new for the purpose of broadening the mind and narrowing the waist line – or was that the other way round? The list of destinations so far has been Dublin, Wicklow Mountains, Mull of Kintyre, Isle of Man, Majorca, Holland, Bruges, Prague, Berlin, Riga, Pula, Krakow, Budapest and Bratislava.

The Yellow Arrows name originated in 2003 after a visit to an outlying Belgian Brewery that was selling off redundant millennium T–shirts cheaply – bright yellow ones. Later in the day and after some 'refreshment' we endeavoured to put on a show of formation cycling to the waiters and diners in the main square in Bruges. The programme of straight, T, diamond and V formations all went down so well that we were likened to that splendid aerial display team the 'Red Arrows' and so the Yellow Arrows were born. I'm sure some of the Red Arrow pilots are former rugby players too and so will not take any offence!

As we look forward to the era of high oil prices and strong measures to curb carbon emissions we can safely predict that cycling will once again enjoy mass appeal as a social and recreational activity.

The camaraderie engendered by the shared experience of travelling along on bikes and discovering what is just around the corner is very strong and long lasting and of course the blueprint that defines how the cycling system should operate in Northern Ireland was established in the 1950's and has been beautifully presented in this book. The Yellow Arrows fully intend to take an active part in the rediscovery of those fun times – after all the best things in life are free – well almost.

DAVID SURPLUS
Managing Director **B9 Energy Larne**
Son of Raymond Frank (Norman) Surplus

Missing from the group is my brother Norman who is circumnavigating the world in a gyrocopter. He left his hometown Larne in March this year, for the 27,000 mile trip and was making steady progress until forced to crash land his machine in a lake in Thailand. He was unhurt. Unfortunately his plane was damaged and he was grounded in Patteya for ten weeks while the plane was repaired and the necessary 'Red Tape' taken care of. However numerous delays and the prospect of extremely bad weather have forced Norman to postpone the final leg of his journey until Spring 2011. He has already flown into the Guinness Book of Records, achieving the longest distance ever flown by a gyrocopter.

Above: my father, Norman Surplus, Cyprus CC, on duty as a motorcycle marshall, on the day when my Aunt, Isabel Clements, set her record for Mizzen Head to Fair Head. The record stood for fifty two years.

Pictured left: The Yellow Arrows, in Bratislava.

Tribute to Joe Bell - by Isabel Woods

Joe Bell lived in Gt. Northern Street and was a Slocitor's Clerk in the firm of Hugh J. Catchpole in Belfast. He had a clever business and legal mind which ably suited him to administrate for the sport of cycling. Along with John Lynn who had been ex-head of Police in Kenya, he was responsible for the negotiations which brought about the formation of the NORTHERN IRELAND CYCLING FEDERATION. He was renowned for his integrity and attention to detail. Negotiations had commenced in 1948 but it was 1949 when final agreements had been reached.

Joe was a Partner in ENTERPRISE PRINTING SERVICE 1977/1979 at Upper Library Street, Belfast and in 1954 the first N.I.C.F. Year Book was published. He had a great team of legislators, according to this first issue. The Executive Committee member was: J.M.Bell, A.Dickson, and F.O'Brien, R. Moore, W.L.Smith and P. Woods.

Officials 1954

Joe Bell

Committee		Secretaries of Standing Committees	
President:	J.M. Bell		
Chairman:	A. Dickson	Track:	W.L. Smith
Vice Ch.	R. Moore	Massed Start:	P. Woods
General Sec:	F. O'Brien	Time Trial:	J. McCarron
Ass.Sec:	P. Woods	B.A.R. comp.	T.R. Millar
Treasurer:	J. M. Bell	Records:	J. Trimble

Vice Presidents: J Keenan, G.H. Thompson, T. Taylor, J.E. Cassidy — Millar, Head Constable, Roth well.

Other working teams were: Timekeeper, Judges and Handicappers

Joe was not just a pen pusher, he could be seen out on the course of almost all the races, sending the results into 'Irelands Saturday Night' and other newspapers. Billy Kirk recalls on one occasion when competing in a 25 mile T.T. on the 'H Course' on the Antrim Road in 1955, he spied Joe frantically waving a newspaper with excitement and shouting "you're doing a 58!" Billy's time was 58mins. 28 secs. It was a record which wasn't beaten until 1967. As a Veteran in his 70's Billy has improved his best time in 2006 with a 57mins. 59 secs!! Technology or what?

My Hero the flying machine

George Wilkes of Windsor CC was the object of my early teenage hero-worship in the early 1950's, only slightly behind Billy Dowds in my regard, but in a completely different way. The 'iron man' persona of Dowds contrasted with Wilkes professional style and charisma. He used to say "*If you cant be fast, at least you can look fast!*"

He rode his French Foucaux bicycle with a hunched back that looked great and I coveted the pronounced veins in his legs, even though they were probably varicose!

One balmy summer evening in 1950, I sat, aged 13, feeling strangely alone, among a crowd of spectators on the sea wall of the Portaferry Road where an Ards CC '10' was in progress. Listening to the hum of animated discussion and banter I suddenly overheard Hugh McKibben (an Ards CC member) say "There is that fellow Geordie Wilkes, he is a flying machine!" Wilkes had come along to watch the Ards event.

He was Irish 50 miles T.T. champion that year beating Dublin's Matt Marlow by 12 seconds. His success was a surprise for he was seen as a pure road racer.

He won the N.I. road championship in 1952 and represented Ireland and N.I. in numerous International races. In 1950 he set two place-to-place records which stood for years: Belfast to Londonderry in 3 hrs. 4 mins. and Belfast to Dublin in 4 hrs. 32 mins.

He devoted much time in later years to coaching junior riders and was an expert frame builder and repairer. From the 1980's until his death in 2006 he was a member of Ards CC.

BILLY KIRK

N.I. Cyclist's at the Isle of Man in 1952

Back Row L-R: Albert Ewart - Maryland Wheelers, John Fee - Cyprus CC, The guesthouse owner and Raymond Moore - Chairman of N.I.C.F. Front Row L-R: Aubrey Brown - East Ulster CC, George Wilkes - Windsor CC and Gordon Reid - Cyprus CC.

The unstoppable Australian, well almost ....

1966 was a good year for me, but not without incident.

The Commonwealth Games were in Jamica and Morris Foster and myself were there. We were in the winning break on the climb of the Blue Mountains. On the descent, a big Australian hit the deck. He got up, caught us. He fell on the next descent, got up, and caught us again. We got to the halfway point – 60 miles and went around an oil drum in the middle of the road. We were passing the riders coming the other way and the poor Australian hit a rider head on. He hit the deck, but did not get up this time. One less to worry about.

On the way to the finish a rider had to retire. He was kicked by a donkey!

As all this was happening the racing at the front was fast and furious! I climbed well on the second climb of the Blue Mountains and finished 5th - photo-finish for 3rd place. Morris Foster finished 8th. Good result for Northern Ireland.

The race was won by the late Pete Buckley.

DAVE KANE   Northern CC,
Dave Kane Cycles

This photograph of Debbie Kane, daughter of Davy was taken just one week before she had her accident.

Dave Kane

Below is a rough summary of his carrer compiled by himself. However, a startling fact is that he was fourteenth in the Isle of Man international, 1964 - in which Eddy Merckx was eighteenth!

Belfast to Dublin Record 1964	Tour of Britain
Belfast to Dublin Record 1971 (This record stood for 27 years)	Tour of Belguim
3 Commonwealth Games (still best road place 5th)	Brittany, France
4 World Champs	Pursuit Track Champion
13 Tour of Ireland's	N.I Road Race Champ.
6 Tour of Scotland's	All Ireland 100 TT Champ
13 Manx Internationals	All Ireland Grass Track Champ
18 Tour of the North's	Tour of Wicklow
Tour of the Gaps	Tour of the Glens
Track League Champ	Regal Grand Prize
32 Irish Reps Team	Coronation Cup
80 N.I.C.F. Reps Team	Star Trophy
N.I. Road race 5 times (2nd)	5 Dilan Men
All Ireland Road Race 2 times (2nd)	Red Hand Trophy
Tour of Ards 3 times (2nd)	Dover-London
Most pleasurable result – Regal Grand Prix 1965	Lurgan Grand Prix

The Ballymena boys were going well and had hammered us. (Northern CC) at Cookstown.
   S. Kerr, G. Caldwell, W. Cardwell, S. Connor, Beggs. But at the 100 mile Regal Grand Prix over Spelga etc. I was in the leading break and finished up with 4 Ballymena men. I attacked on the Tandragee Hill with 10 miles to go. Head down and ass up. Never looked round and held off untill the Finish. Great result!
Northern CC. 1st. Ballymena 2nd, 3rd, 4th and 5th.

Little red Fiat

Just down the street from where I live, turn right and you are on Meetinghouse Street.

It was there that Stephen McDowell lived in 1954 and was working in McEllains Chicken Store in Castle Street. We had met up at James Warnock's garage in Main Street. James was the main B.S.A. Dealer in the district and Stephen was saving up for a 'Tour of Britain' model and I, a Standard Model. He was therefore the first rider that I really helped in the sport of cycling and he went into competition with the old Ballymoney & District C.C.

I was their Secretary until 1960 when I started Route Wheelers.

The early riders were Robert McLean, James Simpson and Raymond Carson.

In 1970 I changed the name to team ROUTE CRT and took a deeper interest in Coaching and as a result formed a small training group of four riders. There were two boys in the group, Richard Nicholl and Stephen Hunter and two girls, Vanda McVicker and Mary Davidson.

Vanda went on to represent Northern Ireland at the 1990 Commonwealth Games in Auckland, New Zealand. At the end of 2000 work commitments and marriage had made changes and there was only two young riders left. They had both been coached to a high level by Vanda but one, Jonathan decided not to continue and the other, Robert went on to win the East Tyrone C.C. road racing league over the next two years. The only rider outside ET to do so.

The red Fiat car that had become the image of the team throughout Ireland, Scotland and UK was the subject of a children's address in a local Presbyterian Church just a few days before it was sold on to a Fiat Dismaltler.

WALLACE McNAUL

Unusual cycling shoes

In June 2000 Mervyn McComb and a few of us decided to ride the 'Border Trek Challenge'.

On day one we cyclied from Ennikillen to Sligo. On Day two Mervyn was quite excited as we arrived at the start and he immediately headed for the baggage truck and handed in his bag before signing on and collecting drinks and freebies. When we met at the start line he was pleased as Punch with himself that all his plans were complete. Suddenly he exclaimed "Oh hell!"

He stared down at his feet and realised he was still wearing his brogues and immediately ran back to the baggage truck only to find it full and the doors being closed. "Ah well" he said "it's okay" as we set off for Enniskillen singing "These shoes we made for cycling"

Nothing was going to stop him from cycling and nothing ever did.

CORMAC McLYNN (Maryland Wheelers)

156 years of cycling between them

Wallace McNaul of Ballymoney and Harry McCartney from Dromore photographed at The Island Civic Centre in Lisburn.
They were attending Isabel Wood's book launch (Wheels of Change)
In November 2008.
Harry was showing Wallace some of the early End to End of Ireland record attempts.

A tribute to the late David McCall 1962 - 2008

David McCall was a top class cyclist at International, National and Club level throughout his life on the bike, with many road and track honours, plus three Commonwealth Games appearances.

Following his retirement from International racing, he served as an Executive of the Ulster Cycling Federation (Cycling Ulster) for several years. He qualified as a Level Three Coach and Commissaire, plus was the driving force behind the motorcycle marshall training scheme which he launched.

He was the inspiration and founder of SportActive cycling, walking and triathlon camps and continued to promote the sport he loved until his sad and very untimely death in August 2008. He was involved with Scottish Cycling and the Braveheart Fund, which raises funds to help young riders achieve their potential.

In 2007 he, along with the Blazing Saddles charity, cycled the length of Ireland in less than 24 hours purely to raise money for charity. David made an equal impact off the bike with a large and enthusiastic personality that will be fondly remembered by everyone who knew him.

During the 1970's David attended Knockmore Primary and Lisnagarvey High School when he started cycling with Maryland Wheelers under the guidance of Mervyn McComb and Joe O'Neill. Around this time he and another schoolboy in Maryland, Eric Mackin became quite dominant within the sport and won many school-boy races in Ulster and around Ireland.

As a junior David had less success in the sport but when turning senior he started to raise his game and within a couple of years was promoted to senior 'A' which in later years became recognised as 1st category, a licence he held for the full 20 years or so it took to reach veteran class. During his time as a senior rider there weren't too many of the major one-day races in Ireland that David either didn't win or almost won. Well, that's what he liked to tell everyone because David was more than just a very good cyclist, he gave his utmost in each and every race and had a good story to tell about it.

David had a long career at a high level in the sport of cycling by anyone's standards, but if I was asked to narrow down the period in which he was most dominant, I would have to focus on the years from 1983 until the early 1990's. During this period David rode for Maryland Wheelers, Banbridge C.C. then formed the sponsored 'Kieran Trainor Solicitors Racing Team' before returning to Maryland wheelers in 1993 where he remained for the rest of his cycling career.

David won over 76 Open races in Ireland with approximately 60 of these being between 1983 and 1993. He also rode the Ras Tailteann on at least 6 occasions during this period and although a stage win eluded him he always finished well in the overall general classification and earned himself a reputation among his peers of being a 'hard man' on the bike who you could always depend on to ride for his team.

Joe Smyth (a cycling legend himself) managed the 1989 Ras team which David rode for that year. Joe had great praise for David's ability to give his last ounce during the race which saw the team with three top ten finishers overall in GC while David finished that year in 15th overall. David and Joe were to remain great friends - their mutual respect for each other would remain a feature of the 'Dunmurry run' in the 1980's and 1990's. David and Joes' combined physical and mental strength was an endurance test for all the regulars who turned up for those Wednesday and Saturday runs over the hardest roads imaginable. Many turned up once or twice and were never seen again but those who stuck it out went on to be champions.

Of the many highlights in his career David was particularly proud to have represented Northern Ireland at 3 Commonwealth Games – Edinburgh 1986, New Zealand 1990 and Kuala Lumpur 1998.

Known as a great motivator and very knowledgeable tactician to his fellow cyclists and club-mates, one particular period would have been in the mid nineties when Scott Hamilton was dominant in all championship

David McCall, winning at Moneymore in the nineties

time-trials in Ireland, while he was
winning all before him.
David encouraged Maryland Wheelers to
be part of the success, backed up by Tom Mateer,
Billy Bothwell and Billy Knowles, Maryland won all
individual golds in Ulster and Ireland in 1995 (Hamilton).

In 1996 the club helped themselves to team golds for all
championship time-trials in Ulster and Ireland. Hamilton, McCall
with Phil Holland, Alan Hodgen and Alan Quinn, the Ulster road-
race championship was the prize of Denis Easton, McCall and
Hamilton. We would not have been that successful without his
drive and self-belief.

In later years David's enthusiasm helped Mark Greer, Peter Wilson and more notably Heather Wilson achieve
great success at home and abroad.

In 2000 David founded 'SportActive' a holiday company which provided specialised cycling and walking
holidays. David's passion for people and sport quickly developed this new enterprise into a successful company.
As the company grew, David talked Sean Kelly into joining him for a few weeks in Majorca during one of his
camps. Now Sean is a regular member of the SportActive team.

Of his many nicknames, 'Morale' was one that suited him best. An enthusiastic club secretary for many years,
he was behind the success of the Maryland/Phoenix club league and the Motorcycle Marshalling Team and in
earlier years a member of the UCF executive.

In August 1987 David married Shirley and they had two daughters, Carolyn and Emma.
David left behind a legacy unsurpassed in not only cycling but with his many friends and family.

PHIL HOLLAND   Maryland Wheelers

The village of Tyrellspass

The Village of Tyrellspass in County Westmeath presents a very English appearance as three members of Cyprus Cycling club rest during a tour of Ireland in the summer of 1952.
They are (left to right)
Fred 'Earl' Granville, Marshall McAdam (studying the map) and Alex Dalgety.
Alex Dickson, then Chairman of the N.I.C.F. took the photograph.
In the background four schoolboys make sure they are in the picture – where are they now?

Rab Collim

Champion Tommy Talbot (centre) with Rab Collim (left), and Billy Dowds (right).

Rab Collim is handed a drink by Ronnie Millar after a 25 mile time trial, on the Ballyhenry Road, Glengormley.

Three greats of Northern Ireland (and Irish) cycling photographed at the Irish 50 miles T. T. championship on Dublin's Navan Road in June 1955.

The champion was Tommy Talbot (centre) of East Tyrone C.C. with W. J. Dowds of South Lurgan C.C. 2nd and Rob Collim of Cyprus C.C. (left) in 3rd place.

Much has been written elsewhere in this book about Dowds and Talbot, but it would be remiss of us not to include Collim's achievements down the years.

He was Irish 50 champion in 1954, N.I. road champion in 1956 and set a new 25 miles competition record for N.I. of 59 mins. 09 secs. on 9th June 1955, as well as taking silver in that year's Irish 25. He also won three open 25's and a 30 in 1955. A very strong mass start rider, he won many road races including a stage in the Tour of the North. This gained him selection to Irish and N.I. teams for International races such as the I.O.M. International.

In the 1980's and 90's his Heating and Ventilating firm of McCaig Collim generously sponsored Ards C.C. to bring great time trialists such as Dave Lloyd, Graham Obree and Chris Boardman to compete in various events on the Portaferry Road.

A tribute to the late Mervyn McComb

Mervyn McComb with Davy McCall
MERVYN McCOMB,
who sadly died in March 2010
Pictured here with DAVY McCALL and
Kieran Trainor.

Mervyn McComb was a member of Maryland Wheelers cycling club for over 50 years and held various positions within the club, including Chairman and in 1996 he succeeded his friend, Billy Stewart as club President. Mervyn along with Joe O'Neill began a recruitment drive for the club in the mid Seventies, primarily focused on getting under 18's into the sport. During the first year of this initiative it was not uncommon to see 50 or 60 schoolboys turn up on Saturday afternoon in Wallace Park for the weekly training runs. On Tuesdays during the cycling season the schoolboy section of the club met in Lisburn and supervised by Joe and Mervyn they cycled to Orangefield for track racing. Morris Foster (Cyprus CC) organised the track racing but Maryland still had close links with track racing through Tommy Givan who loaned his track bikes to the schoolboys each Tuesday evening.

David McCall was one of the schoolboys who joined Maryland Wheelers in 1974 and had much success in the sport both as a school boy but more notably as an accomplished senior racing cyclist.

Mervyn's passion and commitment to Maryland and cycling in general over the years cannot be overstated as many successful cyclists who have been in Maryland have all benefited from Mervyn's commitment and words of encouragement.

Over the past few decades Mervyn was the club run captain and he set a high standard in the role, while another of his key roles was each year on our Reliability Trials He and his team would have tea and sandwiches ready for the hungry cyclists in all weathers.

He will always be remembered throughout cycling circles with great fondness.

ALAN HODGEN *(Maryland Wheelers)*

Darrell Erwin, an inspiration to us all

Darrell was always 'sporty' and at school he excelled at sport by playing for *all* the sports teams and nearly all the teams a year above him. (basketball, football, rugby and athletics) and set many records in athletics. When he left school he played basketball for the Ballymena Basketball Club until his accident in 1999.

He also took up cycling in 1989 and joined Ballymena Road Club and went on to win over 40 Championship medals in Time Trials, road racing and team events.

He represented Northern Ireland Internationally for much of his racing career.

Darrell remembered well the morning of his accident. It was 27th November 1999 and it was 7.45 am. He worked for the local council as a road sweeper driver, lived at home with his mother and life was good. He had a day off work and was driving out to his brothers to help him in the building of his new home. Darrell recalls how suddenly the car hit black ice and skidded of the road up a grass verge and hit a telegraph pole. The car landed in a field on its roof. He says that the damage was done almost immediately as he could not feel anything from the chest down and petrol was pouring over him. He managed to pull himself from the car which took all his energy and then waited until some passers by came and helped him. His injuries were so severe that if he had not been such a fit young man it would have been doubtful that he would have survived. Darrell had broken his back and crushed two vertebrae which left him paralysed from the chest down. He also broke two ribs, punctured a lung and fractured a bone in his neck. He had to spend over two months in Musgrave Park Hospital Spinal Injuries Unit. He cannot speak highly enough of the tremendous care the staff and all the help from the different departments he received on his road to recovery.

As ever Darrell was determined to get on with life and after 4 months of strenuous re-habilitation he was finally ready to leave hospital. Now wheelchair bound, he returned home and his mother was a true inspiration to him and helped to care for him when needed. She even bought him light weight for his birthday to get him started on developing his new sports careers. Quickly he moved on to training at his local gym and began to play wheelchair basketball for The Northern Ireland Knights where he excelled.

He also started wheelchair racing (athletics) where he won his first ever race which was the 2001 Belfast Marathon and went on to win it 5 times, overall he has won over 25 marathons including Longford 7 times, Cork twice and a few others as well as wins at varying distances from 10 ks. to half marathons.

Darrell started handcycling in 2008 when he set up the Ulster Handcycling Association who are affiliated to Cycling Ulster and Cycling Ireland.

He went on to win the 2008 Ulster cycling 10 mile Time Trial championships and retained it again in 2009. He was also 2nd in the Irish National championships and first in his HC2 category.

In 2010 he has been a member of the Para cycling development squad and has competed in Dubai, Spain and Austria and will be taking part in further races throughout the year.

Darrell's latest achievement was a new Ten Miles Handcycling record of 34 mins15 secs, in Co. Antrim.

Always one for encouraging others to try sports the club received a grant from Sport NI and have purchased two kids and two adult handcycles and have taken part in various taster days, come and try it events etc. and hope to keep progressing with more opportunities for people with disabilities to get into handcycling as well as other disability sports. Darrell continues to be a true inspiration to people with disabilities and will continue to help people to rebuild their lives after disability. We wish him well. We love his positive attitude to life and know we will hear more about him in years to come.

MAY FARRAR

Darrell on route in Co. Monaghan.

My Mizen Head to Fair Head experience

From the 8th to 13th September 2009 I completed a charity handcycle from Mizen Head in County Cork to Fair Head in County Antrim – a total of 390 miles.

I was the first ever handcyclist to attempt this gruelling challenge and had to prepare myself by training for six hours each day, three to four days a week in the build up to this event. I had the pleasure of having Alan Mark and Patsy McGurk of the Ballymena Road Club to assist me. They are two good friends and they helped by driving the Road Club bus as a backup vehicle and one to ride behind me and also as a marshal through towns and at corners etc. After months of meticulous preparations and organising I had our hotels and B & B's sorted and my route all planned out with each day being around 65 to 90 miles.

Tuesday 8th September 2009
We knew the trip down to Mizen Head would be quite a long drive in the mini bus, but the time flew by with old stories and reminiscing of the old days and good jokes the whole way down.

Unfortunately the weather was very nasty with torrential rain the whole way down but the weather forecast gave it to change for 10 days so we were quite optimistic as to what was to come, but I was well prepared with enough clothes for the worst of weathers. We arrived in Durrus in Co. Cork in the evening and had a very warm welcome by Mike and Julia of Carbery Cottage B & B and it had also stopped raining which looked promising.

Wednesday 9th September 2009
After a good night's sleep we awoke to a glorious morning with the sun shining over the Peninsula and we knew it was going to be a lovely day. After a hearty breakfast we took the short drive down to Mizen Head where we were greeted and set off by Cllr. Dermott Sheehan. Our journey was to take us 90 miles to Mallow Co. Cork through some very rough roads after the start. With a head wind for the whole journey each day to Fair Head we set off. Our spirits were good as we cycled off in the cool morning air, with lovely sunshine. Progress was slow for the first 30 miles with very rough terrain, but I settled down to the task ahead and made good time until the last 30 miles which started to climb as we made our way to Mallow. At this point it seemed like the roads just kept climbing and never seemed to drop again and it got very warm as we cycled into the afternoon. Our first day which was to be our hardest and longest took us 7 hours and 50 minutes which was only 20 minutes down on my slowest schedule. Thanks to my good friend Sean Wright who supplied us with Powerbar food and drinks which was really needed for this journey. My arms and shoulders felt quite fatigued after today's effort but, 'onwards and upwards'.

Thursday 10th September 2009
Today wasn't going to be as long with just 68 miles from Mallow to Nenagh in Co. Tipperary. We were started off today by Cllr. Richard Dempsey from the Hibernian Hotel. It was a cold and misty morning but I actually felt very good and was looking forward to today's cycle. I set off steady and then as it got warmer I started to lift the pace and made good progress until we reached Limerick. This turned out to be a nightmare with road works in which we got lost a few times and actually ended up going down the motorway for 2 miles. A diversion sent us from a major road onto the motorway which was an experience in itself! When we eventually

got back on course I put the foot down and we reached Nenagh well within my schedule in a time of 4 hours 45 minutes.

Friday 11th September 2009

Today we were let down by the Mayor and the Newspapers which was disappointing. There was a cold mist to start the day off on the 82 miles from Nenagh to Grannard in Co. Longford. Once again today I felt good and set off steady and really built the pace up, despite a few sharp and very hard hills along the way. The weather got really warm again and we made excellent time in 5 hours 45 minutes - again we were nearly 30 minutes ahead of my fastest scheduled time. We arrived to be greeted by Martina Brady of The Cuckoo's Nest B & B, Ballinalee who made us the loveliest home cooked dinner which was well and truly needed.

Saturday 12th September 2009

Today started of sunny and quickly warmed up and we were sent off from Grannard by Cllr. Tommy Stokes and again today I was feeling in excellent form and we set off at a flying pace. We maintained this pace all day and finished our 89 mile leg to Cookstown in a time of 6 hours 18 minutes which was 30 minutes ahead of my fastest scheduled time. This was helped along by the guys from Emyvale C.C. who accompanied us through Monaghan and up to Dungannon and their knowledge of the roads and great marshalling helped keep the pace high for me. So a big thanks has to go out to them. We had a lovely meal at the Glenavon Hotel where we were staying and a lovely cold pint of Guinness to refresh me and some music in the bar lounge to help us relax.

Sunday 13th September 2009

This was our final day and we were in good spirits as we knew we had only 65 miles to go from Cookstown to Fair Head and again the weather was absolutely gorgeous. I didn't really worry about schedules today as I wanted to enjoy every moment of it, which I did every day of my journey.

I knew the roads would be quite tough today but was helped along by some friendly banter from the Ballymena Boys who met up with me along the way to Ballymena where we stopped for a Reception by local Mayor, Cllr. James Currie and a big crowd of family and friends to support me. We kept a steady but light pace along the way and fatigue was starting to finally creep in with about 20 miles to go, but knowing I was so close to the finish was a big morale booster. The last 3 miles climb to Fair Head from Ballycastle was quite hard but I had good company with Tom Dowds (a cyclist who completed Mizen Head to Fair Head) telling me great jokes to keep my mind from the pain. It was so good to see all my family and friends at the finish in Fair Head and people who came along to congratulate me on my achievement.

The Finish at Fair Head
L-R: Alan Mark, Patsy McGurk, Isabel Woods, Darrell Erwin
and Tom Dowds.

The feeling of accomplishment and exhilaration at doing such an event was evident by the big smile across my face and it was really great to get photographs with everyone including my family, former end to enders: Isabel woods, Alan Marks Tom Dowds and Patsy McGurk. I was also greeted by Foyle Councils Cllr. Cara McShane who presented me with a plaque for my achievements. I was only 15 minutes behind my slowest schedule but that didn't matter today.

DARRELL ERWIN

Top N.I. Cyclists - the early years

We asked Harry McCartney if he would list his 'Top Riders' for our book. An awesome task for a gentleman who will be 90 years old at the end of April. This was Harry's reply:

Owing to my illnesses I am hardly able to write this, so what I have decided is to cover up to about the end of the 1960's with both road and track top men.
Then you could possibly get Morris Foster to sort out the last 40 years.

Starting from the late 1880's, just after the introduction of the Safety Bicycle (similar to to-day's roadster) and the Pneumatic tyre, **W. HUME** *of the Belfast Cruisers C.C. who had retired a year or so earlier when Champion on the Old Ordinary or Penny Farthing. He was attracted to this new outfit, acquired one and took part in the Queens College Sports on 18th May 1899. He won all 4 races from the opposition which included the famous Du Cross Brothers, of Dublin who were the Irish Champions then.*
Track record breaking was a feature at many Sports Meetings, both on cinder and grass tracks with distances varying from a quarter mile to 50 and 100 miles. The latter were mostly tandem paced.
HARRY MUSSEN *the outstanding Road Time Trial rider made a great onslaught on these, collecting almost the lot in the late 1890's. Willie Murray from Belfast collected several a few years later, but as Ireland was under the same ruling at that time, many were taken by Southern riders before the practice died out.*

Between 1900 – 1914 there was a fair sprinkling of good track riders including such names as: **W.P MURRAY, H. MURRAY, O'REILLY, RUDDELL, DEANE, GUY, MAGEE, R.BARR, KELLY, POTTS, POWER, WILLIAMSON, McGREEVY, SPENCE, JONES, GRANT, MULLEN** *and several others, including* **SAM COCHRANE** *who later owned a chain of cycle shops in Belfast and other towns.*

WILLIE MURRAY *was undoubtedly the outstanding rider of this era. For quite a number of years he distinguished himself in Belfast, Ballymena and Dublin. On the 27th July 1912 at the Oval Track, Belfast he won the half mile Sprint and the 10 mile Motor Paced Championships of Ulster. Three weeks earlier at the Empire Championships* *(now Commonwealth Games) held in Dublin, he finished third in the 'Half mile Empire Championship'. V. Johnston, English Champion was 1st and W. Payne 2nd.*

W.S.MAGEE from North Belfast, who rode under this assumed name, won the 'All Ireland one mile Track Championship' in 1904 and 1905. This was the recognised Championship distance then, later changing to 1000 yards and then to 1000 metres. Magee also reduced HARRY REYNOLDS one mile track record by 10 seconds. His family name was McAlourum, mostly professional people who resented him competing with common cyclists.

JAMES GRANT from Saintfield was another top man before the start of World War One. In 1912 he won both the 1 mile and 5 miles Ulster Championships. He had 3 sons who rode on the Track in the mid 1920's.

World War One upset cycling to a great extent. Then just over 2 -3 years later came the split in Irish Cycling, which took a long time to heal. Even today almost 90 years later there are many not happy with the present system. After 7 – 8 years the cyclists in the North became affiliated to the 'National Cyclists Union' in London. This set up remained for almost exactly 20 years.

In the 1920 decade many riders carried on as before to be joined by many newcomers. Such names as: JACK SCOTT, Dromara CC. HERBIE KNIGHT, Belfast CC. C.GIBSON, Dundonald CC. W. ANDREWS, S. NEILL, Belfast CC G.JONES, Belfast CC.

Towards the end of the 1920's they were joined by McCUTCHEON, R.U.C., A.SUMMERS, W.POLLOCK, J.HARRIS - All Northern C.C. There was also W.E. and J. McKEE, Belfast C.C. and SAM THOMPSON, Leapough CC. Dromara. Time Trial men often took the longer track races.

On the Track the most prominent rider was GEORGE STEWART for more than the 1920 decade. During his long career he won numerous Championships including the 'Northern Ireland 25 mile title' as late as 1928. It was unfortunate for him that there was no cross channel competition, other than at ones own expense in those days.

CULVENOR (Cubby) GIBSON, Dundonald CC was George's closest rivals. His best year was 1924 when he won the '1 mile and 5 mile Championships' at the R.U.C. Sports. Then at Celtic Park he won the '25 mile All Ireland' beating Jack Barnes of Dublin Harps C.C. and J Jones, Belfast C.C., taking 3rd place.

The 1930 decade was probably the best of the last Century where track racing was concerned. There was a meeting every Saturday and frequently in mid-week in provincial towns, or the early closing day, when shop owners would contribute some valuable prizes like large clocks and barometers.

There was also a large number of competitors, some from the previous decade and some new in the second half of the Thirties.

Amongst the general run of winners especially in Handicap events were names like: McCUTCHEON, BEAUFORD, DAVIS, MAXWELL, HANNA, COLE, CRAWFORD, CRANE, CORR, SARGEANT,

LIVINGSTONE and PARTRIDGE.

It was the last five mentioned who dominated the first half of the decade. They also had the advantage of several invitations from across the water. Expenses paid, to Manchester, Birmingham, Ibrox Park, Glasgow, Dundee and several others.

BILLY CRANE from Dromore was quite good and had several invites. DENIS CORR, from Portadown who rode for the R.U.C. was particularly outstanding. He held both British and European Police Championships. He finished 5th in the '1000 yards Time Trial Championship' at the Empire Games (now Commonwealth) held in Manchester in 1934. Sergeant also rode at Manchester. In 1936 he won 8 Northern Ireland Championships and 2 Scottish Titles, 1 at Ibrox Park and 1 at Dundee.

In the last 2 years of the decade BERTIE HUGHES of Ballymoney C.C. and JIM STEWART, Northern C.C. George's son and brother of Billy, jumped to the fore.

In 1938 Bertie won the '5 mile English Grass Track Championship'.

In 1939 there were Olympic Trials for who would represent Great Britain. Both these riders rode out the Final of the Northern Ireland section at Shrigley when Bertie came out on top. Then in August he went to Manchester, where he reached the Final against Reg Harris, who beat Bertie 2 – 0. The judges weren't satisfied as it was Harris' home track. So it was agreed both would go to the 'Meeting of Champions' at Herne Hill, London on the 10th September, but World War Two ended it all.

As I am not feeling well I shall have to simply give the names of the very top Riders from here on:

The 1940's commenced with WALTER ADAMS, R.U.C. and TOMMY GIVAN, Maryland Wheelers. Then there was C. HENDERSON, JOE (Artie)CRAIG and W. FUNSTON. With the War and the reduction in road time trials many short distance men were turning to the Tracks. These included F.McKEOWN, JOHN KELLY and TOMMY TAYLOR – all Kings Moss C.C.

Belfast and Bangor Councils also helped out in promoting 'Holidays at Home' cycle events at Belfast Water Works and the Castle Grounds. Here on the 1 mile circuit DOWDS of Lurgan, (but Northern C.C.) from the Scratch mark had to ride 3 laps to catch the limit riders.

In 1946 Adams won 2 British Police Championships in England.

One other rider I must mention was JOHN JESS from between Dromore and Dromara. After the North and South came together in 1948-49, the Dublin representatives Jim McQuaid, Emerald C.C. and S. Byrne I.R.C. came to Paisley Park where Jess beat both of them in the 1000 yards Scratch Race. Later he went to Dublin, Lansdown Road, repeated this performance and also caught every rider in the 8 Up Pursuit race, finishing alone.

JIM DARRAGH, ALBERT EWART and BILLY STEWART (Georges other son) and LEO FEENEY carried the colours on to the Sixties where SEAMUS HERRON and JACK JOHNSTON followed.

NORTHERN IRELAND T.T. CYCLING

Like the start of the Track cycling, bikes, equipment etc. brought something of a change to T.T. racing. It also had the advantage of the formation of the Belfast and Dublin centres of the Irish Road Clubs in 1890. Their ambition was to promote long distance Time Trials. They finally got it going in line with the English system, following **SHAFTO KERR'S** visit to the Bath Road 100 in 1904.

At this time Kerr, Spencer Street C.C. was already at the top. Shortly afterwards Harry Mussen from Dunmurry took over. Then there was **FRANK GUY**, Belfast C.C. and **SAM COCHRANE**, Ivy C.C. very close rivals as were **PHIL DUFFIELD, HERBIE NEILL, TOM WATSON and SAM JENNINGS.**

The First World War had now started.

A year or more after the end of the War, cycling was back to normal and it was **JACK McCARTNEY** who took over for the next 8 years. He was ahead of men like **McCLURE, FINLAY, JONES, SPENCE, GARDINER, KNIGHT** and a few others, including **KENNY YOUNG.**

The late 20's and early 30's produced names like: **T.STEWART, J. KEENAN, WEBSTER BROTHERS, W.J.McNEILLY, W.McAVOY, W.BLAIR and BOB KIDD** from Kilmore outside Lurgan. It was Bob who proved most outstanding by winning practically every race he took part in and lowering many existing records. He joined the London Police in 1931.

After his departure, **TOMMY STEWART and JIMMY KEENAN** took over, with Keenan going for the real long distances, including the 24 hour where he held the record. **JACK LAMONT** held the Dublin and back.

In the short distance events it was **BOB GRAHAM, BILLY VOKES**, Belfast C.C, **JOHN ENGLISH** and **BILLY LIVINGSTONE**, Banbridge.

Bob Graham with a 1.5.59 in the Northern '25'. He not only won the Championship but was the 1st man to do under 1.6.0.

In 1935 there was a big shake up when **VICTOR PIGGOTT** and **BILL KERNAGHAN**, both Northern C.C. wiped out all previous times. Kernaghan up to 50 miles and Piggott up to 12 hours with a distance which was 5th longest in Great Britain in 1939. He also won the Belfast – Dublin 5 years in succession.

The 40's were back to War years again when **JIMMY GRAY**, Northern C.C. **T. SMYTH, T. STEWART** (both Kings Moss) **W. CAIRNS, T. GIVAN**, Maryland Wheelers, **W. J.NELSON**, Northern C.C., **I. MATIER**, Belfast C.C.

It was Dowds from Lurgan who joined Northern in 1941 that eventually took over from Gray and the others. In

1943 he won nearly every race.

In 1945 he was invited to take part in the '100 Guinea' Muratti Gold Cup at Manchester. There were French, Belgium, Dutch and English teams competing. The French made a gap of 200 yards when Dowds took up the chase, with the English hanging on. He caught them and finished 3rd behind Alan Bannister the 'English Sprint Champion'

The following morning he rode the British 25 Championship and after going twice around a large traffic island he finished 12th just over a minute behind C. Cartwright.

He was off racing for nearly 5 years during this period. It was **JOHN HARVEY, A. McILLHAGGA, FERGUSON BROTHERS** and **FORDE** of Kings Moss C.C., **DAVE McNUTT** and **GORDON REID** and **W. SANDS who were prominent.**

Dowds was back in the 50's going faster than ever. He won all 3 Northern Ireland Time Trial Championships. The same in All Ireland. He represented Ireland in 3 World Championships and came 2nd in the Isle of Man 2 Lap time trial.

In 1954 he set a new Irish 25 Record of 57 mins 56 secs.

He died 5th November 2000.

HARRY McCARTNEY

Top N.I cyclists - the last 50 Years

In the early Nineteen Fifties we were reaching the end of the 'Dowds' era. He rode his last races in 1955, winning both the Northern Ireland and Irish twenty five mile titles. As well as two other open 25 mile time trials in which he beat an up and coming BILLY KIRK by 7 secs and 57 secs respectively.

RAB COLLIM of Cyprus C.C was the record holder for twenty five miles at 59 mins. 9 secs. The road racing scene threw up a very good junior in TOMMY BURNS of Windsor C.C. who won both the Junior and Senior road races in its one year.

The middle Fifties saw the emergence of the good East Tyrone CC team of TOMMY ALLINGHAM, TOMMY TALBOT and JIM SLAINE. Allingham reduced the hundred mile record to below four hours with 4 hrs. 18 mins. 59 secs. and increased the twelve hour record to two hundred and fifty five miles.

The Ards CC turned up with a good short distance team led by BILLY KIRK and JOHN FENNELL. Billy Kirk reducing the twenty five mile record to 58 mins. 28 secs. Also along at this time came the Ballymena Road Clubs team of SAMMY KERR, SAMMY CONNOR and the CALDWELL brothers, GORDON and WALLACE with Sammy Kerr reducing the hundred mile record to 4 hrs. 14 mins. 47 secs.

The late Fifties brought us a good road rider in the name of HERBIE MAGOWAN of Borough Wheelers who won the road championship and was placed in a couple more.

The early Sixties started with the formidable Northern Road team of SEAMUS HERRON, DAVY KANE, RAYMOND AULD and ALFIE STERNE, with the Ballymena Road Club still considerably strong in the results. It was also the start of the dominant Cyprus squad of JACK JOHNSTON, MORRIS FOSTER, STEVIE CHIVERS, JOE SMYTH and BILLY HUDSON. Between them they won a multiple number of Championships and road Championships and set many new records at all distances. Morris Foster also broke all the Place to Place records during this period, some of which stand to this day.

The beginning of the Seventies brought to the fore Banbridge C.C.s NOEL TAGGART and NOEL GALLAGHER along with up and coming DAVY BEATTIE of Kings Moss and Ballymena's RONNIE GRANT. Kings Moss had another Junior rider at this time, KELSO RITCHIE who was extremely fast, breaking senior records and setting a new record for the ten miles track which still stands at 22 mins. 30 secs. Unfortunately when he reached senior age he packed it all in.

The mid Seventies saw ARCHIE CUNNINGHAM Northern C.C. come to the head of affairs and also BILLY KERR who had returned to racing after a long lay off from junior racing. DAVY KANE and JOE SMYTH were still being placed in many events.

At the end of the Seventies, AIDEN McKEOWN of Pheonix C.C. turned up as a strong Time Trialist and along with Billy Kerr formed part of one of our best teams on the road scene. In the space of a couple of months, Kerr went on to win three major road rides: The Tour of the North, the Sealink International and the Tour of Ireland. Three junior riders, LENNIE KIRK and ALASTAIRE IRVINE and TOM GREEN were starting to get good

Three junior riders, LENNIE KIRK and ALASTAIRE IRVINE and TOM GREEN were starting to get good results - Kirk and Green making its Commonwealth Games team in Edmonton, Canada. The full team included Kerr, Cunningham, Smyth and PAT SHEAROR.

In the early Eighties the new kid on the block was MARTIN QUINN of Kings Moss who as a junior was challenging the senior competitions records. DAVID GARDINER and Kirk road well in the National Road Race championship and along with Alastair Irvine were to form our best time trial team at Brisbane – just missing the Bronze medal by 28 seconds to the Australians. Gardiner would go on to gain eighth place in its Road Race.

The mid Eighties were dominated by the Edinburgh Games of 1986 and a lot of training was done. We had the riders: IRVINE, CORMAC McCANN, MARTIN QUINN, JOE BARR, SEAMUS DOWNEY, IAN CHIVERS and DAVY McCALL It was a matter of getting the best for who gelled together. The selected team of Irvine, Quinn McCann and Barr were the first cyclists from Northern Ireland to ever get a Games medal - 'Bronze' – beating the Aussies by 28 seconds on the wind blown Edinburgh By-Pass. When it was announced that Ladies were to be included in the Auckland Games we knew we had an excellent young lassie in DEBORAH KANE who would be a superb competitor by the time the Games came around. She was very capable of riding with our reasonably good juniors and was soon able to hold her own in the Men's Handicap Races and could turn up a good gallop in the sprint.

Unfortunately fate was to deal her a cruel hand. She was riding an International race in England when a truck came out onto the course and stopped at the entrance of a bend at the bottom of a hill. When the bunch came down there was panic trying to squeeze through. Debbie, being on the outside went straight into the radiator of the truck. A horrible accident which confined her to a wheelchair for life. She has borne the handicap very well and lives life to the full. She runs a very successful cycling Boutique shop along side her fathers well known cycle shop on the Newtownards Road.

The late Eighties were dominated by CORMAC McCANN, QUINN, McCALL of Maryland Wheelers, BARR and the new young riders in MARK KANE of Northern, ANDREW MOSS of Ballymena. Moss reducing the twenty five mile competition record to 54 mins. 21 secs.

South Derry Wheelers JOHN BOONE appeared in the records for the first time. The Auckland team of Irvine, McCann, McCall, Barr, Moss and Kane and for the first time we would have a lady rider, VANDA McVICKER of Route Wheelers. As the Games were held in the early February, (New Zealand's start of summer) the riders were sent out early for training in the better weather. By the time the Games started the riders were in fairly good condition but we hadn't done much competition racing. It turned out that the team were a bit sluggish over the hundred kilometre course and finished a disappointing sixth. We also targeted the points race on the track the following Thursday night and Irvine was successful in winning another Bronze medal in a very competitive race against the Aussies, New Zealanders and English trackies.

The early Nineties were dominated by Andrew Moss and John Boone and another fast junior, RAYMOND

Top N.I cyclists - the last 50 Years

BROWNFIELD Toyota N.D. We were again targeting the Team Time Trial at the Commonwealth Games in Victoria, Canada and again a lot of training took place. Moss, the McCann brothers, Cormac and David and JOHN McCLELLAND of Welland Wheelers formed the team which did a good ride.

The main riders at home at the start of the new Century were JIM McCONNELL and RYAN CONNOR of Ballymena R.C. MICHAEL HUTCHINSON based in London area was cleaning up in most of the British Championships and ALWYN McMATH.

N.I. was progressing through the Track World cup events based in Manchester. David McCann continued to progress on the World Road scene and by the time the Manchester Games came around the chosen team was McMath for the Track. Hutchinson and McCann for the Time Trial and a Road Race team of TOMMY EVANS, DENNIS EASTON, STEPHEN GALLAGHER, DAVID GARDINER and BRENDAN DOHERTY plus McCANN.

The Mountain bikes had been included in these Games and we were represented by GLEN KINNING. The course for the time trial suited McCann, more than Hutchinson and he had an eighth place finish. Hutchinson managed fifteenth and on the Road our best placing was Evans in twelfth.

The changes in funding by the Sports Council meant that individual riders were able to follow a selected programme in racing in big events around the world, so we didn't see so much of them on the home front. Another link up with Continental teams also improved their status. RYAN CONNOR was dominant in the home scene and by the time the Melbourne Games came around the Team had high hopes of good results.

This Team had CONNOR, HUTCHINSON and McCANN for the Time Trial with STEPHEN GALLAGHER, ROGER AIKEN, RYAN CONNOR, TOMMY EVANS, McCANN and LEWIS FERGUSON who was mainly a mountain bike rider.

Hutchinson came fourth just 15 secs. adrift and McCann fifth, a further 15 secs. back. Behind were exceptional riders on the twisting course. Aiken, Gallagher and McCann were well up in the Road Race being in with a chance of medals. They were half way around the last lap, but the strength of Australians Tour de France riders were so strong in the run into the finish.

The preparations are now in place for the forthcoming Commonwealth Games in Dehli and the most improved rider is McCann after finishing eleventh in last years World Championships time trial. He is now a full time professional with Giant Asia and has won a couple of major Tours on the Asia Continent. He also set a new record of 50 mins. 30 secs. for the twenty five mile distance on our local course and also beat Hutchinson by a few seconds on one of their fast courses to set a new British Record of 45 mins. 54 secs. for the twenty five mile distance.

MORRIS FOSTER

The top ladies since the 1930's

Isabel with stiff competition coming up behind. Belfast to Enniskillen, 1953.

Two girls, worthy of note, DEBORAH KANE and VANDA McVICKER have already been mentioned by Morris Foster.

Now I will tell you about the ladies who were exceptional cyclists. In the past, The ULSTER LADIES ROAD CLUB had been active for approximately twenty years – from 1937 to 1957, with the exception of the War years 1941/1944.

I joined in 1949 and competed in all club races that year and also in 1950. Family matters prevented me taking part in 1951/1952. From 1953 till 1956 I was concentrating on Place to Place records. I have however in my possession the result sheets of races from 1937 to 1951, from which I have been able to assess the top lady cyclists in each year, based on their performances in every race held each season.

Unfortunately I have not been able to trace the missing details for 1952/1953/1954. Joy McVeigh who now lives in Canada produced the results for 1955 in her article included in this book.

top ladies since the 1930's

1937 E HUTCHINSON, R.TAGGART, E.McCLURE
1938 R. TAGGART, I. NEILL, L. KANE
1939 R. TAGGART, I. NEILL, L. NEILL
1940 I. NEILL, L. NEILL, A. BROWN
1945 M. GORDON, I. NEILL, A. BROWN
1946 M. GORDON, I. MATIER (nee NEILL), L. KANE
1947 E. McCLURE, I. MATIER, L. KANE
1948 E. McCLURE, M. GORDON, I. MATIER
1949 E. McCLURE, I. CLEMENTS, R. RAINEY
1950 I. CLEMENTS, E. McCLURE, E. SMITH
1951 M. McCORMICK, E. McCLURE, R. RAINEY
1955 J. McVEIGH, H. BREEN, M. WARD

Track: I. NEILL, E.McCLURE, R. RAINEY
Rollers: R. RAINEY, H. BREEN, I. CLEMENTS

Place to place riders:
1953 E. McKEOWN, nee McCLURE, Derry to Belfast
1953 ISABEL CLEMENTS, Enniskillen to Belfast, Irish End to End and 7 other records which remain unbroken.

Massed Start Road Races were not organised for Ladies at this time in Northern Ireland.
Top female riders at present are Heather Wilson of Lisburn, a member of Maryland Wheelers, *(Road)*
and Wendy Houvenaghel, professional *(Track)*.
Both have been selected to represent Northern Ireland at the 2010 Commonwealth Games in Delhi, India.

ISABEL WOODS

Riders representing N.I. at the Commonwealth Games in Delhi October 2010		
Heather Wilson	Maryland Wheelers	Lisburn
Martyn Irvine	Planet X Cycles	Newtownards
Adam Armstrong	Eurocycles	Newtownards
David McCann	Giant	Belfast
Philip Lavery	ROI	
Wendy Houvenaghel	GB	Upperlands
Michael Hutchinson	GB	

Record breakers

When an individual in any sport creates a record in an event they are setting down a marker or challenge to any future competitor to beat it and that is precisely what the riders mentioned below have done over the years. To the general public their results are just another statistic, but to the riders who have done place to place records, it has involved very much more that just riding the bike.

Initially they have to get themselves into a good level of fitness by riding many miles throughout the year, riding in all weather conditions. Secondly they would plan and organise their attempt on the record by studying road maps and working out the shortest route possible. Finally they would apply to the Association who would nominate an official Timekeeper and an Observer to be present on the date of the attempt. The back-up team would consist of a mechanic with spare cycle and parts and a suitable vehicle or van with a relief driver. A few other assistants would be required to supply food and drinks when necessary and one person to provide dry clothing and personal help if necessary (such as a masseur). Other cars would follow the event carrying the officials and enthusiastic supporters and possibly one with medical experience in case of an emergency. All this organising costs money which the rider has to provide, unless they have some trade support or help from friends.

RAB COLLINS

IRISH END TO
END EXPONENTS

ORIGINAL COURSE (386 miles)

Year	Name	Club	Time
1937	Phillip Brady	Shamrock CC	23 hrs. 50 mins
1949	Isaac Matier	Belfast CC	22 hrs. 55 mins.
1952	Paddy McNeilly	Kings Moss CC	21 hrs. 2 mins.
1953	Eddie McArdle	Cyprus CC	20 hrs. 47 mins.
1955	Isabel Clements (Woods)	Belfast CC	23 hrs. 2 mins. *

Men's time 2 hrs. 15 mins. faster than I. Clements (Woods)

NEW COURSE (368 miles)

Year	Name	Club	Time
1964	Morris Foster	Cyprus CC	19 hrs. 47 secs.
1993	Joe Barr	Clarks Bros.	19 hrs. 3 mins.
2006	Paul Donoghue	Sorrento CC	18 hrs. 37 mins.
2006	Padriag Marley	Western Lakes	17 hrs. 48 mins.
2007	Rose Leigh	Sorrento CC	21 hrs. 40 mins.

The Kingdom of Mourne

I must be up and away again to where heather clad hills abound,

Where the silvery Shimna gently flows and the golden gorse is found.

I will wend my way at the break of day, with never a backward turn

Till I am riding along with the larks clear song, away in the Kingdom of Mourne.

I must be up and away again to where misty Donard frowns

Where mountain sheep on her slopes so bleak, scamper at the slightest sound,

Where the skylark, curlew and moorhen rest and the Autumn sun sinks in the west

Ah! That is the place that I know is best, away in the Kingdom of Mourne.

I must up and away again to where Spelga's beauty calls,

There I'll sit down midst the bracken brown and the murmur of water falls,

I will dream of those hills where my thoughts ever lie,

Of those lofty peaks that reach the sky,

Of those mountains whose beauty makes me sigh, away in the Kingdom of Mourne.

ROAMER

Bill Murray 1914 - 1996
This poem was written by Bill in 1945.

Sponsors

Our grateful thanks to the following people whose financial support made this book possible.

DAVID SURPLUS B9 ENERGY	Larne
THE GIVAN FAMILY	Belfast
FRANK THOMPSON	South Africa
RAB COLLIM	McCaig Collim, Belfast
LISBURN CITY COUNCIL	Lisburn
JONNIE AND CATHY WILKES	
SPORT Northern Ireland	Belfast
Rev. JOHN WILSON	Iowa, U.S.A.
THE SMYTH FAMILY (CICLI SPORT)	Moneymore
BILLY GORDON	Lisburn
AUBREY BROWN	Ballycastle
THE MUSSEN FAMILY	Formerly of Dunmurry
JACK JOHNSTON	South Carolina, U.S.A.
ROY and MARY TWEEDIE	California, U.S.A.
BILLY STEWART	Belfast
IAN MOORE	Yorkshire

Other contributors:

BILL JEBB	Ballyclare
MIKE McCONAGHY	Newtownards
RONNIE MILLAR	Portrush
BILLY McCORMICK	Craigavon
JIM McGUIRE	Saintfield

DUNREE HEAD

Thanks

*The decision to invite cyclists
past and present*

to submit their memories and personal stories, some of which may also be accompanied by photographs, has evoked wonderful memories and stimulated a huge response from many cyclists. These personal recollections of the contributors have now been recorded and printed in this book so that members of the cycling fraternity and others can share and enjoy them. If this book had not been printed the contents would, through time, have been lost to posterity.

Finally, it would be appropriate here, on behalf of all cyclists, both past and present, to acknowledge that this great sport which we have taken part in and enjoyed over the years, would not have been possible without the dedication of numerous backroom people such as Administrators, Club Officials, Judges, Time Keepers, Turn Stewards and Marshals etc who have applied themselves to their various duties, which they have done freely and voluntarily.

So spare a thought for them at least the next time you attend a cycling event because without them there would not be any.

RAB COLLINS